LAURA LEE DOWNS

➤ *Childhood in the Promised Land*

WORKING-CLASS MOVEMENTS

AND THE COLONIES DE VACANCES

IN FRANCE, 1880–1960

DUKE UNIVERSITY PRESS   Durham and London   2002

Designed by C. H. Westmoreland

Typeset in Granjon by

Tseng Information Systems, Inc.

Library of Congress Cataloging-in-

Publication Data appear on the last

printed page of this book.

Chapter 6 uses material from a
previously published article, "Municipal
Communism and the Politics of
Childhood: Ivry-sur-Seine 1925–1960,"
Past and Present 166 (Feb. 2000): 205–41,
and is reprinted with kind permission.
World copyright, The Past and Present
Society, 175 Banbury Road, Oxford,
England.

We are grateful to the John Simon
Guggenheim Memorial Foundation for
support of this project.

for Alain

CONTENTS

ILLUSTRATIONS

ACKNOWLEDGMENTS

I would like to thank the many people whose generous assistance has allowed me to complete this book. The staffs at the municipal archives in Ivry and Suresnes provided a warm welcome to the American researcher who had traveled, improbably, to their remote city archives in search of material on the *colonies de vacances*. I would like to thank in particular Michèle Rault, Ginette Lagarde, Haude de Chalendar, Michel Guillot, and Renée Courbe for their tireless efforts in helping me unearth local sources. I would also like to thank the staff at the Archives Départementales du Val-de-Marne, the Institut National de la Recherche Pédagogique, the Musée Social, the Bibliothèque Historique de la Ville de Paris, and the Bibliothèque Nationale de France. Thanks are also due to Karl Longstreth, Map Librarian at the University of Michigan.

I owe a particular debt of gratitude to Lucien Laborie, former director of Ivry's *colonie* at Les Mathes, and to current directors Robert and Christine Duchâtre, who spoke with me at length of their experiences and understanding of the *colonie* movement in interwar and postwar France. I also thank Monsieur and Madame Chéron, Madame Favre, and Monsieur and Madame Robin, citizens of Ivry and of the erstwhile children's republic at Les Mathes, for sharing with me their memories of Ivry and its *colonie*.

Many friends and colleagues have read and commented on various parts of the manuscript, and it is a pleasure to thank them here: Jane Burbank, Sueann Caulfield, Herrick Chapman, Clare Crowston, Sarah Downs, Geoff Eley, Patrick Fridenson, Nancy Green, Tom Harrison, Gabrielle Hecht, Gabrielle Houbre, Pieter Judson, Sue Juster, Valerie Kivelson, Peg Lourie, Leslie Pincus, Donald Ried, Paul-André Rosental, and Tara Zahra. At Duke University Press, I have enjoyed the great privilege and pleasure of working with Valerie Millholland, who has been unwavering in her support of this project since it first crossed her desk. Finally, I thank the Fulbright Foundation, the John Simon Guggenheim Memorial Foundation, the National Endowment for the Humanities, and the Office of the Vice President for Research at the University of Michigan. Without their generous support, this book would hardly have been possible.

I dedicate this book to my husband, Alain Boureau, whose wise counsel and ready laughter have lightened the burdens of academic labor, transforming mere work into a joyous search for deeper understanding.

Childhood in the Promised Land explores the location and significance of childhood in the political and cultural life of working-class cities in modern France. This exploration is anchored in a comparative study of the municipal *colonies de vacances,* organized by the working-class cities of the Paris red belt (*banlieues rouges*). Located in remote villages or along the more inexpensive stretches of the Atlantic coast, the municipal *colonies* gathered their young clientele into variously structured "villages enfantines" within which they were to live out particular, ideal visions of the collective life of children throughout the summer holiday. Social hygienic plans to reinforce the fragile bodies of urban children thus entwined with the ancient dream of remaking humanity by removing the young from the corruptions of the city and placing them in a pure, natural setting where they could be nurtured and educated for a better society.

The book has its origins in my longstanding curiosity about France's gradual and comparatively recent transition from an agrarian and small-town to an urban and industrial society. While much has been written about this process from the standpoint of middle-class observers, no scholar has yet undertaken a study of working-class people's perceptions of the transformation, and loss, of the countryside across the late nineteenth and twentieth centuries. My search for an institutional base through which I might focus and anchor such an ambitious project led me swiftly to the working-class suburbs of Paris, where most provincial migrants landed in these years. Here, I found a host of municipal institutions that were intended to maintain or repair working-class ties to the land—regionally based friendly societies of migrants from Berry, Savoie, the Creuse, or Auvergne; *jardins ouvriers; colonies de vacances.* The archives for the friendly societies proved less forthcoming on these questions than I had hoped, while those for the workers' gardens proved disappointingly thin. But the *colonies de vacances* are quite another story, as I learned first in Ivry-sur-Seine, and then Suresnes, where box after box of ill-sorted papers, dossiers, newspapers, and reports slowly yielded up the untold tale of these collective, and distinctively proletarian, institutions.

It was at this point that I began to realize that I had somewhat unwittingly stumbled upon a genuine *lieu de mémoire,* for each time someone

French asked me what I was up to in all those municipal archives, I would reply "oh, well, I'm looking at the *colonies de vacances.*" At that point, a certain look would cross my interlocutor's face as she or he recalled summers *en colonie,* an episode in one's youth that was sometimes followed up by a stint as adolescent *moniteur* and militant in the popular education movement. No one has yet written a full history of the *colonies,* but in the postwar generations, it seems that nearly everyone has spent a summer or two (or ten) in one of these children's summertime collectives.[1]

Childhood in the Promised Land is thus no longer centered on the problem of working-class ruralism and memories of the land, though these questions form a recurrent theme throughout the book. Rather, the book now focuses on the question of working-class childhood, and the changing institutions, practices, and beliefs that have shaped such childhoods in France since the end of the nineteenth century. Organized by a range of public and private foundations that sought to extend the benefits of country holidays to the children of the urban poor, the *colonies* would gradually reach upward to include children of the middle class as the institution expanded over the first half of the twentieth century. By the late 1940s, the *colonies* would be assuring summer holidays to thousands of middle-class children as well, in a kind of trickle-up movement that, in my view, has characterized the development of the welfare state in France—a development that has proceeded less by top-down impositions than through the central state's gradual adoption and expansion of private and local initiatives.

The "trickle-up" movement of the *colonies* toward embracing middle-class children in the late 1940s and early 1950s forms the denouement of the history I recount in this volume, which follows the *colonies de vacances* as they shape-shifted in time: from charitable work bestowed by late-nineteenth-century do-gooders on meritorious but sickly proletarian children, to a robust institution of popular education in interwar France, to the preferred institution by which children's universal "right" to health, happiness, sunshine, games, and a piece of the French countryside was disbursed across the households of France. It is a curious tale, one whose lineaments are, in essential ways, peculiarly French. Yet at the same time, the *colonies* are clearly linked to parallel movements in Germany, Austria, Italy, the United States, and Britain.

Until the very end of the 1970s, children of the popular and middle classes in France would continue to spend their summer holidays in these rural children's collectives, far from their families and in the presence of one another. Only then did the *colonies* start to fade from contemporary life, as more individualist and consumerist models of leisure began to replace earlier practices whereby the bodies and spirits of urban children were renewed through collective holidays in the countryside or by the sea.

CHILDHOOD IN THE PROMISED LAND

The *départements* of France, ca. 1920
(an * indicates the *colonies* of Suresnes and Ivry)

Introduction

In the summer of 1919, the municipal government of Ivry-sur-Seine created a new semipublic charity, Les Petits Ivryens à la Campagne (The Little Ivryens in the Country), whose sole purpose was to provide cheap summer holidays for the city's neediest children. Raymond Lagarde still remembers those summer months with the "Little Ivryens," lodged on peasant farms in the remote and marshy countryside of the Deux-Sèvres:

> I was nine years old. We each had a black beret with P.I. [Petits Ivryens] stitched in white and surrounded by oak leaves. We were very proud of these berets . . . We spent our vacations in the Deux-Sèvres, near the town of Niort. It wasn't a *colonie* like we have today; we were housed with the local peasants. Our departure was a most picturesque event; we rode out in the backs of trucks that were normally used to haul wood and other merchandise. They would put up a few benches and, voilà, off we set for the Montparnasse station, where we caught the [overnight] train to Niort. When we arrived, our peasant "hosts" were waiting at the station, to take charge of us. So all the kids were spread out in farms across different communes: Coulon, Bel-Air, Garrette, Masset, etc. We stayed a month and a half (for which our parents paid very little). We each carried a change of clothes in our rucksacks, like soldiers. Some of us ended up on farms, others with private families. Personally, I did not fare well on my first vacation. I was put with a farmer who went out each evening to harvest reeds from the marshes, which were very numerous in the region. I was left alone throughout the evenings and the days as well. Some of my friends were housed together at the same farm, but me, I was left alone. Worse, the farmer drank, with all the mood swings that brings; it was not always very pleasant. I could hardly wait for the vacation to end, and looked forward to each departure with impatience and joy . . . For many of us it was the first time we had seen the ocean. Because even though we weren't really that close to the sea, the "Little Ivryens" would periodically gather us all together and take us to the shore for a swim. That was the rule; you had to see the sea at least once. Once we went to the Ile de Ré, another time to the Sables d'Olonnes.

Saint-Denis

Bobigny

Clichy

Levallois-
Perret

Nanterre

Puteaux

Suresnes

Rueil-Malmaison

Paris

Saint-Cloud

Boulogne-
Billancourt

Ivry-sur-Seine

Villejuif

Paris and its suburbs, ca. 1930

> We would spend the whole day, traveling there and back again on the backs of those trucks . . . The last year I went on vacation I went with the [six] Moreau sisters. We were all seven settled with a big peasant family in Bel-Air. It's one of my happiest memories, because there were so many of us, all in one big family.[1]

For nearly a century, children of the popular classes in France have enjoyed (or endured) summer holidays in the countryside, thanks to the *colonies de vacances,* a vast network of summer camps, privately and publicly funded, that provide cheap holidays for working-class children. Since the dawn of the twentieth century, hundreds of thousands of French children (and over a million each summer since 1955) have left home each summer for a long (six-to-eight-week) vacation "en colonie," in an annual mass migration of children that has become a familiar rite of social life in France. In that *colonies de vacances* have shaped working-class childhoods since the turn of the century, they are a part of the social, political, and educational history of contemporary France, an experience common to the lives of working and lower-middle-class children throughout the country. Yet, curiously enough, no one has ever written a history of the *colonies.* This lacuna seems especially sad in view of the fact that the *colonies* are just now starting to vanish from contemporary life, as private family vacations supplant the earlier model of children's holiday collectives in the countryside or by the sea.[2]

Childhood in the Promised Land explores the *colonies de vacances* movement in France from its origins, at the end of the nineteenth century, through the mid-1950s. At the heart of the study lie the municipal *colonies* established in the working-class *banlieues* (suburbs) of Paris; private and semipublic *colonies* organized by various parties concerned with the health and well-being of local children: republican primary schoolteachers, Catholic seminarians, Socialist and Communist municipal councilors. For despite the profound political differences that divided Socialist left from republican center, or Catholic activists from their *laïque* (secular) counterparts, the generation that came to power in the aftermath of defeat (in 1870) at the hands of a newly powerful Germany were in agreement upon one central verity: the demographic future of France rested on the fragile bodies of urban, working-class children—delicate beings whose spiritual and material well-being were seen to be at constant risk, owing to overwork, undernourishment, tuberculosis, and the generally unhealthy climate that was held to prevail in the modern industrial city.

Childhood in the Promised Land analyzes comparatively the organization and pedagogical structures that developed across a full range of municipal *colonies*—Catholic and republican, Socialist and Communist—in order to better comprehend changing perceptions of, and practices around, working-class childhood in early-twentieth-century France. But it focuses in particular on the *colonies* that developed in two key industrial *banlieues:* "red" Ivry and the Socialist garden city of Suresnes, bastions of Communist and Socialist municipal power from the 1920s on.

The comparison is a revealing one, both for what unites the two cases and for what distinguishes them. Hence, the multiple currents that cut across all *colonies de vacances* emerged most sharply in leftist settings: tensions between the nascent social politics of the new left-wing *mairies* (municipal administrations) and popular child-rearing practices; the uneasy intersection between municipal socialism/communism and broader movements for pedagogical reform in light of changing notions of children's physical and cognitive development. Yet these common problems found very different solutions in Ivry and Suresnes, where the usage of municipal authority was governed by two distinct conceptions of the relationships among politics, childhood, and society in the working-class city. The Communist administration of Ivry thus saw in the *colonie* a way to build the utopian future here and now, for in the daily experience of collective life in the *colonie,* the souls and bodies of working-class children might be prepared for the better world they would surely inherit. At the same time, the *colonie* was a way to bind parents' loyalties to the Communist *mairie,* to bring them directly into a communal project that was organized on behalf of their children. The Socialist administration of Suresnes took an entirely different route, constructing a network of municipal social services—model schools and medical dispensaries, elegant low-cost housing blocks—that was managed by the city's own staff of trained social workers. As such, the Socialist garden city was also an experiment in large-scale social engineering, a striking (and well-publicized) novelty in a country where professional social work was only just starting to develop. Standing at the confluence of social assistance and public education, the city's *colonie de vacances* was placed within this larger network of social services, thus establishing a more distant relationship between electorate and administration in Suresnes, a relation that was mediated at all levels by the intervention of social and medical experts.

There are a number of fascinating comparisons to be made between Catholic, republican (secular), and Communist *colonies,* which all borrowed various practices from each other, even as they competed for the same children. Together, they elaborated a vision of working-class childhood in bourgeois society that was at once quite poignant and highly politicized. Hence, pedagogues speculated on the function of play in children's lives at the same time that particular, and allegedly nonpolitical, forms of child welfare became a terrain of sharpened political struggle. This is especially visible in the interwar period, where one can see some of these battles reflected, enacted even, in the organization and function of the *colonie* itself. The children of the *banlieues rouges* thus found themselves living in little "républiques enfantines," each presided over by its own mayor and municipal council, who handled the day-to-day business in the *colonie.* (Leftist pedagogues were concerned above all with encouraging a kind of self-determination among these children, who were between the ages of six and thirteen.) And throughout the 1930s, inspired by the Popular Front dream of a worker-peasant alliance, leftist municipalities throughout the Paris region saw their *colonies de vacances* as little "ambassades rouges," missions of urban children implanted in rural districts from which they could reach out to the local peasantry.

An entire pedagogical practice thus took shape inside of an institution that had begun as a kind of public health measure, "colonies sanitaires" that transplanted pale and spindly children from the thick, gray smog of the city to the good clean air of the French countryside. While the concern with child health would never fade entirely, the obsession with healthy cheeks and kilos gained gradually ceded pride of place over the interwar years, as Communist councilors, (republican) primary schoolteachers, and Catholic seminarians all came to realize what might be accomplished, educationally speaking, during the six-to-eight-week holiday.

A range of ethical, political, and spiritual concerns thus wound through the structures of everyday life in the municipal *colonies* of the Paris red belt. This is most clearly visible in the case of the Communists, for childhood, revolution, and the coming socialist utopia were linked in an avowedly political relation that placed children at the heart of the social transformation to come. But the echoes of ethical and political conviction also resound in Catholic and republican literature on their *colonies de vacances:* in the Catholics' stress on imparting to their young *colons* a "complete spiritual formation"; in the republican insistence on the freedom that their young charges enjoyed, living *en famille* with a peasant *mère* and *père nourricier(e)* under whose watchful and affectionate eyes the *colons* might develop (through an unconscious process of emulation) a love for the rustic simplicity being modeled by this family.

The multiple political valences of life *en colonie* remind us of the complexity of the analytic task before us: how is one to understand a social politics of working-class childhood elaborated by parties and movements that sought to root themselves in the milieu by a conscious strategy of improving the lives of working-class children?[3] How does one pick one's way through the layers of propaganda and self-promotion that gathered around this, the central social program in the poor neighborhoods that ringed early-twentieth-century Paris? For such self-congratulatory prose surely abounds in the promotional literature produced by the directors and patrons of the various *colonies,* as each strove to draw the offspring of the local working class into their particular version of a rural French idyll. Ivry's Petits Ivryens à la Campagne (secular and republican) thus vaunted the independence and freedom that their *colons* enjoyed, "playing peasant" in the green meadows of the Deux Sèvres: "Of course no one forces them to lead the cattle into the fields, but they so love to follow the shepherd or shepherdess, to climb on the wagon, to gather in the hay . . . [T]he simple country life [and] the relative independence with which its seasonal labors are accomplished give the children a taste for the charms of peasant life."[4] In the meantime, the city's Communist Oeuvre de Vacances Populaires Enfantines (ovpe) had built its own rural utopia amidst the fresh, pine-scented winds of the Charente-Maritime: "The air of the *colonie,* filled with the scents of the sea and the woods, is absolutely pure and possesses all the qualities necessary to cure the little lungs of our kids, who, for the rest of the year, are forced to breathe the smoke from the factories of our industrial city . . . We must insure the health [of our children] from infancy onward so that they may better resist the vicissitudes and evils which await all workers under the capitalist regime."[5]

The partisan feeling of each party proclaims itself without shame; indeed, the ovpe made no effort to veil the fact that for the Communists, the "protection of childhood" stood at the heart of their agenda. But theirs was an agenda that pursued serious social policy achievements as a means to an end (reelection) as well as ends in themselves (ameliorating the worst ills of capitalism while building the bodies and souls of those proletarian children who would someday inherit the earth). Is it appropriate, under these circumstances, to approach this material, these records of daily life and pedagogical innovation in the *colonie de vacances,* with the jaundiced eye of Foucauldian suspicion? This is precisely what sociologist Alain Vulbeau recommends in his study of the "governance" of children in modern France.

This suspicion clearly stems (in part) from the kinds of organizations Vulbeau looked at: *colonies sanitaires,* founded by bourgeois and government health agencies in their battle against tuberculosis, rickets, and other maladies of the urban poor; or state-run *colonies disciplinaires,* intended to transform youthful working-class offenders into productive citizens. The municipal *colonies* of the *banlieues rouges* quite disappear in this welter of "barracks *colonies*" ("colonies casernes"), where bourgeois overseers sought to bring wayward young proletarians to heel, to compel them to accept bourgeois norms of comportment and the very limited social role that contemporary society expected of them: to become "disciplined" and "conscientious workers," as the director of one such *colonie* put it.[6] This disciplinary mission was accomplished, Vulbeau tells us, by cynically manipulating the children's need for affection and their dependence on adults; after all, "children submit to adults through a relation of intimacy." The working-class children in these "colonies casernes" thus confronted authority in the guise of affection, "a form of authority that is rendered all the more efficacious by its familial and affective appearance . . . an authority that smiles (and makes you smile back)."[7]

Vulbeau's chilling portrait no doubt captures important aspects of childhood experience in such "charitable" *colonies de vacances.* It nonetheless seems to me that there is a gaping space in French history where one might begin to sketch the outlines of a less Foucauldian history of French educational practices and theories of child development. And the municipal *colonies* of the *banlieues rouges* seem an ideal place to begin. For in the case of Socialist and Communist *colonies,* one is struck by the fact that so much of the archival material was written by leftist pedagogues and supervisors who were themselves artisans and factory workers: women and men who, elected to municipal posts during the era of the *banlieues rouges* (1919–1958), found themselves charged with organizing and developing the local *colonie.* The records from these "red" *colonies* — journals and notebooks kept by the young *colons,* and records and logbooks kept by the young adult supervisors (*moniteurs*) hired to watch over them — offer periodic glimpses of a set of distinctively working-class ideas about what constitutes a healthy and happy family life (much of which was conveyed via discussions of food), and what it means to have a "good" childhood, when the future that stretches before one is a life of manual or industrial labor.[8]

In the practical, day-to-day experience of life *en colonie,* then, the *moniteurs* forged new understandings of childhood, understandings of the physiological and cognitive dimensions of child development that were grounded in their daily activities and interactions with the children. The municipal archives are thus filled with dossiers from the *amicales des moniteurs* detailing the painstaking process whereby young men and women from the milieu, employed at the *colonie* or municipal after-school child-care center (*patronage municipal),* gradually built an entire pedagogical approach from the ground up, an approach that was rooted in daily contact with the city's children and in weekly, collective reflections on the pedagogical challenges and opportunities this work presented.

At the heart of these activities lay a very rich and complex concept of children's play as the central, defining act of childhood. The child thus plays out of instinct, acting on an inborn need to play. In so doing, he or she defines a kind of intermediate space, poised between an inner world of fantasy and the implacable realities of the external world. Within this liminal space, the child plays in order to work out what it means to be an individual who acts in the world, in this case, the world of peers and young adult *moniteurs* with whom the child interacts. A wise parent would thus never seek to prevent her child from playing, for "it is through playing that the child develops all his faculties, and acquires all understanding," or so advised Abbé des Graviers in the winter of 1938, while speaking to the parishioners of Saint-Pierre-et-Saint-Paul (Ivry-Centre) about their duties as parents.[9] Though voiced by a Catholic seminarian, these words could just as well have come from a *moniteur* in a Communist *colonie,* or from the mouth of a republican schoolteacher, particularly one involved with the movement for "l'éducation nouvelle," a movement that sought to renew education by placing it more squarely in tune with the creative energies of the child. For the perception that games and play are central to the child's development as a self-activating agent shaped educational practices across the full range of *colonies*—Communist, Catholic, and republican alike. And it is precisely this vision of education, in which the child constructs him or herself as an agent through various forms of play, that cannot be grasped by a formula that views education as mere indoctrination.

A second question posed by the study of *colonies de vacances* is that of gender. If, from their very origins, the *colonies de vacances* sent at least as many girls as boys out to the countryside, these subsidized summer holidays were all governed by a clearly gendered organization of space and activities. In some cases, this organization followed the sex-segregated structures of the republican primary school, with which the early *colonies scolaires* were so closely bound up. In other cases, it followed the overtly segregated pathways of Catholic education. But even in cases where *mixité* (coeducation) was the rule, in the "children's republics" of the Socialist "Red Falcon" youth groups, or the *colonies de vacances* in Communist municipalities, actual daily practice in the organization of the *colonie* — hygiene, games, a social life organized via subgroups of ten to twelve — tended to group boys and girls separately.

Curiously, however, the *colonie de vacances* movement in France never produced an overarching discourse on the significance of gender difference in the collective life of children on holiday, nor on the orientation of those differences toward preparing the man and woman of the future — as citizens who would accede to their gendered places within the nation thanks to their preparation for these roles in family, school, and *colonie de vacances*. This is curious because, from the very outset, this institution, whose roots lay in the hygienic anxieties of its founders, acquired a strong pedagogical orientation that was defined and distinguished by its unique context: the child, living in a collectivity of peers throughout the long summer holiday, presented "an entirely new situation, a vast field for pedagogical experiment." [10] Yet the pedagogical mission that the *colonies* defined for themselves was always understood in terms of that gender-neutral being "the child," a creature who was defined primarily through his or her difference from adults. For late-nineteenth- and twentieth-century pedagogues were captivated by the gulf of difference, both physiological and cognitive, that distinguishes children from adults, and by the process of human development that, properly guided, unfolds to bridge it. Any distinctions of gender that arose on the ground in the day-to-day practice of individual *colonies* were nearly always subsumed under this larger categorical divide: a primary difference around which discussions of pedagogical practice — of the *colonie de vacances* as a privileged terrain of pedagogical experiment, and of the child as the unknown being at its center, waiting to be discovered — were organized.

Distinctions of gender thus rarely entered into the larger discourses that the *colonie de vacances* produced around its own, distinct contribution to the education of French children, with the *colonies* of the Catholic Church constituting the sole exception to the rule. Here, gendered practices in individual *colonies* — the strict separation of boys and girls from a very young age, and the explicit orientation of their education toward distinctively male and female versions of adulthood — reached out to meet a frankly gendered discourse on the role of *colonies de vacances* in preparing children to assume their distinct and complementary adult destinies. Nowhere else did a gendered discourse of the *colonies'* social/educational mission arise, not even in the republican *colonies scolaires:* adjuncts to a school where gendered educational ideals were enshrined in a longstanding discourse-and-practice of preparing children for lives in which a functional complementarity of the sexes would later be enacted in the sphere of private family life. Aside from the occasional debates that arose over the establishment of coeducational *colonies* — debates that reveal the very gendered presumptions about the innate natures of male and female children that governed the organization of republican *colonies* — the literature generated by the *colonie de vacances* movement was, until the 1970s, quite silent on the topic of gender.[11]

This silence poses some very interesting questions of interpretation: what are we to make of an institution that was gendered at the level of local practice, but which made scant expression of such gendered practices? If feminist historians have often worked in the gap between a heavily gendered discourse (for example, the campaign to return working mothers to the home in 1930s France) and a quite differently gendered social practice (employers' pragmatic refusal to do without these inexpensive workers), the counter-case, where a gendered social practice is covered over by a stubbornly gender-neutral discourse, has yet to be explored.

The analytic difference is not inconsequential. After all, the fundamental structures that govern the workplace — job descriptions, wages, perceptions of skill — were, until quite recently, unabashedly and explicitly gendered. Further, these structures were invariably upheld by some kind of rationale around male-female difference in relation to the technical requirements of particular tasks. In the workplace, then, gender difference carried clear consequences for the individual man or woman's position on the wage-and-skill hierarchy. The historian's task is thus fairly straightforward: to describe the gendered structures of work and then sketch out the ontologies of sexual division, both explicit and implicit, that underpin them.

But in *colonies de vacances,* male-female difference generally passed unspoken, as whatever on-the-ground distinctions a particular *colonie* made in its treatment of boys and girls were either quietly naturalized, or worked with under the hopeful sign of a *mixité* that was installed not for purposes of gender equality but rather to build more "natural" (i.e., less sexually charged) relations between the sexes:

> Living together under the same roof creates between boys and girls the bonds of fellow-feeling and a sense of mutual understanding which can only be gained through experience. Subjected to the same discipline, whose liberal contours are intended to encourage initiative and the taking on of responsibility, experiencing the same joys, enduring, at times, the same privations, being shaped in the same mold, as it were, surely these young children will help build a better society tomorrow.[12]

Sometimes the staff in these mixed *colonies* worked to curb or overcome the particular sexual divisions that defined social groups and activities (especially in children's choice of games) in the hope of creating more frank and open relationships between the young (which, in turn, would presumably lead to more frank and open romantic and marital relations in later life). At other times they simply sought to work with these differences, setting up a harmonious interaction between girls and boys that, over time, would curb the worst and bring out the best in each sex. This approach, of course, rested on the proposition that the observed dispositions of boys and girls in their *colonie* were direct manifestations of a distinct, unitary, and self-evident nature that appertains to each sex: "Girls' natural concern with their appearance has prompted an equivalent concern for good grooming among the boys, which manifests itself in more careful attention to combing their hair, and to maintaining a more scrupulous level of bodily hygiene. Thanks to their daily contact with the boys, the girls have gained in frankness and simplicity."[13] Throughout all these discussions of gender mixing in the *colonie,* no one ever challenged the proposition that gender difference defines a stable, knowable, and meaningful set of distinctions in human character and capacity.

On the basis of their own experiences, individual directors sometimes questioned the particular content of these sexed dispositions, especially when it came to sexual divisions of play, the central activity *en colonie:* "Games are not at issue in the question [of *mixité*], for there are girls who play just as roughly as the boys and boys who spend their recreational hours weaving or modeling with clay."[14] But whether gender difference was accepted as a stable, natural, and self-evident division of the human species (the usual case) or contested in its particular manifestations by the odd maverick, no one ever made the leap from the allegedly natural differences to the political problem of gender inequality. Discussions about co-education thus turned on anxieties about social relations between children, behind which hovered the bogey of child sexuality; rarely did such discussions touch even glancingly on the question of gender equity.

Hence, what no one inside the *colonies* spoke about, at least not before the 1970s, was the fact that in the larger society, gender difference ultimately got transcribed into gender-based inequalities before the law and at work. In other words, what distinguished little girls from little boys was not mere, innocent "difference"—a "natural" concern with appearance on one side, "frankness and simplicity" on the other—but a difference that organized and undergirded the social, political, and economic inequality of women and men. The futures that the two sexes could look forward to were thus shaped not only by "difference" dressed as a purely functional and complementary division of labor within the family, but by structures of gender inequality in the wider world that proved remarkably resistant to state efforts to install a regime of formal equality between the sexes after 1945.

The discussions of *mixité* thus reveal that the organization of daily life in French *colonies de vacances* was underwritten by the conviction that gender difference constitutes a stable and self-evident distinction within the gender-neutral (and misleadingly universal) category of "childhood." And yet these convictions never rose to the level of *colonie* discourse, which remained a gender-neutral conversation that turned around the needs and qualities of that singular being "the child" (or, sometimes, the working-class child).

The study of the municipal *colonies de vacances* thus promises to deepen our understanding of the meanings of childhood in contemporary urban culture, giving us access to those perceptions of the moral natures, cognitive structures, and social possibilities of working-class children that found institutional expression in the *colonies*. This was, moreover, a setting that linked working-class children's moral and physical development to the fresh air and good earth of the French countryside. The *colonies de vacances* thus pose the question of childhood and child development in relation to conceptions of "nature," or, more precisely, to the various and often contradictory perceptions of village life and labor in interwar France.[15] Finally, the study of working-class childhood opens out one promising avenue by which to explore how social change—urbanization, industrial rationalization—interacts with subjectivity. For in deconstructing, and then reconstructing the child's developmental process, pedagogues render explicit the often unspoken presumptions contained in a particular society's conception of what it means to be a human being—our strengths and frailties, motivations and obligations, in relation to ourselves, to the natural world, and to larger communities of people.

CHAPTER ONE

❧ Repairing the Body, Restoring the Soul

THE ORIGINS OF THE COLONIES DE VACANCES
IN FRANCE, 1881–1914

The *colonies de vacances* were not an indigenous development in France. Indeed, Europe's first *colonies* were organized in the mid-1870s by the Swiss pastor Wilhelm Bion, who, in the summer of 1876, gathered some sixty-eight children of the urban poor from his own parish in Zurich and took them on a three-week holiday in the mountain villages above the city. Once conceived, the idea spread swiftly across France's alpine frontier, where it took root in the real material needs of working-class children, many of whom suffered chronic poor health as they grew up ill-fed in the crowded slums and smoky streets of France's rapidly expanding industrial cities.

A mounting uneasiness over the state of public health in working-class cities and neighborhoods thus gave the *colonie de vacances* ready advocates in France. But hygienic anxieties alone cannot account for the nation's swift adoption of the *colonies de vacances;* educational ambitions also played an important role, for the *colonies* presented a unique pedagogical terrain whose defining qualities—far from home and in the open air—resonated with a powerful Rousseauean current in French pedagogical thought. The Napoleonic reforms of the early nineteenth century had driven this current underground, suppressing it under a blanket of traditional educational practice: rote memorization, respect for the teacher, and a rigorous containment of youthful energies within the four walls of the school. But in the mid-1870s, as the French strove to design new institutions worthy of the young Third Republic, these currents began to surface and circulate once again. Let us begin, then, with the Rousseauean pedagogic tradition in France, a tradition that nourished the soil into which the Swiss graft would swiftly plunge new roots.

Pedagogy and the Politics of Republican Virtue

"Travel allows the imagination to soar; it hones the spirit while lending vigor to the soul, strength and flexibility to the body . . . it expands one's horizons, develops his understanding, and destroys received ideas . . . Citizens, you can all appreciate the potential in a school that, with the arrival of fine weather, moves out into the countryside, and there, in the immediate presence of the Supreme Being, hears the lessons of virtue and love of nation, delivered in the shelter of a rocky escarpment, or from the bottom of a valley, in the lush depths of the woods." [1]

Thus did Citizen Portiez open his urgent plea to the Convention in Year II (1794) of the French Revolution, declaiming to his fellow citizen-legislators a revolution in educational technique that might build men equal to the tasks of republican citizenship. [2] At times, Portiez sought to persuade with appeals to the imagination, painting a vivid portrait of eager French youth, shouldering their packs and braving mountain-side and valley, ill-weather and fair. With a patriotic song on their lips and a far-away look in their eyes, the hardy youngsters looked out over the constantly changing landscapes and dreamed already of the tales they would tell back home of their adventures abroad. [3] Most important, though, were Portiez's arguments that linked a more "natural" education of children, in the open air and in direct contact with the force and beauty of nature, to the stern demands of republican citizenship. Inspired by Rousseau's ardent depiction of the child Emile, raised in the woods and fields into a vigorous, independent-thinking adult, Portiez developed this vision before the Convention, stressing in particular the importance of harmonizing the child's intellectual growth with his physiological and moral development. Hardened by life on the open road, the children would grow strong and tough, "their bodies reinforced against attack from all illness, and their spirits from the empire of prejudice." Ultimately, the austere pleasures of outdoor living would change the very shape of their desires, leading them gradually to acquire "a taste for pleasures that are simple and pure, and so recasting their passions." [4]

In the course of his long and eloquent speech, Portiez laid out a method of instruction that would (much later) come to be called the "étude du milieu," in which the world traversed became a kind of school of experience, a living textbook from which all abstract learning was banished in favor of direct encounters with the objects and forces of the natural and social world: a mountain valley where springtime reigned, thanks to the protective embrace of the snow-topped peaks around it, as well as the dreary sight of sterile fields, whose unturned earth bore mournful testimony to the laziness of the local peasantry.[5] Students would thus pass easily from contemplating the world of nature to analyzing the labors of man. From there, they could move to a more systematic investigation of the manners, morals, and politics of the world as it unfolded beneath their tireless march. At every stop along their way, then, the students were to inquire carefully into the shape of local public opinion, and to make direct study of political institutions by attending sessions of the courts and administrative corps.[6] This comparative study of morals would lead them naturally to abandon those arbitrary judgments and narrow prejudices that find fertile soil in the restricted perspective of one's home province.[7] And yet the journey came full circle with a return to home and nation, a point of origin that was now doubly cherished with a love warmed by the light of reason and a patriotism grown fierce, yet also more generous and informed, thanks to the broad experience of the voyage: "Having traveled [the diverse lands of Europe], how much more the young Frenchman will cherish the constitution of his native land!"[8]

Clearly, such voyages of discovery depended crucially upon the guidance of a skilled pedagogue, wise in the ways of Emile's tutor, a teacher who discreetly shaped the personal journey of the student as he traversed the "great book of nature and society."[9] Indeed, without the teacher's skillful, light-handed direction, the student's "natural" progress would soon be stymied. Portiez thus closed his discourse with an appeal to the Committee on Public Instruction, urging that they "develop the means to perfect the system of education by travel." But it would be nearly a century before such "voyages scolaires" found their way into the public school curriculum; for until the last quarter of the nineteenth century, Portiez's Rousseauean vision of students and teacher, at home in the school of nature, building relations of comradeship and learning as they journeyed the world together, lay dormant in the archives of the First French Republic. More dominant by far was the model laid down by Napoleon's 1802 reform of secondary education, a model that was based on Jesuit pedagogical strategies in its stress on hierarchical and one-way relationships of learning, where knowledge was passed down from teacher to students, and all learning took place within the four walls of the school.[10] Not till the early years of the Third Republic, as France strove to build society anew in the ashes of defeat and civil war, did Portiez's *voyages scolaires* return, as part of the plan whereby republican educators strove to renew the nation's outmoded structures of public education.

The reformers were uncompromisingly critical of a system that, "inspired by the monastic or military ideal of the middle ages," locked captive youth inside grim, barrackslike quarters and subjected them to a suffocating discipline, mainly learning by mere rote. In place of such "jails" they proposed to erect truly "modern" schools, where a more "collaborative" relationship with the teacher would gradually awaken the students' spirits and open them up to new experiences.[11] By the early 1870s, some ten years before the national constitution of the republican primary school (Ferry laws of 1881–82), individual educators such as E. Porcher, director of the Ecole Turgot in Paris, were already undertaking a complete renovation of both educational method and content within their own schools, replacing the traditional Greek-and-Latin-based curriculum with a more modern, practically minded syllabus based on math, science, and living languages. Portiez's revolutionary dream of open-air schooling, fallen on hard times since Napoleon's law of 1802, was shaken out and revived as a part of a series of reforms that, in Porcher's estimation, was working toward the same goal: "to bring light and air, movement and life, into the dreary, closed walls of the school of yesteryear."[12]

For the next ten years, first the public lycées and later Jules Ferry's primary schools would experiment with Portiez-style *voyages scolaires,* rewarding their most successful and hard-working pupils with brief, one-to-ten-day excursions at the end of the school year: trips to Versailles and Fontainebleau, Le Havre and Honfleur. "After a year of continuous intellectual effort, what rest and restoration these journeys bring!" reported Porcher with no small satisfaction, noting how the pale faces of book-weary students brightened with new life as they marched two by two in the fresh country air, drinking in the unfamiliar sights and experiences of rural and maritime France. But he underscored with particular pleasure the educational rewards being reaped, as each field and village became a living textbook that opened its pages under the students' feet, presenting them with objects whose vibrant reality "illuminated" the dry, abstract descriptions of ordinary classroom lessons.[13]

The expense of these holidays was to be borne by the *caisses des écoles,* school assistance funds that had been established in each school district in 1882 in order to encourage school attendance by rewarding the best students with prizes—illustrated books, *voyages scolaires*—while extending assistance-in-kind—shoes, textbooks, and warm clothing—to the very neediest.[14] It seemed that Portiez's dream had at last found a place in the system of public education in France. But in June of 1887, when the Paris municipal council reviewed the overall deployment of funds in the city's twenty *caisses* (each arrondissement constituted a separate school district), it was found that the comparatively expensive *voyages scolaires* were diverting a substantial portion of these resources away from the poorest students in order to reward those stronger and more resilient souls who were already flourishing. Should not the order of priority be reversed, so that the bulk of these funds reached those who were most in need? Several months earlier, the city council's Fourth Commission on Public Education had heard a report from Protestant philanthropist Edmond Cottinet, administrator of the *caisse des écoles* of the ninth arrondissement, on the rather singular use to which he had turned the resources of the *caisse*.[15] Since 1883, Cottinet had been using these funds to take his poorest and sickliest pupils on restorative holidays in the country, battling the all-too-common blights of anemia, tuberculosis, and undernourishment with a three-week "cure d'air" whose benefits, he argued, were both dramatic and enduring. The members of the Fourth Commission were moved to a man by Cottinet's stirring account of these trips, and recommended that the *caisses* reverse their order of priority: rather than leaving the poorest students behind to languish, pale and anemic, in the dust and smoke of the city while their stronger, more successful colleagues disported themselves on holiday, the commission urged that the *caisses* reduce their *voyages scolaires* to cheaper, simpler day trips and place the bulk of the school assistance funds behind Cottinet's *colonies scolaires*.[16] The staunchly republican city council voted accordingly and the primary schools of Paris immediately set about organizing *colonies scolaires* for their neediest pupils. By 1888, thirteen out of twenty arrondissements had organized *colonies* in their primary schools, and by 1890, nineteen out of twenty were sending their poorest students on restorative country holidays with the schoolmaster.[17]

Cottinet patterned his *colonies scolaires* after the model pioneered by Wilhelm Bion, of whom Cottinet had learned while on holiday in Switzerland, in the summer of 1880. But Edmond Cottinet was neither the first nor the only Parisian to hear of Bion's work. By the time the city council had placed its stamp of approval on the *colonie scolaire,* proclaiming it "an institution that is particularly to be recommended" (10 June 1887), at least two private *oeuvres de colonies* were already flourishing in

Paris, sending hundred of children each summer to peasant villages in the countryside and along the Atlantic coast. What was it in Bion's initiative that so captured the imagination of Protestant evangelicals in late-nineteenth-century France?

Protestant Charity and the Colonies de Vacances, 1880–1900

In the autumn of 1880, Pastor Théodore Lorriaux and his wife Suzanne, recently arrived in the industrial district of Levallois-Perret, on the northwestern edge of Paris, received a visit from two neighbors. Mme Bonnet and her daughter had just returned from their annual holiday in Switzerland, and were still marveling at the results of Wilhelm Bion's first *colonies de vacances,* which they had witnessed with their own eyes: "Could we not organize something similar in France—in Paris," they inquired of their hostess? [18] Seized by the vision of transporting sickly children from the industrial faubourgs to the fields of rural France, the Lorriaux set to work immediately in search of practical solutions. [19] The following summer, the pastor and his wife sent three young girls from the smoky streets of Levallois-Perret to a peasant farm in Nanteuil-les-Meaux (Seine et Marne), where the three spent twenty-one days restoring their weary bodies and breathing in "the perfumed breeze of woodland and meadow." [20] The experiment was an unqualified success, and the girls returned home, "cheeks glowing with health and their hearts filled with joys hitherto unknown to them." [21]

Thus it was that Pastor and Mme Lorriaux came to organize France's very first *colonie de vacances,* the Oeuvre de Trois Semaines. From this modest beginning the program expanded rapidly, sending seventy-nine boys and girls to peasant farms in Burgundy and the Loire during the summer of 1882. That same year, charitable activist Elise de Pressensé decided to add a *colonie de vacances* to her own Oeuvre de Chaussée de Maine, a workshop and school that she had opened in 1871 to assist impoverished widows and orphans in Paris's Chaussée de Maine district. [22] As the women worked, sewing clothing and lingerie, their youngest children played in the workshop's infant school, while the older ones learned to read and write in the program's primary school. With the establishment of regular public primary schools in 1882, which, in her view, had "every advantage" over private ones, Mme de Pressensé decided to close the program's schools and turn her energies to organizing a *colonie de va-*

cances.[23] News of the Lorriaux's Oeuvre de Trois Semaines had already reached her ears via the small and tightly interconnected networks of Protestant charity in Paris,[24] and Elise de Pressensé designed her own *colonie* with this model clearly in mind.

France's earliest *colonies de vacances* were thus organized by Protestant evangelicals, working in the rather different settings of the public school and the private charitable foundation. Yet these early ventures shared a number of common features—a primary concern for the hygienic (versus pedagogic) value of the *colonie,* and a common organization by family placement in peasant households—for they all drew their inspiration from the same original source: the "Ferien-Kolonie" of Wilhelm Bion.[25] Bion was alive to the potential educational benefits of fresh air, travel, and direct contact with nature. But his initiative sprang above all from his concern with the children's fragile physical state, a concern that led him to organize the holiday so as to integrate these children into the peasants' more robust way of life. Placed inside of individual peasant households, such children were, in his words, to be "colonized with the peasants," that is, to eat as the peasants ate and to participate in their daily labors.[26] Bion was quite clear about the moral and intellectual benefits of a structure in which the children were assimilated into the rhythms of peasant family life, for in Bion's estimation, these rhythms were far more supple than those of the school or any other large collectivity of children, which must of necessity run by the bell and according to a single schedule. By allowing for the different needs of individual children, the peasant family provided a climate propitious for the flowering of individual liberty, or so the theory went. For Bion was convinced that the family was the only unit within which individuals could develop on their own account, with no fear of pressure to conform to the limits and demands of a larger community. At the same time, the children were not simply left to blossom within the structures of peasant life; on the contrary, Bion assembled a team of eight teachers, who accompanied the *colonie* and provided a kind of collective pedagogic animation, reuniting the children several times a week for games, hikes and songfests.

In dubbing his invention a "Ferien-Kolonie" (literally "vacation colony"), Bion invoked a utopian tradition of collective migration to new and unspoiled settings, movements that were illuminated by the hope that the very act of relocation would enable the migrant colony to create a new way of life for itself. Bion had adopted this term quite consciously, in order to underscore the fact that the *colonie* constituted a rupture with

the narrow streets and stifling poverty of these children's past lives; for
at least three weeks each summer, the children of the urban poor would
lead an entirely new life "colonized among the peasants."[27] At the outset, Bion's Parisian disciples all followed the original model quite closely,
appropriating both the organization by family placement and the term
"colonie de vacances." Over time, however, the various *oeuvres de vacances*
evolved in a variety of directions, as each devised new goals and organizational forms while retaining some part of the original inspiration
as well.

The Chaussée de Maine and Oeuvre de Trois Semaines rooted their
colonies in a network of personal contacts among the rural Protestant
notability — a "class" that included not only landed wealth but also the
smaller notables of bourg and village — mayors, schoolteachers, doctors.
These individuals contributed to the material organization of the *colonies* in a variety of ways. Wealthier, landed families sometimes donated
a part of their own rural properties for the summer, housing twenty
or more children at a time and participating directly in the day-to-day
operation of the *colonie*. Village notables of more modest means might
also take in a child or two, but the single most vital contribution of the
local notability, both large and small, lay in their direct surveillance of
the children's placement with local peasant families. As director of the
Chaussée de Maine Alice Delassaux observed, the surveillance of peasant guardians demanded an individual of independent means who could
not be tempted by bribes or gifts, someone who, in Delassaux's blunt
formulation, "dominates the peasants, so to speak."[28] Such a task fell
quite naturally on the shoulders of the rural notability, whose long-term
acquaintance with the inhabitants and, more importantly, positions of
local preeminence, endowed them with a kind of "natural" authority
from which the surveillance of peasant host families flowed easily. Living
in close proximity to the families in question, such notables could drop
in and have a look around at any time, especially, as Delassaux noted
with great relish, when the peasant wives least expected it.[29] Overseeing
the *colonie*'s peasant guardians thus took its place alongside other, older
forms of social hierarchy and command.

The Chaussée de Maine offers a classic example of a *colonie* organized via interlocking networks of rural and urban charitable activism.
Hence in the summer of 1883, when Elise de Pressensé decided to endow her program with a *colonie* of its own, she called upon a dense network of wealthy and like-minded associates whose ready benevolence

underwrote the endeavor and shaped its initial structures. An old friend, Louise d'Eichtal, proved especially responsive to the call; no sooner had Mme de Pressensé announced her intentions than Mme and M. d'Eichtal placed a portion of the family property, "La Poste," at the disposition of the young *colonie*.[30] The d'Eichtal family had dwelt some thirty-six years on this large and well-appointed farm, just outside the village of Les Bézards (Loiret), which made them exactly that type of rural notability suited to oversee the implantation of a *colonie de vacances*. That first summer, the Chaussée de Maine sent thirty-eight children to Les Bézards, twenty of whom lived at "La Poste," where Louise d'Eichtal and her large domestic staff saw directly to the daily details of their well-being. The remaining eighteen *colons* were lodged with the peasants of the village and surrounding hamlets, in households carefully chosen by Mme d'Eichtal and her daughters, who inquired meticulously into the morals and domestic habits of each would-be "gardeuse." Under the watchful eye of this châtelaine, the thirty-eight "petits Parisiens" of the Chaussée de Maine spent the entire summer (some two to three months, versus the eponymous "three weeks" provided by the Lorriaux program) playing in the woods and fields of the Loiret countryside. "La Poste" thus formed the living heart of a *colonie chez les paysans* whose flexible structure allowed for rapid expansion. Over the next two decades, the *colonie* grew steadily, until, by the turn of the century, the Chaussée de Maine was sending well over a thousand children (1,387 in 1902) to spend their summers in peasant households of Mme d'Eichtal's choosing. Back in Paris, Elise de Pressensé energetically worked the urban networks of Protestant charity in order to raise the necessary funds and recruit the *colonie's* young clientele.

A similarly supple structure, rooted in local contacts, allowed the Oeuvre de Trois Semaines to expand nearly fourfold over the period 1882–1914: from 79 *colons* in 1882, the organization mushroomed, reaching 1,134 in fifteen years (1897), and topping 3,000 on the eve of World War I.[31] Unlike the Chaussée de Maine, which concentrated the vast majority of its *colons* around the single center of Les Bézards, the Trois Semaines met the sharply rising demand for rural placements by diversifying the location of its *colonies* until, by the turn of the century, children were being lodged in five different villages across the Vexin and Burgundy countrysides and along the Normandy coast as well. Yet the real heart of the *colonie* lay in Montjavoult, a small village perched high on a hillside in the Oise, about seventy-five kilometers outside Paris. "This

tiny village of 300 souls seems made to order for our children," wrote
Suzanne Lorriaux in 1906, not only because of its high elevation (read:
good, clean air, invigorating to young lungs) but also because of its relative isolation: the nearest railway station lay in Magny-en-Vexin, a good
nine kilometers away, which kept day-trippers at a safe distance while
discouraging the parents from "excessive" visiting.[32] The inhabitants of
Montjavoult were "calm and gentle," sharecroppers for the most part
who possessed but a few fields and cows. These cash-poor households
doubtless rejoiced at the twenty-to-thirty franc fee paid for each "petit
Parisien" lodged therein, and most took in as many as the farmhouse
could decently shelter: sometimes only two, but more often six or eight,
even ten *colons* at a time.[33]

   During the first decade at Montjavoult (1882–91), the Oeuvre de Trois
Semaines organized its *colonie* by family placement alone, benefitting
from the enormous flexibility and extremely low overhead that such
an organization entailed. The local notable who ensured the system's
smooth operation was a Protestant schoolteacher, M. Benech. For some
twenty-five years, Benech served as the Trois Semaines' "right arm" in
Montjavoult, carefully selecting the host families each year and then
traveling up to the railway station in Magny in order to meet the children.
Throughout their stay, Benech watched over the children with "paternal
solicitude."[34] The system of family placement allowed for a prolonged
personal encounter between rural folk and urban gamins, encounters
from which, it was generally presumed, the *colons* would draw the main
benefit, living for weeks on end amidst "these humble laborers who,
rising each day with the sun, return once again to their relentless daily
round of work." As these "humble laborers" prepared the harvest or completed "with gusto" the arduous job of making the hay, they offered their
young guests object lessons in "patience, perseverance, and economy."[35]
But the benefits of this rural-urban encounter could run both ways, and
the deeply religious organizers of the Trois Semaines were fond of recounting the tale of five *colons* from the working-class neighborhood of
Belleville who set their humble peasant hosts a gentle example of religious devotion: "When the children came together each day for morning
prayers, the entire household would draw near, gathering round them
with reverence and emotion."[36] As time went on, however, and the *colonies* expanded, Pastor and Suzanne Lorriaux grew increasingly anxious
over the adequacy of local surveillance, particularly when it came to the

delicate question of sending adolescent girls to live in peasant house-holds.

This was no mere detail, involving but a few individuals on the margins of the Trois Semaines, for the Lorriaux sent not only school-aged children but hundreds of young workers and apprentices, male and female alike, on the three-week "cure d'air" in the country.[37] As the urban founders of the program soon discovered, the interior space of the typical peasant farmhouse was, to bourgeois eyes, surprisingly undifferentiated. Even in households where interior walls had been added, it was frequently necessary to pass through one room in order to reach another, while in two-story houses, the stairway generally led directly into the bedroom of the master and mistress: "No matter what guarantees the chosen peasant families offer (and we are most demanding in this regard), such a system leaves much to be desired, particularly when it is a question of the older adolescent girls."[38] Under these circumstances, even the firmest structures of surveillance seemed an insufficient guarantee, and in 1891, the Trois Semaines constructed "La Clé des Champs," a large house on the edge of the village for the teenaged girls and young women *en colonie* in Montjavoult. Five years later, it built a similar house on the other side of the village, "La Sapinière," where adolescent boys took their three-week rest cure. The younger children, who formed about half the total number of *colons,* continued to be placed on local farms.

Once the system of collective houses had been added to the Oeuvre de Trois Semaines' repertoire, the *colonie* began to expand in that direction, purchasing two houses by the sea (one for the girls and a second for the boys) for those children whose weak and anemic state of health dictated four weeks of good, salt air.[39] By the turn of the century, the Oeuvre de Trois Semaines had abandoned family placement for all but the youngest children; despite the higher cost entailed in maintaining and staffing collective houses, the Lorriaux seemed to feel that a more direct control of the summer holiday was required, particularly where adolescents were concerned. But the partial abandonment of family placement did not signal the abandonment of the *colonie*'s "familial" organization; on the contrary, the annual reports of the Trois Semaines from the mid-1890s onward feature handsome photographs of these houses, bearing the telling caption "our houses are not barracks but real families."[40] As we will see, the assertion that one's *colonie* possessed an "air de famille" constituted a key aspect of its claim to serve the interests of working-class childhood, and organizers from all ends of the political spectrum hastened to advertise the "familial" nature of their particular *colonie.*

Freedom as an Educational Method:
The Protestant Pedagogy of Family Placement

Throughout its long existence, the Chaussée de Maine would remain faithful to the system of family placement; indeed, this charitable organization, built entirely on the collaboration of women activists, was among the most unreservedly pro-peasant of France's *colonies de vacances.*[41] Where other philanthropists expressed reservations about the level of hygiene in peasant homes, the quality of the food (which was often quite different from urban food), or the morality of the peasants (doubting, in particular, that their interest in taking in large numbers of *colons* was nourished solely by a spirit of selfless solidarity), Chaussée de Maine activists vigorously upheld family placement on three grounds: that it (a) was inexpensive, (b) was familial in its very nature, and (c) vouchsafed a maximum of liberty to the young *colons.*

The arguments over family placement turned endlessly around these three points, finding no real resolution, precisely because visions of the peasantry in fin-de-siècle France were highly unstable, prone to run to both extremes. Peasants thus represented all that was good and stable, healthy and strong, natural and unspoiled in a nation where the dramatic physical and geographical transformations of urban and industrial growth served as visible reminders that the human world, as they knew it, was continuously moving in uncharted directions. At the other extreme one finds the peasants as Balzac and Zola portrayed them, rough, primitive, and filthy, thanks to their greater proximity to nature: men and women condemned to a hard existence, painfully extracted from the earth, a life that made them avaricious and mean, deficient in practically all human feeling. The ceaseless turning of the debate over family placement stems from the broad spectrum of images and beliefs that urban bourgeois held about those who still worked the land. As a result, even those programs that placed their children in peasant households often retained a certain reserve about the moral and hygienic value of those placements, and maintained a very close local surveillance.

In a world where paeans to the tranquil virtues of the peasantry traveled hand in hand with the certainty that these people were fundamentally separated from the urban world by their inferior housing and habits of hygiene, different manners of dress and speech, and a lower level of general culture, the Chaussée de Maine's unreserved enthusiasm for family placement constitutes an interesting exception. Indeed, I found only one other foundation, the Lyon-based Oeuvre des Enfants à la Montagne, whose director, Pastor Louis Comte, expressed an equal confidence in the peasant family. These are exceptions whose contours are worth exploring in further detail, as the arguments for and against family placement offer fascinating glimpses down some surprisingly deep wells of feeling about those who populated "la France profonde."

No one ever bothered to contest the claim that family placement was an inexpensive and highly efficient way to organize a *colonie de vacances*, for the evidence lay before all eyes in the hard figures of annual *colonie* budgets. Hence, the primary overhead cost—the payments made to the peasants—was extremely low: one and a half francs per day per child in 1903, which was half the daily cost of keeping a child in a boarding facility.[42] Moreover, this minimal expenditure could be adjusted precisely to the number of children sent each summer; rather than spending precious funds on custom-built facilities—collective houses, dormitories—that might, for a considerable time, lie unused, the *colonie* could put all its resources behind sending the maximum number of "petits Parisiens" on a long and restorative summer holiday.

Opponents of family placement claimed that the system's widely touted cheapness was in essence a false economy; after all, if the purpose of the *colonie* was to deliver fresh air, rest, and hearty food to the anemic and ill-nourished offspring of the working class, then a *colonie* that operated by family placement was working at cross-purposes, delivering a fragile population into the hands of peasants who would probably "feed them nothing but chestnuts" and then demand in return that they contribute to the heavy summertime labors of haymaking and harvest.[43] The accusations against peasant eating practices were fairly easily laid to rest, for outside the very poorest, mountain districts, there were very few peasants still nourishing themselves on chestnuts at the end of the nineteenth century. While the robust meals of the peasantry might seem odd to urban children—a thick, salted soup at breakfast in place of the familiar café au lait, for example—there was nothing unhealthy or lacking in the overall balance of ingredients—or so argued Alice Delassaux: "Our children are fed meat at least four times a week and drink one litre of milk per day."[44] Against more generalized suspicions that ingrained

peasant avarice might lead them to skimp at mealtime, Delassaux cited
the Chaussée de Maine rules: the children were to be fed four times
daily—breakfast, dinner at noon, late afternoon snack, and then supper
before bed. The meals at noon and evening time were to include meat,
fish, or eggs plus vegetables, fruit, and cheese. The proof that their hosts
applied the rules faithfully lay in the healthy cheeks and rounded limbs
of the returning *colons,* "who always come back glowing with health."[45]

The fear that peasants might demand excessive labor from their urban
guests was less easily laid to rest, in part because the Chaussée de Maine,
in keeping with the spirit of Bion's original "Ferien-Kolonie," wished to
see the children fully integrated into the daily life of the peasant household. Inevitably, this meant accepting, even welcoming the possibility
that the *colons* would participate in the work of farmyard and field. The
Chaussée de Maine thus elaborated a vision of daily life in which work
and play were inextricably mingled, with each contributing to the health
and happiness of the young *colons:* "The children are happy in the fresh,
clean air, and they run through the fields, gathering flowers, gleaning
the corn, guarding the herds. Their limbs develop, their skin takes on
a golden hue, and they return to their families filled with energy and
joy." The thought that peasants might work their young guests to excess
was never explicitly raised in the Chaussée de Maine literature; rather,
the baseline presumption was that in the ordinary course of things, the
adoptive family would exercise its delegated parental authority appro-
priately. The first rule, that the *colons* "owed obedience" to their *parents
nourriciers,* clearly rested on this presumption.[46] Moreover, this rule implied that if asked to do so, children should make some contribution to
the labors of household and farm, with the level of services demanded
being left to the discretion of the peasant hosts—subject, of course, to
the ultimate control of the local *surveillant(e).*

Pastor Comte, a man of peasant origins, was far less inclined to rely
on peasant discretion when it came to setting limits on the labor services
that might be demanded of the young *colons.* His "Recommendations to
the *Parents Nourriciers*" thus stated in no uncertain terms that beyond the
occasional errand, *parents nourriciers* were not to use their authority to
demand labor services from their young guests. Under no circumstances
were the children to be used for heavy labor in the fields, nor were they to
be sent off by themselves to guard the herd, lest the solitude of the open
fields frighten them. While tending animals was a common occupation
for very young children in rural districts, Comte worried that urban chil-

dren, unaccustomed to such great, empty silences, might grow anxious and afraid, and so develop "crippling disabilities."[47] Perhaps he recalled long and lonely hours of his own childhood spent watching the cows in some distant meadow, far from the bustling activity of the farmhouse and yard. In any event, Comte's trust in the peasant family did not extend to implicit reliance on their self-restraint in matters of work, for as this peasant son well knew, such restraint was utterly foreign to a world where hard labor was the daily lot of all concerned, including very young children.

On the other hand, the bourgeois charitable activists of the Chaussée de Maine retained some sense that the active emulation of "healthy" peasant labor would serve well the children of the urban working class, offering them an alternative vision of work from those familiar and implicitly less healthy models of urban shop and factory, where long hours of hard work were too often mixed with the rancorous leaven of syndicalist discontent. "The children have, before their eyes, the example of these good laborers, with their simple ways, living the peaceful and orderly life of the countryside. This life, with its sweet, calming influence; the healthy simplicity of this decent milieu in which the children live throughout the months of the summer holiday; the frugal meals, eaten with a robust appetite, sharpened by life in the open air; all these rich influences leave a positive trace in the minds and bodies of the children."[48] Chaussée de Maine activists thus left hanging the question of child labor, which would remain one of the murkier points in the "familial" organization of holidays for a class of children for whom hard physical labor constituted both a certain future and, too often, a present reality as well.

If cheapness constituted a prime virtue of family placement, the system of lodging children with individual families was seen to carry a number of psychological and spiritual benefits as well, benefits that no dormitory, however "familial," could deliver. Entrusted to the care of "carefully selected" peasant families, the child "lived with them as if he were their own child," reported the editors at *La Vie heureuse,* a popular women's journal of bourgeois fashion and philanthropy.[49] The familial setting was thus thought to ease the child's transition from city to countryside, balancing the abrupt change of scenery with the familiar rhythms of family life. Moreover, as Louis Comte observed, placing urban *colons* in peasant households allowed the directors to leave the child within his "natural milieu," the family. This, in turn, granted the child a "certain measure of freedom" which he could never enjoy in a collective, school-style setting, whose system of rules and discipline, though necessary to organizing the collectivity, would "deprive him of all initiative and prevent him from fully engaging in country life."[50] Hence, to the Protestant activists of the Chaussée de Maine and Enfants à la Montagne, the family unit was an efficient and adequate educational structure precisely because it was the child's "natural" milieu: "By placing [the children]with private individuals, you extend their family life while according freedom to these dear little ones," explained Comte. "Their vacations are real vacations; they can relax to their hearts' content. They can shout, sing, and run about, they can follow their *père nourricier* to the fields, the peasant wife into the garden, they can take an interest in the life of the farm, and so begin their apprenticeship as men and women."[51]

While other Protestant *oeuvres de colonies* shared this familial bias, the Chaussée de Maine was practically unique (Pastor Comte aside) in viewing ordinary peasant families as equal to the task of education by example. This confidence was partially rooted in the conviction that the urban working class, recently sprung from peasant stock, retained a living bond to its rural ancestors: "The vast majority of Parisian children are uprooted," observed Alice Delassaux, "and once they go out to the countryside, they find themselves back in their land of origin."[52] The peasant family was, therefore, the ideal landing place for urban and working-class *colons,* for as Delassaux further noted, "the children we take in are poor. If we were to place these children in institutions where they were far better off than at home, they would be completely disoriented upon returning to their families."[53] If the peasant way of life was a healthier one than that of the urban worker, the two were nonetheless bound by a common, low level of material comfort, and a roughly equivalent place near the bottom of the social hierarchy.

The idea that the popular classes of rural and urban France were one (or almost one), separated by at most a single generation's migration, was not unique to the Chaussée de Maine. On the contrary, the notional harmony of urban and rural "classes populaires" formed the implicit ground on which journalists and politicians constructed their anxious proposals for a great "return to the land," a reversal in the tides of migration that would enable the urban working class to resolve its own social misery.[54] But if the mental linkage of peasant and worker was widespread in fin-de-siècle France, the Chaussée de Maine and the Enfants à la Montagne were the only *oeuvres d'enfance* that organized their *colonies* on the basis of this precept. All other *colonies,* pro-peasant and return-to-the-land rhetoric aside, retained some notion that urban and rural constituted separate worlds. For these *oeuvres,* the exportation of "petits Parisiens" to the farms and villages of France necessarily entailed some degree of adjustment on both sides, some kind of break with the "traditional" practices that shaped daily existence within these two worlds. Urban children would thus learn to eat soup for breakfast, while peasant wives would learn to wash the children daily, rather than fortnightly.

Enforcing the rules of this encounter would fall to the lot of the *surveillant(e)s,* whose role as cultural/hygienic intermediaries and pedagogical overseers would only expand over time: "Our children are not simply dumped with their host families and left to their own devices until the day we return them to their parents," wrote Louis Comte in 1902. "We follow them closely at every moment, we watch over them daily, keeping close track of their behavior on the farm, of their health and moral condition . . . Our *surveillants* are truly the linchpin of our organization; it is on their shoulders that our entire *oeuvre* rests."[55] Of course, the *surveillants'* timely counsel was not always graciously received, as Comte was the first to acknowledge: "In the beginning (1893), the *nourriciers* regarded the *surveillants* with open mistrust, as if they were spies sent into their households to question the children and to take their side in all cases, no matter what the circumstances." Fortunately, the *surveillant(e)s* seem to have overcome peasant suspicions rather quickly; by 1902, Comte was delighted to report that the *nourriciers* now saw the *surveillants* and *surveillantes* as a "resource, precious auxiliaries whom they receive with open arms."[56] Perhaps through patient work toward greater mutual comprehension; more likely thanks to the peasants' hard-nosed appraisal of the conditions of cash flow, since refusal of the *surveillant(e)*'s intervention meant loss of the *colon* and the small income attached to his or her care. Whatever the cause, the ultimate outcome was the swift implantation of a dense network of *surveillant(e)s* who accompanied the children to their villages. Each one would pass the summer making tours of duty to some seventy to eighty children, distributed across thirty to forty families, and ensuring the hygienic and pedagogical organization of the *colonie:* "From time to time they gather a group of their children together and take them out for a walk through the countryside. During these walks they chat with the children and seek to effect a moral cure, insomuch as the fresh mountain air is effecting a physical one."[57]

Finally, the Protestant *colonies,* and the Chaussée de Maine in particular, were most insistent on retaining family placement for the freedom (*liberté*) it guaranteed the young *colons.* The notion of *liberté,* understood as a kind of primacy of the individual conscience over the needs of the collectivity, stood at the heart of all Protestant *colonies,* endowing their claims to a "familial" organization with a very specific ethical content: the individual should be shaped not with reference to the larger collectivity but rather according to the rhythm of his or her own internal needs and inclinations. For the activists of the Chaussée de Maine, then, the valorization of *liberté en famille* ultimately contained a powerful critique of the organization of the collective *colonie,* which, in their eyes, was merely an "extension" of school, and marked by "that same discipline that weighs so heavily on children."[58] Louis Comte concurred heartily in this judgment; indeed, he was even more severe in his condemnation: "If you shut children inside a house, their stay in the country will be nothing more than a continuation of school. All will pass methodically; the requisite walks and meals will all be taken according to the sound of the bell. You will make the countryside odious to them, even as you prevent these children from savoring life in the open air."[59] From its very origins, then, the *colonie de vacances* movement contained a powerful critique of the republican school, and of "that schoolhouse discipline that furrows young brows, strains their attention or turns them into machines."[60] Over time, and as the organizers defined more precisely their distinct educational mission, the *colonies* would come to constitute a site of opposition to the school, not only for its collective pressures and discipline but for its conservative pedagogical methods as well.

The family and collective living thus stood for opposing values that were inscribed in their contrasting ways of life, with the former upholding "the true instincts of mothers fighting against petty officiousness [*caporalisme*] in all its forms," wrote the organizers of the Limogeais *colonie* La Clef des Champs: "However well-intentioned they may be, schoolmasters have, in this case, a singular defect, and that is that they are no longer children; they can no longer imagine the kinds of wonderful things they were dreaming up at age twelve. What a small child discovers when left to frolic like a kid in the fields, drunk with elation at his own freedom, and with the light and the sun! Teachers have no idea about plants and flowers; they are too wise. They have the entire school year to straighten out these unmannerly kids and awaken them to solemn and learned things. The ladies who organize *colonies de vacances* have decided that this is more than enough. Long live the happiness of children having fun *en famille*! —an adoptive family when the real one is

lacking."[61] Further, the intimate and familial basis on which the young
Parisians encountered the peasant world would nourish ties of solidarity
between country and city, Protestant philanthropist and urban gamin,
a project whose efficacy rested on the small, human scale of the units
involved. In Bion's estimation, the results could be quite profound, as
"these unhappy children, who could well believe themselves abandoned
by all, have discovered that there are still in this world people who love
them and care for them. This awakens in them a sense of recognition
and satisfaction, and pushes back that spirit of rancor and discontent that
great social inequality sows so easily in the hearts of the young."[62]

Underlying the Protestant pedagogy of *liberté,* then, one finds a solidarist vision of the human community, held together by good will and
good works, alongside a conceptualization of individual child psychology in which physical, mental, and moral health were inextricably linked.
At the individual level, reinforcing these children's prematurely worn
and ill-nourished bodies would inevitably brighten their spirits as well,
in a simple child psychology in which familial attention to the children's
very basic and often ill-attended needs for physical care and affection
would build a certain self-confidence. At the social level, the women and
men of the Chaussée de Maine envisioned a chain of solidaristic bonds
linking rich and poor, peasant and urbanite in a redressive project that
reserved the privilege of country vacations to the youngest and least-
favored of Parisians. "How many poor children have no idea what a
bush or a leafy pathway looks like," wrote Elise de Pressensé in 1868.
"I am a born solidarist: my heart is with them."[63] Her faith that God
loved all his creatures with an absolute equality underwrote a solidarist social vision that was nourished by her contacts with the avant-garde
circles around philosopher Victor Considérant and Socialist leader Be-
noît Malon.[64] Mme de Pressensé thus organized her *colonies de vacances* in
the conviction that all children had a right to happiness, and to enjoy the
beauties and benefits of nature. The realization of this *redressement social*
rested only partially on the shoulders of the urban bourgeoisie. After all,
the goods of the world are plural, and even the modest families of rural
France had genuine gifts—a healthy environment and a family life that
was believed to be more continuous, unbroken by the stresses of modern urban poverty—to share with the children of the urban poor. "One
young girl . . . who lost her mother while on holiday, was lovingly taken in
by her adoptive parents, who asked as a favor if they might keep her for an
extra month for no extra salary," wrote Alice Delassaux in the Chaussée

de Maine's report for the summer of 1905. "These fine peasants set a shin-
ing example of solidarity and selflessness."[65] Collaboration in the effort
to save urban children would thus activate the very ties of solidarity on
which the realization of a more fraternal and "social" republic rested.[66]

The liberal Protestant activists of the Chaussée de Maine thus placed
their trust in the peasant family, a setting within which, it was believed,
the child could grow and develop in liberty, as an end in himself, rather
than with reference to a larger community, before whose exigencies
such individual development must necessarily conform itself. Here in
the peasant family, a more "maternal" spirit of solidarity would prevail against the regimen of group life; or so it was hoped, for curiously
enough, there is no whisper in the Protestant literature, not even in the
writings of peasant son Comte, of a peasant family ordered by paternal
authority, in which youth bows to age, and female to male. Rather, this
literature explicitly paints these families as imbued with a kind of liberal spirit that the Protestant founders tended to cast as "maternal" and
individualist, by contrast with the more paternal spirit of impersonal authority and strict collective discipline that governed the school. In this
auspicious environment, the individual *colons* would develop, physically
and intellectually, as individuals, in the liberty vouchsafed them within
the peasant family.

The mode of family placement would remain extremely widespread
in France, lasting up through the end of the 1930s (then finding new life
during the war, as children were sheltered with peasant families for the
duration), for it was no sooner adopted by Protestant charity than municipalities throughout urban France followed suit, organizing *colonies
chez les paysans* for their neediest and sickliest young citizens. As we will
see, the *colonies scolaires* formed the sole exception in this era, rejecting
family placement in favor of *colonies* that were structured by the forms
and goals of the republican school. Cottinet and his colleagues nonetheless insisted that their *colonies scolaires* retained a "familial" air, and made
much of the organization by small groups of eight to twelve students, and
the paternal/maternal bonds of affection that would, in theory, arise between teachers and students, nourished by the three to four weeks spent
living together on holiday. The notion that the *colonie* stood in for the
family, understood as the exemplar of a human group bound by non-
instrumental relations, was thus underscored at the very outset even in
this most collective and schoolroom-inspired context. Throughout the
life of the institution, and in all its many incarnations, whether Catholic

colonie with the seminarians, family placement with the peasants, even
the "red" *colonies* of the Paris suburbs, the notion that the *colonie* somehow constituted a family stood at the heart of its claim to provide a genuine moral, educational, and emotional benefit to its young *colons.*

Colonie de Vacances or *Colonie Scolaire?*
Edmond Cottinet and the "Propaedeutic" Deviation

The Calvinist tendency to mistrust institutions and fall back on the
family as a basic social, educational, and spiritual unit thus produced
a paradoxically anti-institutional institution, one that hovered uncer-
tainly between placing children with actual peasant families and housing
them inside a variety of small-scale collectives that were deemed familial
(which meant that they strove to imitate the family insofar as possible,
mixing age and gender groups among both *colons* and the directors). Republican schoolteachers and Catholic seminarians approached the organization of *colonies* with a quite different sense of the problems, priorities,
and possibilities contained therein, for these were educators by training
and experience, women and men whose familiarity with collective pedagogical settings inclined them to conceive educational ventures inside
such frameworks, and to view the absence of a larger collectivity as an
active flaw that necessarily limited the scope of any family-based system
of education.[67] Alongside and completely independent of the Protestant
colonie familiale, then, arose an entirely different model of *colonie,* one
that was based on the collective structures of the primary school and *patronage* (Catholic youth club).[68]

   This predilection for the collective certainly marked Edmond Cottinet's *colonie scolaire* from its very origins, despite the fact that those origins lay far more explicitly in the schoolteacher's crusading concern for
the children's health than in any vague pedagogical hopes he may have
held. Indeed, as we have seen, Cottinet took especial pains to distinguish
his "purely hygienic" *colonies* from the pedagogically driven *voyages scolaires* with which his colleagues rewarded the meritorious elite at the end
of the school year: "Our goal is completely different . . . it is the goal
of preventive hygiene. We wish to extract all the pale and sickly schoolchildren from the sulphurous fumes of the big city; from the confine-
ment, indolence, and world-weariness that are rife among them."[69] His
overweening concern with hygiene shaped the entire venture, from his

preferential selection of "the poorest and puniest" schoolchildren, to the organization of daily life on the holiday.[70] And yet its origins in the primary schools, its ongoing attachment to the *caisses des écoles,* and to deploying schoolteachers as *surveillants,* ensured that the *colonies scolaires* would closely echo the rhythms of the republican school.

Hygienic and pedagogical aims thus dwelt in uneasy coexistence in the *colonie scolaire.* At the outset, Cottinet maintained that the pedagogical dimension was of "secondary" importance.[71] By the turn of the century, however, the teachers who staffed the city's *colonies scolaires* had gradually reversed Cottinet's original formula, reducing the institution's hygienic and benevolent character to second rank in favor of their own increasingly well-defined pedagogical goals. In the space of a single generation, the schoolteachers of the Third Republic had produced a summertime complement to the school. Let us return to Cottinet's first *colonies scolaires,* in order to see how the shifting balance between hygiene, benevolent purpose, and pedagogical aims shaped the evolution of this institution.

In 1887, journalist Francisque Sarcey recalled the day, five years earlier, when he first heard the term "colonie de vacances" on the lips of his good friend Edmond Cottinet: "He came over to my house one day in a fever of excitement, and spoke of his idea with such warmth of heart, with that elegance of expression that comes over him when he speaks of things that truly capture his heart. It was a question of taking a certain number of poor children from the primary schools of the IXe arrondissement . . . to choose the frailest and puniest among them and take them far from Paris during the summer holiday, to the mountains or forest, for a rest cure."[72] Cottinet had it all figured out: by using funds from the *caisse des écoles,* and relying on the benevolent aid of the teachers who, for a "modest emolument," would surely agree to lead the *colonie* (and so benefit themselves from the "cure d'air" being vouchsafed to the children), the ninth arrondissement could organize summertime rest cures for some of its neediest pupils.[73] That the need for such restorative excursions was urgent none could doubt: "How do the children of our primary schools spend their summer holidays?" Cottinet asked his friend. The question was a purely rhetorical one; before Sarcey could get a word in, the agitated prophet had supplied the answer: "Most of them hang about in the streets, breathing in the poisonous air of the big city, drinking water from the Seine and eating the food provided by their families, which is usually insufficient in quantity and nearly always adulterated; in sum, replacing the hygiene of the school, which is hardly of the best, with a hygiene that is far worse yet."[74] Cottinet thus sought to enlist the forces of nature—sunshine, fresh air, vigorous exercise, and hearty food—in a program of preventive hygiene that would reinforce the fragile bodies of urban children before any real illness had taken hold of them.

It is easy enough to look back from the well-fed (and medically well-defended) vantage point of the late twentieth century and dismiss the hygienic concerns of those who organized the first *colonies,* to locate therein the Foucauldian enterprise of controlling the popular classes by imposing an increasingly strict bodily discipline on its youngest members. But this is entirely too simplistic and one-sided a view, one that ignores the pressing material context of late-nineteenth-century France. Indeed, to attribute dark Foucauldian purposes to these minions of the republican school, placed by chance in neighborhoods where youthful misery did not hide itself, is to catch but one small piece of the picture while missing the larger point. For whatever the various "civilizing missions" that impelled these women and men to action, they all arose in a context in which the mixture of city plus poverty spelled a genuine crisis of public health. Hence Dr. Grancher's famous studies of Paris schoolchildren revealed that in 1904, 62 out of 438 schoolchildren in the rather well-to-do sixteenth arrondissement had tubercular lesions on their lungs.[75] Another of Grancher's studies declared fully one out of six of the Paris school-age population to be in a tubercular or pretubercular state of health.[76]

But in the great "social scourge" of tuberculosis lay only the most dramatic side of the story; working-class children suffered homelier ailments as well—anemia, rickets, bronchitis, and a generally lethargic, or overly nervous, air, owing to chronic malnourishment and childhoods spent curled in the cramped, damp, and generally unclean housing of the urban poor. As the schoolteachers in Paris's poorest neighborhoods well knew, this wretched state of affairs only deteriorated over the summer months, when the closing of school, far from being a welcome release, consigned these children to the "disastrous" months of vacation: "Rather than being a return to paradise lost, their holidays are a foretaste of hell . . . No more games, no more schoolmates; their parents dare not let them roam the streets, for fear of accidents, or that they might fall in with the wrong sort, and so they are kept inside their apartments, and God knows how swiftly relations must sour among all these recluses."[77] Locked each day inside their narrow, dark apartments from the moment their parents left for work (six or seven in the morning), until their return some twelve

The following four photographs courtesy of the Bibliothèque Nationale de France, service reproduction, FOL-Z-953, *La Vie heureuse,* July 1903, 139.

The Departure, Gare de Lyon, ca. 1902. Under the watchful eye of the Chaussée de Maine's *dames charitables,* the children file quietly onto the train that will carry them to the rural hinterlands of the Loiret.

Children from the Chaussée de Maine *colonie* in a
Loiret farmyard, ca. 1902, feeding the "avid beaks"
of hitherto unfamiliar beasts. "The *colons* now live
on familial terms with these good, faithful, and
happy companions," declared *colonie* directors.

Four very young Parisians confront their
dinner at a peasant table. "Soup and bread,
meat four times a week, and one liter of
milk per day—this is the solid, healthy diet
by which the provinces fill out the sunken
cheeks of our little Parisians," proclaimed
the *dames charitables* of the Chaussée de
Maine in 1903.

Despite its original caption—"raised on
the arid paving-stones of Ménilmontant,
the *colons* roll in the grass and meet that
unexpected and astonishing phenomenon,
a flotilla of ducks"—the soberly clad
colons give no sign of such wild abandon
in this photo, taken on the grassy banks of
a pond near the village of Choux, in the
Loiret, ca. 1902.

hours later, gnawing at whatever meager provision for lunch and dinner might have been left on the table, these children returned to school in the fall more listless and pale than ever. For as every schoolteacher knew, summertime, "the most beautiful months of the year," was for the vast majority of working-class families the "dead season," when work was scarce, "and the children grew as slender as their mothers' wallets."[78]

These hungry, half-attentive children were doubtless no gift to teach, and Cottinet and his colleagues were surely moved by that self-interest of educators who, wishing to succeed in their mission, found themselves blocked at every turn by the poor health of their pupils: "When school starts up again in the fall, and our own children return fresh, rested, and alert . . . from country holidays spent close to nature, in Edenlike proximity to man's first friends, the animals and plants . . . those children from poor families return more pale, nervous, and frail than ever, more disposed to catch every wintertime illness."[79] One does not need to dig deep into the Foucauldian underside of the bourgeois soul in order to comprehend schoolteachers' interest in effecting a rest cure via the *colonies scolaires*.

Conveniently enough, Cottinet sat on the administrative board of the ninth arrondissement's *caisse des écoles,* from which strategic spot he ably raised the funds for that first *colonie scolaire,* in the summer of 1883.[80] Eighteen children were chosen for the initial experiment—nine girls and nine boys, sent in sex-segregated groups (recalling the model of the republican school)—to pass a full month of summer in empty school buildings at Chaumont (Haute-Marne) and Luxeuil (Haute-Saône). Prefect Favalelli of the Haute-Marne took a strong interest in Cottinet's hygienic/pedagogic experiment and initially proposed to support the venture by organizing a series of family placements for the *colonie des garçons.* But Cottinet would not hear of it: the schoolteacher's *colonies scolaires* were to be organized solely on the basis of the small, school-based collective.[81] Only then did the prefect think to propose the normal school at Chaumont. Perched on a high promontory overlooking the broad valley of the Marne, the sunlit, airy village of Chaumont admirably met the needs of the boys' *colonie.* For the girls, Cottinet chose the town of Luxeuil. Though situated at the same altitude as Chaumont, Luxeuil was protected from the winds, and so offered a steadier climate and more "sheltered" pathways for the daily promenades—all in all a far more suitable setting for the girls' more "delicate constitutions."[82]

The *colons* were recruited from a single neighborhood school—the boys' and girls' schools of the rue Blanche—so that the director would know his/her flock "intimately," and they were chosen according to Cottinet's scale, which reversed the normal order of things and reserved this benefit to "the very poorest of the frail, and most deserving of the poor."[83] Cottinet later explained this principle of selection in terms that recall Elise de Pressensé's "socialism" of solidarity: "The very poverty that condemns them has also saved these dear little ones; it has given them a reverse privilege, it has taken them out of the contaminated air of the city, it has marked them for the first places in the healthiest resorts, so that they might benefit from the prescriptions of health, from the maternal care of their teachers, and from a new kind of lesson as well, in which their teachers become nature's tutors. It has marked them for the welcoming smiles and occasional treats from the good folk of ten provinces."[84]

The teachers who took charge of those first *colonies,* Mlle Mercier and M. Lécart, were chosen for their ardent support of the project, as well as for personal qualities of intelligence, energy, and patience. Their "inborn love of children" and a "most happy coincidence of lively temperament and firmness of character" suggested they would handle well the challenge of living day in and day out with these children for a full summer month.[85] M. Lécart presented an additional advantage: until the age of twenty, he had worked the land alongside his peasant relatives, and so seemed an especially well-chosen guide to the life and ways of rural France. Finally, Cottinet strove to ensure that a certain familial spirit encircled the venture, a spirit that rested crucially on the active participation of women. The male teachers in charge of the boys' *colonies* were thus adjured to bring along their wives, so that the boys would not suffer the lack of "maternal" attention. Happily for the success of that first *colonie,* Mme Lécart proved entirely equal to the task: "Young, lively, and warmhearted, she was both sister and mother to our boys, and their gratitude to her still burns brightly."[86]

By recruiting his *colonies* along the "class" lines of the schoolroom, Cottinet renounced the mixed age-and-sex groups of the *colonies familiales* so beloved by Protestant charity in favor of single-sex groups of children between the ages of ten and twelve, thirteen at the very limit: "Any younger and there is the risk that the children will miss their mothers too much, besides which their lack of endurance slows up and curtails the daily promenades. Any older and they can no longer bring back to the school the benefit and example of their cure."[87] The notion of mixing boys with girls in the same *colonie* was too remote a possibility to even bear comment, although the following summer, the *directrice* at Chaumont did arrange for the nearby *colonie des garçons* to pay a strictly supervised visit to the girls' *colonie,* in the garden of the school where they were lodged: "We were in the study hall working on our essays," Antoinette Fauconnier later wrote in her journal, "and at each sound of the bell we raced to the windows to see who was there, because we knew the boys from the normal school would be coming, and we were eager to see them arrive. Just when everyone had finally settled down to write, the bell rang once again and we all ran back to the window. They were here. They entered though the great formal garden, then came into the hall where we were working. As soon as they began to arrive in the hall, we ran away, out into the little courtyard. Later, the boys were brought into the little courtyard as well, where they sat down on the benches along the wall, waiting to be fetched back to their *colonie.* We girls played merrily at all sorts of games, and did not pay them the least attention."[88] This icy reserve melted only a bit when it came time for the boys to receive the girls in their *colonie* several weeks later: "They hardly mixed together at all," Cottinet later admitted, "rather, one after another, each rose to recite verses of prose and poetry, and to sing. There was, however, no dancing."[89]

In order to assure the internal cohesion of these little communities, Cottinet made small groups of nine or ten the rule. After all, nine "anemic" children, freed from the classroom and let loose in an unfamiliar countryside, could stir up plenty of mischief to occupy a teacher's attention full-time: "during the train ride, in the forests and mountains, on the banks of rivers, . . . at all hours of the day and night."[90] In addition, he urged that each *colonie* form a "homogeneous contingent," drawn from the same school, so that the teacher might know as fully as possible the "delicate" troop that she or he would be heading up.[91] Cottinet thus reposed his hopes on rendering "familial" the rather different (and decidedly nonfamilial) forms of solidarity forged within the contours of the public school. With such guidelines, his *colonie* grew slowly: from 18 in 1883, to 100 in 1884 (10 groups, 5 boys, 5 girls), reaching 120 by 1886. In the spring of 1887, armed with four years' experience (covering some 350 children, all told), Cottinet presented the results of his work at a meeting of delegates from the city's twenty *caisses des écoles* and other crusaders who sought to "extend M. Cottinet's excellent work."[92] The group had been called together by Director of Primary Education Ferdinand Buisson, and included such luminaries as Victor Duruy, Alexandre Dumas (fils), and Abel Hovelaque, president of the Paris municipal council. Before this august company, Edmond Cottinet elaborated in eloquent detail the hygienic and pedagogical advantages of the *colonie scolaire*. To this end, he skillfully deployed the narrative of his own experiences with the *colonie* of the ninth arrondissement, contrasting the poverty and emptiness of his poorest students' homes with the variety and color of the weeks spent *en colonie:* "What haven't they discovered in this school of nature? Are they not now familiar with the oak and the reed, the hare and the frog, the miller and his son, and the donkey? Have they not now seen with their own eyes that the 'green hemp-plant' and 'surrounding fields of ripening wheat' are real things that exist outside of [La Fontaine's] fables?"[93] By the meeting's end, the Comité Parisien des Colonies de Vacances had been launched; Cottinet's *colonies scolaires* would henceforth enjoy the financial and promotional benefits of patronage from the highest literary and educational circles in Paris.[94]

   Daily life in the *colonies scolaires* was structured around the founders' signal desire to impart a visible measure of immediate good health along with the longer-term benefit of lessons in basic hygiene. The former was to be achieved by hearty, well-balanced meals, long hours of rest each night, and a daily "dose" of fresh air, taken on long afternoon hikes through woods and fields. The hygienic instruction began in the weeks before the departure, with the family's assemblage of the rather elaborate trousseau demanded of each *colon,* with multiple changes of clothing and a toilet kit that contained brushes for teeth, shoes, and clothing: "We hail the toothbrush, which is by no means a luxury item," wrote Edmond Cottinet in his 1887 report to the Oeuvre des Colonies de Vacances. "Everyone knows the role that cleanliness plays in preserving the teeth, and that preserving the teeth is, in turn, essential to a healthy digestion."[95] The lessons in basic hygiene were then continued inside the *colonie*'s daily routines, which opened each day with a thorough airing of both bedding and dormitory: "Rising like soldiers at six in the morning, our boys polish their shoes, brush their clothing, and sweep out the dormitory, washroom, stairs, and study hall, under the direction of the teachers' wives. Then, when they have washed themselves with soap from head to toe, they make their beds. Many parents have thanked us for imparting these new habits to their boys. For the Colonies de Vacances, you will recall, were first conceived as a school of cleanliness."[96]

The presumption that families too poor to assure their children's basic daily nutrition would, nonetheless, somehow magically produce the elaborate trousseaux on which the *colon*'s daily hygienic ritual rested seems rather at odds with Cottinet's original definition of the *colonie scolaire* as "an institution of preventive hygiene, aimed at the sickliest children in the primary schools, and the very poorest among the frail."[97] He later offered a gloss on this definition, reminding his colleagues that while the target group was indeed children from poor families, "we do not restrict our definition of poverty to extreme indigence . . . We consider 'poor' any family that cannot afford a rest cure for a sickly child"— a definition that reached well beyond the poorest classes to embrace a wide swath of the urban "classes populaires" (artisans, shopkeepers) as well.[98] Perhaps he had been driven to downplay the original scheme of priority for the very neediest students by four years of constant complaint from directors who faced an enormous job of mending and repair each summer, thanks to the shabby and incomplete state of their *colons'* trousseaux; or perhaps he had never really envisioned sending the very poorest of the poor *en colonie*.[99] But in specifying the *colonies'* mission as one that favored "poor" but not necessarily "indigent" children, Cottinet himself began to gnaw away at the institution's purely benevolent statute, and this opened a space within which the less zealous of his colleagues might begin to shift the criteria of recruitment away from the most deprived children in favor of the "good" students, whose company was doubtless more interesting to their teachers, and whose success in the classroom bore witness to their capacity to get along well with the schoolmasters and mistresses. This understandable preference to spend the summer with students whom they enjoyed, rather than with more difficult children—sickly, perhaps irritable, with intellectual horizons that were no doubt limited—emerges in the earliest reports from Cottinet's colleagues in the city's other nineteen arrondissements. Hence one school director opened the annual report on his *colonie scolaire* by expressing frank regret at the substitution of *colonies* for the old *voyages scolaires,* for, in his view, the good students were more "interesting" than the poor, sickly *colons*.[100] And in the summer of 1887, Cottinet noted with sorrow that the sixth arrondissement had chosen its *colons* from the most "delicate" of the "meritorious" students, rather than from among the very poorest, while the *colonies* of the seventeenth arrondissement included children who were neither poor nor frail "but simply those who had gotten the best grades."[101]

Through the Eyes of Children:
The Journals of the *Colonies Scolaires*

The deviation toward a more "pedagogic" organization of the *colonie,* and toward a somewhat less ill-favored student population, was surely exacerbated by Cottinet's decision to fill the summer holiday with instructive hikes, veritable *leçons de choses en plein air:* "The promenades . . . lie at the heart of our enterprise; they have entirely replaced the school. And what a new pedagogy is arising therein!" celebrated Cottinet. "It is Nature herself who conducts the class . . . not a single day passes that the children don't go out to hear the 'lectures' of the fields and woods, the teachings of the donkey and the cow, the solfège sung by all the birds." [102] A portion of these visits were devoted to the creations of man: quarries, lighthouses, ports, factories, abattoirs, even a prison, which left a "grave impression" on the young visitors.[103] And each day, the "school of nature" provided its own *leçons de choses:* "The children caught for themselves the fish for last night's dinner, in the river where we swim. Tomorrow they will make an illustrated book of plants from flowers they have gathered, and then follow the beasts back to the farm. The other day they followed them to market, to see how it is they are sold, then, finally, to the abattoir, where the veterinarian, M. Desnouveaux, explained the function of each internal organ in a most successful anatomy lesson. As for the grain that was being threshed on the farm, now they see it arrive at the mill, where the miller himself explains its transformation into flour. When they took their leave of the obliging M. Friesenhauser, the children were covered in flour and science." [104]

   The girls engaged in a quieter round of activities, more oriented toward the domestic affairs in which they were presumed to be interested: "Here, no visits to the quarries, slaughterhouses, and prisons, thank you very much!" wrote Cottinet in the winter of 1884, after perusing the journals kept by the young girls over the previous summer holiday. While the girls did explore the weaving sheds at a nearby textile mill, and then wrote up a "perfect" account of their visit, they took no trouble to hide the fact that it was the concierge's cow, and her two white goats, that stirred their greatest enthusiasm.[105] Every morning after breakfast the girls would clean and sweep out both kitchen and dormitory—tasks that were not incompatible with more childlike forms of amusement, as one young girl's journal reminds us: "We spent the morning putting our things away and setting our room to right; making the beds, sweeping and dusting. When we had finished we climbed up to the hayloft and rolled in the hay, then went back down to the garden." [106] In addition, "Madame" made it clear that each girl would take her turn assisting with the preparation and clean-up at mealtimes: "This pleased us because we like being useful, but also because it teaches us how to do such things back at home," wrote twelve-year-old Régine Orner. If her honeyed words betray an unfailing sense of what "Madame" would like to see when reviewing the pages of her journal, they also suggest that the self-esteem of these young adolescent girls was bound up with acquiring competence in the basic household tasks performed by adult women: "Our parents must say that we made good use of our vacations, that we are not lazy things, that we know something about keeping house." [107] Of course the boys performed precisely these same domestic chores in their own *colonie,* but these acts were unburdened by any rhetoric of home economics. [108]

In the afternoons, the girls took their own "little" promenades, wherein the domestic theme was often pursued with a vengeance: "What interested them most was the market," observed Cottinet, "where they went twice a week and compared prices with those in Paris. Then there was the mill, where they were every bit as well received as the boys." [109] "Madame" was careful to see that her young charges take in the "picturesque" side of the country as well, in a series of visits to the churches and cemeteries that graced the episcopal city and its nearby villages: "The altar is surmounted by paintings of very fine quality," wrote ten-year-old Gabrielle Lachaud of the chapel at Saint-Dié. "It is Madame who told us so, but I think her guidebook helped her enormously in discerning precisely what is meant by 'quality.' " [110] Marthe Savantré especially appreciated a guided tour of the city library, where the librarian opened, page by page, the city's great treasure, an illuminated missal of rare beauty: "Once again, a man who takes us seriously and imagines us capable of understanding his explanations." [111] Others were more taken by the field trips to forge and factory, where one fervent young *patriote* learned "with joy" that the steels used in Edouard Magot's filemaking works at Vesoul came from Firminy, "and are, thus, French." [112]

If the weather was especially fine, the girls would renounce sightseeing altogether in favor of outdoors occupations: a swim in the cold waters of the river, a hike out to Frouard's farm in search of fresh milk, a walk through a nearby wood to a clearing, where they might pause to hear "Madame" read under the welcome shade of a dogwood tree.

Or they might spend the day in the fields helping out with the harvest: "They taught us to turn the hay, to bale, tie, and bring in the oats, and to harvest the hops."[113] If a tinker happened to pass along the way, the girls would stop his wagon and surround it with eager curiosity, posing all kinds of questions about his métier, "which touches so closely on their future lives as housewives."[114] It would seem that the orientation toward home economics, already well installed in the Republic's *écoles de filles,* structured daily life for girls *en colonie* as well—or so went the official program. But the journals kept by the young girls suggest that lessons in domesticity frequently lost out to more playful occupations: "In the afternoon we went to Robach and then into the Châtel wood, where we were to read, crochet, and rest ourselves, or so Madame told us. Upon reaching the woods, we didn't do any crochet work, we didn't read, we didn't rest; rather, we ran, we balanced on the trunks of fallen trees, we gathered flowers and made bouquets."[115]

Cottinet crowned his "nouvelle pédagogie" with the requirement that each child keep a daily journal. The *colons* devoted an hour each morning to the redaction of these documents, which were intended to serve both as a daily intellectual exercise and as proof positive to the directors of the *caisses des écoles,* on whose patronage the *colonies* rested, that the children were indeed developing intellectually while on holiday.[116] As Cottinet repeatedly emphasized, this visible intellectual progress owed primarily to the pedagogy of experience, which reigned supreme in the *colonies scolaires.* Hence the point of the journals was not simply to maintain the "habit" of writing, but for the children to develop an active awareness of how they were spending their time: "By explaining a rural task, the location of a building, the use of a machine, or simply recounting their own impressions . . . some of the most backward boys, hitherto incapable of taking down the simplest dictation, have found themselves able to *write from nature.*"[117] Where traditional, schoolroom methods had failed, Cottinet's "new" pedagogy of experience was scoring real success, as boys from the sixth form who had never managed to write a thing during dictation, "no matter what the subject," were now producing "quite respectable journals on the basis of things they had *seen,* and this impressed their schoolmasters deeply."[118]

In addition, the journal would serve the teachers well in their struggle against the twin dangers—boredom and laziness—that lurked around the edges of daily life *en colonie.* Cottinet thus claimed that the obligation to write each day would break up the time into differentiated moments;

without it, "the days might seem too long, the games less delightful, and boredom would quickly lead them to pine away." [119] The time for personal reflection afforded by the daily sessions with one's journal was doubtless appreciated by those introspective spirits accustomed to reflecting on their feelings via the written word. But for school-weary children, fatigued not only by poverty, ill-health, and the stresses of city life but also by ten months of relentless "bourrage de crâne" in the regular school classroom, the official consecration of an hour a day to this "devoir de vacances" was surely no treat. Moreover, the journal doubtless reinforced that "propaedeutic deviation" of the *colonies scolaires* for which Wilhelm Bion would later criticize them, lamenting their "obsession with instruction" and mocking the "childish and cumbersome inanities" such pedantic obsessions produced: "books of plants, collections of insects, rocks, and butterflies; it is a triumph of the born schoolmaster. And the child finds no time to act in the spontaneity of his own young spirit, to admire nature in its august and magnificent glory, to give himself over to the mysterious essence of things." [120]

But the journals also provide a unique perspective on country life in France at the end of the nineteenth century, as seen through the eyes of children, and are therefore worth examining in some detail. Particularly interesting are the glimpses they afford of rural-urban relations at the end of the nineteenth century, of the mutual suspicions and preconceptions that shaped these encounters. Young Marthe Savantré spent a month in the episcopal "city" (bourg, more likely) of Saint-Dié in the summer of 1884, an experience which seems to have reinforced her preexisting certainty that urban life is innately superior, or at least more lively and interesting, than rural folkways: "The town is quite clean, but that is hardly surprising; we've met no more than four people." [121] But it was her comrade, Gabrielle Lachaud, who captured quite precisely the unexpected quality that attended the encounter of city child and peasant under the sign of these first *colonies:* "As we walked back through the village, we stopped for some milk at the home of the funniest woman, who at first thought Madame was mother to all of us. She then peppered us with a host of questions in order to find out who we were, where we came from, what we were doing there in her village. Nearly all the country people we've met have been like that. They want to know everything, and then nearly always finish by saying: 'Ah, you're from Paris, I have a sister in Paris—or it might be an aunt, or a cousin—she works for a grocer, near the railway station. Perhaps you know her; her name is' And then they tell you her name. Oh, these country folk are so funny!"[122]

Not every village dweller betrayed such charming enchantment with the colony of young Parisians in their midst, and "Madame's" report on the *colonie* that same summer unfolded a catalog of indignities to which various village demons had subjected her young charges: not only had "naughty urchins" followed the "young ladies" about, throwing stones and tugging at their straw hats, but one man had actually chased after them with a broom, yelling "dirty Protestants"! It seems he had mistaken the *colons* for the wintertime occupants of the "heretics' house"—that is, the Protestant boarding school—where the *colonie* was lodged: "It is an offense to some in this ancient episcopal city. But what annoys our girls the most is the constant gawking. When they stop a peasant dairymaid as she's going to market and drink up her entire stock right there in the street, people gather round them to stare."[123] After several weeks, the role of urban exotic must have grown tiresome indeed to these young girls: "One can only conclude that the people of Saint-Dié haven't got anything better to do if they stop to stare at young girls drinking milk," wrote one fed-up Gabrielle.[124] At the same time, one can well imagine how utterly unexpected these young ladies must have seemed as they paraded through town and village in two straight lines, straw hats planted firmly on their heads.

Cottinet's 1887 report to the newly organized Comité Parisien provides a parallel commentary on the children's lives and experiences *en colonie,* a commentary that in some sense retells the tales of Gabrielle and Marthe from the perspective of the teacher. The schoolmaster thus cast in a more positive light the experience of being gawked at and questioned at every turn, remarking that in the *colons'* reactions to such treatment, one could read the positive impact that "temporary exile" from home and family was having on the children's social and moral development: "In this new way of life, lived under the eyes of strangers, our little Parisians show the instinct to do their native city proud. They watch themselves; their conduct and language have improved. With no possible recourse to their absent families, they undertake to support each other, to help each other, to care for each other, in this temporary exile which unites them."[125]

Cottinet's report also underscored the importance of this direct contact with rural life for the broader education of the young Parisians: "We so often bemoan our children's ignorance regarding rural life, and the *colonies de vacances* are thus praised for the incomparable opportunity they give for various *leçons des choses*. Few, however, choose to speak of the opportunities they offer for *leçons de personnes*. It is all well and good to distinguish wheat from rye, but how much more important to distinguish true peasants from mere louts. As useful as it is to know the plough, the sower, the reaper, how much more important to know the laborer; he who sows, he who reaps. And when the Parisian has admired these great laborers at work, struggling under wind and rain to draw plants or fruit from the miserly, ungiving earth, and has then seen them smile . . . or reach up to shake down the desired fruit that dangles from the tree, then the little Parisian is no longer inclined to believe the terrible things that are said about those who feed France." [126] A valuable lesson for the peasantry as well, who could now discover "the good will, sweetness and courtesy of these so-called urchins, who reveal themselves to be the very flower of our people." [127] Yet in the end, the tone of Cottinet's commentary, with its frequent reference to Parisians' low opinion of the peasantry, quite reinforces the suspicions raised on reading these girls' journals: proponents of a *retour à la terre* would have to work very hard indeed to convince these young Parisians of the wisdom of such a move. As one young girl recorded with vehemence, "It seems that the people of Saint-Dié eat boiled meat every day. Well, I can grow up and I can grow old, but I will never marry a man from Saint-Dié for fear that he will guard his unhappy love for that daily stew." [128]

The *colonies scolaires* thus staked their claim to a distinctive place in the structures of public education on the basis of successes scored in both hygienic and pedagogic realms—successes that, in Cottinet's estimation, flowed from the novel pedagogical practices that arose therein. These practices targeted the child's overall development, conceptualized as an interdependent unity of physical and moral, social and spiritual/intellectual needs, and defined the rhythm of daily life accordingly: "We rise early each day, much earlier than in Paris . . . Every *colon* starts by making his bed. If he refuses to do so, or if he is too little, we help him for a few days. Each *colon* cleans his shoes and brushes his clothing . . . Once this is done, we move on to the toilette, and the entire body is soaped up and then rinsed in plenty of water." All meals were taken together, for the *colonie* was "a family," and Cottinet recommended that children set and clear the table, "so long as there is not too much destruction to be feared from their clumsiness." In this pedagogy of family life, passed in the company of one's teachers and schoolmates, each moment *en colonic* contained opportunities for expanding the children's repertoire of those ordinary, everyday accomplishments that were "every bit as useful as they were foreign to the majority of poor children."[129]

Once these basic tasks of daily life had been seen to, it was up to the individual schoolteachers to decide how to organize the rest of the day, "to vary the hikes, which are the central business of life *en colonie,* while never forgetting that the training must be progressive. One should be neither too tough nor too timid ... And bring along a lunch, for the more they live in the outdoors, the better off they will be." Nor should they shrink from applying the beneficial effects of "hydrotherapy," weather permitting: "A few short river baths on hot days ... these great cold dips whose efficacity has proven almost miraculous, should be prudently applied, so long as they are carefully surveilled."[130] On days when it rained, "aside from the games, songs, and dances common to both sexes, girls will have their needlework and mending; boys will have rural chores, which are always easily found, and gymnastic exercise. They can also write more frequently to their parents ... When evening comes, we have seen *colonies* that have succeeded with theatrical games and impromptu dances." And if worst came to worst, there were always the back pages of one's journal to be filled.[131]

Over time, public advertisement of the *colonies'* hygienic benefits grew steadily more elaborate. Hence Cottinet's earliest reports close with statistically unverifiable exclamations over the color restored to city-pale cheeks, over the abundant force and energy that surged through the bodies and spirits of children so transformed by the four-week *cure d'air* as to be unrecognizable to their own parents when they came to collect them upon return.[132] By the mid-1880s, however, Cottinet and his colleagues were gathering a most precise array of statistics and data on which to rest the *colonies'* hygienic claims: inches and kilos gained, the rise in red blood cell count, the increase in thoracic perimeter.[133] This passion for results culminated in a system of detailed "psycho-medical certificates" on which the particular health trajectory of each *colon* was recounted in scrupulous detail. The certificates give a good idea of the chronic ill-health suffered by the children of the urban poor, a host of interlocking minor ailments that stripped the child of that very excess of energy and joyful spirits that was supposed to define this period of life:

Au départ	*Au retour*
Faded gums	Healthy color
Pallid face	Good color
Morning cough	No more cough
Frequent bloody noses	No more bleeding
Upset stomach	No more nausea
Headaches	No more headaches
No appetite	Normal appetite
Very nervous	Quite calm
Interrupted sleep, trouble breathing	Peaceful sleep, breathes easily
Rickets; can walk only short distances, slowly, on a flat terrain	Gradually comes to follow his comrades everywhere, to climb hillsides and walk quite quickly
Can only climb to the 5th floor with help	Now climbs to the 5th floor unaided (to the great surprise of his family)
Knows neither how to dress himself nor make his own bed, nor brush his own clothing; can hardly wash himself	Dresses himself, makes his own bed, brushes his clothes, enjoys washing himself
Uneven temper, very irritable	Sweeter-tempered, less cheeky, happier; has acquired orderly habits.[134]

In sum, we get the very picture of the sickly child, with his sunken chest, wasted limbs, and pale, anxious face, for whom a month of hearty meals and open-air, country living provided a rapid and efficacious cure.

Alongside the hygienic balance sheet, the *colonies scolaires* recorded with equal pride their annual pedagogical record. First came the acquisition of new habits of cleanliness, which was next of kin to godliness, or at least good health in this newly pasteurized world: "Filthiness, the abandonment of the self, disorderliness of things and people, these are the vices of poverty. Where can their children rid themselves of all this if not in the *colonies*?"[135] If not an absolute guarantee of good health, rigorous hygiene nonetheless provided the strongest shield available against the epidemics that still mercilessly stalked the children of the popular classes:

"Among the poor, hygiene is hardly better than in the streets," noted the editors of *La Vie heureuse,* "and if an epidemic of measles or typhoid strikes, one sees the long line of little white coffins marching toward Ivry and Pantin [cemeteries]."[136] Of course the children were not meant to be the sole beneficiaries here: "For don't working-class households gain something in the habits of cleanliness, orderliness, and politeness that the *colons* bring back with them?"[137] Once again, we find ourselves in the presence of that extraordinary faith in the personally and socially transformative power of education peculiar to late-nineteenth-century France. While Ferry's primary schools were clear standard-bearers in this realm, Socialists and Catholics also shared the confident hope that education of the whole child, not just in mind or intellect but in body and soul as well, constituted the high road to individual and social improvement.[138]

Second came the benefits of contact with nature, to whose beauties children were thought to be especially attuned: "They are highly sensitive to all of nature's spectacles, which are entirely new to them: the depth of the woods, the majesty of the mountains, the infinite space of the starry sky. Their souls are permanently uplifted by all this."[139] Hand in hand with this spiritually elevating experience traveled the homelier lessons brought by contact with those "noble souls" who worked the land. Significantly, the children did not undergo this education individually, as with family placement, but in the company of their peers, with whom they shared the common condition of adapting to a new world and a new way of life.

But the ultimate guarantee of the *colonie scolaire*'s pedagogical efficacy lay in the constant and mindful presence of the schoolteacher, on whose long experience and "innate love of children" Cottinet posed the success of his project. This latter advised the teachers to throw their schoolbooks by the wayside and follow the path of Rabelais: "You will find it most appealing to toss your books away over the windmills, to forget all syllabi and inspections, to declaim outdoors in the countryside, as Rabelais recommended, to take a field of alfalfa as your text and a peasant as your tutor."[140] One can imagine how rare a bird was the "maître" or "maîtresse" who actually applied the spontaneous pedagogy of the woods and fields; nonetheless, the simple fact of enjoying a more intimate and familial relationship to his or her pupils would, hopefully, sow educational benefits that the teacher could then reap throughout the following year: "How differently they regard their teachers once they have seen them get up in the night to cover them as soon as they hear them coughing, sometimes rising more quickly than their own fathers would. How differently they see the schoolmistress who helps them make their beds, bandages the wounds of the girl with scrofula, or carries on her back the girl with the sprained foot . . . What sweetness spreads in their relations once they are back in school! Their studies will benefit from this surplus-value of affection as much as their health." [141] In his most utopian and optimistic moments, Cottinet identified that "surplus-value in affection" as the most enduring and potentially transformative benefit of life *en colonie,* for the teachers, to be sure, but also for the students, who, upon experiencing the "maternal devotion" of the teacher, would open their hearts and spirits to the good in life: "Their hearts are won over, their gratitude, like their health, will endure. The *colonies de vacances* have put something more than good scholarly relations between teacher and pupil, and that something—affection—transforms life." [142]

Cottinet had brought the *colonies de vacances* to the schoolchildren of Paris under the sign of the public primary school. If the organization by school class brought certain functional advantages—ease in locating and identifying the neediest candidates, grouping together pupils and teachers who already knew one another—this organization carried certain dangers as well, notably the temptation to simply transport the schoolroom, with all its *devoirs* and disciplines, into a new, rural setting. The trick, then, would be to temper the collective disciplines of the *colonie scolaire* with that intimate and easy friendship, bridging the hierarchical divide of teacher and pupil with what Cottinet liked to call an *esprit familial.* Perhaps then the need for collective order would not overwhelm the individual initiative and spontaneity of the children. As the *colonies scolaires* expanded, however, many *caisses* abandoned Cottinet's "familial" principles and moved inexorably toward the familiar models of the classroom: twenty to twenty-five students, rather than nine or ten, came to constitute the modal *colonie* for most Paris arrondissements by the turn of the twentieth century, a size that implied a resort to familiar techniques of learning and control. As more than one schoolmaster discovered, these pedagogical techniques, so admirably suited to imparting the multiplication tables, or the location of France's Far Eastern colonial possessions, were far less well adapted to imparting the kind of holistic education that Cottinet had so movingly preached before the Comité Parisien des Colonies de Vacances. [143]

Against the Propaedeutic Deviation

With the solid patronage of the Comité Parisien behind them, the *colonies scolaires* expanded rapidly in the last decade of the nineteenth century, rising from 847 in 1888 (415 girls and 432 boys) to 1,246 *colons* in 1899.[144] With the expansion in numbers came a turn to more permanent facilities. Whereas empty rural schoolbuildings had sufficed for Cottinet's small "familial" *colonies* in 1885, the *caisses* of turn-of-the-century Paris deemed an investment in larger, year-round facilities essential to the expanding hygienic and pedagogic mission of the *colonies scolaires*. During the last years of the century, the hygienic ambitions of these *colonies* had grown more elaborate, with coastal villas being added to the traditional rural locations, feeding dreams of sending children to spend not just four weeks but four to six months, even the full school year, in the restorative atmosphere of the *colonie*. The *villas scolaires* slowly multiplied, the off-season *colonies* expanded, yet when it came to sending children to live year round *en colonie,* the *caisses* hesitated; was this not merely a veiled way of extracting the child from its own family? "When a child lives far from his family for so many months, his maintenance in the countryside being underwritten by the *caisses des écoles* of municipal government, it seems to constitute in reality a disguised placement, one that will lead to a relaxing of the family tie."[145]

Along with the growth and development of the *colonies scolaires* came renewed criticism of the collective approach from philanthropists who feared that children's freedom to develop and do as they pleased on holiday would be utterly crushed by the weight of institutional forms and routine. It was, after all, difficult to believe that the simple fact of passing a month together in some rural schoolhouse could displace the familiar, hierarchical lines that shaped pupil-teacher relations over the regular school year in favor of easier, more "familial" relations, let alone relax the strict habits of discipline. Indeed, reports from the fin-de-siècle *colonies scolaires* suggest that such fears were quite justified: "I must point out . . . that the *colonisation* is too long," wrote the director of the *colonie* of the eighth arrondissement in 1889. "I noticed that the majority of the children find that after about two weeks, the days grow quite wearisome. Such boredom is perhaps surprising, especially in the midst of such a lovely countryside, with the great variety of hikes and sights to see, each more remarkable than the last."[146]

If boredom plagued some *colonies,* other directors reported the difficulties they had in getting children (especially the boys, it seems) to write
in their journals each day. The directors of the *colonies* in the sixth arrondissement were so despairing on this latter point that in 1889 they
decided to gather the *colons* in a room at the town hall a few days after the
return, so that they could "acquit themselves of this obligation" under
the surveillance of a member of the *caisse.*[147] One is struck by the grim
adherence to school-based notions of duty and achievement, and the felt
need to counter what the mayor of the second arrondissement termed
"the monotony of the sojourn," an ever-present danger that led the teachers to fill the children's days with ultraorganized and closely surveilled
occupations in order to "ward off boredom and nostalgia for their families."[148] And while the *caisses* all adjured their directors to share the children's lives and maintain a "most paternal discipline" among them—
"to look after them; in a word, to replace their families"—the accounts
of daily life as it actually unfolded in the *colonies scolaires* suggest that
Cottinet's vision of pupil-teacher relations being "transformed" by a few
weeks of day-in, day-out contact was a utopian one that was rarely, if ever,
achieved.[149] It would seem that Cottinet's original "familial" design had
been utterly overwhelmed, engulfed by the traditions and practices of the
republican school. This impression is reinforced by journalist François
Ponsard's account of his official visit to the eleventh arrondissement's
colonie scolaire at Mandres-sur-Vair (Vosges) in the summer of 1905.[150]

Though clearly aware that the Mandres *colonie* constituted something
of a showplace, Ponsard took no pains to hide his own cynical amusement
at the less-than-splendid spectacle that unfolded before him in this decidedly unpicturesque corner of the Vosges countryside: "It is without a
doubt one of the more dull countrysides in France: no trees, no bodies of
water, not even real mountains. The term "Vosges" here is nothing more
than an administrative convenience, the name of the *département,* for one
can see no hint of the slightest foothill." The *colonie* itself was lodged in
the quite unexceptional family estate of M. Duval-Pihet, former mayor
of the eleventh arrondissement, who had pompously dubbed his property "the ancient château of Mandres-sur-Vair." Though utterly uninter-
esting from a historical or architectural point of view, the "château" was
still a most pleasant abode for the little street urchins of the eleventh
arrondissement, "accustomed to the decor of the rue Popincourt."

Upon arriving, the ministerial commission found all two hundred
colons assembled in the courtyard, waiting to perform for the honored

dignitaries: "The two hundred little gamines were lined up in the courtyard, defying the sunshine and singing the music of Rouget de l'Isle, accompanied by a piano, the only one in the region." But many of the young
girls were too distraught to contribute to the patriotic hymn, as their tear-
ful eyes searched the audience in the vain hope of seeing their parents;
"several were sobbing outright." It seems the ministerial visit coincided
with the annual invitation to parents to come out and tour the *colonie,*
an invitation that precious few parents had actually accepted: "Having
placed the girls facing the entryway, [the directors] had had the bizarre
idea of hanging above this charming company an immense red placard
bearing the inscription LOOK FOR ME. But out of two hundred young
girls, more than one hundred expected no visitor, for their fathers and
mothers had already written to say that they could not come, and their
little hearts were breaking at this reception from which their own parents were absent. After this charmless "Marseillaise," the privileged ones
broke ranks and ran to kiss their parents. The others cried, sentimental
girls of ten and still not adjusted to the separation from their families,
after five days in the *colonie.* At this moment, how the cramped abode
in la Folie-Méricourt, or at number five rue du Chemin-Vert, must have
seemed like very heaven."

With this tragi-comic conclusion, the children's patriotic pageant gave
way to a solemn banquet, garnished by speeches from M. Darnay (current mayor of the eleventh arrondissement), M. Duval-Pihet, and — inex-
plicably — Minister of the Navy M. Thomson. The child who had gained
the most weight (three kilos) was given a prize for her excellent performance, while the unfortunate creature who had failed to gain a single kilo
was awarded a consolation prize for her sorrows. The entire company
was then invited to take the tour of the *colonie.* All too soon it was time to
leave: "We kissed the girls, whose grief was already forgotten, and who
were playing with all their hearts . . . we then climbed back aboard our
special train, acknowledging all the while that this *colonie scolaire* was
an extremely fine work perched in an extremely ugly countryside." [151]

Ponsard had no special ax to grind in favor of one form of *colonie*
over another; in fact, he clearly found the entire visit a source of great
amusement, from the grim Vosges countryside, with its much-vaunted
yet rather tawdry "château," to the climactic prize-giving ceremony for
kilos gained — a bizarre parody of the annual prizes for academic excel-
lence distributed at the end of the school year. It is precisely his lack of
any stake in the matter that makes Ponsard's testimony so valuable, for

as the narrative of the visit unfolds, it reveals just how far the *colonies sco-laires* had traveled down the road of reproducing the republican primary school in summer dress.

At the same time, it is important to recall that the directors' failure to transform traditional student-teacher relations in the *colonies scolaires,* let alone reproduce an *air de famille,* did not necessarily signal disaster. On the contrary, as one young girl's account of her *colonie*'s "grand bal" reminds us, the *colonies scolaires* continued to provide opportunities for novelty and amusement to the children of the urban poor: "There were Venetian lanterns strung through the trees, and we were allowed to dance with the boys, but they, luckier than we, were allowed to keep dancing until 10; the young ladies were expected to go to bed at 8 P.M., like every other night."[152]

By the turn of the century, the critics of the "illiberal" structures of the collective *colonie* had joined voices with a wider-ranging chorus that accused the *colonies scolaires* of having turned their backs on their original, benevolent mission. Rather than assuring a restorative month in the country to the very neediest and sickliest pupils, the directors and teachers had simply extended into the summer months the disiciplines and petty favoritism of the schoolroom. The debate was pursued in an especially vigorous exchange among members of the Société Internationale pour l'Étude des Questions d'Assistance, which in the spring of 1903 devoted two long meetings to the study and review of the organization, function, and impact of *colonies de vacances* at home and abroad.[153]

At these meetings, the *colonies scolaires* were criticized less for their propaedeutic deviation from Cottinet's original scheme than for having created structures whose comparatively high per-pupil cost necessarily excluded the broad mass of needy and anemic children. Critics thus cast a jaundiced eye at the relative luxury of the villas, to whose comforts these children were utterly unaccustomed, and whose expense forced the *caisses* to restrict the numbers sent *en colonie* each year. Directors of the *caisses* bristled at the accusation that the newly acquired villas constituted an excessively luxurious setting, claiming, rather, that they were not "luxurious" but simply "healthy and clean": "We teach them to behave properly and to eat well, and they can easily maintain these habits of personal hygiene back in their families."[154] But there was no denying the fact that the cost per child was far higher than for the private foundations of Protestant charity: from 53 F to 120 F per child per month, versus the 42 F per child monthly pension that the Chaussée de Maine and Oeuvre de Trois Semaines paid to their peasant host families.[155] If the *colonies scolaires* had expanded since the days of Edmond Cottinet, that expansion seemed to have reached a ceiling by the early twentieth century; in 1902, only 3.75 percent of the primary school population (5,329 students—an average of 266 per arrondissement) left the city for a restorative country holiday with their schoolmates.

Debate grew more heated when one Dr. Drouineau observed that the *colonies scolaires* did not always send the poorest children from the neighborhood, but rather those who benefited from some kind of local patronage: "Poverty is, thus, not the central criterion, at least in some arrondissements," he hinted darkly.[156] Arthur Delpy replied to the criticism with a ritual invocation of Cottinet's formula that it was "the most anemic among the very poorest" who were selected for this benefit, for the *colonies* were, in essence, a form of social assistance.[157] At this point Alice Delassaux of the Chaussée de Maine leapt into the fray: "But that principle is not always respected . . . I have a certain experience with *colonies de vacances,* for we take children from all the arrondissements in Paris and from the industrial suburbs as well, but I know that in most [*colonies scolaires*] children are sent to the countryside by favoritism. Why? Because the children who are not sent are too ill-clad, or get bad grades in school, or simply don't please the teacher."[158] By this point tempers had risen sufficiently that the president deemed it wise to adjourn, with the promise that M. Delpy would open the next session with a full exposé of the relative advantages and disadvantages of group living versus family placement. Before he could actually bring the session to a close, however, Alice Delassaux waved her hand once more: "I must add—there are no teachers in the room? . . . The greatest stumbling block in the *colonies de vacances scolaires* is the schoolmaster himself."[159]

The discussion that unfolded at the following session reviewed a number of arguments we have seen before: family placement cost less and gave the children a gift of freedom, the chance to stretch their limbs and run with abandon after ten months of living cramped under the twin disciplines of insufficient space at home and of a school whose pedagogy rested on children sitting quietly at their desks. Moreover, life on the farm would give these "little city dwellers" an invaluable apprenticeship to a rural life "of which many know nothing."[160] To which the teachers replied with some rather strong points in favor of the collective *colonie,* whose centralized form allowed the directors to watch over their charges more closely and to provide them with a level of comfort and hygiene that was generally not available in peasant households. The implied critique of peasant hygiene came through loud and clear. Moreover, urban resources, it was argued, gave the directors access to a wider range of food products and to the latest dietary wisdom, allowing them to provide a more balanced and healthy regime to their anemic young clientele. In the "relentless" struggle against tuberculosis, did this broader hygienic control not count for something?

But in the end it was the argument from pedagogic advantage that held the day, an argument in which the teachers invoked their classroom-based knowledge of children to criticize family placement for its lack of attention to the intellectual and social aspects of child development, in particular to the child's need for the company of peers — shaped and directed, of course, by the conscientious oversight of the schoolmaster: "Our *colons* must be able to leave their urban milieu without feeling too much like fish out of water. They need to find themselves among friends who, sharing the same preferences and the same education, are ready to frolic with them. They need to be watched over by schoolmasters who know their characters and can appreciate their good points and judge their failings." [161] No system of *surveillants* could make up for the absence of this context; however active they might be in their efforts to provide a collective animation to their *colonie chez les paysans,* the "intellectual benefits of the common life," guided by the "moralizing and educative influence of the schoolmaster *surveillant,*" would always be sorely lacking. "In a collective *colonie,* the child is never alone, he always has something to do," added Louis Delpérier. "His life is never monotonous, as it becomes after several days in a family placement. From the intellectual standpoint, the collective *colonie* develops the child's intelligence considerably because trained educators are there to stimulate and guide this intellectual flowering . . . the lectures, discussions, and [cinema] projections increase the small capital of his knowledge." [162]

We are a long way indeed from the pedagogy of *liberté en vacances,* wherein the child ingests peasant virtues — those modest appetites and habits of hard work that spring from proximity to the land — by a process of unconscious emulation that is, in theory, analogous to the cognitive process that unfolds in the bosom of his or her own family. The directors of *colonies scolaires* doubted very much that such a learning process ever actually unfolded in peasant placement for the very simple reason that such organization blithely ignored the fundamentals of child psychology: children who are lonely, isolated in unfamiliar surroundings, do not make avid pupils. As a Dr. Noir testified, "One can be sure that a child from Paris, placed with peasants, no matter how well-meaning, will feel out of his element. The mode of life, hygiene, and education in Paris are, in fact, completely different from those of the country; the mores and language are utterly different."[163] At least one *surveillant* from Pastor Comte's program agreed that family placement demanded an often difficult adjustment on the part of urban children to the more taciturn and isolated world of the peasantry: "The farms are certainly far from cheerful; they have an austere, even sad air about them, although they are well-kept. The inhabitants show the effects of this austerity; they are not very talkative, and seem a bit rough, but they are, at heart, scrupulously honest . . . The children whom you have placed here were a bit homesick at first, and I had a hard time getting them to buck up. Happily that did not last long; three or four days later, their good spirits had returned."[164]

As far as the directors of *colonies scolaires* were concerned, the absence of peers, and of trained educators, willing and able to oversee the hygienic and moral/intellectual education of the *colons,* weighed heavily against the looser system of family placement. And if the collective format demanded a structure of discipline, well, this was in the interests of the entire community, and did not prevent the children from profiting from their rural surroundings. On the contrary, in the company of friends and the familiar faces of their teachers, the *colons* could draw the maximum benefit, expanding their horizons with the minimum pain or effort. "Many of these children have never been outside their own neighborhood," wrote M. Delarasse of the tenth arrondissement. "For them, the universe is reduced to the two or three streets where they play, or make mischief, to be more precise. All of a sudden they find themselves in the midst of the woods and fields. Their eager eyes open wide to contemplate this natural world, unknown to most of them. The great spectacle moves them, enchants them, and instructs them. They exchange their impressions with a most vivid joy. And in this family setting, the schoolmasters and mistresses are so happy to give them true *leçons de choses.* In this fashion they learn many new things with astonishing rapidity, yet without mental fatigue, things that will remain graven on their memories forever."[165] The *colonies scolaires* thus presented many of the same advantages of family placement—proximity to the land, a healthy regimen of long rest, good food, and plenty of exercise, all in the good country air—without the main disadvantage, namely, reliance on the peasantry for a host of hygienic and pedagogic tasks it was simply unfit to perform.

These were two structures, two ways of life, two views of the peasantry, and of the potential long-term benefits, hygienic and intellectual, that might be drawn from a month or more *en colonie*. The activists from Protestant programs remained unconvinced by the pedagogues' arguments, and continued to militate on behalf of family placement in the name of cheapness and *liberté*. One activist, Dr. Beauvisage (deputy mayor in the Lyon city council and director of the city's Oeuvre Lyonnais des Enfants à la Montagne), went so far as to suggest that the *colonies scolaires* might be exaggerating their hygienic record — by incompetence if not downright treachery — at the all-important weigh-in of the *colons* as they returned from their summer holiday, for "upon their return . . . some children filled their pockets with heavy objects in order to weigh even more."[166] The partisans of family placement were thus equally prepared to argue that their organization carried the decisive hygienic advantage; it was, after all, as a program of preventive hygiene that the fin-de-siècle *colonies de vacances* staked their distinctive claim on the benevolent/public health landscape: "Dr. Landouzy has said that if we believe tuberculosis to be an enemy which must be thrust back, then the pediatric health care given in the *colonies de vacances* must be seen as our first line of defense against this powerful enemy, the second being the sanatorium and the third the hospital. Among these three lines, he added, it is clear that the strongest and most important is the first, for it is better to prevent than to cure."[167]

But if both parties were prepared to argue that their organization met children's true health needs more precisely, the real gulf that separated the two lay elsewhere, in their respective understandings of children and child development in relation to nature and the French countryside. Teachers and directors of the *caisses des écoles* thus seem to have held an unspoken agreement on the matter of *animation:* without an intense organization of daily life in the *colonies,* a constant round of hikes and visits to natural and historical sites, a ready supply of games and schoolroom tasks (notably the journal) with which to distract the children on an overly hot or rainy afternoon, life in the countryside would rapidly lose interest for these children. They would grow bored and nostalgic for home, and then get up to mischief, or simply fall into lassitude, waiting for the moment when the holiday would finally end and they could see their families once again. Protestant advocates of *liberté en vacances* assumed quite the opposite: place a child in the unfamiliar setting of farm and countryside and she will immediately devise all the animation needed out of her own skull, or in the company of two or three companions. On the one hand we find the Protestant faith that the child is sufficient unto itself; on the other, the schoolteacher's conviction that without his or her active intervention, the child will lapse into mischief or listless inaction. The two views, and two organizations, utterly incompatible on the essential points, coexisted uneasily from the 1880s through the end of the Second World War. But as the individual *colonies* gradually coalesced into a national movement, over the first half of the twentieth century, one structure was bound to displace the other.

In the short run, the national supply of *colonies de vacances* would remain divided between the two forms, and in 1910, over half the 72, 866 French children sent *en colonie* found themselves settled in with peasant families. By 1936, this figure would plummet to 10 percent (out of 420,000 children sent nationwide).[168] Protestant accusations that teachers favored the intellectually talented (or the offspring of "better" families) over the truly needy were not without foundation, and in fin-de-siècle and Belle Epoque France, the two forms seem to have catered to slightly different clienteles, with the Protestant programs (and especially the Chaussée de Maine) recruiting from the very poorest industrial districts. Thus it was that in 1891 the working-class city of Clichy chose the Chaussée de Maine as intermediary for the city's first municipal *colonie de vacances;* Suresnes, Courbevoie, Asnières, Neuilly, Choisy-le-Roi, Clamart, Pantin, and Montrouge soon followed suit.[169] By the turn of the century, the Chaussée de Maine had become intermediary for the municipal *colonies* organized in a dozen of Paris's most densely industrial suburbs. The *colonies scolaires,* on the other hand, continued to recruit a more varied segment of the urban "classes populaires," sending children whose parents could well afford to pay alongside those who could not.[170]

In the long run, however, the group living formula would come to dominate the *colonie* landscape, displacing family placement with astonishing rapidity in the interwar period. In 1928, Dr. Georges Dequidt (president of the Comité National des Colonies de Vacances) attributed this secular trend to a generic "crisis" among the peasantry, provoked by the hardships of the war. By the late 1920s, he estimated that suitable placements had grown quite scarce, and that they must always be "supplemented" by local surveillance that is "competent and devoted." But the origins of the shift lay deeper than the mere lack of suitable placements. As Dr. Dequidt himself made quite clear, the criteria of desirability, and people's notions of what can and should happen *en colonie,* had also shifted, growing more elaborate and ambitious: "Collective placement has tended to take the place of the other for practical reasons, but even more for technical reasons, since this seems the only way to effect the kind of moral and physical education that is the indispensable complement to the benefits of life in the great outdoors."[171] Clearly the action and propaganda of the *colonies scolaires* and their partisans had influenced the national picture. So, too, had the *colonies catholiques,* relative latecomers to the *colonies* movement whose innovative pedagogical strategies, firm commitment to the collective format, and unwavering suspicion of the peasantry would exercise decisive influence over the shape and direction of the *colonies de vacances* movement in France throughout the first half of the twentieth century.

The *colonies de vacances* were imported into France at the very moment that Jules Ferry established the national network of republican primary schools: free, secular, and compulsory for all citizens aged six through thirteen. The Swiss graft took immediately, for obligatory schooling traveled hand in hand with the abolition of child labor in France, and this in turn produced new problems of child care in working-class districts.[172] For if children no longer spent the greater part of their day at home or in the workshop, playing or working alongside their elders, what were the children of working mothers to do during the long summer holiday, when school was no longer open and the child's presence in the factory or workshop no longer legally permissible? The *colonies de vacances* were to provide one very popular response to this novel problem, a response that, moreover, accorded well with the social doctrine of the republican school, in which children were separated from their families (hierarchically ordered by age and gender) and reassembled in more egalitarian, single-sex peer groups, horizontally grouped by age.

The organization of *colonies de vacances* thus rested on the same underlying pedagogical principle as the republican primary school, for in both cases the social basis of education was transferred from the family to the network of relationships with peers and, of course, the relationship of the group to the teacher. An institution that was founded to meet the multiple needs of poor urban families was thus able to stake an important pedagogical claim from the outset. On the strength of this claim the *colonie de vacances* would ultimately spread upward and outward to the children of the middle classes, realizing by the late 1940s Edmond Cottinet's dream: "that someday thousands of children of the people will scatter by turns to the mountains and the seaside."[173] From its origins as charitable outreach to the very neediest urban children, the *colonie de vacances* would evolve into a far-reaching social right: the collective summer holidays in the countryside that became the right of every French child.

CHAPTER TWO

⚮ *Toward a Pedagogy of Child Leisure*

THE POLITICS OF CATHOLIC DEFENSE, 1882–1914

The first Catholic *colonies* were organized in the late 1890s, some fifteen years after the pioneering initiatives of Protestant charity and the republican primary school. They developed out of an existing network of *patronages:* after-school programs that organized children's leisure activities while providing them with basic religious instruction. But if not the first to organize *colonies,* the Catholics were undoubtedly the most active and innovative force in the development of new pedagogies of child leisure in France at the turn of the twentieth century. Indeed, the pioneering influence of Catholic youth organizations — scouts, *patronages, colonies de vacances,* and, after 1927, the Jeunesse Ouvrière Catholique (JOC) — is nowhere more visible than in the working-class cities around Paris, where the sociopolitical mission of re-Christianizing the "heathen" proletariat in this moment of acute religious crisis (separation of church and state, secularization of primary education) imbued these organizations with an especially strong pedagogical purpose. The Catholic Church thus defined its presence in the Paris red belt primarily through its innovative intervention in the lives of working-class children and youth. In so doing, it provided an important model of effective intervention in the collective life of children on holiday, setting a pedagogical example that would strongly shape the form and direction of secular *colonies* in the interwar years, republican and Communist alike.

In April of 1906, directors from *colonies de vacances* all across France traveled to Bordeaux for a two-day conference, organized by Louis Comte. The rapid growth of the *colonie* movement had prompted Comte to organize this conference in the hopes that the many and diverse programs (some 150) that were, by this point, sending over 26,000 children on vacations in the countryside or by the sea, might construct a national federation through which to coordinate their wide-ranging efforts.[1] The men and women who gathered in Bordeaux represented organizations of all stripes, from the avowedly neutral *colonies* of Protestant charity, to the openly crusading *colonies catholiques,* to the militantly secular *colonies* of the republican school and municipality. Comte's aims were modest: to build an umbrella organization that could coordinate campaigns for public financial assistance to the *colonies,* and to create sufficient uniformity of practice among the federated programs (especially with regard to the medical reports) that the federation might serve as a kind of clearinghouse where national statistics on children's health, patiently gathered over time, could serve as the basis for future scientific and medical research.[2] By the second day of the conference, however, whatever hopes for unity Comte had nourished were foundering hopelessly in the face of vehement secularist opposition to the presence of Catholic programs in the company.

As tempers rose among the directors of proudly secular *colonies,* Comte sought to lure them into a more cooperative stance by invoking an older version of secularism as that "neutrality that respects liberty of conscience."[3] It was a doctrine that harmonized easily with liberal Protestant notions of freedom and individual conscience, a doctrine that had served well in the early years of the Third Republic, when the first battles of secularism were being fought around the constitution of Ferry's public primary school. But the tone of secularist politics had hardened since the early 1880s, particularly with the wrenching crisis of the Dreyfus Affair, which had unleashed an outpouring of venomous, anti-Semitic, and frankly antirepublican sentiment on the Catholic right.[4] This vicious attack had reawakened lightly sleeping visions of the Church as a bastion of backward-looking bigotry and obscurantism on the republican left, which rose in defense of Dreyfus and of the republican notion of justice that would ultimately vindicate him.[5] By the first decade of the new century, anti-Catholic passions were running at their very highest pitch: "The Church, Catholicism, even Christianity itself, are utterly incompatible with a genuinely republican regime," thundered radically anticlerical Maurice Allard from his seat in the Chamber of Deputies in the spring of 1905: "Christianity is an insult against reason, an offense against nature . . . How much progress have we failed to make because we've been dragging behind us this dead weight of Judeo-Christianity, with its tradition of lies and prejudices."[6] Comte's gentle invocation of a "neutrality that respected all convictions" could hardly stand up in a world riven by such fierce hatreds. As he strove vainly to impose the calm *laïcité-cum-neutralité* of yesteryear on the assembled delegates, militant secularist Gustave Théry leapt to his feet and cried out in protest against the presence of "black cassocks" among the invited company: "The cry went up: 'It's a disgrace!'" At this point, the "cassocks" all rose, and with Abbé Charles Vallier at their head, swiftly withdrew from the meeting. The president of the session rapped his gavel sharply, struggling to restore order to the agitated meeting. But the cause of unity had already been lost; when the final balloting came, not one Catholic program was prepared to join in any such federation.[7] A long-term separation of Catholic and secular *colonies* thus received an official, and rabid, imprimatur at the height of the religious "wars" around the separation of church and state. It was to be a breach of long enduring. Although Catholic and nonconfessional programs continued to find some limited ground for cooperation, the ultimate outcome of Comte's campaign for national unity was the creation of two national federations, one nonconfessional, the other most assuredly Catholic.[8] From this day forward, the two organizations would develop along divergent paths, building two networks of patronage, two reservoirs of pedagogical wisdom, and two traditions of theory and practice on how to organize *colonies de vacances,* and to what end.

Against the "Godless Schools" of the Republic: The Rise of the Catholic *Patronages*

Secularist distaste for the "cassock" was matched by the Catholics' equally powerful dislike of the "godless" Republic, whose principle of public neutrality (*laïcité*) represented, in their eyes, nothing less than a savage attack on the capacity of the Church to organize social life along Christian lines. The first blow had come in March of 1882, with the declaration that religious instruction could no longer be given on the *laïque* terrain of the public school. Four years later, the Goblet law (30 October 1886) banned all clerical teaching staff from public instruction, and the wholesale secularization of state schools followed swiftly thereafter.[9] Within five years, the teaching orders had disappeared entirely from the *écoles des garçons.* The *écoles des filles* were permitted to phase out their clerical teachers more gradually, and in those rural districts where regular

teachers were scarce, these women often continued teaching until retirement (or death) took them from the classroom. At the turn of the century,
then, many girls' schools still remained in the hands of the *bonnes soeurs*.

   The architects of the *école laïque* had thus approached their task with
a certain flexibility that was characteristic of this earlier period of *laïcité
ouverte*.[10] While many Catholics perceived the secularization of public
schools as a vicious attack on the Church, Jules Ferry and company had
in fact shown themselves willing to bend on matters of principle when
faced with practical concerns like the staffing of girls' schools in remote
regions. Twenty years later, policymakers would find that the space for
such compromise had been utterly closed off, swallowed up in the extreme postures adopted by anticlericals and Catholics alike. Hence, in
the aftermath of the Dreyfus Affair, when the Republic decided to move
decisively against the remaining congregations, exiling first the Assumptionist and Jesuit orders, which had played an especially odious and vocal
role in the conflict, Emile Combes finally took aim at those last remaining
teaching orders in the girls' schools. In the late spring of 1902, he closed
down some three thousand "unauthorized" schools, public and private
alike, declaring that religion and republican education could share no
common ground. This time, Catholics did not accept the renewed wave
of secularization quietly; on the contrary, the sudden, massive expulsion
of the good sisters (many of whom were, by this point, quite elderly)
stirred considerable local protest, some of which ended in violence.[11]

   The crisis and resolution of the Dreyfus Affair had thus radicalized
secularist politics in France, supplanting the relatively accommodating
spirit of *laïcité ouverte* with a more hard-line *laïcisme militant,* under
whose crusading banner the full separation of church from state was
finally achieved, in 1905–6. Throughout the struggle, long-smoldering
hatreds between religious and secular Frenchmen finally burst into
flame, igniting the great drama of church/state separation that would
divide the nation until the German invasion of August 1914. For secular republicans, this was the final step in the realization of a fully secular
state, the need for which had been painfully underscored by the divisive,
even subversive role played by sections of the clergy during the Dreyfus
Affair, and they pursued their ideal of public neutrality with zealous conviction. For many Catholics, however, disestablishment seemed nothing
less than a partisan attack on the Church, launched by the occult forces of
Freemasonry, who cloaked their deadly assault under a perfidious mantle
of "neutrality." As the "enemies of religion" completed the seculariza-

tion of public life, severing church from state by the unilateral rejection of Napoleon's Concordat, many Catholics felt ejected from the national body altogether, "exiles in their own land," as one contemporary put it.[12]

During the first wave of laicization, as Ferry and his cohort secularized public primary teaching in a spirit of *laïcité ouverte* (1880s), individual parishes had responded by expanding local programs of social assistance and popular education. Central among these was the chain of urban *patronages,* initially founded in the second quarter of the nineteenth century to ensure the perseverance of young apprentices once they had made their first communion and entered into the adult world of workshop and factory. The origins of the term "patronage" derive quite literally from the function of patron/protector that a lay confrère assumed vis-à-vis the young apprentices whom he took under his wing: "It was in the first instance a relationship of 'personal patronage,'" writes Gérard Cholvy, "with the lay brother stepping in to assist parents who were failing in their duty. He would seek to convince them of the importance of giving the child a real métier and would himself handle placing the child with a master. In the name of the parents, he would review the clauses of the apprenticeship contract . . . [and] ensure that they were being respected, by visiting the master's shop where necessary." Among the many clauses in this contract—assuring a minimum number of hot meals per day for the child, or protection from corporal punishment at the hands of the master—was a clause promising that the child would not be obliged to work on Sunday, "unless it were to clean up the shop," and would be sent instead to spend the day at the *patronage.*

In its origins, then, the *patronage* was a small company of apprentices, each bound to the confrère by a relationship of individual patronage. This structure was soon amplified by a system of group patronage, in which small groups of apprentices met together every Sunday with their patron.[13] The confrère thus had to devote his Sundays to the apprentices, and, moreover, to find a space for their meetings (usually on the parish grounds) and a minimum of resources to cover expenses. In the effort to attach these adolescents firmly to the world of parish church and daily devotions, the early *patronages* combined religious instruction with recreation—games, singing, and the occasional promenade outside the city walls. The *patronages* thus offered an alternative to the cultures of street and café, filling the Sunday afternoons of young apprentices—and, after 1851, young female factory workers—with healthy and uplifting diversion. With the establishment of the Third Republic, some of the more forward-looking directors organized weekly discussion groups as well, "study circles [where] they discuss[ed] matters among themselves, with the participation of an educated ecclesiastic." The *patronages* of the early Third Republic thus constituted themselves as a kind of secondary school for working-class youth, offering an ongoing education whose prime objective was to prepare them for the duties of republican citizenship, but in full consciousness of their status as Catholic citizens of a republic: "The young men of the working class who emerge from the *patronages* must be Catholics in every dimension—and in each Catholic, we must not forget, lies a *citizen*."[14] The *patronages des filles* offered an analogous combination of religious instruction, civic education, and recreation, but devised in accordance with Catholic notions of gender-appropriate activity. Rather than gathering to discuss the duties of citizenship, the girls were brought together under the sign of charitable activity, and, with a sewing or knitting project in her hands, each child joined the circle where religious themes met with charitable conceptions of women's public activity. At the end of the afternoon, the handwork would be set to one side as the girls joined hands to dance, sing, and play games in rounds.

With the secularization of primary education, the Church was suddenly faced with a novel problem: until 1881, catechism and primary education had marched hand in hand within the four walls of the same school building. Ferry's secularization abruptly severed this tie, forcing the Church to scramble for some means to catechize those children who remained in the republican schools. The stakes here were quite high, for these children represented the vast majority of the school population: over 75 percent of school-aged children, suddenly slipped from the tutelary grasp of the parish priest. In the flurry of pastoral letters that addressed this urgent problem, bishops gradually turned their thoughts to the existing network of *patronages*.[15] Might not these "high schools of the people" be retooled and expanded to meet the needs of a younger clientele, released from the public schools every Thursday afternoon to pursue their religious education? Almost overnight, the *patronages* were transformed from a program for adolescents into institutions of mass popular education, as urban parishes hastened to carve out classroom space (for catechism classes) in the parish hall, and fit out the adjoining courtyards with swings, monkey bars, and climbing ropes, to entice the new, younger recruits, aged five or six to thirteen. Sometimes the parish was able to provide an elaborate and quite spacious installation: "Right next to the church, a vast courtyard stands open, and on Sundays, one sees hundreds of children frolicking joyfully, breathing in with all their might the lovely spring weather and nourishing themselves on sunlight and fresh air," wrote François Veuillot of the parish of Sainte-Anne, in the densely industrial thirteenth arrondissement. "The courtyard is surrounded by large buildings, barns, and halls, even a theater and festival hall, which, on rainy days, become the refuge for this bustling company."[16] More often, though, the urban *patronages* were founded on a much narrower material base, for directors soon discovered that in most working-class neighborhoods they needed only to open the parish courtyard and hang a swing or some gymnastic ropes and rings in order to draw in flocks of children.[17] By 1901, the Church counted at least 3,588 *patronages,* up from the modest 155 listed in 1866, most of them located in poor and working-class districts.[18] On the eve of World War I, nearly ten thousand *patronages* were flourishing in parishes all across the nation.[19]

The secularization of public schools thus moved the *patronages* from the margins of Catholic activism to its very center. No longer just a meeting-place for the occasional evening study circle, the *patronage* had become the site and source of religious education for the mass of public-school children, "an indispensable counterweight to education without God," in the words of social Catholic activist Max Turmann.[20] But if the enormous expansion of *patronages* was fueled primarily by increased supply, rising demand played a role as well, as families in working-class neighborhoods were always in search of reliable modes of child care: "The *patronage,* which plucked us off the streets Thursdays and Sundays, gave working mothers peace of mind," recalled working-class militant René Michaud. "For us kids, it was prayers and services, of course, but it was the games which made the rest all go down more easily."[21] Plenty of "de-Christianized" parents, though rarely attending services themselves, were nonetheless quite happy to see their offspring spend their Thursday and Sunday afternoons playing and praying at the local *patronage.* The programs further extended their reach by assuming a range of charitable functions analogous to those of the *caisses des écoles.* The childen were thus assured some kind of snack every Thursday and Sunday afternoon, though in the poorest districts this was often no more than a chunk of bread washed down with water.[22] More substantial were the coupons for shoes and second-hand clothing that the abbé distributed to those children whose threadbare garments and broken shoe leather bore testimony to the poverty of their homes. These coupons could be redeemed in local shops, and for families in real distress might be the

sole source of an almost-new winter coat or pair of shoes for their growing child.[23]

As important as the care-giving function was, however, the *patronages*
were above all institutions of Catholic education, aimed at those children
who were condemned by poverty to attend the "godless" (but also fee-
less) schools of the Republic. As we will see, the combined force of the
sudden expansion in numbers, the shift toward younger children, and
the enhanced pedagogical and political importance of the *patronage* as
the Church's prime riposte to school secularization would force a wholesale rethinking and renewal of pedagogical technique in the *patronages*
at the dawn of the twentieth century.

Catholic educators were quite frank about the role that church-state
conflict and the progressive "de-Christianization" of France had played
in expanding the network of urban *patronages:* "If our society were truly
Christian and the family what it should be, the *patronage* would never
have been called into existence."[24] And yet, as Max Turmann pointed out
in his influential book *Au sortir de l'école,* it was precisely the *patronages*
that would allow the Church to continue playing an active role in educating the young, so long as Catholics were willing to pursue actively
the struggle for these youthful hearts and minds. In this era of secularism triumphant, too many had already succumbed to the temptations of
withdrawal from public life: "Like veritable 'internal migrants' . . . they
refuse to have anything to do with the republican government, and stand
scrupulously aloof from everything of an official or public nature, thus
forming little closed circles that are clearly cut off from the rest of the nation."[25] Such internal migration, however comforting to the individual,
put the long-term future of the faith at considerable risk. Now more than
ever the Church needed its members to come forward and participate actively in programs of education, in particular the *patronages,* whose brief
was to educate young workers into a resilient and pro-active Christianity:
"It is not enough to make of them obliging boys of the genre 'Yes, Father'
or 'Yes, Monsieur l'abbé' — docile instruments in the hands of any mod-
erately powerful individual, agents who are too often unreflective and
unconscious . . . [I]t is only with robust young chaps who are resolute
and 'have their wits about them' — and not with submissive 'good young
men,' obedient and obliging — that we can take up the heavy burden that
the Church expects of us."[26]

Paradoxically, then, it was the second, more radical phase of *laïcisme
militant* that seems to have shaken Catholics from the half-sleep of in-

ternal migration and into a more vigorous and engaged militancy. For if the second wave of church-state separation (1902–10) further poisoned Catholic/secular relations, leaving a legacy of bitter memory and mutual suspicion on both sides, it also ushered in what one scholar has called "the century of militants": a kind of Catholic renaissance marked by a profound shift in the structure, orientation, and social reach of Catholic activism. Much of this shift owed to the freshly mobilized energies of new, lay populations—notably women and young people. Spurred by the crisis of separation to an unprecedented and wide-ranging activism on behalf of the embattled Church, these women and men turned increasingly to "the people," reaching out with new organizational forms and new ways of linking spiritual life and social being. This was an era in which the papal injunction to "go to the people" produced a flourishing array of social action and popular education initiatives: Marc Sangnier's Sillon, which targeted youth of the popular classes, the *universités populaires,* and the *cercles d'études,* where bourgeois students and working-class autodidacts met to study social questions together.

But nowhere was this social Catholic dynamism more evident than in the realm of education and its surrounding terrain of educational/leisure activities, where the politics of Catholic defense produced an extraordinary creativity and innovation in the structures and pedagogies of Catholic education and child leisure.[27] Let us look more closely at the inner workings of the *patronage,* that immediate ancestor to the Catholic *colonie.* For in much the same way as the republican primary school shaped Cottinet's *colonie scolaire,* the *patronage* would form the social and pedagogical base of the *colonie catholique.*

"Those High Schools of the People That We Call *Patronages*"

The priests and lay activists (*confrères d'oeuvres*) who collaborated in the organization of *patronages*[28] quickly came to see that in order to attract and maintain their youthful clientele, it would be necessary to offer them something more than the weekly catechism, or the austere atmosphere of the study groups. One part of the solution clearly lay in tailoring the religious offices to the briefer attention spans of the young: "It is important that services not drag on for too long, that they not bore the children, that they be shaped by children and for children," wrote Abbé Schaeffer of the *patronage des filles* at St. Joseph de Plaisance. Worse, too many priests had succumbed to the temptation of filling their half-empty churches with children dragooned from the *patro,* hoping thus to convey a sense of energy and enthusiasm for religion in these de-Christianized neighborhoods: "We seize upon the children simply to fill the church," railed an exasperated Abbé Schaeffer. "We make them attend vespers, the sermon and salutation; the entire afternoon is spent inside the church. And we are talking here of poor young girl-apprentices, who have only this day to restore themselves, and to get some fresh air! The inevitable consequence is that they hastily quit the *patronage,* carrying a most disagreeable memory of church that stays with them forever."[29]

But the pedagogical creativity of Catholic educators extended far beyond the mere tailoring of offices to childish proportions; after all, children were not meant to devote all their time to "exercises in piety." Abbé Schaeffer explained: "Human nature claims its right to distraction, and games hold pride of place at Saint-Joseph de Plaisance. We head out on a long promenade two or three times each year, and these hikes are the object of long weeks of planning and conversation, for our *petites Parisiennes* do so love the countryside!"[30] By the turn of the twentieth century, the organizers of *patronages* had developed a pedagogical scheme that mixed spiritual, practical, and political instruction with a variety of recreations intended to reinforce "the associative spirit," those bonds of solidarity that bound members to the *patronage,* and to each other: "We begin by attending mass," wrote Abbé Foucher in the summer of 1910, advertising the virtues and pleasures of his *patronage de vacances* in the working-class city of Suresnes: "It is an excellent way to start the day. Then comes catechism, which lasts throughout the morning hours, but the class is surrounded and broken up by periods of play and recreation." But the real fun began after lunch, when the *patro* was transformed into the site of a game, pageant, or theatrical production that might go on for hours, lasting throughout the afternoon until the *patro* closed its doors at 5 P.M.: "It is here that the imaginations of our directors give birth to wonders. They still speak in Suresnes of the festival of mid-vacation— I do not know if this term is French—with its grand procession worthy of the Mardi Gras. At its heart marched the queen of the Singalhais surrounded by a battalion of sharpshooters and followed by her monkey, bear, and tiger. And let us not forget the fifes and drums which celebrated the occasion with a most successful concert."[31]

Festivals, parades, and games of imagination, as well as more formal theatrical productions, filled many a long Thursday or Sunday afternoon at the *patronage.* "Faces covered with shoe polish, jackets turned inside out," children found scope for artistic expression in the sketches and plays produced at the *patro,* even as the directors seized this opportunity to impart the basics of public speaking, showing the children how to "carry themselves," even seeking, at times, to "shape their taste."[32] The game of putting on a play thus engaged the children in a collective project while serving the pedagogical purposes of priest and confrères in their desire to complete the education of their young charges.

A similarly pedagogic conception of recreation as the means to more precise lessons—in team spirit, cooperation, the organization of a complex endeavor—underwrote the periodic war-games that pitted the boys of one *patro* against their peers in a nearby suburb. The *Bulletin mensuel* of Notre-Dame-de-la-Salette (Suresnes) periodically reported on these mock battles, often adopting the form of a communiqué sent from the field of battle: "The boys' *patronage* received the following message, which was doubtless found in the office of the chief of staff," reported the *Bulletin* in October 1910: "Coming to you from Garches, site of hostilities. A telephone call announces the arrival of the enemy: Courbevoie... Our army, divided into two wings, makes a highly successful turning maneuver, so successful that Courbevoie is cut in two, their flag is captured, and eighty of its soldiers taken prisoner." The remaining enemy troops beat a hasty retreat toward the park at Saint-Cloud, and ambulance drivers from the allied suburb of Puteaux rushed to clear the dead and wounded from the field before distributing cigarettes (of sugar) to the battle-weary young soldiers. The victors then tucked into a well-earned meal prepared in the field kitchen nearby: "And so our chefs light the fire and the aroma of strong coffee rises in the air, giving our soldiers the desire to attack . . . their lunch." The afternoon was passed in hot pursuit of the enemy, who vigorously defended the entry to the park at Saint-Cloud, "but our leaders' topographical skills allowed us to bypass the enemy and take them prisoner. It was a complete victory, and our entry into Suresnes was a triumphant one. Behind us floated the enemy flag, which was hung in the hall at the *patronage,* to remind us of the glories of that day."[33]

The *patronages* thus gave free rein to what Christian Guérin has called the "pedagogy of the imaginary," engaging children and confrères in a wholehearted game of war whose preparation and enactment awakened the children's organizational skills and demanded no small effort of collaboration and team spirit as well.[34] In reading through the pages of the *Bulletin mensuel* one is struck by the total engagement of priests and confrères in the children's games and imaginary worlds: reporting the "battle at Garches" in the form of a communiqué from the field, drawing the children into the story through their own unabashed involvement. We will have occasion to return to this point in exploring the daily life in Catholic *colonies,* where the entire three to four weeks could pass as one long, continuous game.

The *patronages des filles* proposed a somewhat calmer round of activities to their adherents: games, theater, and song were thus combined with religious instruction, sewing lessons ("a great way to make the *patronage* popular with their families, especially those who are drawn in for purely material reasons"), and some technical courses as well, which generally meant the eternal home economics, but classes in business and secretarial skills also found their way onto the menu.[35] The *patronages des filles* were thus organized along the same basic lines as the *patronages des garçons,* offering a similar mix of recreational and instructional activity that was oriented, ultimately, toward a single, common goal: building robust young Christians imbued with the fighting spirit. At the Patronage St. Joseph de Plaisance, the girls received the message through a pair of conventional, gendered images of feminine spirituality, where the negative stereotype of "excessively pious" women, attached to their "petty devotions," was contrasted with the "deep and simple piety" which the girls were encouraged to cultivate, "a piety whose accent is placed on our larger duties and *based on firm conviction* . . . A spirit of initiative, a readiness to fight for one's beliefs, a sense of vocation."[36]

Despite their common basic organization, male and female *patronages* were also distinguished by important differences in day-to-day practice. This emerges most strikingly in the place that theater and games of imagination held in girls' and boys' *patros.* Where boys were encouraged to invest themselves unstintingly in gymnastic competition or games of war, the literature from the girls' *patronages* places greater stress on the practical, material aspects of life, both inside the *patronage* and in the wider world beyond. The girls' study circles thus devoted long hours to discussions: "their labor in the workshop, family life, the thousand and one little details in the life of a young girl."[37] The focus on practical life was by no means intended to exclude a sense of pleasure and recreation; on the contrary, much time was also devoted to singing and other amusements: "Naturally the young girls love to sing, and we must encourage them. Singing ought to have a special place in the life of the *patronage* . . . secular songs included."[38] Yet there is no trace in this literature

that anyone sought to construct a female equivalent to the vibrant, imaginary worlds that livened activity in the *patros des garçons:* worlds where
boys met on suburban fields of battle, spurred on by abbés and confrères
whose investment in the game was every bit as wholehearted. It would
seem that the pedagogy of play, with its stress on the game's unconscious
action in the formation of moral character, was judged to be in some
way less central to the education of young girls. Indeed, far from wishing to stimulate young girls' imaginations with games of war, priests and
directrices sought to limit such stimulus. Hence, Abbé Schaeffer urged
his colleagues to measure carefully the girls' contact with the world of
make-believe contained in the theater. The girls could put on their own
plays, to be sure; they should even be encouraged to do so, but in scrupulously surveilled moderation: "These amusements are not dangerous if
approached in the right spirit. It is more a question of shaping this spirit
in the girls than of suppressing these plays altogether. So go ahead and
set up a theater, with costumes and scenery, so that the children may play
naturally and with joy, so that they do their best to play as well as they
can. You will build in them neither vanity nor a love of theater if you take
care to have only conscientious Christians take part in the play."[39] Perhaps girls were felt to be more impressionable, more deeply affected by
works of the imagination. Whatever the reason, similar cautions simply
never appeared when the children in question were male.

The transformation of the *patronages* into institutions of mass primary education did not efface their original function as organizations for
the benefit of adolescent workers, and the *patronages* continued to organize after-work study groups. The *cercles d'études* prided themselves on
their nonhierarchical and dialogic structure, in which the young came
together "not to hear from a professor but rather to learn from each
other."[40] Each week, then, youthful moderators led their peers in discussions that ranged across a broad array of political and religious topics. A
few of the subjects discussed in Suresnes's study group during the spring
of 1912 were the guild system, monks ("yet another subject on which
misconception abounds, and which belongs as much to the domain of
history as to apologetics"), the priest, and finally socialism ("This question is the order of the day, and we studied it from a practical standpoint,
which gave rise to the most generous resolutions").[41]

In addition, the *patronages* usually offered some kind of technical instruction—evening courses in industrial design, or in fields where the
priest or confrère had some technical expertise. The eminently prac-

tical craft of shoe repair thus accompanied the annual class in industrial drawing on the roster of courses at Suresnes's *patronage des garçons* in 1912.[42] Alongside this practical training, the *patronages* sought to
give their members some kind of vocational guidance as well, to the extent that Abbé de Pitray, director of the Patronage Olier (Saint-Sulpice)
dreamed of making them into "elementary vocational schools." "Too
often, the choice of profession is left to chance or the whims of caprice,"
wrote the abbé in 1898. "One chooses a métier without giving the matter
much thought, by looking at the offers posted on the town hall doors; or
he decides to join a particular workshop because the boss gets his shave
at the local barber shop. And yet this decision is not so simple; the child
must be up to the task of choosing for himself. We must therefore first
awaken the child's most important aptitude, his judgment."[43] In addition, the confrères strove to impart the basics of good (that is, bourgeois)
conduct to their younger proletarian "brothers," an act that in this era of
social Catholic activism was perceived to carry substantial mutual benefit: "Even as the young men from high society impart to our workers
habits of politeness, good language, and manners, they also have something to gain from these children of the people: an ease and simplicity in
relationships that is precious to everyday interaction."[44]

But in the end it was the variety of organized sports that drew large
numbers of adolescents to the *patronage*. The initial impulse behind the
gymnastic clubs and shooting societies mixed pedagogical intent with
a bottom-line desire to attract the maximum number of adolescents
for whom, it had to be admitted, the study circles held scant appeal.[45]
The sports and gymnastic societies flourished from the outset, and in
1898 the *patronages* founded the Fédération Gymnastique et Sportive des
Patronages de France (FGSPF), in order to facilitate inter-city matches and
gymnastic competitions. By 1906 the FGSPF had already enrolled some
50,000 adherents, which number had tripled by the eve of World War I.[46]
Troubled by the growing place that sports and physical culture occupied
in what were meant to be institutions of popular education, tradition-
alists raised the occasional protest against a massive turn to games and
national competitions that seemed all too redolent of "paganism's favorite amusements."[47] In defense of the wildly successful FGSPF, directors
of *patronages* invoked the moral and patriotic aspect of such competitions, underscoring in particular their positive impact on the young boys'
overall moral condition: "A scrawny and sickly body often houses a bitter soul, [while] a healthy body can become an efficient instrument of

discipleship."[48] The emphasis on bodily health as a means to moral and spiritual strength captures very neatly the dominant attitude toward hygiene among the directors of Catholic youth programs: though never neglected, hygiene was always a secondary purpose, a means to the true, spiritual end of the *colonie* or *patronage*.

The *patro* thus became a site of intensive neighborhood activity: what one Catholic pedagogue would later call "the house where the youth of the popular classes—drawn as much by the healthy pleasure of planned recreation as by the friendship of the priest and Christian comrades—find all that they need to complete their religious, moral, intellectual, professional, and physical education."[49] On the basis of this novel combination of sports and prayer, games and song, priests and lay activists gradually developed a set of pedagogical techniques in which the active engagement of the child in his or her own education became the guiding principle: "Look out in the great courtyard where the gymnastics course is just starting. We have about ten squads of twelve children each . . . you can easily imagine the advantages of this method: the child grows attached to his squad, and is conscious of the progress he makes therein. As he gains on his comrades, his success spurs him ever onward."[50] As institutions of learning, the *patronages* sought to make of each activity an educational opportunity. This emerges most clearly in the large-scale projects organized collaboratively by directors, staff, and children, such as the August 1913 Congrès des Patronages, which was run by the children themselves. Abbé Vallier proposed this exercise in limited self-government as an especially efficient means of engaging the boys and focusing their energies and attention: "The children take a very active and personal part in all this . . . There is nothing more educational, nor an education that one recalls better . . . for they have had to make an effort, albeit a joyous and personal one; they have drawn conclusions, ideas, and principles from their own common sense and experiences (ratified by a 'president' and underscored by the applause of an entire assembly)."[51] The "active pedagogies" in early-twentieth-century *patronages* thus took as their fundamental guiding principle the full investment of the child in the learning process. In this sense, they prepared the way for later developments in both *colonies de vacances* and the interwar scout movement.

Through such concrete and self-reflexive experiments in educational technique, the *patronage* made itself into a kind of laboratory of pedagogical research. Directors and staff thus carefully scrutinized the actions and states of feeling among the children as they moved from worship to play and back again. In so doing, they sought to deepen their understanding of children's cognitive process, so as to intervene more effectively in shaping the moral characters and spiritual lives of their young charges: "The priest should study each child's temperament," wrote Abbé Bruneau, describing his work with the children of the *patronage* at Saint-Augustin (Lyon). "If he has a good heart and a little tact he will soon learn that all children cannot be approached in the same fashion: there are the shy ones, the hotheads, the touchy ones, and the good children."[52]

The results of this reflection can be read in the internal organization of the *patronage,* which was progressively elaborated over time, and in the explicit discussions of discipline and educational technique to which the daily business of running the *patronage* gave rise. The children were thus divided by age group into smaller sections — pre-catechism, preparation for first communion, and *persévérants,* sworn to keep the vows of that first communion. The instructors for these were lay activists who were generally recruited from the bourgeoisie — students or young professionals with a vocation toward education and social activism in poorer neighborhoods. Usually, the confrères would met weekly with the priest or abbot who directed the program, in order to coordinate the activities of the *patronage* and to exchange pedagogical advice. "In these councils, we freely exchange opinions and hear the news from near and far. We speak of supervision, of games, of hikes, of progress yet to be made," recalled Abbé de Pitray of his pioneering Patronage Olier, organized by the parish of Saint-Sulpice in 1895. "In general, each leader is free to organize his section as he sees fit; the councils are simply meant to render his task easier . . . One leader gave a series of lectures at these meetings on the way to conduct oneself with children, on the importance of justice in our relations with them, on the superiority of one-on-one education, and on the study of child character and the means of changing it. We all know that children study their teachers; it is about time that teachers began to study their children."[53] In the era of the secular school, with the educational mission of a complete Catholic formation now resting squarely in the *patronage,* the staff and directors undertook a thoughtful study of the children in question, reflecting on their natures and their openness (or lack thereof) to new experiences and to the adoption of a more Christian way of life, despite the "pagan" milieux in which these young "Apaches" of working-class cities were growing to maturity.

Over time, the close attention to child learning in this unschoollike set-

ting would produce the foundations of a novel pedagogy of child leisure
that could be adapted for a number of different settings. At the base of
this developing Catholic pedagogy lay the conviction that in order to
prosper and develop, children require a "familial" atmosphere, illuminated by bonds of genuine affection in which setting the child could grow
in confidence. By using the term *familial,* Catholic pedagogues intended
to invoke the spiritual family of the *patronage,* and not the gender-mixed
atmosphere of the biological family of origin. In working-class districts
especially, this family was likely to be a most defective structure for a truly
Catholic education—lax (at best) in religious observance, worn down by
heavy labor and the struggle to gain mere material existence: "Poor parents, they are more to be pitied than blamed," wrote Abbé Bruneau in
1902. "Can you imagine them explaining the catechism to their child at
the end of a long day in the factory, shop, or office? It would be an act of
pure heroism. The mother herself has far too much to do; all that one can
ask of these good people is that they confide their little ones to us, for not
only do they lack the time, they have neither the interest, the knowledge,
nor the means to educate them."[54]

The directors of *patronages* thus regarded the working-class household
with a profound and frank ambivalence, and some did not hesitate to
compare unfavorably these mere biological units with the ideal families
of spiritual and fraternal union being forged in the *patronages:* "We are a
family," wrote Abbé de Pitray in 1899. "I think I can even say that many
families would envy the harmony and mutual charity that reign among
us here."[55] The "family" of which they spoke was that hierarchical and
single-sex structure of spiritual affiliation, forged in the round of games
and spiritual exercises pursued each week at the *patronage* and nourished
by the bonds of love and confidence that developed over time: "a society
of children and youth who love each other like brothers and practice their
faith together, a society with an accepted and respected hierarchy but
no means of constraint ('. . . the sections loving their leaders, the confrères loving each other, all united by the bonds of friendship and the
profound confidence that surrounds the most loving director')."[56] The
will to make of the *patro* a living alternative to the family of origin was
no less powerful in the *patronages des filles,* where the *directrices* were enjoined to establish an equally "familial" relationship with their flock, to
create an all-female analogue to the male "families" of priest, confrères,
and boys being forged in the *patros des garçons:* "For the young girl, the
directrice is a friend, and for many, a second mother. She must be affec-

tionate, and have the girls' complete trust . . . she must strive to develop their character and initiative. But she can never force the girls' trust, for this can develop only gradually, inspired by her affection and devotion."[57]

We are a long way here from the mindset of those Protestant and secular organizers who anxiously considered the possibility that the *colonie de vacances* might further strain the ties that bound poor families. By separating children from their parents for so many weeks and placing them in easier, pleasanter circumstances, did the program not run the risk of rendering these children dissatisfied with their little worlds back home? Far from worrying over such matters, Catholic educators strove to build on precisely this kind of dissatisfaction, to extract the child from the anticlerical milieu of origin, from those "prejudices" nourished in conversations with "bad" company, "or even with one's own father," and encourage him to seek after something better: a new way of life, a different kind of community, relations built on things of the spirit rather than the ties of flesh.[58] Of course the individual programs varied considerably on this point, from crusading priests like Abbé Vallier, who sought to recruit boys from his *colonie* at Verrières directly into his junior seminary (and from there, he hoped, to the priesthood), to more open-minded souls like Abbé Picquet, whose parish lay in the notorious slums of the cité Jeanne d'Arc. Picquet never asked that the parents who sent their children to his *patronage* attend mass themselves: "He never spoke of religious practice to these sorely tried men and women; he never demanded that they attend services nor sought to force an outward compliance that could never be anything more than a hypocritical posturing by the most obliging and obsequious souls."[59]

In between these two extremes we find the pragmatic moderation of a de Pitray, or Abbé Schaeffer, whose *patronages* embraced working-class children from a range of religious backgrounds, including children from nonpracticing households. At the very least, such sociological variety demanded a different approach, more open and supple than the unabashed proselytizing of an Abbé Vallier: "As far as relations with the family are concerned, we must always remember that . . . the *patronage* is nothing more than a stopgap measure that is, alas, all too necessary," wrote Abbé Schaeffer in 1898. "We must therefore endeavor to undermine family life as little as possible and give preference to its legitimate needs . . . Moreover, we must not require the children's presence at the *patronage* whenever they wish to go out with their parents." Not only was Schaeffer alive to the tensions that were likely to arise between Church/*patronage* and family in the "de-Christianized" neighborhoods of working-class Paris, he was prepared to go some distance toward smoothing over these tensions by acknowledging the "legitimate" demands of family.

No sooner had he uttered these conciliatory phrases, however, than the abbé revealed his true opinion on the matter: working-class families being what they were, the girls would naturally prefer to spend every afternoon at the *patronage*. In the interests of maintaining harmonious local relations, however, the abbé and his staff could not allow this: "We even compel those girls who prefer the *patronage* to the company of their parents not to render the *patronage* odious by their exaggerated fidelity... We often stress the duties of family life to our girls, and the *directrice* stays in touch with the parents in order to show them that we wish simply to be their associates, their basis of power in the education of their children." The oblique indictment, followed by hasty protestations of a collaborative action *with* the parents, suggest that the abbé may well have shared his colleagues' essentially negative estimation of the working-class family — "a family dismembered by vice or the demands of labor," in Félix Kérivan's pithy formulation — whatever tactical differences may have distinguished Schaeffer's day-to-day interactions with such families.[60] The ambition to create a rupture, to divide children from their families and encourage them to strive after a better way of life, would grow considerably once the priest had his flock under continuous control, day in and day out, in the Catholic *colonie de vacances*.

Catholic educators thus came to define the *patronages* as institutions for the education of the full human being, an education that embraced both the practical and spiritual aspects of life. As Abbé de Pitray observed, this larger education was the best way to anchor the spiritual and religious formation that the *patronages* strove, ultimately, to impart, for without first educating the "entire human being in all his aspects," the priest, no matter how "renowned" he might be in matters of education, risked wasting his efforts in a merely superficial action, laying down his teachings in a kind of "surface polish" that was destined to "disintegrate" at the first testing. For without that prior education of the whole child, such teachings could find no deeper purchase in the child's soul.[61]

In this era of sharp and prolonged religious strife, the directors of *patronages* conceptualized their mission in explicit opposition to the narrowly intellectual and overly materialist mass education of the public schools, where, it was claimed, sheer numbers drove teachers to rest their pedagogical method on pressing each individual into a single mold:

"Established for the average intelligence and character, this mold produces a level of decent mediocrity. The more gifted natures put up some resistance to the intellectual and moral pressure to which they are subjected. The triumph of this mass education will be to suffocate, rather than guide, all that is too noble and too generous in these souls, reducing them to the common, mediocre standard and producing minds and hearts shaped 'according to the formula.'" The product of these schools was the child who molded his actions to conform with those of his peers, on the one hand, and with the force of duly constituted authority, on the other—a child who had lost, or, in truth, never developed the capacity to think for himself: "The result is the withering of all initiative, and the child never learns to make use of one of God's greatest gifts to man, freedom of choice."

Against the mediocrity of mass education the directors of *patronages* proposed a more individually tailored and complete formation of the whole child, through the active methods being developed in *patronages* all across France: "All effort in our *patronages* is turned toward guiding our children, *while teaching them to will and think for themselves. We seek to develop their sense of initiative* and not to suppress whatever vital forces God has placed in each soul . . . We also believe that *children should not be withdrawn from contact with the world, nor should one seek to save him from the moral difficulties strewn along his path.* He must learn to overcome these obstacles, and if he falls, to pick himself back up again. He must know how to act in our absence, for we will not always be close by him."[62] The goal was to create more resilient young Christians, and if the methods tended toward the creation of a moral elite, so much the better. A remarkably similar set of concepts and practices would inform the Catholic scout movement some twenty years hence. In the meantime, the pedagogical vehicle for this "total" education remained the *patronage*.[63]

The success of the Catholic *patronage* can be measured, in part, by the efforts of secular educators to found an equivalent. For in the Catholic creation of after-school programs, republican pedagogues discerned the outlines of a broader possibility for continuing education programs that could complete and extend the work of the republican primary school: "It is apparent to all that we must provide some kind of continuing education," wrote Edouard Petit in his 1896 report on public primary education to the minister of public instruction. "Even in the most backward cantons, it has become clear that the school years are too brief, and [once they are completed], the child quickly falls prey once again to indolence and a lack of curiosity."[64] In 1896, Ferdinand Buisson and Léon Bourgeois launched the secular continuing education movement at the annual congress of the Ligue d'Enseignement, in Rouen, exhorting their colleagues to create a network of *laïque patronages* that could match, if not outshine, the existing Catholic one: "What is a *patronage scolaire?*" asked former prime minister Léon Bourgeois: "It is everything that might be useful to the child . . . it might be lectures, games, a brass band . . . [or] gymnastic society, it can be anything and everything . . . , [for] a *patronage scolaire* is anything that captures the child's imagination, anything that accustoms him to solidarity, to putting into practice the great principles of mutuality and brotherhood. All this is called the *patronage,* and this is good!" The solidarist politician was especially excited by the potential for enacting social peace and mutual solidarity through a network of *patronages scolaires:* "The child must find assistance and protection in the milieu that is his own commune, for it is in everyone's interest that the school from which he has graduated become a community hall of public peace."[65] While the network of *laïque patronages* would never equal the Catholic one, the broader push for continuing education bore fruit in a host of initiatives that expanded opportunities for adult education among the popular classes—continuing education in the "upper" primary schools, more attention to technical education.[66] Ultimately, however, the concern with creating a secular equivalent to the Catholic *patronages* would come around in a renewed focus on the *colonies scolaires* as the ideal complement to the school—sites of leisure and open-air instruction where the structure and content of learning bore little resemblance to the disciplines of Ferry's schoolroom. But it would be another thirty years or more before *laïque colonies* turned from their hygienic preoccupations toward a more pedagogic orientation.

From *Patronage* to *Colonie de Vacances,* 1898–1914

The dynamic era of *laïcisme militant,* in which the renewed attack on the Church unleashed new and creative energies, also saw the birth and rapid expansion of the Catholic *colonies de vacances.* These *colonies* generally issued from the *patronages,* rather than the parochial schools, for, as we have seen, the former gathered in children from the public schools— children whose families were too poor to pay the Catholic school fees, hence, children whose need for intensive exposure to a more fully Catholic way of life was presumably far greater. The continuity from *patronage* to *colonie* facilitated the organization and control of the *colonie:* "Indeed, what more certain guarantee of the discipline and good influence of the Oeuvre [des Saines Vacances] than the authority, confidence, and affection that the confrères exercise so naturally over the children throughout the year in their generous, Christian dedication to the *patronage?* What better way to render surveillance bearable . . . than to confide it to those who know our little 'Apaches' best, and are beloved by them?"[67]

But this continuity had important pedagogical consequences as well, for it ensured a greater openness to the "active methods" being deployed in the *patronages,* which here found a whole new field for application: "But yes, after the *patronage* comes the 'colonie,'" wrote "E.P." in his 1905 brochure on how to organize a *colonie de vacances:* "In the *colonie* we can exercise a continuous and unceasing action, we can advance continuously without having to start up again each day the work accomplished yesterday and destroyed since by evil influences. We don't lose ground before we've had a chance to consolidate our position." The life of the Catholic *colonie* was thus utterly bound up with the urban *patronage* from which it sprang, at the same time that it extended and transformed that life in ways that were sometimes quite unexpected: "The child sees us in all the acts of everyday life, and so appreciates us more fully. We, too, see all aspects of the child's character, and nothing that might help us in guiding him escapes our notice. It is indeed a genuine family life, lived on intimate and confident terms with the priest."[68]

Of course, plenty of Catholic families had been sending their children to *colonies de vacances* since the 1880s, using the *colonies scolaires* of the republican school or municipality, or the nonconfessional programs of Protestant charity (some 80 percent of the children who participated in the *colonies* organized by Louis Comte and Elise de Pressensé were Catholic).[69] During these years, most parishes were preoccupied with organizing their first line of defense against Ferry's "godless schools": the parochial schools and *patronages,* intended to assure the continuity of religious education for children of the faithful. But as positions hardened in the renewed struggles of the Belle Epoque, the directors of educational programs turned their thoughts to those young Catholic gamins being sent to spend their summer holidays lodged with ignorant (or, worse yet, Protestant) peasant families, or with the teachers of the "godless" republican school. In 1902, Abbé Bruneau, vicar of St-Augustin in Lyon, wrote with typical paranoia of the subtle action that these *colonies* were doubt-less exercising on the many Catholic children who left the city for the country in the company of Protestant directors each summer: "The state does its all here [for the *colonies scolaires*], while the Socialists and Protes-tants have organized their 'Voyages à la Montagne' on a grand scale . . . [I]t is important to realize . . . what our enemies are doing in order to de-Christianize the souls of our children . . . Given the rapid spread of the 'colonies scolaires' organized by the enemies of religion, it is our duty . . . to counter these secular works with competing works of our own."[70]

But the goal was not simply to compete with the *laïcs* for bodies; in this era of religious crisis, the *colonies de vacances* were widely perceived as one key to maintaining a positive Catholic presence in the lives of children and their families: "In these ill-starred times, the *colonies de vacances* have a more urgent mission," declared the Société de Saint-Vincent-de-Paul in 1904, for "with freedom of instruction [i.e., Catholic education] in a state of grave crisis, the *colonies* hold out a last, desperate hope." Hence, during that single month of day-in-day-out contact with the children, working to "elevate their souls" and "shape their judgment," the Church could acquire "more influence over the children than the teachers in the public schools gain over the ten months of classes."[71] Or so it was be-lieved. By 1905, Catholic programs in the Paris and Lyon regions were already sending some four thousand children on holiday with the priests and lay brothers of the parish.[72]

The very first Catholic *colonies* were quite loosely organized, by com-parison with what was to follow: literal offshoots of the urban *patronages* of Saint-Sulpice (Paris) and Saint-Augustin (Lyon). Abbé de Pitray (Saint-Sulpice) thus founded his Colonie Edouard when, in the summer of 1898, he took the first *colonie* of eleven boys, aged seven to thirteen, from the Patronage Olier to his family's hunting lodge in the maritime pine forest of the Landes, near the village of Porge. Here the boys spent several weeks in a loose round of games, meals, and then more games, leavened by the weekly hike into Porge, where the children attended mass, then spent the afternoon "fraternizing" with the boys of the village, who shared in their games and afternoon snack. Religious exercises were kept to a bare minimum: a morning and evening prayer, the Salve Regina sung each night before bed. The rest of each day was spent playing on the château grounds, or swimming, building sand castles, and hunting for sea shells on the shores of the nearby beaches: "There is all that sand, and we can play at 'Carotte' [throwing knives] for two days on end," wrote

one satisfied young *colon.* "After lunch . . . the youngest organize a croquet match, which usually ends like croquet matches elsewhere: after a
long series of interminable discussions, one player finally quits."[73] Aside
from making their own beds and setting the table before each meal—
"a small effort that interrupts their games, but initiates them into solidarity"—the children had no other duties and precious few constraints
on their time.[74] The abbé organized several "grandes promenades" to
nearby points of interest: a fully secular itinerary that avoided sites of religious significance—cathedrals, shrines, and woodland chapels—in favor
of such tourist delights as the lighthouse at Cape Ferret, or the fishing
village of Arcachon, on the Bay of Biscay. For the most part, however, the
children were free to organize their time and their games as they liked.

It was a formula that seems to have pleased both abbé and *colons,* for
each year the *colonie* grew, from eleven in 1898, to twenty in 1899, rising
to forty in 1900 (sent in two separate groups), before reaching the maximum of seventy-two in 1903 (which was all the château could hold, even
when the *colons* were sent in a relay of two groups).[75] The abbé took
care to see that the children ate well, putting special emphasis on len-
tils, which "boost energy." But he also favored mutton, for the Landes
sheep were "particularly renowned."[76] But there was no hygienic campaign comparable to that being waged by the Protestant programs or the
école républicaine. Hence, children were neither weighed nor measured
at the departure and return; as with most Catholic *colonies,* a smiling face
and round pink cheeks were generally regarded as sufficient testimony
to the *colonie*'s hygienic virtues: "The children's healthy and vigorous
appearance, which everyone remarks on at their return, testifies more
eloquently than could any scale that in terms of their bodily well-being,
the children lacked for nothing."[77]

Each year, the abbé published an account of his Colonie Edouard in the
patro's monthly "Nouvelles du Patronage Olier." In the summer of 1903,
this report took the form of a journal, culled from the letters home of
a young schoolboy in the *colonie* (who was doubtless the fictive creation
of the abbé's imagination). His "journal" recounts the ups and downs
of daily life in the *colonie* with a humor that is rarely seen in this age of
acute religious tension: "We were on the road with the schoolmasters
when along came a priest, like the one from the *patronage* . . . some of
us greeted him, but can you believe it, mother, when he had passed far
behind us, Garichoux shrieked all kinds of insults at him at the top of
his lungs. The assistant teacher pretended not to hear, but my teacher,

red with shame, gathered us all together and declared that it was a disgrace and that Garichoux would be deprived of two promenades."[78] But
Garichoux continued to poison the atmosphere of the *colonie* with his
anticlerical swagger. On the fifteenth of August [the Assumption of the
Virgin], not one child dared reply 'yes' when the abbé asked who would
be going to mass: "He repeated the question . . . [but] no one moved
(thanks to the influence of Garichoux)." Of course, the young Garichoux
was ultimately cured of his anticlerical ways when, one week later, he
found himself the sole stay-at-home in a *colonie* full of boys eager to attend Sunday mass: " 'Well then, I'm going along too.' And that was how
it came to pass . . . that the entire *colonie scolaire* went to mass today."[79]

De Pitray's program was the first and last *colonie catholique* that cheerfully accepted the appellation *colonie scolaire*. When, just four years after
the Edouard *colonie*'s maiden voyage, Abbé Bruneau (Saint-Augustin,
Lyon) decided to follow de Pitray's example, he made sure to adopt a
name that avoided all references to school: l'Oeuvre de Saines Vacances.
"What, in fact, is the goal of this oeuvre?" asked Abbé Bruneau in 1902.
"It is to extend and perfect the education given throughout the year at
the *patronage*, it is to remove children from pernicious idleness, and from
the evil influence of the street, as well as from the nasty air of the big
city." The hygienic motive was tacked on almost as an afterthought, following the far more central moral and educational goals of Church and
patronage, to which all-important topic Abbé Bruneau swiftly returned
in his peroration on the deadly perils that lurked during the *grandes vacances d'été:* "For the child, it means the street, and several days on the
streets quickly destroy ten months in the *patronage*. Even this latter is
insufficient and needs a complement, for the child's sojourn therein is
brief—just several hours each week—and for lack of time, the director
cannot really accomplish his mission as an educator."[80] If the *patronages*
were already doing the Lord's work, saving young proletarian souls for
Christ, then how much more efficacious and enduring a *colonie catholique?* Here, the children would enjoy weeks of uninterrupted contact
with a fraternal, Christian community, living in a kind of rural retreat
where nature's beauty might turn their thoughts more swiftly to God.

In order to realize the pedagogical mission, however, the *colonie* had
to be adapted to the purpose in form as well as intent. And this meant
collective living, however appealing on grounds of cheapness the family
placement alternative might seem. After all, one had to consider realis-
tically the families with whom these children were being placed: "It is

Protestant or Catholic, but much more often Protestant — I am speaking of the Lyonnais and Stéphanois regions here . . . And even if the family is Catholic, in what sense is it Catholic?" Could this simple fact offer any real guarantees against the renowned avarice of peasant farmers? Abbé Bruneau was highly skeptical: "I believe that those who consent to take in an unknown urban child do so largely for the twenty francs they are paid for its keep, and often they use the child as a shepherd or for work around the farm."[81]

Beyond the risk that individual peasants might exploit their young guests lay a deeper problem: in organizing *colonies* by family placement, the directors were asking families to take on educational responsibilities for which they were unsuited, not because the individual families in question were defective but because the family as a structure is too self-interested and too oriented toward its own material survival to rise above the particulars of its own situation and function as a genuine institution of learning. Be it a Catholic family or a Protestant one, "in neither case will the child be given any religious or moral instruction, for as soon as the good weather arrives, the peasant has more immediate concerns than the moral interests of his young ward. The child will go to mass if the family goes, he will say his prayers if given the time, but no one will monitor his friendships, his choice of reading material, his daydreams, his conversations. At the very least he will find some child of his own age and make friends to the detriment of each — for we all know that city children develop differently from country children."[82]

Unlike the directors of secular *colonies,* who hoped to make of the young *colon* a kind of living link between countryside and city, "a powerful element in the social rapprochement of peasants and urban workers," Catholic educators believed the young child was morally too fragile and unformed to sustain such a burden.[83] Cut off from his normal routines, isolated from both peers and priest in some remote hillside hamlet, the child lost all pedagogical benefit that a well-organized collectivity might deliver, and became even more vulnerable to corruption: "In family placement there is no surveillance, and there are no promenades, no lessons in hygiene, hardly any intellectual pastimes, no talks, no jollity. Family placement means isolation, idleness, and boredom, perhaps even immorality," wrote Abbé Vallier in 1904. "You have uprooted children from the four walls of their homes, or from the sidewalks of the streets, and transplanted them to the feet of the haystacks, or to the farmyard, where they wander with the poultry. If they meet up with some village

urchin they latch onto him, smoke cigarettes together—which everyone knows stunts their growth—sing popular songs and play at being
the urban sophisticate. Or perhaps they follow their host into the fields,
where they are left to themselves with no other occupation than to chat
with the shepherdess; their idleness is complete."[84] Rather than striving
to link the rural world to the urban, then, one should hold them in strict
separation, at least where young, unformed citizens were concerned.

The real heart of the matter thus lay in the educational ambitions that
Catholic directors had for their *colonies de vacances,* and in the firm and
highly developed pedagogical conceptions that underwrote those ambitions. They were, thus, utterly uninterested in the moral lessons that
peasant families might impart by example—those values of hard work,
proximity to nature, and a life of scrimping and saving so vaunted by
Protestant programs. Hence, the rare cleric might comment on the relative merits of placement with a pious rural family, whose sturdy Catholicism might give the urban child a more virile sense of Christian practice:
"Many of these young 'colons' were students in the secular schools and
had only the vaguest religious training, for back home in the big city,
they never saw their fathers go to mass. But the peasants with whom we
placed them were good Christians; their Catholic practice and way of life
quite struck our young boys, who thus saw that it is not only women and
children who fulfill their duties to God."[85] But I found not one instance
in which a Catholic educator even alluded to (much less lauded) that
table of ordinary virtues—hard work and saving—that constituted the
Protestant curriculum for the peasant school of hard knocks. For Catholic educators, this kind of "familial" education-by-osmosis was simply
beside the point, a mere acclimatization to rural ways of life that hardly
even merited the title education. By 1903, just five years after de Pitray
had launched the first Catholic *colonie,* Abbé Vallier could report that in
the diocese of Lyon, all purely Catholic programs had adopted the collective structure in the conviction that it was "the simplest *and best means
of gaining the desired moral result.* Several went so far as to declare that it
is the only structure possible."[86]

By a distinct, yet in some ways analogous route, Catholic pedagogues
had arrived at the same conclusion as their enemies, the teachers of the
republican school, in favor of the *colonie collective.* Perhaps this should
not surprise us; after all, the organizers of Catholic *colonies* and the republican *colonies scolaires* shared a common faith in the importance of
the collectivity as the ideal, nay essential context for any real education.

The family was simply too private, too involved in assuring its own continuity to perform the disinterested and universalist task of education.
Two distinct and powerful streams of opinion thus fed the trend toward
colonies collectives in France. Over time, then, France would distinguish
itself by comparison with its neighbors to the north and east—England,
Germany, Denmark, Switzerland—where vigorous *colonie de vacances*
movements continued on the basis of family placement.[87]

How the Catholic Church Transformed a Program of
Public Hygiene into an Institution of Learning

What, then, did life in a Catholic *colonie* look like? How did the young
colons of Douvaine and Verrières fare under the strict surveillance of an
Abbé Bruneau or Abbé Vallier? What kind of lessons did the directors
of such *colonies* hope to impart, and by what methods? Let us look more
closely at the techniques and approaches that were engendered by the
priestly ambition to impart a "complete religious formation." For it is in
the Catholic *colonie* that we will find the first systematic efforts to create a full-blown pedagogy of the collective vacation, based on the active
methods of the *patronage.* For if Protestant charity and the republican
school first introduced the *colonie de vacances* into France, under the twin
signs of charity and public health, it was the Catholic *patronage* (and later
colonie) that openly and self-consciously transformed what was above
all a charitable program of social assistance and hygiene into a program
whose primary focus was educational.[88]

   The first priority was to win the child's trust and affection: "In living
alongside the children, and by *loving them,* one soon wins their hearts,
brings them closer to the priest, and so does them the greatest good possible. The director is a real friend and brother, and the children treat him
as such even as they maintain all due respect for him."[89] The Evangelist's
exhortation to love one another thus became not only Christian duty but
shrewd pedagogical technique as well, for if the road to the child's will
and understanding passed by the heart, then gaining his affection was
the indispensable base on which the priest could begin the work of total
education for which the *colonie* was designed. This mission was accomplished by having the children live day in and day out with the priest,
"who, at every moment and in every way, however small, works to accomplish his educational mission, and to win the esteem and affection

of the child, to make him more confident and open."[90] In the intimacy
of daily life, helping the child to tie his shoes or cut his meat at the table,
passing by his bedside each night for "a little private chat," the abbé and
his confrères wove the bonds of the spiritual family's affection ever more
tightly around the child: "We were a real family," wrote "René," from
the *colonie* at Mesnières (Suresnes) in 1909: "M. the abbé was our father,
and practically our mother as well. Every night after we were in bed,
he came to say goodnight to us and blessed us each with a small sign
of the cross on our foreheads, so that we would sleep easily."[91] On the
basis of this "continuous intimacy" with the children, the young abbés
would begin the work of moral education: "to open their eyes to their
own shortcomings, to watch over their efforts and failings, to encourage
some and console the others . . . and then clinch their education at the
most propitious moment, in the evening, for example, when we take the
place of the absent mother and tuck the little ones in . . . Ah, the salutary
tears that one can provoke at that moment!"[92]

A strong presumption of in loco parentis thus defined the basis of
action in Catholic *colonies*. For the period of the holiday, at least, the abbé
and his co-directors were prepared to place themselves, quite literally,
in the position of collective parent to the *colons,* receiving their obedience, but also the trust and affection that children normally reserve to
their parents. The guidelines at Douvaine underscored the centrality of
this substitution of priestly for parental authority and insisted that it be
absolute and undivided. The *colons* were thus adjured to place their trust
and affection in the directors, to grant them "that openness of heart that
one has for a beloved mother and father." Moreover, they were to accept
these men as their friends: "their companions in their games and their
confidants in all their sorrows, troubles, and difficulties."[93] The parents,
for their part, were warned that if they wished their children to benefit
physically and morally from their time *en colonie,* they had to accept un-
conditionally the director's "absolute authority," to relinquish all control
of their children for the duration of the *colonie* and "entrust" them entirely to him: "He will watch over them with the tenderest solicitude."[94]

Like a strict parent, the director should keep a close watch on the child
at all times: "You must be with them at every moment, day and night, and
never let them out of your sight," wrote Abbé Bruneau of his experiences
with the Douvaine *colonie,* on the shores of Lake Leman. The motive
behind this counsel was less anxiety for the child's physical safety than
concern for the state of his soul: "The *colonie* must be one big family, with

the abbé as its father. You should of course give them a bit of freedom and plenty of initiative, but you should never leave them to themselves. Watch over them constantly without seeming to do so, get them used to chatting among themselves in front of the director, as if he were not there, and never allow them to form groups of two." These young objects of priestly concern were, after all, vessels of original sin, in need of the close and explicit moral surveillance-cum-guidance that arose under the propitious circumstances of a one-on-one encounter with the priest or confrère, or when the entire group played together under the abbé's watchful eye. What had to be avoided at all costs was the devilish combination of two *colons* on their own, cooking up mischief together, for as any right-thinking Christian knew, "the devil will always make three."[95]

Abbé Bruneau's demanding stricture for a "constant surveillance" expresses in unequivocal terms the underlying anti-Rousseauean premises of Catholic education, namely that as heir to original sin, the child was not sufficient unto him/herself, but a constant prey to temptation and error. One could not simply place the child in a propitious setting and then confidently wait for the good to emerge from within; rather, the educator had to strive consciously to reshape the children's fallen nature, to make of education an act of re-creation, so that they might take an active place in the supranatural order into which they had been introduced at the moment of baptism. Such active intervention was particularly urgent for the children of the popular classes, raised and educated in the de-Christianized cultures of proletarian neighborhoods and republican schools, for these milieux could only confirm man's fallen nature. While this all may seem rather obvious, it is nonetheless worth underscoring, for it meant that the Catholics were the sole practitioners of child-centered learning who did not proceed from the premise that education consists merely in calling forth what already exists in the child. Arising at the confluence of a child-centered method and faith in original sin, the Catholic pedagogy of child leisure possessed great internal coherence, and defined a distinct and crucial profile on the pedagogical landscape of early-twentieth-century France.

This being said, we should also realize that Abbé Bruneau's ideal of perpetual surveillance was perhaps more rhetorical than realistic in its extreme and totalizing ambition. Accounts of daily life in Catholic *colonies* suggest that Abbé Evrard's more measured call for an "active presence" approximates more closely the atmosphere that directors and confrères strove to create: "To ensure that familial life that we all agree is essen-

tial, you must assure an active presence, rather than a constant surveillance. There must be frequent and relaxed contact between teacher and
child if the educational mission is to be given its full scope."[96] Obviously,
such an intensive involvement with the *colons* dictated a relatively small
group, and Catholics consciously limited their *colonies* to some one hundred children or so. Moreover, directors were careful to ensure that the
ratio of adults to children never exceeded one to ten or twelve.[97]

But the strict attention to size and adult-child ratios was only one
means to the end of realizing a truly "familial" *colonie,* one that could
work effectively against the children's "depraved habits, lack of stead-
fastness, weak character, and, sometimes, indelible hereditary defects."[98]
The real linchpin of Catholic pedagogy in the *colonie de vacances* was the
strategy of joining the world of adult directors to that of the children:
"The best approach is to join in their games, to take part in their schemes,
to grant them all reasonable wishes or explain to them why you are refusing." This was the age when priests and seminarians hiked up their
habits and, basketball shoes flapping underneath, joined in games of soccer, basketball, capture the flag, or the *jeu de piste:* "Despite his age and
his cassock, M. l'Abbé often becomes a big brother to them; he takes part
in the children's games, joins them at recreation, and is interested in all
their antics . . . He takes part in their conversations and follows them with
as much attention as if he were speaking with adults. He never grows
tired of listening to them, and answers all their questions."[99]

This is the ideal portrait of the "big brother," who surfaces repeatedly
in the Catholic literature on *patronages* and *colonies* — someone who en-
gages with the child at the child's level, and not from on high, as a schoolmaster; someone who is, perhaps, a little childlike himself: "His prodigious imagination invents, recombines, and varies the games infinitely.
He loves to move and race about just like a child."[100] Toward the end
of the 1920s, as *laïque colonies* developed more overt pedagogical aims,
their directors began to seek *surveillants* on this same model until, by the
time of the Popular Front, the "big brother" had become the prime meta-
phor for the job of *moniteur* (the term *surveillant* having been scrapped
in the meantime as implying a soulless, joyless, authoritarian duty; the
very opposite of child-centered action). But until that time, the Catholics were the sole organizers of *colonies* who devoted such sustained and
thoughtful attention to ensuring that the whole was bound together by
a sufficiently "familial" pedagogical structure.

This kind of adult engagement in the imaginative and play-centered

lives of children lies at the heart of the *nouvelles pédagogies,* and its outlines doubtless seem familiar to readers from the more child-centered
cultures of England and the United States. In pre-Popular Front France,
however, one rarely saw such things outside the Catholic *colonies,* for the
republican school had explicitly rejected play-based and child-centered
pedagogies even for its network of pre-school *écoles maternelles.*[101] In fact,
the pioneering role of Catholic *colonies* and *patronages* in developing such
pedagogical techniques in France has been forgotten by historians of
education, Catholic and non-Catholic alike, who, distracted by the triumph of secularism in the official school, have neglected the far more dynamic (and autonomous) terrain of the *périscolaire* (extracurricular education). Until the early 1930s, Catholic *colonies* constituted the main site
of experiment for *nouvelles pédagogies* in France; only gradually would
laïque colonies begin to shake off their hygienic obsessions and elaborate a pedagogical framework of their own, borrowing liberally from the
Catholic tool kit as they did so.

In the struggle for the child's soul, the priest had the powerful force of
childish affection on his side: "The child loves to be taken seriously and
treated as an adult. He always knows when he is loved, and if he feels
loved, he will avoid doing anything that might upset you."[102] Properly directed, this eagerness to please, to be loved and appreciated, would allow
the beneficent force of the abbé to push back the innate force of original sin, and so help the child resist the inner demon: "If you only knew
how susceptible children are to management, in the spiritual sense of the
term. Thanks to their natural expansiveness, you can see into their souls
quite clearly, and from there, it is easy to show them their faults, to point
out their weaknesses, and to guide them toward virtue, specifying the
ways they might exercise it."[103] As we will see, the physical organization
of life in Catholic *colonies*—the early morning wash-up in the icy waters
of an outdoor fountain, long hikes across arduous terrain in all sorts of
weather—became integral aspects of this moral hardening, which operated through the child's body as a means of reaching his spirit.

Father Vallier's *colonie* at Verrières gives a good sense of how such an
austere program was realized among the offspring of the Catholic working class. Verrières was an exceptional case in that it was one of the rare
Catholic *colonies* that was organized without reference to a *patronage.*
Rather, the children were recruited by Lyon's Société de Saint-Vincent-
de-Paul from among their poorest client families, most of whom dwelt in
the slums of the city's notorious Croix Rousse district. At the end of July

1903, the first *colonie* of forty young boys arrived at the Montbrison train station: "After being relieved of their bundles, they set off bravely on the long road to Verrières"—ten kilometers by the main road and much of it straight uphill.[104] It was a most fitting introduction to the active life they would lead over the coming weeks, hiking across the Auvergnat hills in pursuit of health, toughness, and spiritual uplift. Happily, the twenty-three-year-old Abbé Vallier, who marched vigorously at their head, had foreseen a small pause for refreshment along the way at the château of the viscount Camille de Meaux: "Tables had been set up under the great trees in the park; the forty *colons* sat down and their dinner was served to them by children their own age, who were M. de Meaux's own grandchildren. At the same time the three directors (Father Vallier and two young seminarians) were received at the family table."[105] At the end of the meal, the small company rose and continued on their journey, reaching at last the small hillside school, which was only half-built and, like many Catholic institutions, stood empty and abandoned in the wake of Emile Combes's renewed campaign against the congregations: "The Brothers had been driven out, and so there were no classrooms, only their dwellings."[106]

Like many fin-de-siècle Catholics, Abbé Vallier saw great virtue in the disciplined, almost military organization of educational institutions. Upon their arrival, the boys were lined up in the courtyard and divided into smaller companies of about twelve *colons*. Each division was headed up by its own "corporal" (a seminarian), who was assisted by a "sergeant," chosen by the directors from among those *colons* who seemed most apt for the job. This microdivision into groups of twelve was then overlaid by a larger division of the entire *colonie* into two teams, the *Rouges* and the *Bleus,* who would meet each other on the field of battle in the *grands jeux* that filled many a long afternoon over the summer holiday. Well before the arrival of scouting in France, then, the directors of *colonies* were employing a remarkably similar blend of games and pseudomilitary organization, two aspects of life *en colonie* that were fully interpenetrated in the frequent games of war organized by the abbé and his co-directors. And yet the children were awakened each day not by the harsh tones of the cornet but by the gentle sound of the flute, intoning the canticle "Nous voulons Dieu." Vallier's technique with the children seems to have combined a certain gentleness of approach with an insistence on the firm ordering of the collectivity in units small enough to enact the kind of intimate interactions and close surveillance upon which the "familial" life of the *colonie* rested: "At Verrières, the children have come to understand that discipline and the sense of brotherhood are necessary and good in all contexts—as necessary in school, the barracks, or the factory, as they are here, in the *colonie*."[107] This approach, at once individual and yet firmly anchored in the collectivity, had its basis in the strong bond that the perceptive and charismatic abbé established with the children.

Religious offices occupied a prominent place in the life of the *colonie,* and each day began with the entire *colonie,* assembled in the courtyard, yelling out at the top of their lungs "My Lord, I love you!" This high-volume mantra would be repeated at unpredictable intervals throughout the day—at the end of lunch, in the midst of a tough contest for the ball in a match of soccer or *ballon prisonnier.* The entire company would then shuffle into the chapel for mass. After a quick breakfast of bread and café-au-lait, the children were free to play in the company of their directors. The morning activities tended to be less formally organized, as individual seminarians ("corporals") took their groups out to a broad, flat meadow for some gymnastic training, or off on a short walk to the nearby Ance River, where the boys would splash about in the icy waters, hunting for frogs and crayfish, or any other life-form that had the misfortune to swim by at that moment. If the weather turned nasty, the *colons* would troop back to the school for an hour or two of quieter activity: a "little chat" with the abbé or one of his associates, a game of cards or marbles in the courtyard. Some *colons* took the opportunity to discharge themselves of the obligatory weekly letter to the family back home. This was one activity from which the seminarians maintained a certain distance. To the child who sat anxiously chewing his pencil before a blank sheet of paper, they might suggest a few topics of interest, help him find something to say beyond the usual "I'm eating well, I'm having fun," or to close with some formula besides the peremptory demand to "send me this or that thing." But the actual redaction of the parental letter was left strictly in the hands of the *colons.*[108]

The afternoons were devoted to more sustained activities that involved the entire group. This might be a long hike over the hills and into the next parish, where Abbé Vallier would stop to bless the Holy Sacrament. Or the "corporals" might organize a large-scale game of war that would unfold its twists of plot in the woods and fields around the school: "One day each week, the afternoon was given over to a 'little war,' the *colons*' favorite sport," wrote Mgr. Lavarenne in 1953, as he recalled the Verrières *colonie* in its early days, just before World War I. "Once the theme of the maneuver had been established and the objective determined, the two camps each headed out separately under the leadership of a director, who refereed the operations. The young abbés were almost as fiercely engaged in the struggle as the *colons*. The projectiles were pinecones, which we had carefully soaked in water so that they would close up and grow heavier." The trick, then, was to have the wind at your back, so as to carry these homemade missiles as far as possible. At the end of the day, the abbé himself would appear on the field of battle to determine the victor, "which was usually pretty clear. The two camps gathered face to face and yelled out reciprocal cheers. The victors returned to the vanquished their captured flag, and on the way back, we passed by the village church in order to announce the outcome of the battle." [109]

Strenuous activity, and long, arduous hikes in particular, were thus the order of the day at Verrières. Even if the children found them tiring, Vallier always said that his goal was "not to fatten his kids but to strengthen them . . . [W]hat he sought above all was to give children the habit of endurance and energy, so that none would ever declare himself vanquished." [110] And in fact, the long promenade as test of endurance (versus protracted *leçon des choses*) was at this time rapidly becoming the keystone in the physical organization of Catholic *colonies*: "With the flag flying before you, bugles if you have them, and the pace set by marching songs, you can advance like the Nippons at the conquest of Port Arthur," wrote "E.P." in his 1905 manual "Comment organiser une colonie de vacances." "With a little training, a ten year old's little legs can easily march thirty kilometers." [111]

The contrast with the republican *colonies scolaires* could not have been greater: "We choose our itineraries so as to increase progressively the distance covered, to give a gradual training, without exhausting them," wrote the director of the eighth arrondissement's *colonie scolaire des garçons* in his 1910 report to the *caisse des écoles*. For as the good director well knew, overly strenuous exercise would burn off precious calories, and so tip the scales in the wrong direction at the all-important weighing of the *colons* at their return. [112] But Abbé Vallier was not burdened by such weighty material concerns; on the contrary: "*Le Père* held administrative formalities in profound contempt, all those weighings and measurings and statistics that now burden the life of a *colonie* director and which have never restored anyone's health. He relied, rather, on his own vigilance and that of his associates, on the benefits of mother nature and the protection of the Holy Virgin Mary as well." [113] As well he might have, for at Verrières the prime concern was not to put meat on the *colons'* scrawny young bodies, but rather to strengthen their wills by imposing tests of physical endurance, "to instill in his children . . . a taste for exertion and the habit of sacrifice, to shape energetic wills capable of dominating the instincts and resisting the pull of ready-made opinion or everyday example." [114] By toughening the children's bodies, Vallier sought to endow them with sufficient discipline and strength that they might master both anger and pain. And this, in turn, was the condition for a truly free will, servant neither to the demands of passion nor the pleas of physical weakness.

It is important to recall that Vallier's disdain for the hygienic preoccupations of his republican counterparts represents one extreme along a spectrum of Catholic opinion about the role that hygienic concerns should play in *colonies de vacances*. Overall, the directors of Catholic programs agreed that such bodily concerns were of secondary importance by comparison with the all-important spiritual and educational goals of the *colonie*. Yet this should not be taken to indicate a complete lack of concern for the children's health; rather, it signals their coming down on the opposite side of the equation from their republican and Protestant colleagues. Where secular directors continued to stress the hygienic virtues of the *colonie,* invoking in particular their near magical faith in its power to turn back the terrible inroads that tuberculosis made on the child population, the Catholics constantly underscored the unique educational opportunity presented therein. The *colonie de vacances* thus allowed the Church to extract children from a plethora of evil influences— the street, the republican school, lax or de-Christianized parents—and immerse them in a world ordered by Catholic principles. In order to accomplish their mission, directors of *patronages* and *colonies* alike acknowledged the need to develop the body along with the mind and spirit. Moreover, these women and men were painfully aware that their young clients suffered physically the effects of a lifetime of poverty, and that anemia, rickets, and chronic bronchitis marked their young bodies and cried out for attention. The vast majority of Catholic programs thus gave the children a thorough medical examination before allowing them to participate in the *colonie*—a novel event in the lives of such children: "One of the mothers innocently remarked that no one had ever examined her daughter so thoroughly, that it was as if she were the child of a rich man," wrote a reporter in a 1907 account of the *colonies catholiques* in Saint-Etienne.[115] Thus Father Vallier's professed contempt for the *colonies scolaires'* ritual weigh-in must be placed in its proper context, within a broad conception of Catholic *colonies* as first and foremost institutions of popular education and spiritual training.

Educating the Educators for a "Truly Catholic" *Colonie:* The "Ecole de Cadres" at Verrières

Far from being a mere "food farm" for malnourished children, the Verrières *colonie* was "an eminently sacerdotal work, infinitely productive, that leaves its mark even more deeply in the soul than in the blood." [116] Such seriousness of pedagogical purpose demanded that sustained attention be given to the training of young seminarians for this singular educational task, and the following academic year (1903–4), Father Vallier organized a course at the seminary to prepare some forty young priests for service in twelve local *colonies* the following summer.[117]

In this, the first "école de cadres" for *surveillants* in *colonies de vacances,* students read treatises on education (particularly the works of Mgr. Dupanloup) in order to prepare their own pedagogical plan. They sought out new games while reviewing the rules of their old favorites; some even struggled to master the technique of Swedish gymnastics.[118] Those who had done their military service were consulted on the finer points of organizing games of war; others put their talents to work writing plays and songs for the upcoming *colonie.*[119] The students also compiled a list of topics for "little chats" with the *colons* each morning after breakfast: courtesy, domestic animals, the Sillon, electricity, games, the Catholic mass, volcanoes, and missionaries are but a few of the subjects that were actually covered that summer at Verrières. Finally, the students considered the *colonies de vacances* in more general, institutional terms, reviewing their history in France and the variety of forms they might take. When one novice timidly suggested that family placement seemed like a good idea, the other students booed him down in no uncertain terms: "While family placement might be splendid from a physical point of view, from the moral standpoint it is simply revolting," declared one of his more experienced colleagues.[120]

Vallier's "école de cadres" climaxed in the actual *colonies* that departed in August 1904 for two months in the foothills of the Massif Central: "What an opportunity to correct their ideas on a multitude of subjects, to broaden their horizons and develop their reason! It seems to us that this vocation tends to attract educated and profoundly Christian spirits, but in order to truly do good, one needs more than loving kindness; he needs broad and genuine knowledge, for the young boys quickly discover any gaps in the knowledge of he who dares to try and indoctrinate them . . . [Moreover,] they easily understand the inevitable limitations of 'bookish' science." [121] But even as the *colonie* was revealing to its *colons* the limitations of their lessons at the *école républicaine,* it was providing the seminarian with "a sacerdotal training" of great practical value: "the love for children, and the desire to orient them toward God. It is the science of all sciences, and it could save the nation, if all truly possessed it." [122] More important still was the social understanding these sons of the bourgeoisie drew from their prolonged contact with the children of the people: "The *colonie de vacances* lays before the seminarian's very eyes the immense physical and moral poverty from which God's people are suffering; it also shows him the most effective remedy: Jesus Christ, and the best means to apply it: the most perfect devotion of the souls that live in their bodies." [123]

But what about the girls? For, as the foregoing paragraphs suggest, the children in the earliest Catholic *colonies* (Edouard, Douvaine and Verrières) were all boys. How were all those girls in the *patronages des filles* spending their summer holidays? After all, by the turn of the twentieth century, fully one third of all Catholic *patronages*—1,637 out of 4,168— were aimed at young girls. Ten years later the numbers would double, reaching some 3,500 *patros des filles* in 1910. Much of this rapid expansion owed to the tireless efforts of Mme Aline Duhamel, who, from the moment of her marriage in 1887, had devoted herself to the *patronages* of Saint-Clotilde, and later, of all Paris. [124] Blessed with abundant energy, sound common sense, and a real genius for organization, Mme Duhamel worked ceaselessly to expand the network of *patronages des filles,* and to secure their prolongation through *colonies de vacances.* In 1910, Cardinal Amette, archbishop of Paris, named Duhamel president of the national secretariat of the Archiconfrérie des Patronages des Filles. From this position she redoubled her efforts to secure rural holidays for the young girls of urban *patronages,* recalling, perhaps, the boredom and loneliness that she had known as a teenager, cooped up for two long years behind the walls of St-Odile's convent school, *en pension* with the good sisters. [125] By the immediate prewar period (1910–14), the effects of her work would manifest themselves in the sudden take-off of *colonies des filles* in parishes throughout Paris and its suburbs.

But at the turn of the century (1898–1903), as priests and confrères were

establishing the first *colonies des garçons,* the girls were left to languish
in the city while their brothers marched off for three weeks of adventure in the woods and fields of rural France. Max Turmann bemoaned
this gender inequity in his 1904 treatise on popular education, adding the
shamefaced excuse that where girls were concerned, there were "additional complications." These were left studiously vague and implicit,
linked to a cloudy notion of "particular differences": "as it entailed sending thirty children far away, we were more reluctant to send young girls
than boys; it was a matter of particular differences." Parents undoubtedly manifested a greater reluctance to part with their daughters for such
long periods of time, but the directors, too, showed a marked slowness in
organizing for girls the equivalent of what their brothers enjoyed. One
might wonder whether this delay reflected a shortage of personnel, and
yet Combes's campaign against the congregations had surely freed many
a *bonne soeur* from her normal teaching duties. In truth, the delay in organizing girls' *colonies* was linked to a combination of factors: first, the presumably greater religiosity of women and girls made the need seem less
urgent to a Church bent on the missionary conquest of de-Christianized
workingmen. In addition, however, the organization of *colonies* for girls
by a Church whose religious hierarchy was entirely male presented un-
foreseen problems of control. In the *patronage,* sheer physical proximity
obviated any such difficulties, as the abbé was always nearby to handle
the religious education of the girls and (if need be) guide the work of
the *directrice.* In the *colonie de vacances* such direct priestly control was
no longer possible, and many a parish priest no doubt hesitated before
releasing an autonomous female band into the French countryside.

   The Société de Saint-Vincent-de-Paul was the first to step into this
gap when, in 1904, just one year after establishing its *colonie des garçons*
at Verrières, the Société decided the time had come to do something for
their sisters as well: "In the convent at Monsols (Beaujolais), they found
the ideal locale and direction . . . The devout sisters of Monsols, who can
no longer teach and yet remain schoolmistresses, wish for nothing more
than to take up once again their mission, which is, once more, education." Twenty girls were sent on that first *colonie* with the good sisters of
Monsols, where they divided their time between short hikes, prayer, and
reading, their hands at all times occupied by the inevitable needlework
or knitting: "When she returns home, each little girl brings her mother
a towel that she made herself under the guidance of the good sisters,

which proves that up [at Monsols], they never forgot practical matters, nor family life."[126]

Hiking, gymnastics, and pseudomilitary exercise played a scant role in these *colonies,* nor were directors concerned to build character by toughening the girl-child's physical endurance. The girls thus arose each morning at six, heard mass, then prayed and sang a hymn before heading out for their morning constitutional, "properly provided with bread for their meal." Breakfast was a picnic taken in the fields: "We got the milk at a farm. We then played, relaxed, and worked with our crochet hooks or needles. We had even brought a book, and as our little knitters sat on the green carpet of the clearing, fingers flying . . . the wise and motherly *directrice* imposed a rest-break on their tongues."[127] The *colons* then returned to the convent for a real dinner, the main meal of the day. En route they stripped the bushes of berries and shook hazelnuts down from the trees, munching eagerly "these simple fruits that city children consume with such alacrity." The afternoons looked quite similar: after a brief nap, the hottest part of the day was spent indoors at various tasks: writing letters, reading, and sewing, followed by a second departure in the late afternoon, with a snack of bread and chocolate tucked into their baskets. "On the way home each evening, the joyful troop stops to pray at the church." The regime was less physically harsh than the boys' *colonie,* but in its own way equally unconcerned to pursue a rigorous program of hygiene, as the Société de Saint-Vincent-de-Paul conceded in its 1905 report: "As you can see, the mission that is accomplished up [at Monsols] is more moral than hygienic. It is as much a retreat as it is a vacation."[128]

In the meantime, Mme Duhamel's energetic push to expand the *colonies des filles* was producing swift and dramatic results, as *patronages des filles* in the Paris and Lyonnais regions established their own network of *colonies* over the first decade of the twentieth century. The new *colonies des filles* often drew on the important resources that the former teaching orders provided—empty convent schools and unemployed women with a vocation for teaching. In addition, the austere convent-based program of a Monsols *colonie* soon gave way to more active vacations, with the *colons* hiking, climbing, and exploring in the company of younger, lay activists. The *colonie des jeunes filles* of Notre-Dame-de-la-Salette in Suresnes thus passed an eventful three weeks in Bologne (Haut-Marne) in the summer of 1913: "The banks of the Marne, where you can safely wade and paddle about, give the impression of an ocean beach, while

the slopes of Saint-Bologne recall a mountain landscape; we were able
to climb it only with the aid of a pickax, cutting our way through the
underbrush." [129]

The turn toward more vigorous outdoorsmanship prefigured the tremendous leap forward that gymnastics, organized sports, and scouting
for girls (the Guides, in the organization of which Duhamel would play a
key role) would make in the 1920s. And, as always, these vigorous physical
activities were located in a broader context of pious observance: "What
memories Bologne will henceforth evoke! Domremy! Rising at 3 A.M.,
as valiant as their patron saint, the girls left on a pilgrimage to the land of
la Pucelle. Every site that was marked as a souvenir of Jeanne recalled the
humble shepherdess to them, the model young girl, pious and devoted to
home and family, who later became the liberator of all France." [130] The
girls also visited Langres, Chaumont, Notre-Dame-de-Mechines, and
Sesfontaines, "where we made the trip in a wagon" — sites of Catholic re-
membrance spread across the Lorraine countryside. But the high point
of the *colonie* was surely the pilgimage to Domremy, and this reminds
us of the singular importance that a vigorous and engaged female piety-
cum-activism was acquiring in this period where new forms of political and civic organization met the stirring of lay activists in defense of
the Church to produce movements of unprecedented amplitude among
Catholic women and girls. For if Joan of Arc was a model of female piety
and devotion to home and family, she was also a girl who marched forth
in soldier's dress to lead entire armies in the defense of her nation. Over
the interwar period, the Church would continue to propose such models
of female activism, even while counseling the virtues of domestic life.

At the end of the nineteenth century, from the midst of the worst political crisis it had known since 1790, the Catholic Church moved decisively
onto the terrain of popular education, defending its role in public education by founding *patronages* and *colonies de vacances.* As we have seen, the
clergy and lay activists who collaborated in these ventures became the
first architects of a full-blown pedagogy of child leisure in France. The
renewed vigor and singleness of purpose that made the Church such an
active and innovative force in this domain emerged, ironically, out of the
same crises — school secularization, then church-state separation — that
gave rise to the myth of a secular triumph in the field of primary education. And so Catholic dynamism in the growing domain of the *périscolaire* was quickly forgotten, overlaid by the blanket presumption that

secularization ultimately deprived the clergy of any authoritative voice in matters of education. But as we have seen, the reality was far more complex; contrary to the public memories of both republican "victor" and Catholic "victim" alike, the clergy continued to sound a vigorous alternative note. This was certainly quite audible at the turn of the twentieth century, when the *colonie de vacances* emerged as a site of contest between the clerical educators and secular hygienists as they battled for control over the definition and organization of the *colonies.*

In the course of this debate, Catholic pedagogues revealed that they had something quite unique to offer in the organization of child leisure, namely, a set of active methods that had been developed in the unexpected company of a vision of fallible human nature, stained by original sin. Where the secular and left-wing practitioners of the "new pedagogies" in Belgium and Switzerland, Italy and Britain reposed their methods on a confidence in the basic goodness and self-sufficiency of the individual child, France's Catholic pedagogues of the *périscolaire* joined their active methods to a fundamentally pessimistic view of human nature. This curious hybrid shared with its secular counterparts a rejection of passive and rote forms of learning in favor of techniques designed to draw the child into an active participation in his or her own education. As such, the Catholic pedagogues of *patronage* and *colonie de vacances* were the avatars, creating the first forms by which the international movement for a "new pedagogy" found expression in France. It would be another thirty years before the interwar flowering of initiatives in popular education provided secular proponents of active methods with any comparable ground for application.

But this singular coupling of "pédagogies actives" with the doctrine of original sin also posed novel questions about the role of discipline, liberty, and individual initiative. After all, Catholic educators could not simply let "nature" take its course, referring themselves to an individual and child-centered definition of what was necessary and right in order to establish the content or structure of instruction in the *patronages* and *colonies de vacances.* Rather, the educator had to work from the outside, to reshape the child's fallen nature. The Catholic vision of education as an act of re-creation applied to human creatures of all social classes, for when Adam and Eve fell, so did we all. But the need was especially urgent for the children of the poor, raised in the de-Christianized cultures of working-class streets and republican schools. For Catholic educators, then, an "active education" did not mean waiting for the creative forces within the child to lend that education its inspiration and direction. It meant, rather, providing both structure and content to the child, securing his or her active engagement in learning things of which he or she was presumed to have no natural inkling, let alone any natural inclination. The implicit tension between the mobilization of child energies and the ongoing need for guidance and discipline, thanks to our universal heritage of original sin, propelled Catholic educators to adopt the *colonie collective* as the only viable setting for a truly Catholic application of the new methods. Here, the children's collectivity, organized by priests and seminarians who were trained for the task, shaped the form and content of learning while defining the limits of individual liberty by linking individual children to the broader needs of the child community. By this route, Catholic educators arrived at the same form—the *colonie collective*—that had found favor with the republican "enemies of religion." Their convergence on the collective format reminds us that what linked secular republicans to Catholics in this era, namely their shared conviction that education requires a collective and public (versus private and familial) setting, may be as important as the passions that divided them.

British and American readers will perhaps be surprised to discover how lately the *nouvelles pédagogies* (secular style) arrived in French schools, and what a long and hard road they traveled before finding any kind of secure purchase therein. From an Anglo-American perspective, child-centered educational techniques seem a logical, natural, and desirable way to impart knowledge to the young, for they permit teachers to avoid hierarchical and one-way relationships of power/knowledge by inviting them instead to participate actively in the imaginary and play-centered worlds of children. The entire practice is undergirded by faith in the inherently pedagogical nature of children's play, and its outlines are so familiar as to seem utterly banal from within the more child-centered cultures of Britain and the United States.

By this I do not mean to say that the French take any less interest in their children; rather, I wish to draw attention to a peculiarity of Anglo-American adults, which is their underlying sense that there is something ultimately positive about remaining childlike into your adulthood. As Alison Lurie recently observed, this is particular to modern Anglophone cultures, where, "since the late eighteenth century, poets and philosophers have maintained that there is something wonderful and unique about childhood: that simply to be young is to be naturally good and great." Such attitudes are far less common in France, where, as in many other nations, "there is nothing especially wonderful about being a child of school age. For the first four or five years boys and girls may be petted and indulged, but after that they are usually expected to become little adults as soon as possible: responsible, serious, future-oriented." [131] French institutions of child rearing and education — schools, *colonies de vacances,* children's literature — thus stress the temporary nature of childhood: one does (or should strive to) ultimately leave it behind, and it is the job of these institutions to help children leave the condition of childhood as gracefully and swiftly as possible. When the priests got down with the children, then, it was a means to the end of helping that child to exit from the childish state, rather than an effort to preserve and valorize some childlike innocence or spontaneity in themselves. This same understanding would reappear at the heart of secular and leftist initiatives in the interwar years — Célestin Freinet's *école du travail,* and the Centres d'Entraînement aux Méthodes d'Éducation Actives (CEMEA). [132] Rather than attributing the slow penetration of child-centered methods in France to any Gallican exceptionalism, we can perhaps more usefully read this history as pointing toward a singularity in modern Anglo-American cultures, perceptible in the attitudes that adults hold toward children and notions of childhood. [133]

CHAPTER THREE

✑ *Family Placement in a Socialist Mode*

THE FOUNDATION OF THE COLONIE

MUNICIPALE OF SURESNES

By the turn of the twentieth century, the *colonies de vacances* had already won their reputation as France's "first line of defense" in the struggle against tuberculosis.[1] In the aftermath of World War I, with widespread undernourishment among children, especially in the occupied zones of northeastern France, and newly rising rates of tuberculosis among the population in general, the hygienic virtues of the *colonie* would gain an even greater luster.[2] Indeed, preserving and reinforcing the health of French children, on whose slender shoulders rode ever more heavily the burden of future repopulation, lent the *colonies de vacances* a heightened national significance that organizers hastened to underscore in their annual campaigns to raise funds: "It is now more necessary than ever that we bolster our children's health, for when the war is over, the future of our race will depend on them," intoned Victor Diederich, mayor of Suresnes, in his 1916 letter of appeal for the municipal *colonie de vacances:* "So long as they are robust and healthy, and enjoy a perfect mental and physical equilibrium, the next generation will be courageous and strong, ready to work, and to build the economy and national prosperity."[3] While the day-to-day business of organizing individual *colonies* remained largely in local hands, the urgent demographic climate of postwar France had moved the *colonies* to the center of national programs that linked public health to broader schemes of urban renewal and reconstruction.[4] In this climate, the role of private charity inevitably dwindled as municipal administrations increasingly took over the job of organizing *colonies de vacances,* extending their reach across an ever-broadening swath of the local school-age population.[5]

The working-class city of Suresnes offers a particularly rich and revealing instance of the importance that the municipal *colonie* acquired in relation to a larger social politics that linked urban planning, public health, and primary education in a rationally ordered scheme of Socialist municipal administration. Hence, with the Socialist victory in Suresnes in 1919, newly elected mayor Henri Sellier immediately set about constructing a network of municipal social services that were aimed especially at improving children's health. As a first step, he restructured the city's fifteen-year-old *colonie de vacances* along more properly Socialist lines and placed it at the heart of the larger network of social services, which was to be managed and coordinated by a growing staff of municipal social workers. At first glance, the refurbished *colonie municipale,* which placed the city's children with peasant families in the Nièvre, seems a kind of quaint anachronism, quite at odds with the scientific modernism of Sellier's Socialist experiment in rational urban planning. Upon closer inspection, however, it becomes apparent that, far from mere anachronism, peasant placement constituted a vital and consciously chosen element in that plan. For like many municipal Socialists, the new mayor was convinced that urban children suffered above all from the stress of constant submission to the collective disciplines of city life, "one of the major causes of mental exhaustion among children in our great cities."[6] Concerned that the rhythms and constraints of a collective *colonie* would simply replace one set of disciplines for another, Sellier opted for the suppler, more child-scaled rhythms of life in a peasant family. Placing city children in this carefully chosen region, which was thoroughly de-Christianized and solidly Socialist, had the added advantage of giving to those children a resource whose value was unquestioned at the time, namely, a direct, living tie to the French countryside. For through the adoptive peasant family (with whom the child lived at least eight weeks each summer, from the age of five or six until his or her fourteenth birthday), the child acquired a living link to the "forgotten corners" of the French countryside, a kind of adoptive *pays natal* for those young Suresnois whose parents had lost touch with their own rural roots.[7] The *colonie municipale* of Suresnes thus reveals a strong current of left-wing ruralism at work, shaping the Socialist politics of childhood. It is a powerful and distinctively Socialist vision of the land and its relation to urban and working-class life, a vision that has since been obscured in a literature that recalls only the right-wing and Vichyite calls for a "return to the land" that rang forth across the interwar landscape.

From Urban Village to Industrial Suburb: Suresnes, 1890–1919

Like so many of the small cities around Paris, turn-of-the-century Suresnes was a rapidly industrializing city that, for all its recent development, still bore the aspect of a sleepy rural bourg. The mid-nineteenth-century residential expansion to the west of Paris had already reshaped the old wine-growers' village that lay spread at the feet of Mont-Valérien, interspersing dairy farms and vineyards with laundries, dye-works, and perfume factories. But the transformation of peri-urban space came gradually to prewar Suresnes, and in 1914, unpaved roads and pathways still meandered through the fields and terraced vineyards, linking the open spaces of the plateau, with its wheat fields and stone quarries, to the railway yards and warehouses that sprawled below along the banks of the Seine river valley. Traces of the old village survived not only in the open fields and dairy farms, but in the handful of handsome country houses that still dotted the steep hillsides of the growing city, villas long since abandoned by the urban notables whose quest for bucolic tranquillity had led them to the western banks of the Seine some fifty to one hundred years before: "At the bottom of the avenue lay the château," recalled one Suresnois. "There was a great park that ran to the end of the Suresnes road and all the way to the rue des Alouettes. The château was right at the crossroads . . . I don't remember who lived there. When I was in school I knew kids who played hooky there, because there was an English garden, with grottoes and a little stream."[8]

With the industrial push of the 1890s, the entire western loop of the Seine became the site of intensive and highly profitable industrial development, grounded in metallurgy and the new, "high-tech" automobile and aviation industries. From a mid-nineteenth-century population of just over 2,000, Suresnes expanded nearly tenfold, reaching 16,248 by 1911.[9] About half of these new arrivals were factory workers, drawn by the expanding opportunities for employment in the nascent car industry and at the vast state arsenal in the neighboring *banlieue* (suburb) of Puteaux. The remainder were white-collar workers of various sorts, many of whom also found jobs in the district, working in the accounting and time-study departments of the highly modern factories west of Paris. Whether working class or petit bourgeois, however, the new migrants were nearly all of provincial origin, arriving en masse from the

villages and small towns of rural France.[10] Crammed into the dilapidated housing of this lately bucolic spot, the population of Suresnes experienced a rapid and steep decline in living conditions over the early
twentieth century. This grew especially acute during World War I, when
the arms industries' insatiable demand for labor drew some three thousand additional migrants, who filled to bursting the old farms and out-
buildings, and crowded into every available rooming house and furnished flat before spilling over into the shantytowns of tin and tar-paper
shacks that sprang up overnight on the hillsides of Mont-Valérien. "We
called it Little Morocco because there dwelt the blackest misery, people
who drank all the time . . . There were rag-pickers living near the top
of the *chemin du Télégraphe* . . . The more prosperous among them had
a horse and wagon, but others had only dog-carts that they'd banged
together from old car wheels with no tires." [11]

By the end of 1918, 93.8 percent of the Suresnes labor force was employed in the metals and munitions trades, which comprised a full 77.9
percent of the city's industry at that time. Although the prolonged trade
slump of 1919–23 closed many factory gates for good, local industry
remained overwhelmingly concentrated in metalworking, which comprised 60 percent of local firms and employed 70 percent of the city's
workers.[12] Aside from local factories—small-to-medium-sized shops,
engaged for the most part in subcontracting and repair—there was
plenty of work to be had in the nearby giants: Renault, Citroën, or the
arsenal at Puteaux. Local industry thus sought out both skilled and unskilled labor, and drew provincial workers in ever greater numbers during the interwar years. The population of Suresnes soared throughout
the 1920s—from 19,117 in 1921, to 22,209 in 1926, to 26,065 in 1931—and
continued to grow even through the economic downturn of the 1930s,
reaching 32,018 by 1936.[13] By 1925, one seventh of these people were living
in boardinghouses and furnished rooms, and a 1929 survey found that
fully half the population was crammed into lodgings that were deemed
"inadequate" (meaning housing that provided less than one room per
occupant).[14] Small wonder that the first postwar elections, in November–
December 1919, swept into power Socialist militant Henri Sellier, at the
head of a municipal ticket that placed public health, housing, and urban
renewal at the top of its electoral program.

Henri Sellier and the Socialism of Municipal Solidarity

Henri Sellier was one of the most forceful and energetic personalities to emerge in left-wing circles of the early twentieth century.[15] A born activist, he was highly intelligent and imbued with a vision of municipal politics as the crucible of a broader social transformation. He was, moreover, blessed with extraordinary drive and direction, a seemingly inexhaustible reserve of energy, and a gift for public oratory: "With those who knew him, his manner of speech was pleasantly colorful: vivid and street-wise," recalled Sellier's secretary, Georges Goblot, "but when circumstances demanded, he could be dazzling; his precise and decisive mode of argument was irresistibly convincing, and the elegance of his language captivated his listeners." [16] This combination of qualities placed Sellier at the center of municipal and Socialist politics in interwar Paris, and would ultimately bring him to national prominence as minister of health under Léon Blum's Popular Front government of 1936–37.

Like many of his fellow Suresnois, Sellier sprang from modest, provincial circumstances, having been born in Bourges, in 1883, into a family of small means: his father was a skilled metalworker who served as foreman in the cannon foundry at the immense state arsenal at Bourges, and his mother, who sprang from peasant stock, kept a small jewelry and watch shop. Henri was an excellent student, winning scholarships first to the lycée at Bourges (1894), and going on to the prestigious Ecole des Hautes Etudes de Commerce (HEC) in Paris, from which he emerged in 1901 with fluent German and English and an expertise in accounting that would serve him well once he entered local politics. In the summer of 1902, the HEC sent Sellier to the Siemens plant, in Hamburg, where he worked for the summer as secretary to Walter Rathenau. It was in Hamburg that he first encountered Albert Thomas, that "pillar of French reformism" who was to become Sellier's lifelong companion and ideological fellow-traveler.[17]

Upon graduating from the HEC, Sellier combined a variety of commercial and civil service jobs—employee in a bank, *rédacteur* at the Ministry of Commerce—with continued studies, this time preparing a degree in law, which he received in 1906.[18] That same year, Sellier joined the fledgling Ministry of Labor as *rédacteur,* rising within a few years to the position of bureau chief. It was a move that put him squarely in the center of Socialist circles in Paris.[19] During his tenure at the ministry (1906–10), Sellier would labor tirelessly to support the syndicalist activity of the Confédération Générale du Travail (CGT), and the working-class cooperative movement as well.[20] But it was the working-class city rather than the struggle to transform the workplace that would ultimately capture the young Socialist's energies.

Henri Sellier's engagement with municipal socialism stretched back to the late 1890s, when, as a young teenager, he first joined the Socialist Party in Bourges. Here, he encountered Edouard Vaillant, a medical doctor and political activist who had figured prominently in the Paris Commune and in the founding of the Parti Socialiste de France.[21] Sellier discovered socialism largely through the work of this man; indeed, Vaillant gradually became a kind of spiritual father to Sellier, and took Sellier under his wing soon after his arrival in Paris, in 1899. Drawn by the ties of common regional origin, as well as by shared political dreams, Sellier became a frequent guest at Vaillant's table, where his place was laid every Friday evening. Long after "le Vieux" had gone to his grave, Sellier would honor his patron with esteem and affection, recalling the Edouard Vaillant "who honored me with an almost paternal affection. Even as I learned to love the Republic, democracy, and socialism, I also gained a profound sense of current problems in the organization of work, of hygiene and social protection, and of the rigorous method required to solve them."[22]

Edouard Vaillant's revolutionary doctrine rested on the conviction that physical health and well-being are fundamental *rights* of all citizens, as well as the essential material base for any meaningful conquest of political power by working-class people, and he strongly advocated the use of municipal power to achieve those aims. By organizing and operating a host of municipal services—transport, water, gas, and electricity, to be sure, but also schools, hospitals, public baths, social housing, bakeries, police, and municipal workshops—Socialists could render the commune a microcosm of the future, Socialist society: a "laboratory of decentralized economic life," but also a "powerful political fortress" that local Socialist majorities could turn against the bourgeois-dominated central power, once they had achieved a "genuine autonomy."[23] The condescending and aleatory ties of charitable social assistance must therefore give way to the fraternal bonds of social solidarity, organized at the level of the commune. Citizens would then reap the benefits of such mutual assistance on the material level (improved health and welfare conditions) and on the spiritual/intellectual level as well, as the Socialist commune delivered up a practical example of social solidarity at work.

Vaillant thus defined a doctrine and practice of municipal socialism in which the working-class city became both the context within which and the means by which the working class could be organized more generally. The lesson was not lost on the young Sellier, who remained faithful to a communally based vision of social reform. Indeed, near the end of his long career, some forty years later, Sellier would characterize his considerable urbanist achievements as nothing more than an effort to realize the program Vaillant had put forward during his tenure on the Paris municipal council (1884–93): "I never undertook a single municipal or administrative project that wasn't inspired by the thought of Edouard Vaillant. When I was called to the Ministry of Public Health, my fondest dream — alas, never realized — was to introduce reforms that would have allowed us to apply Vaillant's doctrines of social solidarity to the organization of public health and social protection among the French population."[24]

Having thoroughly imbibed the revolutionary doctrines of *vaillantisme,* Sellier would devote his political career to preparing the collectivist society through concrete social reforms in the here and now. Always conscious of "the value of concrete realities, without which the most seductive doctrines are nothing more than a vain and hollow carcass," he did not shrink from nurturing pragmatic contacts with the decidedly nonrevolutionary reformers grouped around the Musée Social.[25] Nor did he hesitate when opportunities for concrete political and administrative action came his way: first in 1910, when the canton of Puteaux-Suresnes elected him to the Conseil Général de la Seine (which post he held continuously until his ouster, under Vichy, in 1941), and second, in 1915, when the Conseil named Sellier director of the newly created Office Public des Habitations à Bon Marché. "We are evolutionists," wrote Sellier in 1925, "and if we were not, we would not join in the struggle nor in city administration, where, by small steps and in the midst of great difficulty, we realize slow but sure reforms." But Sellier never forgot the ultimately revolutionary goals that the reforms of municipal socialism served, for "what distinguishes Socialist urban action is the conscious will to favor all reforms that bring us closer to that [revolutionary] transformation."[26] The stress placed on preparing the future society through each reform taken in the present would give to Sellier's social politics a peculiar anchoring in both present time and in a not-yet-achieved revolutionary time, whose preparation lay above all in the action of municipal *oeuvres d'enfance*—schools, health clinics, and *colonies de vacances*—on the children of the working-class city.

This was the era in which Socialist municipal reform was organized around urban and social planning, with public hygiene and a concomitant rationalization of urban space as the guiding principles. The primacy of planning among turn-of-the-century Socialists owed much to the work of Maurice Halbwachs, whose early publications on working-class family budgets and urban ground-rents recast the problems of urban poverty and unequal distribution among social classes within a whole new framework that linked social relations to spatial ones.[27] His *Politique foncière des municipalités* thus argued that the market in urban land was distorted by an enormous rise in land values, which in turn was driven by the pressure of social forces, notably migration. Under these circumstances, the municipality could no more afford to leave the price of urban land to the impersonal workings of the market than could the state afford to leave the price of bread to such whimsical and aleatory mechanisms. Sellier extended this reasoning in his own 1912 study, *Les banlieues urbaines et la réorganisation administrative du Département de la Seine,* which argued that individual communes had to seize control of urban land by taxing the surplus value of urban housing.[28] The municipalities would then be in a position to organize and control the rapid urban and industrial growth of the Paris *banlieues* by imposing a rational order, the urban plan, on these chaotically expanding agglomerations.

During the first third of the twentieth century, then, Henri Sellier played a key role in making the urban plan the key instrument in the municipal Socialist arsenal. Ideally, such plans combined a more rational organization of urban space—controlling development by dividing industrial and residential neighborhoods into separate zones—with concrete plans for improving the quality of working-class housing by building publicly subsidized houses and apartment blocks. At the same time, the municipality was to create a network of city services—medical dispensaries, *écoles maternelles, colonies de vacances,* municipal libraries, sports facilities, public meeting-halls, and *maisons de culture*—aimed at improving the health, welfare, and cultural/educational level of its working-class and lower-middle-class citizens. The urban plan of municipal socialism thus comprised several integrally linked elements— zoning, social housing, public hygiene, and popular education—which,

taken together, composed a rational and progressive urban order intended to overcome both the anarchy of capitalism and the anomie of the
marketplace. The goals of municipal socialism were thus subtly shifting,
and Vaillant's fin-de-siècle conception of the city as a "laboratory of decentralized economic life" was gradually reshaped until a new vision had
risen in its place, a vision of the working-class city where housing and
services were conceived as a counterweight to the disciplines of work, "an
ensemble of scientifically established sites, regenerative centers of a new,
modern life, well-balanced and positive . . . pointing to the future."[29]

But Sellier and his colleagues did not intend for municipal socialism
to resolve itself into a mere top-down provision of services by the city to
a passive citizenry. On the contrary, the new mayor strove to ground the
reforms of municipal socialism in a kind of local democracy, or "participatory urbanism," in which citizens and administration would engage in
an ongoing dialogue over the development and direction of city services,
with the citizen side of this discussion being developed and sustained inside a network of local cultural and political associations: neighborhood
groups, *amicales des anciens élèves,* brass bands and choral groups, the
municipal historical society.[30] In Sellier's view, such associations offered
a model of daily solidarity and active citizen participation, providing,
moreover, a neutral terrain on which citizens of different social classes
could meet and collaborate in the name of a common cultural or leisure
pursuit. As such, they permitted a democratic and participatory organization of the commune at its grass roots. By organizing the channels
of local democracy through the city's voluntary organisms of leisure and
cultural activity (all of which were subsidized by city hall), Sellier sought
to build a democratically grounded springboard for his politics of municipal services. Social solidarity, nurtured at the grassroots by the "participatory urbanism" of associational life, and at the center by the city's
politics of social assistance, would thus engender new social ties in the
working-class city.[31]

By 1935, with memories of his own workplace struggles now long behind him, Sellier had come to define the goals of socialism in terms of
the city and the expansive sense of the social rights of the citizen that
municipal Socialist ideals generated: "Socialism looks toward a social
organization that gives each citizen a maximum of well-being and freedom, and guarantees the development of each individual's abilities. This
implies organizing institutions that can ensure a state of permanent material security for all, as well as social protections and a level of physi-

cal and intellectual culture that meets everyone's needs."[32] Paradoxically enough, Henri Sellier's great contribution to the municipal Socialist tradition would be the construction of a working-class city conceived in opposition to the workplace, cities at whose gates "the prospective inhabitant ceases to be a worker and becomes once more a man."[33]

Let us turn, then, to the city of Suresnes, which, with the Socialist victory in 1919, became, in Sellier's own words, "a fruitful laboratory of social solidarity ... [and] of education toward social and human progress."[34] It also became something of a fiefdom for the young mayor, who rapidly attained immense local popularity from very early in his first administration, and was repeatedly reelected by ever greater majorities. Within fifteen years, Sellier would transform this awkwardly expanding industrial city into a showpiece of urban planning whose modernist and rational aesthetic proclaimed itself in the handsome art deco buildings of the garden-city district. Nestling at the heart of this ambitious municipal program lay Sellier's oddly archaic Nièvre *colonie,* whose Janus-faced structures—a team of trained social workers using up-to-the-minute medical and social technology to identify those children who would be sent to spend the summer with a peasant family in the southwestern Nièvre—direct our attention to the leftist ruralism that underpinned Henri Sellier's early, and decisive, initiative toward organizing Suresnes as a microcosm of rational, Socialist management.

Building the "City of the Future": Municipal Socialism and the Politics of Childhood in Suresnes, 1920–1940

Within weeks of their resounding victory at the polls in December of 1919, Sellier's "Bloc des Ouvriers, Employés, Petits Industriels et Commerçants pour la Défense des Intérêts Communaux" (which included eighteen Socialists and nine republicans) moved into city hall and embarked immediately on an extensive program of urban development and renovation. The new administration outlined a scheme that called for vigorous action on several fronts at once: housing, education, public health, sports and leisure facilities, and municipal services and infrastructure. Within two years, this scheme had already begun to bear fruit, visible in the changing landscape of the old industrial center along the Seine, and in the newer districts on the northern and western plateaus above, where muddy pathways gave way to paved roads, and modest yet

well-designed neighborhoods sprang up almost overnight: "When we
first arrived, in 1922, the chemin du Télégraphe ["Little Morocco"] was
all wooden houses," recalled one Suresnois:

> Some people even lived in old converted wagons. The roofs were made of
> tar-paper, rather than tile, the "commode" was a hole dug in the garden. No
> one had electricity . . . Periodically, the gendarmes would come by on horse-
> back and invite us to clear out, since we were living in a militarized zone.
> They would pull out their whips, which dangled along the horses' sides,
> and deal us a few blows . . . We were *zoniers*. Father Lapin was a *zonier;* all
> the farmers behind the fort were *zoniers*. And then one day, Mayor Henri
> Sellier, who was also senator at the time, needed the land behind the fort
> in order to build the garden city housing project. He took up our cause and
> succeeded in having Mont-Valérien declassified (in 1926–27). From then
> on, one could build real, solid houses. And little houses begin to spring up
> all over.[35]

Sellier's extraordinary effectiveness as mayor owed in part to the fact
that he functioned on both the local and regional/national planes of government at once, holding a range of positions at the departmental and
national levels that, taken together, describe a series of concentric circles
around the twin problems of urban development and public hygiene:
head of the departmental Office Public des Habitations à Bon Marché,
general secretary of the Office Public d'Hygiène Sociale and of the Association des Maires de la Seine, member of the national Conseil de
Familles des Pupilles de la Seine and of the Union Internationale des
Villes.[36] The combination of functions and affiliations endowed the new
mayor with an unusually varied and dense network of contacts, as well as
access to important financial and organizational resources. In addition,
the city of Suresnes offered the urban reformer certain advantages, for as
Georges Risler later remarked: "Thanks to its location and population,
Suresnes never fell into the utter chaos that is the disgrace of so many
areas in the outskirts . . . [It is] a balanced community, with its workers,
its industrialists, and its shopkeepers, with no excessive specialization,
no over- or underdevelopment of a single social category."[37] This "balanced" socioeconomic structure put greater resources at the disposal of
the *mairie,* in the form of a larger tax base. At the same time, it meant
that the city's deepest problems of poverty were limited to a few areas and
neighborhoods. Unlike Ivry or Saint-Denis, where low incomes, inadequate housing, and ill-health were broadly spread across the majority of

the population, Suresnes's most pressing urban problems were spatially concentrated in relatively few spots: the dilapidated neighborhoods that were interspersed among the factories along the Seine and the shanty-towns of tin and tar-paper shacks that pockmarked the northern plateau.

Yet the solid presence of a bourgeois old-guard also constituted a block of potential political opposition, for these self-appointed guardians of a Suresnes-gone-by were hardly inclined to accept the arrival of socialism in their midst. In order to govern effectively, Sellier would have to win these people over, a task at which he proved quite singularly adept. No sooner had he taken office than the new mayor was inviting industrialists and shopkeepers to join him in building social solidarity across the municipality, proposing projects like the municipal *colonie de vacances* as an ideal terrain for cross-class activism, and (as we shall see) cheerfully coercing, even shaming, those who refused the obligations such solidarity imposed.

The first twelve years of Sellier's twenty-two-year administration passed in a veritable frenzy of construction. In January of 1920, just a few weeks after taking office, Sellier launched the construction of a vast garden city district on forty-four hectares of open field that stretched above the old city, running along the western plateau toward Saint-Cloud/Reuil-Malmaison. By 1922, people were already moving into the 213 houses and apartments that had been built. The following October (1923), the *cité-jardin*'s first primary school, named for Edouard Vaillant, opened its doors to children of both sexes from ages two to thirteen. Vaillant was a pleasing, low-rise structure of red and yellow brick that boasted up-to-the-minute hygienic facilities (showers, lunchroom, and infirmary), landscaped playgrounds, light-filled classrooms, and a full range of handsomely equipped workshops for preapprenticeship courses in wood and metalworking, sewing, cooking, and tailoring. The nursery school (*école maternelle*) had an enviable *jardin d'enfants* at its center, where each morning's activity opened with a collective tooth-brushing session, and Montessori methods ruled supreme.

Four years later, Sellier opened a second school complex, Payret-Dortail, on the northern plateau, in one of Suresnes's very poorest neighborhoods. Standing high on the sun-washed hillside, far above the dust and noise of the factories and automobile testing grounds below, Payret-Dortail was designed to take maximum advantage of the southeastern exposure, which inspired immense bay windows and numerous landscaped terraces. This second school was even more spectacular than

Vaillant, for the architect had included an elaborate sports installation—
track, pool, and a great assembly hall with facilities for cinema projections—alongside the classrooms, workshops, playgrounds, and medical
facilities. "I think it was the only school in France at the time that had a
swimming pool," recalled a pupil from one of the first classes at Payret-
Dortail. "It was so nice to have a new school, and everything was so
big. Our classrooms were very bright and airy."[38] As in Suresnes's other
four city schools, Payret-Dortail sought to reinforce children's bodily
health through its well-stocked cafeteria, where the children were served
a hearty, hot meal at midday (free for children of the unemployed), and
by the provision of regular gymnastics instruction for children of both
sexes. The subsidized meals were a great success and were a source of
much-needed nourishment to children particularly during the difficult
years of the crisis (1932–38).[39] The gymnastics classes were another matter altogether, for their success depended on the training and experience
of the individual teaching staff, which, in late 1920s France, could be
quite rudimentary: "Madame Perrot . . . was very sweet but she did not
take much trouble. She had us walk around and around in the courtyard
singing: 'The little chicks have lost their mother hen . . .' That was gymnastics! All around the courtyard, and when the song was ended, it was
time to go back in."[40]

By the late 1920s, continuing construction on the garden city (which
reached 2,500 apartments in 1937) demanded the addition of a second
school in the district, the Ecole Aristide Briand, which opened its doors
in October of 1932. Here students found facilities that were every bit
as modern and elegant as those of Vaillant and Payret-Dortail, with a
similar array of airy, sunlit classrooms, carefully planted greenery, and
extensive sports and preapprenticeship provision for the elementary and
upper-primary divisions.[41] Built of warm red brick, with elaborate friezes
decorating the doorways, Briand's école maternelle was an especially
striking piece of art deco architecture, and boasted a solarium for the
health and pleasure of Suresnes's youngest citizens.[42] Sellier rounded out
his school-building program with extensive renovation of the city's older
primary schools (Jules Ferry, 1878, and Jean Macé, 1908) and crowned
the whole edifice with the construction (in 1932–35) of a stylish glass-
and-cement open-air school, tucked high on the hillsides of Mont-
Valérien. Built specially for children whose fragile (read tubercular or
pretubercular) condition demanded sunlight, fresh air, and a lighter program of study, Suresnes's open-air school attracted international atten-

tion for its sheer architectural beauty and for the bold alacrity with which the staff applied the "active methods" of Decroly, Montessori, and Freinet.[43]

Assuring the health and education of Suresnes's youngest citizens thus occupied the preeminent place in the municipal program of the successive Sellier administrations, as a comparative glance at municipal budgets confirms. At a time when neighboring cities were placing no more than one tenth to one fifth of their resources behind education and "oeuvres d'enfance," the city of Suresnes consistently devoted at least one third of the entire municipal budget to such programs.[44] Nearly thirty years after his death, Sellier would receive nothing but praise for this comprehensive school-building program, which had made Suresnes a "center of modern pedagogy."[45] At the time, however, the construction of such elegant facilities for the health and education of working-class children provoked the occasional sour commentary from critics who accused him of building "palatial schools that will create a need for luxury among the children of the people that their social situation will never allow them to satisfy."[46] Refusing to rise to the bait, the mayor simply replied that "the human being who learns at school what beauty and comfort are will no longer accept a slum as his dwelling."[47] Ever true to the doctrines of his mentor Edouard Vaillant, Sellier rested his municipal social politics on the conviction that the road to the human spirit passes through the body and the material conditions of its daily existence. Only by improving both individual health and collective living circumstances could Socialists hope to alter the cognitive horizons and reinforce the political combativeness of citizens, for as Sellier was wont to put it, "the new society will be built only by vigorous and strong men."[48]

Sellier's social policies were thus driven by the desire to shape a new kind of citizen. His hopes were undergirded by the neo-Lamarckian conviction that such a reform of human material could in fact be realized through systematic improvements in hygiene, housing, and education. This gave his municipal policies a strong pedagogical orientation; indeed, as sociologist Katherine Burlen observes, Sellier's urbanism, with its structure of imbricated interventions in public hygiene, education, and housing, seems above all to have aimed toward a "pedagogical organization of society."[49] The municipal Bureau of Hygiene, created in 1921 in order to rationalize, and centralize, the work of municipal social assistance, constituted yet one more site on the map of social hygienic/pedagogic intervention. Under the zealous direction of bureau chief Louis Boulonnois, the bureau's functions would expand considerably over the next ten years until, by the early 1930s, the Bureau of Hygiene had come to form the beating heart of an urban plan whose social hygienic aspect was coordinated and implemented through a network of municipal social workers who were dispatched into each and every district.[50]

As Louis Boulonnois himself observed, the municipality had at its disposal two points of entry into the households of its citizens: one was the family's legal obligation to declare each birth; the other was the child's legal obligation to attend school.[51] The bureau chief organized his office with both points of entry clearly in view, beginning with the obligations of the former. Thus, in its earliest incarnation, the bureau was staffed by a handful of nurses who visited the homes of women who had recently given birth in order to render assistance, where necessary, and impart lessons in infant care to the young mothers. There was very little continuity to this structure of home visiting, since the nurses were not assigned to particular neighborhoods, and the same young mother might receive two or three different nurses in fairly rapid succession. In the late 1920s, Boulonnois decided to abandon this structure on the grounds of pedagogical inefficiency, and by 1931, he had reorganized his growing staff on the basis of geographical sector, attaching each social worker permanently to a dispensary, infant health center, or to one of the city's five neighborhood schools.[52] Although she continued to report back to the municipal bureau, the municipal social worker, now titled *assistante scolaire,* was henceforth physically to be found at her desk in the school's infirmary, which became, in Boulonnois's phrase, "a branch office of the *mairie*'s welfare department."[53] Here she helped run the school infirmary, maintained pupils' health records, and assisted the medical inspector in the annual physical exams given to all students in the school.

The job was not an easy one; up through 1925, the reports of the medical inspector repeatedly lament the children's "highly questionable" state of bodily cleanliness—"some of the children are covered with lice and fleas"—and one survey revealed that only one student in six brushed his or her teeth daily. By 1930, however, the medical inspector's report registers considerable progress in the school's campaign to impart the lessons of basic hygiene: "There has been considerable progress in bodily hygiene; dirty children are only found in the lowest grades and among the new arrivals who are not yet educated . . . This year, for the first time, I noted that a large number of bad teeth were being treated."[54]

During the school's annual medical inspection, the *assistante scolaire*'s direct acquaintance with the individual children being examined was especially helpful in identifying cases in which poverty or illness at home indicated a more careful and probing exam by the overburdened medical inspector. It also enabled her to give invaluable input in the selection of children for the *colonie de vacances;* indeed, by the late 1920s, this latter task often fell directly in the hands of the *assistante scolaire* herself. Equally important, her rooting in the school provided both the base and the justification for making contact with the families (especially mothers) of individual students, either by periodic visits to the child's home or by requesting that the parents/mother in question make an appearance at her office in the school. In the words of one interwar *assistante,* these appointments were called for a variety of reasons: "observations about the child's cleanliness, or a plea to take the child to see a doctor — verification of the reasons invoked for a child's absence, or investigation of reasons for nonattendance in the absence of any such excuse — request that the child attend the open-air school, or leave with the *colonies de vacances.*"[55]

The *assistante scolaire* thus became an *assistante polyvalente,* or multipurpose social worker as well; rather than being defined by her specialization in a single branch of medicine or social work, as were the visiting nurses of the early 1920s, the *polyvalente* was defined by her geographical implantation in a particular neighborhood school. Here she coordinated and directed a range of medical and social services that were aimed primarily at the schoolchild. From this base, she sought to draw the families, especially the neediest ones, into her ambit.[56] The *polyvalente*'s bailiwick thus radiated outward from the primary school to embrace the families of all school-age children who lived in the surrounding district. Fifty years after Edmond Cottinet's first *colonies scolaires,* and sixty years after the foundation of the *caisses des écoles,* we see the primary school in the Socialist municipality expanding still further its medical and social hygienic functions through a centrally coordinated team of *assistantes scolaires,* "who, even as they assure a social service within the school, also extend those services to the population at large."[57] To an ever greater degree, the school was becoming a key site in the primitive development of the welfare state in France, with the well-being of neighborhood schoolchildren as the point of departure for a more all-encompassing contact with the entire population.[58]

Ultimately, Sellier's elaborate network of social services was organized more through Boulonnois's team of increasingly active *assistantes sco-*

laires than through any dialogue between the *mairie* and its citizens, mediated by autonomous neighborhood associations.[59] Thrust by the municipal government into the private spaces of working-class and petit-bourgeois families, these women sought to ensure the welfare of individual members (especially the children) while guaranteeing a sound level of public health through a rigorous program of preventive hygiene.[60] The latter entailed careful diagnosis of the family's physical, moral, and financial difficulties, beginning with the initial point of contact, the child at school, with all his or her particular problems: poor attendance, falling asleep in class, failure to register for the *colonies de vacances*. The symptoms were then traced back into the individual homes, where their root causes — contagious disease (especially tuberculosis), chronic unemployment, a sick or alcoholic parent — were identified (or "diagnosed," in the language of the social service), and appropriate measures then prescribed.[61]

There is, clearly, a central ambivalence in the public health and education policies pursued in interwar Suresnes, as its architects and engineers oscillated between fidelity to the participatory and democratic spirit of Vaillant's municipal socialism (Sellier's insistence on the role of local associations in the democratic implantation of a participatory urbanism) and a will to achieve ever greater technocratic control of the population, which tendency was most fully incarnated in the person of Sellier's ardent disciple Louis Boulonnois, aptly titled the "Saint Just of the social service."[62] After all, the Bureau of Hygiene's diagnosis of "defective" families, carried out in the name of protecting the children and guaranteeing public health, could easily slip over into a eugenically conscious kind of natalism, one that was organized less around the push for sheer numbers than around elevating the sociobiological *quality* of citizens through systematic interventions in public health and education ("sauver la graine," in Pasteur's famous and oft-quoted phrase). Like so many interwar Socialists, Henri Sellier periodically issued statements that said as much: "Given the large number of men of all ages who are more or less anemic and probably tubercular . . . given the increased level of urban concentration . . . , the decline in morality and habits of excess and intemperance . . . , we must improve the quality of families and reduce the number of sickly and defective individuals."[63]

Yet it would be a mistake to lift such statements out of their context and then judge their author by late-twentieth-century standards of ideological correctness, not to mention contemporary standards of material comfort, nutrition, and general health.[64] For as Robert Nye has observed, the language of Lamarckian eugenics was broadly shared across the political spectrum in early-twentieth-century France.[65] The Lamarckianism of interwar Socialists thus had less to do with Nazi eugenics or mystical unions of blood—language of preserving the French "race" notwithstanding—than with a distinctively Socialist analysis of the all-too-evident effects of poverty on human bodies and spirits.[66] French Socialists had, after all, a long-standing concern with the health of working-class citizens, a kind of material analysis that saw the bodily health of workers as one essential condition of revolutionary action and change. Henri Sellier and his colleagues set out to enact this social analysis in a comprehensive program of individual and public hygiene that offered nothing less than a new "equalization of opportunity" in life, a revolutionary transformation of humanity through the steady improvement of the social and material conditions of daily life.[67]

Sellier was thus heir to a Socialist and anarcho-syndicalist tradition that had put its own revolutionary spin on the old maxim that a healthy body was the condition of a sound mind. And it was these convictions that imbued French socialism with the strong Lamarckian bias that is so visible in the social politics of a mayor so active as Henri Sellier. From the organization of the municipal Bureau of Hygiene to the shape and design of both garden city and the city's newest school buildings, Sellier's municipal socialism linked public health to the education, and reeducation, of citizens in both mind and body, beginning with school-age children but reaching out, ultimately, to embrace the entire population.

Yet reeducating the older generation remained a secondary concern when placed next to the urgent matter of providing the basic conditions in which the rising generation could enjoy the fullest possible physiological, intellectual, and moral development. Indeed, children were inevitably the central objects of a revolutionary vision that reposed its best hopes for social transformation in the fact that young children represented a genuinely new point of departure, uncorrupted by a lifetime of struggle for existence inside the ancien régime: "By working together on behalf of youth, each of us . . . knows he is placing a stone in the edifice of that ideal city that must be the humanity of tomorrow."[68] Moreover, this new point of departure was understood as both a mental and physical being whose body and mind must, simultaneously, be strengthened for the new world of the future: "To whom should we address our efforts?" asked anarcho-Communist pedagogue L. Rouget in the spring of 1914:

To the old guy who already has one foot in the grave? He no longer needs us. To the mature man, filled with all manner of prejudice, physically, intellectually, and morally corrupt? . . . It is very hard to straighten out a twisted tree, and it is, by the same token, very difficult to implant a firm will and a just manner of thinking in a man of that age . . . It is to the child and youth above all that we must address ourselves, those whose bodies are not yet marked by abuse and whose minds are not yet soiled by official dogma or family prejudice. It is he who is most easily educated and on whom education has the greatest impact.[69]

The older generation, however engaged in the battles of syndicalist warfare, had been raised up inside the very ancien régime against which they struggled—their minds and bodies were, inevitably, produced inside the very society against which they fought. Their children, by contrast, could hope for something different, and this something extended to the realm of biological being: they could enjoy better health and more favorable conditions for their own physiological and cognitive development than their parents had ever known.

Standing at the frontier of public health and popular education, the municipal *colonie de vacances* would clearly play a vital role in this larger project of urban and social/human renovation. Within five months of taking office, Mayor Sellier had created a special municipal commission inside the city council's commission on instruction and popular education, whose task was to ensure that the city sent the greatest number possible to the municipal *colonie de vacances*.[70] Before instigating the summer recruitment drive, however, the existing municipal *colonie,* inherited from the predecessor (republican-Socialist) regime, had to be refashioned from the ground up, replacing a structure that smacked heavily of Protestant charity with a truly municipal *colonie,* one that was managed directly by the Socialist administration on behalf of the city's youngest citizens. From the outset, then, Henri Sellier folded the *colonie de vacances* into the capacious embrace of a municipal socialism at whose core lay the direct management of services by the Socialist *mairie* itself.[71]

Building the Nièvre *Colonie*

Since the turn of the twentieth century, the city of Suresnes had been sending some of its poorest children to spend their summers in the Loiret, lodged with peasant families in the countryside around Châtillon-sur-

Loire. In this initial, prewar incarnation, the Suresnes *colonie* was organized by the local *caisse des écoles,* which raised the necessary funds, identified eligible children, and then engaged the services of the Chaussée de Maine to act as intermediary.[72] The recourse to experienced intermediaries (generally the more neutral Chaussée de Maine rather than the austerely Protestant Oeuvre de Trois Semaines) was a common expedient in the industrial cities that ringed turn-of-the-century Paris, since establishing a *colonie chez les paysans* was no simple matter. First, an appropriate district had to be identified, since much of rural France was in fact deemed inhospitable for a family-placement-style *colonie.* Brittany and Normandy were excluded for their high rates of alcoholism, while poorer regions (parts of the Massif Central and the hill country east of Lyon) were avoided on the grounds that local peasants lived so meanly that they could not adequately feed and shelter urban children, and might even be tempted to use their young guests as much-needed cheap labor during the busy seasons of haymaking and harvest. The ideal setting was neither too sparsely populated nor too close to a major city, a district in which the peasants were relatively prosperous smallholders who lived largely from the fruits of their own labors: "The *nourriciers* must be small proprietors, farmers with a garden and farmyard, a goat or cow, who harvest themselves a part of the children's food, and who do not sell instantly all the fruits of their labor," advised Dr. Armand-Delille of the Oeuvre Grancher in his 1925 speech before the national congress of *colonies de vacances.*[73] Most *oeuvres de placement familial* thus turned their eyes toward the *départements* of central France, to the Loire, Nièvre, Yonne, Cher, and Allier, some of which had long practiced *l'élevage humain,* first through the wet-nursing trade, and later, by taking in orphans from the Assistance Publique's Service des Enfants Assistés.

Once an appropriate district had been located, the real work of organizing the *colonie* began. If the chosen district was sufficiently dense, with a number of villages and hamlets concentrated in a limited area, the program could designate the district a self-contained *centre de colonisation* within which children from a single town could be settled. By the late 1910s, most programs had adopted the method of organizing family placement by *centres de colonisation,* as it avoided scattering the children from a single city across the countryside, and so facilitated the job of surveillance.

But the single most difficult task, on which the success of the *colonie* depended, was the work of locating and patiently building up a network of contacts among the rural notability. For every successful *oeuvre de place-ment familial* had its stable of local collaborators in the shape of those pro-vincial mayors, teachers, and doctors who could be relied upon to select intelligently, and on the basis of precise and local knowledge, a pool of peasant households whose standards of comfort, hygiene, and prosperity met the minimum requirements of the program (generally, a separate, well-aired room for the *colons* with no more than two children to a bed, and no bunking in with the farm workers). As noted above, Protestant *colonies charitables* generally built their relationship with the peasants of a particular district through the wealthy landowning families. Secular and republican programs like Louis Conlombant's Paris-based Oeuvre des Enfants à la Montagne, by contrast, studiously avoided the traditional ties of rural domination in favor of knitting more egalitarian relations between the citizens of rural and urban France, which were to be de-veloped and nurtured during the daily rounds of the program's on-site *surveillant(e)s.*

These latter were Parisian schoolteachers, republican educators whose ardent devotion to the goals of the *colonie* and personal acquaintance with both the *colons* and the local peasants made them the key figures on which the success of the endeavor rested. These men and women were ex-pected, first and foremost, to "love" the children, "with their good points and their faults; to understand them and respect their developing person-alities, to know how to guide them toward beautiful and useful things."[74] But the job also required great stamina, as *surveillant(e)s* had to cover long distances on foot or bicycle, in order to visit the children in their charge and make sure they were being properly cared for. It was in the course of these visits that Conlombant urged his *surveillant(e)s* to strengthen the larger ties of solidarity between the rural and urban citizens of the Third Republic, by sitting down with their rural compatriots to freely discuss matters of mutual interest: "A bit of good advice on the care and feed-ing of young children," to be sure, but the director hoped that his staff would carry still further their role as urban emissaries, and offer the peas-ants timely counsel on modern agricultural methods as well: "We must never forget that, since the peasant does our society a service in giving health and strength to the *colons* we confide to him, the program owes him something as well."[75]

Of course these conversations had to be steered delicately, in order to bring urban knowledge to bear on useful topics without offending peas-ant pride, or appearing to interfere unduly in the family's private affairs:

"Without nosing into their business, [the *surveillant*] should speak with them about insurance against fires, hail, or the death of beasts. He can help them understand those social laws of interest to farmers, the agricultural syndicates . . . , fertilizers, animal hygiene, selective breeding in the farmyard, agricultural schools, etc."[76] Moreover, the *surveillant(e)* had always to keep in mind the differences of culture and discursive style that still separated rural worlds from the urban one: "He must be *simple,* for peasants do not like the monsieur who comes to inspect them; but they like the man or woman who treats them as a friend, chats with them, knows how to keep to the essential things without being trivial." For, all rhetoric of the common ties of citizenship aside, it was, in the end, necessary that the urban world impose itself here, if the rural one was to effectively serve the cause of urban children's health.[77] It was necessary above all because rural and urban modes of child care were different, and if the program wished to capture the advantages of rural life for its *colons,* it sought to do so on its own terms, overcoming the tenacious force of peasant routine through the *surveillant(e)*'s powers of rational persuasion: "The peasants have their own habits, and we know from experience how difficult it is to undo them. You must visit them often and repeat many times and in different ways what it is you wish them to do. They must first of all be convinced." In the vexed matter of leaving the bedroom windows open while the children slept (a key point in interwar hygienic practice), the Oeuvre des Enfants à la Montagne had been carrying on a patient war of attrition for more than two decades: "After more than twenty-five years in the Cantal, my *surveillant(e)s* are still unable to convince all the peasants to leave the windows open on hot nights. But on each of my rounds, I have nonetheless observed that the number of families converted to this practice has risen. I do not despair of someday convincing them all," wrote one persistent missionary to the backward hill people of the Massif Central.[78]

Establishing a *colonie chez les paysans* thus demanded a considerable investment of time and energy, and implied, moreover, a continual work of upkeep in the cultivation and renewal of contacts among the rural population. No wonder the municipalities around Paris preferred to rely on the longstanding contacts and accumulated expertise of the Chaussée de Maine's *dames charitables.* Turn-of-the-century Suresnes was no exception in this regard; once the *caisse des écoles* had selected the children, the municipality played no further role in the organization of its *colonie,* but rather left the entire business in the hands of the *dames de l'oeuvre,* who ran the entire operation from start to finish, verifying the health and cleanliness of the young *colons* before their departure, as well as the physical cleanliness and moral character of the peasant families who would harbor them throughout the long summer holiday.[79]

We know comparatively little about those early, prewar *colonies* in Suresnes, for if any record was ever made of the process whereby the newly elected, vaguely Socialist, and rabidly anticlerical Diederich administration decided to organize that first municipal *colonie,* in the summer of 1904, such record has long since disappeared.[80] What remain are a few figures — thirty-four children sent to the Loiret in that first summer of 1904, rising to sixty the following year — and a passing indication that the cost of these holidays was borne not by the parents but by the municipality, which became more and more active in the business of raising funds as demand curved steadily upward.[81]

But if the origins of the city's *colonie* remain obscure, the shape and timing of its foundation suggest that the establishment of a municipal *colonie de vacances* formed part of the left's larger struggle to define a purely secular structure of public child care and leisure organization. Hence, in the summer of 1904, at the very moment when the municipality first engaged the services of the Chaussée de Maine, the city council was also preparing an inventory of local church property, in ready compliance with the national law that would separate church from state. The official history of Suresnes points out that this inventory was taken without incident, "in perfect calm" even, "thanks to the utter propriety of both mayor and curé."[82] Yet Suresnes had been deeply divided by the Dreyfus Affair, just a few years earlier, and the fact that a second eyewitness speaks quite frankly of the "difficulties that arose between parish and municipality" between 1905 and 1911 suggests that considerable tension still lurked beneath whatever surface calm may have governed Catholic-*laïque* relations during the actual separation.[83] It is probably no accident, then, that the foundation of parallel sets of *patronages* and *colonies de vacances* in Suresnes should have coincided so closely with France's final separation of church and state, as the struggle to sway the hearts and minds of the next generation moved to the center of Catholic-*laïque* struggle in the cities and towns of the Third Republic.[84] Mayor Diederich was thus careful to choose a Protestant intermediary for the municipal *colonie,* one that was overtly committed to the cause of religious neutrality.[85] During their six weeks with the peasants of the Loiret, the young Suresnois would be vouchsafed a summer free from the pressures of priest and seminarian, lodged in the de-Christianized peasant households of central France.

After 1914, the crisis of war thrust the municipal *colonie* into greater prominence, as problems of food supply, already acute by the summer of 1915, drove increasing numbers of families to the *colonie* in search of rural placements for their children.[86] The *colonie* thus expanded quite rapidly, from 96 (48 girls and 48 boys) in the summer of 1914, to 115 in 1916, before reaching 163 by the third, terrible year of war (September of 1917).[87] This swift expansion had, in turn, drawn Mayor Diederich and his municipal council into greater and more direct involvement with the organization and financing of the city's *colonie scolaire*. Hence, in the summer of 1915, we first hear of an autonomous municipal Commission des Colonies de Vacances, whose main purpose was to raise funds from a range of local benefactors, mostly industrialists and shopkeepers.[88] These additional funds were earmarked for the children of fallen soldiers, who, transformed into "orphans of the nation" by their fathers' patriotic sacrifice, would henceforth be sent to the Loiret countryside for free with the municipal *colonie de vacances:* "Too numerous already in Suresnes, alas, are the little, innocent victims of this war of liberation, rendered atrocious by the barbarity of the enemy," mourned Mayor Diederich in June of 1915. "In asking for your contribution today, we are asking your aid in discharging a debt that we must all consider sacred."[89] In Suresnes, no less than across the nation, the war was "nationalizing" the local *colonie,* folding war orphans into the expanding company of *colons* (who had long since ceased to be the poorest of the poor) and giving a more national and patriotic valence to participation in these local programs of social assistance: "Is this not the hour when it is more necessary than ever to intervene in order to create healthy and robust men to replace those who have disappeared?"[90]

That same year, the municipal Commission des Colonies de Vacances began making annual tours of inspection, sending a small delegation to visit the farms and villages near Châtillon-sur-Loire, where the Chaussée de Maine had lodged the young Suresnois: "We visited the 31 farmers and found all [110] of our children, to whom we distributed chocolate and a substantial quantity of *biscuits Plobet* . . . We are pleased to have confirmed that our children are well and decently housed, and that we heard from the children themselves that the food is plentiful and very good . . . At Châtillon we received a delegation of several children who came bearing a bouquet with a card: Our thanks to the delegates of our benefactors." When the children returned in September, the commissioners carefully weighed and measured each one, emerging with the proud statistic: an average of 1.4 kilos gained per child![91] The Sellier administration would thus take office in a municipality where the *colonie chez les paysans,* brokered by the experienced lady-bountifuls of the Chaussée de Maine, was already a well-established tradition.

When Henri Sellier arrived at the *mairie* in the winter of 1919–20, he came bearing his own, rather different experience of organizing a *colonie chez les paysans* for the neighboring city of Puteaux, where, in his capacity as acting mayor, he had been sending the children of mobilized soldiers to spend their holidays with peasant families in the Cher and southwestern Nièvre since the summer of 1915.[92] It was a region known for its long tradition of *élevage humain,* taking in the orphaned and abandoned children of Paris: "It was in this same region that Saint-Vincent-de-Paul created, some three hundred years ago, the first placements for children from the Hôtel Dieu, and the *département* of the Seine still sends its orphans there," noted one local journalist. "The rural population, a significant portion of which springs from Paris roots, has kept the age-old practice of taking in children and raising them."[93] In the aftermath of World War I, family placement remained the mode of choice among the Socialist and republican-Socialist *banlieues,* where the collective approach would not begin to unseat the peasant family before the early 1930s, and Henri Sellier was no exception in opting for this less expensive and more flexible form of *colonie.*[94] But unlike his colleagues in Clichy and Asnières (or his predecessor, Victor Diederich, in Suresnes, for that matter), Sellier rejected the use of a charitable program as intermediary, and constructed his *colonie* on a relationship of formal collaboration between two government offices: the *mairie* of Puteaux and the local office of the Service des Enfants Assistés, at Saint-Pierre-le-Moûtier. The Enfants Assistés had nearly a century of experience in the district, placing the orphaned and abandoned children of the Paris region with peasant families on a more or less permanent basis, and the director's normal routine included periodic tours of inspection of the farms and villages that dotted the countryside around Saint-Pierre. During these visits he paid the *nourrices* their salaries and verified the well-being of the many hundred orphans in his district, while always keeping an eye out for any new placements.[95] The office at Saint-Pierre thus maintained a lengthy and up-to-date register of peasant households deemed suitable for permanent placement, from which reservoir the director could easily draw several hundred temporary summertime placements for the young *colons* of Puteaux.[96]

In the summer of 1918, the scope of Sellier's collaboration with the Enfants Assistés abruptly expanded, as the rapid German advance toward the capital prompted the government to organize a swift and massive evacuation of Parisian children to safe havens in the countryside. As German field guns pounded away at the city, Sellier, working in tight communication with the director of the national Service des Enfants Assistés, oversaw the departure of some 75,000 children for peasant households in the Yonne, Nièvre, and other traditional centers for the placement of children by the Assistance Publique. The entire operation took five days, at the end of which time all 75,000 had been lodged with peasant hosts for the duration.[97]

Sellier thus arrived in Suresnes with a record of concrete and spectacularly successful experience in organizing rural placements for urban children. He also carried with him the fruit of this experience in the shape of some firm and fully worked-out views on the ideal structure and organization of the municipal *colonie* in a working-class city. As we shall see, these views harmonized well with his Socialist-humanist conception of a city whose architecture and services were designed to grant citizens relief from the dehumanizing disciplines of work. Indeed, one could argue that Sellier's *colonie chez les paysans* played an analogous role vis-à-vis the children of Suresnes, offering these weary young creatures a relief from the stress, noise, and collective disciplines that life in an industrial city imposed: "These children are veritable martyrs . . . to this relationship . . . of *perpetual submission to collective discipline,*" wrote fellow Socialist Antonin Poggioli in his 1931 report on municipal *colonies de vacances:* "They must be quiet at home for fear of disturbing their parents or neighbors, while at school, the teachers demand that they sit still and pay attention . . . If they are taken to a park or woods, they hear over and over again the same rules: you may not walk on the grass . . . , or stray very far, or cross such and such a street, etc., etc. . . . Distinguishing that which is forbidden from that which is allowed creates a terrible and continual mental strain for these poor little things."[98] And of course, like all services in the Socialist city, the *colonie* was to be managed directly by the *mairie,* and sustained by the ties of local social solidarity. Hence, no sooner had Sellier taken office than he dispensed with the charitable services of the Chaussée de Maine and extended to Suresnes the collaborative structure he had created for the children of Puteaux. Henceforth the city's *colonie de vacances* would be organized and managed directly by the *mairie*'s Commission des Colonies de Vacances, which, for the next twenty-four years, would work with the Service des Enfants Assistés at Saint-Pierre-le-Moûtier finding suitable families for the ever-expanding crop of young Suresnois who would be spending their holidays *en colonie* with the peasants of the southwestern Nièvre.

Reorganizing the *colonie* as a municipal service delivered directly by the *mairie* traveled hand in glove with the administration's express desire, underscored in each electoral program, to expand the numbers of children sent to the countryside each summer. Although progress was slow at first, the numbers rose fivefold over the late 1920s, peaking at 539 *colons* in the summer of 1933. The total then hovered between 433 and 500 in 1934–35 before starting to fall back toward 350 in the later 1930s, presumably due to the combined effects of economic depression and the 1936 law granting paid vacations to adult workers.[99]

The drive to expand the municipal *colonie* was fitted into the mayor's larger social politics of childhood, a politics that sought to ensure a summer in the country to every Suresnes schoolchild, whether that vacation was secured by the child's own family or through the collective efforts of the municipality.[100] For the sake of their children's health and proper physical development, the Sellier administration urged parents to ensure that, one way or another, their children leave the dust and noise of the city each summer for at least six weeks of rest and relaxation in the countryside. "They will leave you at the end of July, pale and fatigued, and they will return in mid-September rosy and vigorous. Next winter, you will frequent neither the doctor's office nor the pharmacy — the baker will cost you a bit more, but for that you can only congratulate yourselves."[101] This tireless campaign was reinforced by yearly surveys of the entire school population, conducted first by the teachers and school principals, and later by the *assistantes scolaires,* as the *mairie* sought to determine how many young Suresnois were in fact reaching the provinces each summer, and by what means.[102] The surveys revealed that by the early 1930s, about 75 percent of the city's children were spending six weeks in the countryside each summer. Some three quarters of these children were being sent by their parents to live with relatives or family friends back in their native province; a further 5 percent left with the local Catholic *colonies;* and the remaining 20 percent were enjoying their summer holiday in the southwestern Nièvre with the adoptive peasant families provided by the municipal *colonie.*[103]

The *colonie* thus offers a model instance of Sellier's social politics at work, a policy whereby the *mairie* provided the direction—all children must spend the summer in the country—and the means for those who had no relatives left "back there" in the native province, or no money for the trip. In the name of social solidarity, then, the municipal *colonie* particularly extended its welcoming embrace to all those children whose parents could not accompany them to the countryside, for, as city officials put it: "This is not a program of social assistance; rather, it is open to everyone. Those who can pay do so; those families who have trouble bearing the full cost receive substantial aid."[104] The *colonie* also gave Sellier a framework within which to elaborate a politics of childhood that strove to distinguish the fate of working-class children from that of their parents, to separate out the destinies of the young, on whom hopes for the future might be reposed, from the already known, and sharply delimited, hopes of their elders. For as the new mayor well knew, the poverty and long hours of hard labor that marked the lives of working-class adults shaped the lives and destinies of their children as well: "My mother worked in a factory, twelve hours a day," recalled one Suresnois who recounted her childhood on the eve of World War I:

> Each morning, before leaving for work, she would put our dinner on the fire. And so before I could leave for school, I had not only my brothers to look after, and take to school, I had to watch over our dinner, and build up the fire. We would put coal-dust on the fire, in order to keep it going until noon. As soon as I got home each day, I would put the soup on the fire and look after my brothers. I never went out to play. I never went out at all. There was never any question of my playing. We had nothing, nothing.[105]

Such an unchildish childhood, deprived of what had come to seem childhood's most elementary, nay definitional aspect, the freedom to run and play in the sunshine and fresh air out of doors, put the physical and moral/psychological development of the individual child at risk, or so early-twentieth-century pedagogical wisdom would have it. Moreover, the absorption of children in the collective survival of their families left precious little scope for the interposition of any effective municipal politics of childhood. Sellier sought a solution in the policy of systematically creating opportunities for working-class children that their parents could never know, building roads to a qualitatively different future through the available institutions—schools, lunchrooms, and apprenticeship training. Accordingly, he pressed hard on the parents of children most at risk, those who did not wish to part with their children for six (and, after 1932, eight) weeks each summer, in the interest of the proper physiological and moral/psychological development of the child.

The financing of the *colonie* shows how Sellier knit the concept of municipal social solidarity to the local project of social, pedagogical, and hygienic reform, launched in the service of a longer-term revolutionary vision. Sellier arrived in the *mairie* at a moment when revolutionary hopes were running high all across the nation. It was a time when children ran through the streets of the city chanting "Révolution pour que la terre, devienne un jour égalitaire, Révolution pour renverser, l'gouvernment à Poincaré."[106] It was a time when an energetic revolutionary like Henri Sellier, buoyed by the winds of his recent and decisive victory at the polls, could lead his administration in demanding an end to the military intervention against the "Russian Socialist republic" and the swift reestablishment of economic and political relations with the beleaguered young nation.[107] And it was a time when ardent spirits like Sellier did not shrink from asking that local bigwigs contribute handsomely to the city's programs of social assistance, all in the name of that selfsame social solidarity that bound wealthy industrialists to ragged children in the Socialist municipality. Sellier and the Commission des Colonies de Vacances thus addressed themselves to the civic spirit of their "Dear Fellowcitizens," invoking the health of the rising generation, seriously compromised by four years of war and the economic crisis that followed: "The examinations of the inspecting doctor, the daily efforts of the nurses who work in each of our schools have uncovered a most worrisome state of physical degeneration among the very youngest, who are the future of the race . . . Ongoing unemployment, with its parade of misery, dooms many children to a terrible state of undernourishment. We must rebuild them, and six weeks of freedom and fresh air will go a long way toward doing so."[108]

The letter discursively binds all citizens in the common cause of local children's health, underscoring in particular the collective debt the city owed to its fallen soldiers, who had left behind them more than three hundred war orphans: "[These] fathers died to defend you, so please help us give their children a holiday—you owe it to those who have disappeared." But Sellier quite reasonably expected that the captains of local industry would contribute proportionally far more to the municipal program than the good widow Blanchard or the Association des Anciens Elèves.[109] At least one wealthy notable, perfume mogul René Coty, failed to grasp the principle of proportional contribution lurking implicitly in Sellier's appeal that the citizens pull together and "do more" in the struggle to arrest the alarming decline in children's health. Perhaps the eminent and decidedly right-wing *parfumier* did not even bother to open the envelope that arrived on his desk one morning in the spring of 1920; rather, upon seeing that it bore the return address of the "red" *mairie,* he may have simply passed it along, unthinking, to his secretary. But whatever the fate of that first letter from Sellier, the cost of ignoring it was swiftly and mercilessly levied in a public denunciation of Coty before the entire city council in late July, as the mayor solemnly read out the list of sums received from all corners of the city in support of the young *colonie:* "He noted with satisfaction the size of the sums received, but he also noted with regret that one of the most important local industrialists had sent only twenty-five francs, saying that, alas, he could do no more." Rather than accepting the implied insult to his administration, Sellier rallied his colleagues to return the gesture in kind and send the derisory sum back to the disdainful *parfumier.*[110] When Coty returned the following October from his summer holidays in Corsica, he found his twenty-five-franc contribution awaiting him in his château at Longchamp, in the Bois de Boulogne.

Coty decided to make the best of a bad situation, and wrote back to Sellier a lengthy denial of any personal responsibility in the regrettable "misunderstanding" surrounding the *colonies de vacances,* which he laid at the door of some unfortunate underling at the factory: "I will investigate the matter this very afternoon, so that I may understand just how my managers could have made such a gross error, and when I have the answer, I will not hesitate to subject the guilty one to a most severe warning." Coty then proceeded to unfold before Sellier his own grand scheme to build "vacation hamlets" in Corsica so that his "young compatriots" might build their health and strength, "which constitutes a most precious capital." On this basis Coty then embroidered a claim of common interest with Sellier, claiming that the "children's cause is what most moves me, for they represent the future, and the grave task of remaking the France of tomorrow rests with them. Which is simply to say that I agree entirely with your ideas about this major problem . . ." and so on. The vociferous protest of innocence in the affair of the twenty-five-franc subscription was accompanied by a one-thousand-franc donation, "double what I would have contributed had the request been sent directly to me."[111] Sellier's reply was typically laconic, thanking Coty for his letter, which had "utterly dissipated all misunderstanding between you and the municipality," and for the handsome donation, which continued to appear each spring for at least five years thereafter.[112]

Thus did Sellier assure the financial health of the municipal *colonie,* so that the city might continue to realize "that which it regards as its prime duty" vis-à-vis its youngest and least fortunate citizens.[113] The mayor's active construction of a broad and solidarist participation in the municipal program on behalf of the children extended to the parents themselves, who were urged to participate "loyally" and pay whatever amount they could afford in weekly installments to the *assistante scolaire.* After all, in a work of local solidarity, "everyone must make the small sacrifice that the [municipality] asks in order to send the children to the country."[114] Thanks to the *mairie*'s aggressive fund-raising campaign, the city was able to subsidize the majority of its *colons,* extending some financial aid to over half the families of children sent each year. Between 1928 and 1939, anywhere from 39 percent to 48 percent went absolutely free of charge, and the proportion of those receiving some kind of financial assistance rose as high as 89 percent, even 94 percent in 1935–36, the very harshest years of the economic crisis.[115]

As noted above, Sellier organized the Suresnes *colonie* by simply extending the structure he had established five years earlier for Puteaux, a move that was eased by the considerable personal prestige that the new mayor enjoyed, and the good working relationship he had already established with the Service des Enfants Assistés at Saint-Pierre-le-Moûtier. Hence, once the municipal Commission des Colonies had recruited that first summer's contingent of 128 children, Sellier contacted the director of the service in Saint-Pierre, one M. Dépuiset, and asked that he place the children in a region distinct from the "centre de Puteaux," which lay southeast of Saint-Pierre, across the villages Dornes, Chatenay, and St-Humbert.[116] The mayor thus hoped to extend to his *petits* Suresnois the advantages of a "homogeneous placement," in which children from a single town were clustered in their own self-contained center of contiguous villages and outlying farms.[117] In asking that Dépuiset create a center for the children of Suresnes, Sellier sought to minimize the sad bewilderment that often struck urban children who, accustomed to the density and noise of life in the city, found themselves suddenly uprooted, displaced to the strange and empty silence of the countryside, broken only by the lowing of herds or the barking of farmyard dogs.[118] Having children from your same town, even your same school, living in the neighboring farm, or in a house at the other end of the village, would surely ease the transition.

Yet the competition for placements in the Saint-Pierre district was especially fierce in the immediate postwar period, as larger and more long-established *colonies,* including Sellier's old Puteaux *colonie,* plus *colonies* from Boulogne, Nanterre, and other western *banlieues,* jockeyed with the smaller and younger Colonie de Suresnes in the scramble for advantageous placements in their own homogeneous centers. But the sheer size of an urban *colonie,* though important for the potential profit it represented to the peasant *nourrices,* was not the only factor that counted in attracting the benevolent attention of the Enfants Assistés. The personal relations that developed between a municipality and the agency at Saint-Pierre, as well as the conduct and cleanliness of that city's children during their summer *en colonie,* could also prove decisive. Happily for the children of Suresnes, the Puteaux and Boulogne *colonies* committed some serious gaffes on both counts during the summers of 1919 and 1920, and this, in turn, placed the smaller, less obstreperous Suresnes *colonie* in a comparatively good light. Puteaux thus managed to alienate the entire office at Saint-Pierre by sending numerous and interfering "municipal delegations of so-called 'inspection,'" whose members spent the entire summer in the center at Dornes-Chatenay-St-Humbert, conducting their own tours of inspection, "which interfered not only in the running of the *colonie,* but also in that of the services of the Enfants Assistés."[119] One can imagine the slow-burning fury of the staff at the Enfants Assistés, who found their daily round of work hampered by the Puteaux "delegation" — some fifteen to twenty schoolteachers, city councilors, and their wives dropping in unexpectedly on peasant households with whom the Enfants Assistés had carefully cultivated relations over long years, posing questions and freely criticizing whatever struck them as odd, distasteful, or merely out of place. "[It] has a most negative impact on the locals and undermines the moral authority of the placements," was Sellier's understated summary of a situation that surely found less polite description in the mouths of those men and women in the office at Saint-Pierre who saw their "moral authority" over local peasant families suffer and diminish with each day the delegations remained.[120] Boulogne, for its part, offended with the number of ill-clad and lice-ridden *colons* that the city inflicted upon the good Nivernais peasantry: "You cannot imagine the number of lice-ridden and incontinent children," moaned Dépuiset in June of 1921. "What a desolate impact they have on our country folk, who have not seen such parasites for many years . . . If we are not careful, the opportunities for placement will soon dry up." [121]

The errors committed by the *colonies* of Puteaux and Boulogne, though very different in content, threatened the same vital resource on which the Enfants Assistés depended, namely, the stock of goodwill and solid relationships that the agency at Saint-Pierre had built up over many years working with a stable group of reliable peasant *nourrices*. And the Assistance Publique was surely not going to allow the summer holidays of grubby young *banlieusards* to interfere in any way with the carefully nurtured relationships that the Saint-Pierre office enjoyed with the local *nourrices,* relations on which the main business of the Enfants Assistés (namely, placing the orphans and foundlings of Paris) depended. In the winter of 1920/21, the Assistance Publique decided that two summers of ragged, ill-behaved children and interfering municipal delegations had wreaked sufficient havoc with the smooth operation of their agencies in the all-important districts of the Cher-Nièvre-Allier. Henceforth the Saint-Pierre office was to confine itself to orphan placement and cease altogether its collaboration in organizing *colonies* for the children of the *banlieue ouest*. Distressed at the prospect that the children of Suresnes would suffer the loss of their *colonie,* a resource that he himself had created back in the summer of 1915, Sellier stepped forward and lent his personal prestige to the cause, negotiating a settlement with the Assistance Publique in which he agreed to assume personal responsibility for the entire *colonie,* which was to be reorganized as an intercity consortium, "La Commission Intercommunale des Colonies de Vacances." [122] Dépuiset grudgingly accepted the arrangement, and a single, intercity structure, under Henri Sellier's direct management, became the sole and unwavering condition under which the Assistance Publique reversed its initial decision and allowed the Enfants Assistés of Saint-Pierre to continue placing children of the *banlieue ouest* with the peasants of the district. [123]

With Henri Sellier at the helm, the intercity commission held together for the next ten years or so, at which point the constituent *colonies* gradually broke off, one by one, and went their separate ways. [124] At its core lay Suresnes and the surrounding, Socialist *banlieues* of Puteaux, Boulogne-Billancourt, and Nanterre, who, together, sent at least one thousand children each summer to the fields and forests of the southwestern Nièvre. At times, other communes joined in (Pavillons-sous-Bois in 1922, Bezons in 1923, Dugny in 1927), and for ten years (1924–33), the syndicalist Colonie

Enfantine des Vacances of the Travailleurs Municipaux and the electronics firms of Thomson-Houston and Alsthom also sent their *colonies* with Sellier's consortium.[125] But the unpleasantness of 1919–20 had left its mark in the form of a newly tenuous relation with the agency at Saint-Pierre. For the first few years of its existence, the Sellier consortium would work hard to win back the confidence of the Saint-Pierre office and its *nourrices,* keeping a close rein on the municipal commissions of inspection (who did, after all, have a legitimate and important intermediary role to play) while tightening up the procedures by which each commune verified the children's health and cleanliness and the condition of their clothing on the eve of their departure.

Not surprisingly, the onus of proving the worthiness of the *colonies* from the *banlieue ouest* fell most heavily on the shoulders of the young *colons* themselves, who, summer after summer, were asked to demonstrate to the local peasantry, by their cleanliness and personal deportment, the valor of the *banlieue* child: "In the region, the general impression of the *colons* from Suresnes is favorable," wrote Dépuiset in his evaluation of that first Suresnes *colonie* in the summer of 1920, "and certainly much better than that left by their comrades from Boulogne-Billancourt, whose stay here will do much damage to future *colonies . . .* The children from those two towns will surely be refused this year."[126] If the letter opened with words of measured praise for the Suresnois, it was only to underscore the fragility of that achievement, dangling menacingly the negative case of Boulogne-Billancourt in order to spur the children of Suresnes to ever-greater efforts of self-discipline and winning ways. Dépuiset then elaborated the point in the paragraphs that followed, which listed by name those children from Suresnes who required "watching": the ten who wet their beds (which was never a reason for excluding them), the six who arrived carrying head lice, and those five whose tattered and insufficient "trousseaux" had made more work (mending, extra laundry, or both) for the *nourrice*.[127] Writing just twelve months after the Assistance Publique had threatened to close down the Nièvre *colonies* altogether, Dépuiset could rest assured that his comments would not pass unremarked, and indeed, complaints from the *nourrices* of head lice and insufficient trousseaux diminished steadily to the point where, by the late 1920s, such matters disappear altogether from the correspondence between Saint-Pierre and Suresnes, not to be seen again until the harshest years of the Occupation, in 1941–43.

CHAPTER FOUR

✑ Inside the Nièvre Colonie, 1923–1939

Despite the initial difficulties with Dépuiset and his staff at the Saint-Pierre office, a general willingness to work things out ultimately prevailed on both sides, and the Nièvre *colonie* was back on a solid footing within a year or two. Hence, just before his retirement, in 1922, Dépuiset designated a distinct *centre de placement* for the young Suresnois, a cluster of eight to ten bourgs and villages to the west and south of Saint-Pierre (including Saint-Pierre itself), where the children of Suresnes were given first priority, and would always find ample lodging until the demise of Henri Sellier, and his *colonie chez les paysans*, in the autumn of 1943.[1] During periods when drought and/or the high price of bread forced the less prosperous peasants to withdraw their services, the Enfants Assistés extended the Suresnes *colonie* westward into the Cher. Though the children were "a bit dispersed," the region was "lovely," and the smallholding *nourriciers*, "prosperous and motivated by the warmest feelings for our children."[2] Sellier's Nièvre *colonie* thus established a solid link between the working-class children of the Socialist city and the peasants of this solidly Socialist (since 1902), long de-Christianized, and increasingly depopulated corner of the Cher/Allier/Nièvre. As small-scale polyculture declined in this region, hardwood forests gradually overtook the stony fields and vineyards, and by the mid-1920s, the southwestern Nièvre presented a rather woodsy aspect, "essentially farms and forests, which resembles more closely the *Bourbonnais* than the *Nivernais* of which it is a part."[3] Thus did Ernest Blin, local savant and director of the Service des Enfants Assistés at Saint-Pierre, describe the district in which he worked from 1924 through 1931–32. Though it offered no spectacular scenery, the countryside was pleasantly verdant, and slightly hilly. But it must have borne a mournful, deserted aspect as well, for the overall population of the region had fallen by nearly 40 percent since the end of the Second Empire, a rural exodus of young people that flowed largely toward Paris.[4] Even Saint-Pierre (which was the capital of the canton) held a "certain attraction" over the neighboring countryside, as "rural types" retired to the bourg: "The widows close up their isolated country houses in order to come live in what are often narrow, airless rooms," noted Blin in 1929. "A senile population thus accumulates in the capital, which does nothing for its vitality."[5] As the local economy shifted from subsistence polyculture (wheat, vines) to animal husbandry, small property gave way to large, and the farms where the Suresnes children were lodged were substantial and prosperous units of at least forty hectares, often upwards of one hundred.[6] Around them lay the broken shells of abandoned dwarf properties, the empty barns and deserted farmhouses of men and women long since departed for other regions, other lives. With them left the artisans and shopkeepers who animate the centers of rural life. At least four of the hamlets that took in children from Suresnes no longer possessed a post office or bakery, and the once prosperous village of Azay-le-Vif was now half grown over in woods. One can imagine the profound sense of displacement that the children of a bustling and youthful industrial city (where, in 1932, nearly one out of every four inhabitants was a child aged ten or younger) might have experienced upon finding themselves isolated with the aging peasants of the southwestern Nièvre.

From that very first summer, Sellier asked that the Enfants Assistés at Saint-Pierre determine the actual placements, linking individual children to particular rural families on the basis of a list of names sent by the *mairie*. The list indicated the age and sex of each child, any particular desires he or she had expressed (to be placed in the company of siblings or friends, or to return to the home of a particular *nourrice*), and finally the family's "situation sociale" sketched in the lapidary formula of the parents' contribution to their child's *pension*. Apart from the crisis years of the mid-1930s, the figures for this last category formed a shallow, inverted bell-curve, ranging from the various forms of free passage that covered about 35 percent of the *colons* (unemployed, welfare recipient, orphan, or simply "free"), to a wide array of partial payments, distributed across another 20 percent of the children, and arriving finally at the full payments made by the parents of the remaining 45 percent.[7] Most children expressed some kind of preference as to their placement; 136 out of the 172 children reviewed by the Commission de Colonies in the summer of 1923, for example, had asked either to return to the *famille nourricière* with whom they had spent the previous summer, or to be placed with a sibling, best friend, or simply "with an older girl," as ten-year-old Lucette Dubois requested.[8] In some cases, parents wrote directly to the

Municipal Commission, reinforcing their children's request to return to households where they had happily spent the previous summer.[9]

Recruitment for the *colonie* was conducted through the primary schools, where every April the teachers (and later, the *assistantes scolaires*) handed each child a notice asking who would be participating that year in the *colonie,* and what level of financial assistance was required.[10] Sellier was particularly concerned with those children whose "situation sociale" granted them free passage: the *pupilles de la nation,* children with an un-employed parent or those whose families were on the dole. These were the families most likely to be living in the cramped, airless apartments and rooming houses of the old factory district, or in the tin and tar-paper shacks that perched uneasily on the northern plateau and on the slopes of Mont-Valérien. "These little ones who barely have enough to eat and who sleep in basements on mean little pallets": these were the children whose physical and "moral" (we would say emotional or psychological) development was most likely being compromised by urban poverty; these were the children who were in greatest need of the fresh air, restful sleep, and abundant food that a summer in the Nièvre *colonie* offered.[11]

But Sellier was also aware that especially in times of hardship families are often reluctant to part with their children for long periods. He there-fore targeted the mothers in his initial campaign to build up the *colonie,* inviting these women to place their confidence in the *mairie*'s parental concern for the children of the city, and on that basis to give their own children over to the collective care of the *mairie* for six (later eight) weeks each summer: "Those of you who hesitate to separate from your children and hand them over to the care of strangers need only look at your little neighbors in order to see the salutary moral and physical transforma-tion they obtained [last summer]. This year you must decide. You know that nothing is more precious to the municipality than the health and education of your little ones. Have confidence in the city, and make the small sacrifice it asks in order to send your children to the country."[12] Henri Sellier directed his appeal at the mothers, but he did so in the name of the individual child's right to good health, independent of his or her family circumstances. As we shall see, this was a right that the *mairie* was prepared to guarantee, and to support even in the face of opposition from families reluctant to part with their children over the long summer holiday.

Once the children had been recruited, the municipal Commission des Colonies (which included teachers and *assistantes scolaires* from each of

the neighborhood schools) met to determine fee reductions and assistance with the trousseaux (especially with shoes or clogs, but also with
school smocks and the occasional shirt).[13] Parents were then invited to accompany their children to the public baths for an obligatory wash prior
to the equally obligatory medical exam, held in the public dispensary two
weeks before the departure.[14] Here, the child received a thorough medical checkup and, after 1930, vaccinations against diphtheria and small-
pox. In the course of this exam, the particulars of the child's medical history—height, weight, and thoracic perimeter, to be sure, but also lymph
nodes, teeth, history of contagious diseases, skin or scalp conditions—
were inscribed on a series of index cards, one of which was destined for
the "parents nourriciers" in the Nièvre. At the bottom of each card lay a
space entitled "observations," where the doctor or *assistante scolaire* could
include additional information about the child's personality and temperament, or any special dietary needs. In practice, this space was most
often devoted to discussions of the child's bed-wetting habits, for if the
child had any such tendency, it was best that it be known in advance:
"Not that this condition would exclude them from the *colonies*—quite
the contrary," wrote Sellier in the summer of 1921. "The children who
suffer from this condition are those who most need a sojourn in the country. But the director who sees to the placements must be able to warn
the *nourriciers* so that they can take the necessary precautions."[15] Parents
were thus enjoined to openly acknowledge the problem, and to include
a rubberized sheet in the child's trousseau, so that *nourrices* had no unpleasant surprises.[16]

Relieved to hear that nighttime incontinence did not necessarily exclude their child from the *colonie,* some families responded eagerly to
Sellier's invitation to a frank discussion of their child's "condition," mediated (as always) by the *assistante scolaire:* "Mademoiselle," wrote one
Mme Derosiers in 1928, "my daughter, Raymonde Derosiers, tells me it
is time for the medical exam for the *colonies.* I do not wish to hide from
the person who will take care of her that she sometimes wets the bed,
but if you just get her up at night, this can be avoided. For this reason
I have never dared to send her before. It would help me if you would
be so kind as to speak with the doctor about this. I will be quite put out
if he refuses her. In anticipation of the opposite outcome, I hope that
you will forgive me, Mademoiselle."[17] More often than not, however,
parents remained evasive on the subject—or perhaps children who had
not previously wet their beds started to do so upon finding themselves

All of the photographs in this section courtesy of the Musée René Sordes de Suresnes.

(*Right*) The rapidly industrializing city at the turn of the century: the rue du Pont in 1900. (*Below*) The rue du Puits d'Amour, 1927.

(*Above*) "Palace-schools for the children of the people": The "sand beach" at the Wilson *école maternelle,* mid-1930s.

(*Right*) Measuring the success of Sellier's municipal child-health program: the annual school physical exam, mid-1930s.

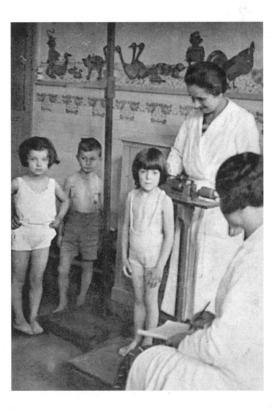

The children of Boulogne-Billancourt await the local
train that will take them to the Gare de Lyon for the
great departure with the Suresnes *colonie* in the Nièvre,
summer 1922.
(*Below*) The children of Suresnes and Puteaux gather
before the Gare de Lyon, summer 1922.

All accounted for, the children of the *banlieue ouest*
proceed into the station, summer 1922.
(*Below*) On the platform at the Gare de Lyon,
summer 1922.

Boarding the train for Nevers, early 1930s.
(*Below*) *Nourrices* and *colons* finally meet, or are
reunited, in the arrival at Nevers, mid-1930s.

Three young *colons* rush out to greet the pony cart that has
come to collect them at Nevers, mid-1930s.
(*Below*) The annual tour of inspection, mid-1930s. The
Suresnes delegate receives an enthusiastic welcome from the
colons placed in this small village.

in unfamiliar surroundings. Whatever the reason, previously unidentified bed wetters would continue to turn up in the *colonie* each summer
throughout the interwar period, to the concern of the municipal Commission des Colonies, and to the considerable aggravation of Director
Ernest Blin, who declared one day in utter exasperation that "those poor
little wretches always cause problems."[18] Yet all parties (Ernest Blin included) agreed that children for whom the stresses of urban poverty expressed themselves in such symptoms were especially in need of the quiet
rhythms provided by a summer in the Nièvre. Unlike the bearers of head
lice or contagious illness, these were children whom no one wished to bar
from the *colonie,* and the *nourrices,* for their part, were invited to accept
bed wetters by the promise of an extra indemnity for their pains.

Once the medical dossiers had been assembled and all children inspected, the parents were asked to present the trousseaux for an equally
thorough inspection (and completion, where necessary), which task was
generally managed by the wives of the municipal councilors on the Commission des Colonies.[19] The *mairie* reminded parents that all this bureaucratic control was necessary in order to ensure a positive reception in the
Nièvre, "for the *colonie* will not be welcome in the Nièvre region unless
the children are sent in a state of irreproachable cleanliness."[20] Head lice,
nits, or insufficient and ragged clothing were an affront to the *nourrices'*
pride and self-respect, and therefore constituted grounds for the child's
immediate and pitiless exclusion. At the end of their sojourn, the children
would return once again to the dispensary, so that the beneficial effect
of their country holiday could be registered in kilos and centimeters.

With the final sewing shut of the trousseaux the night before the departure, the municipality's role in the *colonie* came to a close; the municipal
delegation (four or five city councilors, teachers, and *assistantes scolaires*)
that would accompany the children the next morning on the five-hour
train ride to Nevers would stay long enough only to hand the children
over to their host families, who would be waiting to meet them at the
station. From here on out, then, matters were left almost entirely in the
hands of the *paysans nourriciers,* under the direction of the Enfants Assistés, with the Commission des Colonies stepping in only for the annual
tour of inspection, and to help adjudicate any problems that could not
be settled by the agency in Saint-Pierre.

Parisians into Peasants? Reconciling City Mice to
the Countryside (and Vice Versa)

"We arrived at Saint-Pierre-le-Moûtier on August 19, and on the 20th
and 21st, we visited the placements of our children . . . We were very
satsified overall with the general condition of our children, who had all
been placed with good people who took them in and looked after them
with a most maternal affection." So begins the 1923 report of the delegation's annual inspection tour. Director Birckel of the Enfants Assistés
had done an especially good job placing the children that year; only 3 out
of 160 had to be moved, "mostly in order to make the children happy,
for the placements had been good, but the individuals did not hit it off,"
and the delegates saw all around them evidence that the 1923 *colonie*
had satisfied both *nourriciers* and *colons:* "Placed with these good people,
farmers and such, our children frolicked in the woods and fields . . . The
food is healthy and does them good, the children are well cared for and
breathe in with all their might the fresh air of the fields and the aroma of
the trees." The climactic event of the visit, a distribution of prize diplomas to the most devoted *nourrices,* thus opened with a formal word of
thanks to Director Birckel for the "devoted care" he had shown in choosing the placements. Only then did the delegation proceed to distribute
its awards, "diplomas of recognition for the touching solicitude . . . of the
nourrices, who showed a special affection for our little *colons.*"[21]

In what precisely did the ruralism of municipal Socialists consist? Can
it be meaningfully distinguished from the ambient ruralism of the era?
And why, in the mid-1930s, when the educational *colonie* was fast gaining ground in leftist and secular pedagogical circles, did Sellier and his
colleagues cling so stubbornly to their *colonie chez les paysans*? Before we
can answer these questions, we need to look more closely at the world of
the Nièvre peasantry after 1918, to consider more closely the structure of
the Nièvre *colonie,* the material conditions and the human relations that
made up the interwar *colonie.*

First of all, who were the *paysans nourriciers* of the Nièvre *colonie,* and
on what basis were they selected for the job? The office at Saint-Pierre
composed its register of households for the *colonie* from the ranks of
families that were already harboring foundling children on a year-round
basis, or had done so in the recent past. A glance at the criteria that the
Enfants Assistés applied in selecting families for their foundlings thus

offers a glimpse inside the very households that were taking in young *banlieusards* over the summer holidays. Like the private *colonies* by family placement, the Enfants Assistés had established its offices in regions of prosperous subsistence polyculture, "regions with small farms where the mistress of the household can find the time needed to raise young children, and where young boys and girls of thirteen can find work, perhaps in the households where they were raised, without being assimilated to the domestic staff, as happens on large properties. Under these conditions, the young orphan grows truly attached to the home of his *nourriciers,* and often marries in the district."[22] In the wish to protect foundlings from merely being "assimilated" to the farm labor force, the Enfants Assistés avoided regions of large monocultural production, like the Beauce, in favor of those districts in central France (Burgundy, the Cher, parts of the Auvergne) where the more archaic family farm had managed to survive, "regions which have long been rich in *nourrices* and where the welcoming of orphan children into the family home is a veritable tradition for rural households. We must cite particularly the Morvan, the Nivernais, the Bourbonnais, where Paris has been sending its orphans for over a century now, as the ideal land of adoption for the Enfants Assistés."[23]

But the goal was not merely the defensive one of protecting orphans from being exploited as cheap labor; rather, the Enfants Assistés strove to locate homes where the child would be raised as a member of the family and experience genuine parental affection: "In the best *famille nourricière,* the fate of the orphan seems mingled with the fates of the children of the house, whom he calls brother and sister, as he calls their parents papa and maman."[24] On his thrice yearly inspection tours, then, the director evaluated his placements according to a host of material conditions—the health and appearance of each foundling child, whether she or he was attending the public school regularly, the material comfort of the household. But the crucial sine qua non was always the same: "Does the child seem to be loved by his *nourriciers?* Is he surrounded by affection?"[25]

In this context, it is worth noting that the *paysans nourriciers* had to agree to send to the public primary school not only the foundling child but their own children as well, in order to avoid reproducing within households those divisions of education and culture that had split the nation into mutually hostile camps since the end of the nineteenth century: "In inscribing this prescription into the rule, the *conseil général*'s

sole aim is to ensure that conflicts stemming from differences in education do not divide the children as they grow up in a single household."[26]
Clearly, the Enfants Assistés had given careful thought to the material
and ideological structures that underlay a functional family unit appropriate to the task of raising the orphans of the Third Republic. As a result
(and as Henri Sellier was surely well aware) the households vetted by
the Enfants Assistés were relatively spacious and clean, filled with other
children, and guaranteed secular.[27]

Once the initial material and organizational difficulties that plagued
the Nièvre *colonie* in the immediate postwar period had been overcome,
the children of the Socialist *banlieue ouest* slipped easily into this structure, as the directors' periodic letters of inspection make clear: "You may
reassure Mme Prost on the subject of her children, who are being well
cared-for," wrote Ernest Blin in the summer of 1928. "I found them playing with the *nourrice*'s little girl and an orphan that she is raising." Blin
then went on to explain the origin of the children's complaint to their
mother back in Suresnes: "What irritated the older one was being forbidden to play far from the house and without any possible surveillance. One
can only congratulate Mme Bernardon for the way that she understands
her duty." In this case, the children had little to complain about, for they
had plenty of space to play in the garden, "and the tents they had made
for themselves in the shade of the trees shows they have found the means
and the desire to amuse themselves while staying close to their *nourrice.*"
Indeed, opined Blin, Mme Prost should perhaps be reminded that *nourrice* Bernadon was a person of endless patience and good-will who never
complained about the youngest child's "most unpleasant condition" (incontinence).[28] His report thus concludes on a note of unqualified support
for Mme Bernadon, and so reminds us that one important function of
the Enfants Assistés was to protect their *nourrices* from unjust accusations or exaggerated claims of ill-treatment, launched by the *colons* or
their families back in Suresnes. As we will see, it was not always so easy
to adjudicate the claims of justice between family of origin and adoptive
summer family in the country, for as both the Saint-Pierre office and the
Commission des Colonies discovered, it was sometimes quite difficult
to ascertain where truth and justice lay, working with two sources that
were, in some cases, quite difficult to reconcile: the testimony of children
and subsequent, on-site investigations of the Saint-Pierre officialdom.

The relationship between Suresnes children and individual peasant
families was always initiated by the peasants themselves, who each spring

signaled the Enfants Assistés if they wished to participate in the *colonie:* "I put in my request to M. le Directeur at St-Pierre-le-Moûtier a bit late, seeking two children from your *colonie de vacances,*" wrote Mme Yollet-Fourami of Mornay-sur-Allier to Suresnes's Commission des Colonies in the summer of 1933. "You can get my references from Mme Learouble, from the mayor of Mornay, from the schoolteacher, or from Gisèle Morin, and the little Delormes [former *colons*] who know me quite well." [29] *Nourriciers* could request as many children as they liked, on the condition that they put no more than two children in each bed, which rule was quite strictly enforced. [30] Families generally asked for two to six children per summer (though couples on large farms sometimes asked for as many as ten or twelve), and they showed a marked preference for taking in girls, perhaps because girls were perceived as more useful to have around the house, or believed to cause less trouble (though the files contain as many complaints about troublesome girls as boys). The Enfants Assistés thus had to make an extra effort to place the boys, attaching them to their sisters wherever possible and exhorting host families to accept entire sibling groups, a tactic that was also deployed to combat the initial loneliness that beset displaced urban *colons.* [31]

Children, too, could request placement with their same *nourrice* of the previous summer, and were, indeed, encouraged to do so in the name of solidifying the ties that bound these supplementary family units. But the request could be fulfilled only with the written consent of the *nourrice* in question, a provision behind which the *nourrices* could take shelter, protecting themselves from repeat visits from young urban terrors whose habits and comportment did not always earn them a high place in local affections: "The little boy was shockingly vulgar, and went so far as to call his *nourrice* a w . . . [whore], which speaks volumes about how he's been brought up," wrote Ernest Blin of one especially difficult young boy whom he doubted he would be able to place the following year, and certainly not in the village of Mars-sur-Allier, where his reputation had spread rapidly. [32] In the summer of 1921, following the troubled years of 1919–20 and the bad blood that had arisen between the *nourriciers* of the Nièvre and the children of the *banlieue ouest,* the Enfants Assistés was able to grant only forty out of eighty requests for same placement, largely due to *nourrices* refusing to take back children whom they'd harbored the previous summer. [33] But as conditions stabilized within the intercommunal consortium, relations between *colons* and their hosts seem to have improved as well, and from the mid-1920s on, the Enfants Assistés was once again encouraging families to take in children from a previous summer, in the name of continuity in the program and in the families of adoption.

Philippe Rey-Herme claims that for the nation as a whole, the supply of peasant *nourriciers* always exceeded the demand, and the records from the Nièvre *colonie* suggest that this was true for the Saint-Pierre district as well.[34] Each year that the Colonie Intercommunale fell short of one thousand *colons,* the director had to concentrate the *colonie* across a smaller geographic district, a policy that left entire villages out of the game during short years, and provoked bitter protest from peasant wives whose household budgets depended on the extra income: "I simply cannot understand how there could be no children for St. Parize," wrote a bewildered Mme Vachez in June of 1931.[35] Directors, too, worried about alienating good and reliable peasant *nourrices* during years when the supply of *colons* fell short: "I have at least 700 placements," wrote Director Dépuiset to Henri Sellier in the summer of 1921, "and if I receive only 500 schoolchildren, my many *nourriciers* will be quite angry, which will have a negative impact on future years."[36]

In the early years of the *colonie,* the peasants were paid for each child on the basis of a graduated scale that was differentiated by age and sex, with girls always ten francs cheaper than their brothers of an equivalent age. The Enfants Assistés never commented directly on this differential, but since the *pension* was explicitly intended to cover the cost of feeding the child, it seems reasonable to presume that it was based on the persistent notion that, at any given age, girls would always eat less food than boys—a presumption that Edmond Cottinet roundly criticized in his 1886 report, which denounced the systematic underfeeding of girls in working-class families. Or perhaps boys were presumed to make more work for the *nourrices,* a hypothesis that the marked preference for girls tends to support. Whatever its origin, however, the graduated scale was abolished in 1922 in favor of a single, unified rate of 120 F per child, irrespective of age or sex.[37]

Unlike those of the vast majority of interwar *colonies,* the Suresnes trousseau contained neither a distinctive beret nor scarf nor any other item of clothing intended to unify visually the *colonie* or dress up the moments of departure and return. The Municipal Commission prided itself on this tranquil profile, which, in their view, signaled the no-frills seriousness of purpose with which their *colonie* operated, and which they proudly contrasted with the noisy self-proclamation of neighboring programs.[38] In the interwar *colonies de vacances,* children generally wore their uniforms on collective outings only. Therefore the lack of any unifying insignia points not only to the sober neutrality of the Suresnes *colonie,* its obdurate refusal to join in the hurly-burly of interwar child mobilization on behalf of church, party, and state; it also underscores the fact that the commission organized no special program of games and promenades for the children in the Nièvre.

The commission's apparent indifference to the educational potential of the *colonie* stands in stark contrast to the rapidly expanding peda-gogical ambitions of interwar *colonies,* ambitions that, by the early 1930s, were spreading outward from the collective *colonies* to those using family placement. In the Oeuvre des Enfants à la Montagne, for example, the teachers who accompanied the children on their journey to the villages of the Cantal would gather all the children from their sector once each week for a round of games, song, and gymnastic exercise, rounded out by some informal instruction and the occasional promenade to a local site of natural beauty or historical/folkloric interest: "The *surveillant* thus sees all his *colons,* can question them [about their holiday] and learn a mass of useful details, offer them sound advice on their conduct, politeness, the gratitude that they owe to their *nourriciers* and to the staff . . . He can use these meetings to teach them pretty songs, games, and dances, have them do gymnastics in the open air, even contribute to their moral education, to help them love life in all its forms. For the animals and trees are living things that we must love, respect, and protect."[39] The local gamins of farm and village were generally invited to participate in this weekly *ani-mation* of the *colonie,* by dint of which the *colonies* by family placement sought to capture some of the pedagogical advantages of the collective formula without giving up their distinctive familial structure.

The archives for the Suresnes *colonie* make but fleeting reference to collective games organized in the fields around Saint-Parize-le-Châtel, where the largest number of *colons* were concentrated. Otherwise, there are no indications that the Commission des Colonies made any effort to organize a collective animation of the Nièvre *colonie.* Further, the idea that life on the farm might impart technical skills (how to drive a team or plough a straight furrow) or moral lessons (virtues of hard work and frugality) seems to have held little interest for the men of the municipal commission, who sang no Virgilian odes to the virtues of life among the peasantry as a school of hard work and self-sacrifice to the morally at-risk children of the urban working class. For the Suresnes commission, the *colonie* had a function of leisure and repose in relation to the world of the industrial *banlieue;* it was neither the avenue by which to effect a possible "return to the land" (a term that never once surfaces in the thousands of pages that make up the interwar archive) nor a school of virtue for children of the urban working class.[40]

Over the twenty years of its peacetime existence, I found only one report which made even the most glancing reference to the educational dimension of life in the Nièvre *colonie.* Interestingly enough, the lessons to be learned came not from the peasants but from the relationships that arose among the children themselves as they assisted their *nourriciers.* The labors of farm and field thus furnished nothing more than the context for an education in fraternal solidarity, which family placement was believed to facilitate: "All this shows the educational benefit of these family placements, where the older ones look out for the younger in a spirit of complete brotherhood."[41] The Suresnes *colonie* thus remained faithful to its original brief of securing restful and restorative holidays to the *petits* Suresnois, paying scant attention to the educational possibilities that "colonisation" in peasant villages offered the children of urban workers and focusing instead on their physical reconstitution through fresh air and good food.

The life of the *colonie* thus unfolded within the households, yards, and fields of the individual *paysans nourriciers.* In other words, the success of the *colonie* depended on the human qualities of its peasant collaborators, and this, in turn, required that the staff at Saint-Pierre acquire a certain adeptness in reading peasant character accurately. Beyond the minimum material requirements—a separate room for the children, well-aired and bright, and a kitchen garden from which to feed them fresh vegetables—the Enfants Assistés used two criteria to identify the best placements: love of children and evidence that a certain "amour propre" (pride, self-respect) reigned in the household. If the former was treated as a universally intelligible human endowment whose presence or absence could be fairly easily detected on the face of the child, the quality of "amour propre" carried a more particular significance, one that acquired concrete meaning in relation to local values and custom. Hence, when the directors at Saint-Pierre invoked the "amour propre that sharply determines the behavior of the *paysans nourriciers,*" they referred to that pride of rural women in the condition of house, garden, farmyard, and children, a locally rooted understanding of "amour propre" that the Enfants Assistés recognized and adopted when making its own judgments regarding the quality of its peasant collaborators.[42] Of course it was precisely this sentiment of peasant self-respect that lay at the heart of the difficulties of 1919–20, when the presence of so many lice-ridden and ill-clad *banlieusards* stirred widespread protest among *nourrices,* whose professional pride rested on the visible, outward signs (a clean and well-kept child) that they performed their job well. In the aftermath of this crisis, Sellier urged his colleagues in the intercommunal consortium to be especially rigorous in the matter of head lice and clothing, for in his view, complaints over the ragged, lice-ridden children were dictated by a "quite legitimate *amour propre*" on the part of the *nourrices.*[43] There was to be no question of ignoring or overriding this "quite legitimate" sentiment; on the contrary, in that very "amour propre" that had stirred such vigorous protest among the *nourrices* in 1919–20 lay the surest guarantee that the urban *colons* would be kept clean and properly cared for.

The office at Saint-Pierre, and the *colonies* of the *banlieue ouest,* thus internalized and adapted the criteria of the Nièvre peasantry for judging the quality of individual hosts; if a child returned filthy and tattered from his summer in the country, this was taken to indicate an "utter lack of care and self-respect on the part of the *nourrices,*" and such women were dropped instantly from the registers at Saint-Pierre.[44] At the same time the Enfants Assistés often found itself brokering the rather different relationships to bathing borne by rural and urban inhabitants of interwar France, for the level of cleanliness that satisfied the claims of peasant pride (and so met the hygienic criteria of the Enfants Assistés)—a daily wash of face and neck, feet and hands—struck some urban parents, accustomed (grosso modo) to a weekly bath, head to toe, as somewhat rudimentary, if not downright neglectful. Parents who complained that negligent *nourrices* were sending their children home filthy from their summer vacations thus met with a testy reminder from Director Ernest Blin: "I can well believe that the children were never bathed from head to toe, for such things are not common in the country."[45] Convinced that peasant families (or at least those peasant families vetted by the Enfants Assistés) could deliver a level of hygiene, care, and affection that met the developmental needs of urban working-class children, the directors at Saint-Pierre adopted the cultural relativist lens of the gentleman anthropologist, interpreting in a positive light (or at least neutralizing urban criticism of) local rural practice in the realms of family hygiene and child rearing.

The Enfants Assistés thus found its guarantee of the quality of child care in the ethical orientation of the *nourriciers,* who, in its view, were

"animated by the best feelings for our children." Of course this spirit had
to be underwritten by sufficient prosperity to serve as proof against any
untoward hopes of profiting materially from the transaction; peasants
were to be paid justly for their service, yes, but to perform it out of avarice would make them mere *vendeurs de soupe,* whose sole interest in the
child was the profit to be extracted from lodging him or her.[46] Far better
were the households where a genuinely maternal spirit reigned, households such as that of one good woman, no longer young, who gave up
her own bed to the *colons* and slept on a pallet on the floor.[47] In such acts
of self-sacrifice did the Municipal Commission, and the Enfants Assistés
itself, find the outward manifestation of that benevolent and maternal
spirit that guaranteed a successful *colonie.* Such visible signs of a truly
maternal/paternal affection were eagerly sought out by the directors of
oeuvres de placement familial, who well knew that their project depended,
finally, on the quality of the human relationship that arose between peasants and *colons.* For in the end, success could not be read off some table
of material conditions (although these, too, were important), but, rather,
rested on the human qualities that peasant collaborators brought to their
work: benevolence, a spirit of solidarity that led them to share the benefits of their way of life with the children of the urban poor, a love of
children and pleasure in their company. "They are well-disposed, and it
is not the lure of profit that leads them to take in children," wrote Louis
Conlombant in 1931 of the peasant collaborators in his Oeuvre Parisienne des Enfants à la Montagne. "They know that they are doing their
urban brothers a service, that they are collaborating in the regeneration
of childhood through fresh air. [Moreover], they recall the joys they have
had with *colons* in past years; it is a pleasure for them and they are most
eager to accept the children."[48]

When less benevolent sentiments threatened to emerge, as in the "attempted soviet" that swept a small band of *nourrices* in the bourg of
Saint-Parize-le-Châtel in the summer of 1928, this was cause for genuine
alarm, not only for the threat posed to rates, but for the far more dangerous spiritual corruption it implied; did not the will to force up rates suggest that the benevolent maternalism on which the endeavor rested was
souring to a mean-spirited, penny-pinching avarice? "Five complainants
from Parize-le-Châtel . . . have written to inform me that they cannot
feed the children for the rates posted and that they demand a raise." So
did Ernest Blin inform his friend and colleague Alexandre Joyeux of
the late-breaking unpleasantness brewing on the very eve of the *colonie*'s

arrival, in late July of 1928. The timing itself served to underscore the *nourrices'* true goal: to force up the *pension* on the eve of the children's arrival—the one moment when the Enfants Assistés could ill afford to eliminate a demanding *nourrice* from its registers. But Ernest Blin was not one to be maneuvered so easily: "These are not the best *nourrices*, and I had not planned to send them as many children as they requested, and had even left one of them out of the picture altogether." Having, happily, guarded some room for maneuver, Blin told Joyeux that he intended to move decisively and for good in this matter, "in order to strangle at the outset this attempted soviet." While he had already found other place-ments for the children they were to have received, the director had rea-son to fear that the disgruntled "soviet" might nonetheless appear at the station when the children arrived, hoping to profit from the noise and confusion that inevitably surrounded their arrival (some one thousand-plus in the company of municipal delegates and *assistantes sociales*) and claim the reassigned *colons* for themselves. But the municipal delegates, responsible for the actual, name-by-name distribution of *colons*, could not allow this to happen, for "*they must not have any colons.* One does not wait till the last minute to make such a request; this is an effort to 'force our hand,' a method that we cannot allow to take root."[49] Clearly keeping costs down was at issue here, as was the all-important question of Blin's authority over his peasant "collaborators." But behind all that lurked an overarching conviction that the *colonie* could not function on the basis of mere market logic. For if all depended on the benevolent collaboration and goodwill of the peasantry, then all was lost once that benevolence was allowed to turn to the calculation of *pensions*, a recasting of the child from object of benevolence and affection to a source of cold, hard cash. When, in the summer of 1931, the director had reason to believe that the same "soviet" was once again stirring to life, he reinforced the point in no uncertain terms: "I sent out a circular today to the *nourrices* of Mars, St. Parize, and Luthenay, so that they would know [the rates] well in advance . . . We could find ourselves faced with a 'soviet' whose core con-sists of the same complainants from the rue de la Fontaine in St. Parize, and, at the eleventh hour, find ourselves in trouble. But I hope that the energetic repression of the attempted 'sovietization' of two years ago will bear its fruits this year. We shall see. In any case, we won't be caught unawares."[50]

Before the Occupation, when the long-term sheltering of urban *colons* under conditions of spiraling want strained beyond repair the structures

of the Nièvre *colonie,* the "attempted soviets" of 1928 and 1931 offered
the only hints of collective discontent among the *paysannes nourrices* of
Saint-Pierre. For the rest, their letters to the Saint-Pierre office, to Mayor
Sellier and his deputy, Alexandre Joyeux, and, on occasion, to the families of children taken in during previous summers, all suggest that the
colonie made an important contribution to the peasants' livelihoods, and,
one senses, to the pace and interest of village life as well, judging from
letters that *nourrices* sent to their visitors once they were back in the city.
And when the children returned to Suresnes each fall, they were laden
with gifts from the farmyard: "Chickens, ducks, rabbits, and cats are a
part of the convoy . . . that arrived . . . at the Ecoles Jules-Ferry," wrote
journalist Eugène Gibon as he bore astonished witness to the *colonie*'s
return in September of 1932.[51]

Regulating the Alternative Family

The delicate, human bonds that made up the *colonie,* passing through the
office at Saint-Pierre-le-Moûtier, remind us of the singularity of Sellier's
Nièvre *colonie,* which strove to combine the suppleness and immediacy
of private and familial relations with the distance and neutrality of institutions by institutionalizing a structure of alternative families in the
Nivernais countryside, a district that, over time, acquired a steady relationship to the city of Suresnes thanks to the bureaucratic mediation
of the Enfants Assistés. In order to institutionalize these relationships,
the Commission des Colonies and the office at Saint-Pierre had to establish certain minimum conditions deemed essential to the success of the
endeavor. And this process of institutionalization, in turn, entailed imposing a certain discipline on the three parties to the relationship—the
parents, the *colons,* and the *paysans nourriciers.* Above all, it was essential
to create and guarantee a space within which the *nourrices* could carry
out their task without undue interference from the family of origin back
in the city. The Commission des Colonies thus forbade any direct contact
between the two families and offered its services as official intermediary
in the case of any conflict.[52] "In the interests of fairness" parents were forbidden to make any special gift or payment to the host family, nor were
they allowed to visit their children during the summer holiday.[53] If they
had reason to believe that their child was unhappy, unwell, or being mistreated, the only course of action open to them was to contact the *mairie,*

which, in turn, contacted the Saint-Pierre office immediately and asked that the family's, or the child's, claim be investigated.[54]

If the parents had to accept a discipline of distance from their own children during the long summer holiday, their children were also expected to exhibit a certain degree of self-control, to behave "like a child who has been properly raised in a well-run household."[55] The *colonie*'s "Instructions pour les Enfants" spelled out in some detail precisely what this phrase entailed: to keep themselves and the room they slept in neat and clean, and to behave properly at the table, which meant helping with the service, leaving nothing on their plates, and eating every last morsel of bread they had asked for. They were to treat all animals with respect: no unnesting the birds of the forest or teasing the barnyard animals (which included not only peaceable beings—cows, plow horses, chickens, and ducks—but more mischievous goats, as well as hives of bees, who were quite likely to fight back). And they were asked to play peacefully with the other children—no telling tales, no arguing, and certainly no fighting. The *petits* Suresnois were thus invited to enter into the life of family and village as if they were the well-behaved city cousins of the host family, "to behave as if the farmers were your parents and their children your brothers and sisters."[56]

The *paysans nourriciers,* for their part, were simply asked to remain within the guidelines that the Enfants Assistés established for the orphans in their care, and to give the children no alcohol other than the traditional "eau rougie"—wine cut with water, which children normally drank in this era. Having set forth these brief guidelines, the municipality's short "Instructions pour les Nourriciers" closed by reminding these women that they were to accept neither gifts nor money from the family back in Suresnes.[57]

Oddly enough, the Suresnes "Instructions" make no mention of children's labor on the farm (as opposed to their helping out *inside* the house). This is a curious omission in view of the fact that children housed on working farms were, inevitably, drawn into participating to some degree in the cycle of labor that structures the rhythm of life on any farm; the alternative would be to be left standing to one side of the stream of daily activity. And indeed, as the annual reports from the Suresnes delegation underscore, the children were hardly left aside during these, the most frenetic months of the agricultural year: "An older boy, joined by a few little ones, takes the initiative to lead the beasts out to pasture; an older girl volunteers to help with the laundry, amidst twenty or so good Nivernaises at the local *lavoir;* others help with the housework."[58] The delegates looked upon these scenes with unconcerned amusement, stressing the fact that it was the older children who undertook such labors, children who, moreover, were moved to do so of their own free will—"those who are inclined"—rather than by any coercion on the part of their *parents nourriciers.*

It is thus quite striking that the municipal "Instructions pour les Nourriciers" make no mention at all of limiting children's labor services, particularly in view of the fact that comparable *colonies,* such as Louis Conlombant's Oeuvre des Enfants à la Montagne, took great pains to clearly delimit the tasks that the *nourrices* could ask of their young visitors. Conlombant thus declared in no uncertain terms that the *colons* were not to spend their holidays performing labors that exceeded their physical strength, nor to languish alone in some remote pasture, guarding the herd. This did not mean that *colons* should refuse to help around the house, or to run the occasional errand: "To the extent that their age permits ... they can perform small errands so long as these demand no effort and expose them to no danger ... but we cannot accept that our children serve as little shepherds."[59] The silence of the Suresnes "Instructions" on children's work suggests that in this realm the municipality had opted to rely entirely on the Enfants Assistés' established rules and structures for the surveillance of orphans, which, as we have seen, sought to ensure that these children were being raised as a part of the family, and not simply assimilated to the farm labor force.

The occasional letters of complaint that the *mairie* received from unhappy children in the Nièvre *colonie* suggest that these structures and rules may not always have provided an adequate shield. "I have something to tell you," wrote Madeleine Pichard to her mother in the summer of 1935:

> We are very unhappy here, but please don't tell a soul about it. We go to bed at 10 o'clock each night and get up at five each morning. We drink our coffee and then go out to the fields to sit on a rock, from which we watch the pigs until noon. After [lunch] we return to the fields, for if the pigs break through the fence then we catch it from the mesieur. Every day the pigs break through and every day we get struck with the whip, but please don't write to him about it or he'll just hit me more ... Maman, you know that I cry each night in bed because I want to come home. If only you knew, we sleep on straw and feathers, the bedding is awful and we are so hot ... I don't want to go anymore *en colonie* ... Madeleine et Roger.[60]

Let us set aside for the moment the question of the credibility of Madeleine's tale, an issue we will return to below, and consider first the adults' responses to the child's plea for help. This response combined a certain skepticism on the part of Saint-Pierre Director Desbruyères vis-à-vis the reliability of children's hardship stories with an almost unfailing responsiveness to what was perceived to be the real substance of the complaint—the children wished to be moved elsewhere. Here, the prime mover was the Suresnes Commission des Colonies, which, time and again, overcame the Enfants Assistés' reluctance to offend its peasant *nourriciers* and insisted that unhappy children be moved, especially when children complained of excessive labor or of being struck.

In the course of adjudicating these claims, the Suresnes commission produced those concrete definitions of acceptable versus inadmissible forms of labor that were so strikingly absent from the municipality's "Instructions." Thus Alexandre Joyeux's response to the case of Madeleine and Roger Pichard—a letter to Director Desbruyères requesting an immediate investigation of conditions at the Dupont farm—indicates that the Suresnes Commission des Colonies was well aware that the *colons* were sometimes asked by their *parents nourriciers* to lend a hand with tasks around the house. Further, his phrasing suggests that the commission drew a sharp line distinguishing the admissible tasks of housework from any laboring in the fields: "Clearly we see no harm in the older children's seeking of their own initiative to make themselves agreeable to the *nourrice*. Nonetheless, and I am sure you agree, these little tasks must never acquire an obligatory character."[61] Joyeux's distinction between admissible and inadmissible forms of work for the children was thus drawn along two axes: a physical one separating housework from fieldwork, and a moral one that distinguished the child's voluntary help around the house from labor extracted by adult coercion. Contained within the latter, moral condition was the expectation that it was only the older children who would be touched by such questions during their summer *en colonie,* for the moral condition could be effective only if the children in question were old enough, and sufficiently independent, emotionally, to exercise autonomous judgment and will.

Joyeux's clarification of the line between permissible and inadmissible forms of work would surely serve as a useful guideline in future cases, should the need arise. But as far as Madeleine and Roger Pichard were concerned, such declarations of principle, and indeed the request for an investigation at the Dupont farm, were purely pro forma, for as

Joyeux noted in his postscript to Desbruyères, he had already promised the Pichards that he would have their children moved to another household.[62] Desbruyères' final report on the affair is most interesting, for it reveals how grudgingly he complied with his friend Joyeux's wishes: "I visited Madame Dupont at Dhere [Langeron] this morning, where I questioned the Pichard children. The latter told me, as they had on my last visit, that they were very happy with their *nourriciers;* and declared this, moreover, with conviction. The girl must know that her letter was a tissue of lies. Nonetheless, I moved the children, as you requested."[63] Some of Desbruyères' reluctance arose from confusing signals sent by the children themselves, who had initially requested placement on the Dupont farm — "which shows they were perfectly happy there last year," noted an exasperated Desbruyères. More annoying yet was the fact that neither Madeleine nor Roger had uttered a peep during the inspection tours of M. Desbruyères and the Suresnes delegation: "You visited this placement twice and I myself did so once. No complaint was ever addressed to either of us." To Desbruyères, this all added up, finally, to nothing more than the baffling, annoying antics of children, which surely should not be used to guide the actions of the adults who ran the *colonie.* If Joyeux was prepared to purchase the short-term harmony of the *colonie* at the price of giving in to the Pichard parents and the whims of their mercurial children, Desbruyères was equally prepared to defend the longer-term interests of his office and its relations with local *nourriciers* by banning such troublesome characters from the *colonie* altogether: "I would be grateful if you would inform the parents that next year, I will categorically refuse to take their children."[64]

Throughout Desbruyères' report, one senses the man's inclination to mistrust the claims of children. This skepticism is confirmed in at least one other report from that same summer, in response to a young girl's accusations of sexual misconduct, leveled against the seventy-year-old father of her *père nourricier.* Once again, the affair began with a letter to her mother, written in secret from the stables:

My Dear Maman and Grandmaman
I am writing my letter, which I think will make you happy; I am answering your two letters which I received this morning, I am writing to you on a plank in the stables. Zitite is peeling potatoes with Raymonde. But I have something to tell you that will not make you happy . . . You know the grandfather that grandmaman says is the nicest one, well, he is a bas-

tard—at night he comes in to touch our backsides, I was forced to put the
bed straight up against the wall and lie at the very back, with each of us
taking turns.

We will see you soon, big kisses from Denise and Zitite[65]

It was every parent's worst fear—especially every parent of girls—for in
a *colonie* by family placement it was commonly felt that the older girls
risked being exposed to various forms of sexual misconduct at the hands
of their peasant hosts. In fact, as we shall see, Suresnes parents would
eventually turn away from the Nièvre *colonie* in favor of a collective-style
one not only because the latter was seen as more "educational," but because it was perceived as a far safer structure for girls aged ten to fourteen.
These ambient anxieties about the security of older girls in the *colonie*
made the case of the Chollet sisters an especially sensitive one, and Joyeux
asked that Desbruyères return Denise's letter to Joyeux's office when the
investigation was finished (this is the only time that Joyeux ever specifically requested that a child's letter of complaint be returned to his office):
"Of course I have no advice as to how you should proceed in the inquiry
I have requested. All the same it seems to me that this is a case where we
must take every precaution, without the *nourrices* being aware, in case
what the children say is true."[66] Yet something in the child's letter led
Joyeux to share Desbruyères' customary skepticism regarding the testimony of children, for he closed his request by adding, "If you can get the
information with your customary discretion, I will look into the possibility of leaving the children with the *nourrice* until the end of the vacation."[67] (Clearly the two men had already discussed this sensitive case by
telephone.)

Debruyères' report arrived in Suresnes just four days later, a typically
laconic document that contained few surprises: "I have just looked into
the Chollet children's complaint. The unanimous opinion is that the Fouchez are people of impeccable character. Old man Fouchez is seventy
years old."[68] Once again the director showed himself ever ready to defend
his *nourriciers* against claims of abuse, citing their solid reputation with
local farmers, as if that fact alone rendered Denise's accusations absurd.
But something in this case—the characters of Denise and Zitite Chollet,
the nature of their accusations against the old père Fouchez—led Desbruyères to go even further, beyond mere skepticism, to the point where
he concluded his investigations by turning the original accusation back
upon the girl herself: "The girl seems quite advanced for her age. She

persisted in her accusations, but what she did not tell her parents is that, though she sleeps in a separate room, she leaves that room to sleep with the boys. I warned Madame Fouchez of this incriminating fact and urged her to let me know if the girls start leaving their room again at night. If so, I will put them in the hospice until the departure."[69] Not surprisingly, Desbruyères saw no reason to displace the children, who were left to finish out the holiday in Mme Fouchez's care.[70]

It is tempting to conclude that Desbruyères fell into the old trap of blaming the victim, a habit whose well-worn comforts were perhaps especially alluring in the face of the evident discomfort that children's accusations of mistreatment, and especially of sexual misconduct, raised in the adult organizers of the *colonie*. After all, the reports he sent back to the Suresnes commission show an unbroken tendency to side with his *nourriciers* in the face of children's accusations. At the same time it must be conceded that, on the basis of the letters and reports preserved, we can never be utterly certain of what really happened on the Dupont and Fouchez farms in the summer of 1935; the dossiers are simply too thin to permit any such ex post facto judgments. But if absolute certainty remains elusive, the cases of Denise Chollet and Madeleine Pichard, read alongside the larger dossier of children's complaints over the period from 1919 to 1939 (some twenty letters all told) do offer some clues about the conditions under which such conflicts unfolded, and this in turn helps to clarify why the adults concerned (especially Director Desbruyères) had such difficulty in hearing and evaluating dispassionately the testimony of children in the Nièvre *colonie*.

Nearly all the dossiers comment on the frustrating fact that those children who complained of poor food or ill-treatment in their letters to their parents never spoke up during the various tours of inspection conducted by the Suresnes delegation and the Enfants Assistés: "The little ones [Jeannet and André Rachou] complain that they are not adequately fed," wrote Joyeux to Desbruyères in the summer of 1933. "The children said nothing to us during your visit, nor mine; nonetheless I would be most grateful if you would look into their claim."[71] This remark surfaces repeatedly in the dossiers of complaint, alongside other evidence—children clubbing together to write their letter, or hiding in the stables to do so—that suggests that among the children of the industrial *banlieue,* the authority of adults still carried considerable weight; that it was difficult for them to overcome habits of deference or dissimulation (if not downright fear) in order to speak out forthrightly to grown-ups other than their own parents.[72] Hence the institutionalized mechanisms of review failed time and again in the face of childish diffidence, as children called in their parents rather than trusting the faces of institutional authority. Indeed, the profound doubts that these men entertained about the reliability of children's testimony, combined with children's evident reluctance to speak out directly before adults other than their parents, rendered standard fact-finding procedures a less than adequate tool of investigation and understanding. No wonder the Suresnes commission preferred to resolve things simply by moving the children in question!

One is also struck by the collective reticence on the part of adults when confronted with claims of sexual or physical abuse. Joyeux's letter to Desbruyères in the case of the Pichard children thus adopts a tone of great delicacy in referring to the "blows of the switch" as simply "the second point" in her accusations, the first being Madeleine's claims of excessive labor.[73] Now this reticence could have had many sources—discomfort in the face of the children's claim that they were being mistreated (how hideous if true, and how incriminating to an organization which sought to promote the health and happiness of children). Or perhaps their verbal delicacy in such matters reflected real embarrassment, a hesitation before the task of subjecting their peasant collaborators to investigation of what may have felt like childish invention or exaggeration. This was clearly true in Director Desbruyères' case. And so we return to the question of the credibility of children's complaints, beginning with the letter that Madeleine Pichard wrote to her parents in the summer of 1935. Now Madeleine's letter is one of a handful of complaints[74] from the Nièvre *colonie* that recounts a child's dreary and physically taxing "holiday," spent in performing household and field work at the *paysan nourricier*'s behest, enforced by "blows from the switch": "I was not at all happy with my vacation," wrote one young boy at the end of his summer on a farm in Saint-Parize-le-Châtel. "The house was in dreadful shape, our beds were terrible, we hardly ate anything, and oh, how we worked, even on Sundays. He hit us with the switch and locked us in the filthy stables. In the morning we had to split wood in the pouring rain ... [and] he had us break stones on the road."[75] These letters reveal a familiarity with rural and agricultural chores that would have been unknown to the children of the interwar *banlieue*—cutting wood in the midst of a downpour, watching the herd while perched on a rock in the midst of the pasture, and then chasing after those renegade pigs who had escaped into the woods. Moreover, the widespread concern expressed by organizers of *colonies chez les paysans* that their children not be used as little shepherds suggests that the occasional complaints of excessive farm labor that we find in the Suresnes dossiers were probably not unfounded. Rural children were integrated from an early age into the daily round of chores on the farm, and the specific tasks that the young Suresnois mention in their complaints—lighting the fire, chopping wood, fetching water, leading herds to the pasture and then watching over them—were precisely the kinds of unskilled and physically less demanding jobs that *paysans nourriciers* would have confided to their own children. Small wonder, then, that the integration of urban *colons* into the life of the farm entailed performing such chores, in some cases to an extensive degree.

And what of the "blows from the switch"? We know that on many a farm the *fouet d'enfants* ("children's switch") hung prominently on the kitchen wall, that the peasants' own children periodically felt its sting, and that such practices did not bring down accusations of child abuse from the neighbors. Rather, this fell into the class of acceptable parental discipline and probably passed unremarked unless the switch was employed with unusual violence. But would *nourriciers* who used the switch on their own children have extended this practice to the children of strangers? Apparently the municipal commission felt it was best not to take any risks in the matter, for each time such a complaint was raised, the commission saw to it that the children in question were moved to another household.

Adjudicating the claims of unhappy children who claimed overwork and ill-treatment while *en colonie* thus raised thorny and perhaps insoluble problems around evidence and testimony, and the collusive reticence of Joyeux and Desbruyères in such cases may have reflected their profound uncertainty in the face of claims that contained some insolvable tangle of truth and exaggeration. Were these actual *coups de fouet* that the child had endured, or was this a menace that loomed large in the imagination of a child who had noticed the *fouet d'enfants* hanging on the wall, perhaps witnessed its use on the farmer's own children? Even if the *colons* had been switched, it was not clear that any of the adults involved (perhaps not even the child's own parents back in Suresnes) felt this constituted a shocking overstepping of delegated parental authority on the part of the *nourriciers,* let alone undue brutality toward children. After all, local custom saw nothing objectionable in the occasional recourse to the *fouet d'enfants.* Hence Desbruyères' notable reluctance to press accusations in the households of his *familles nourricières,* a point on which the Suresnes commission did not press him, so long as the children in question were moved.

The Suresnes commission thus found itself caught between the wish to protect the city's children from forced labor in the guise of summer holidays, and the need to accommodate the Enfants Assistés, who sought to protect the good reputation, and self-respect, of its *paysans nourriciers*. In the face of these multiple pressures, the commission fell back on a policy that combined efforts to encourage the *colons'* adaptation to their new surroundings with a policy of moving unhappy children no matter where the precise truth of their stories might lie (a pragmatic solution that avoided making any legal/ethical judgments of who had done what to whom). Hence, by forbidding the family of origin any direct access to the adoptive family in the Nièvre, the directors of the *colonie* sought to reinforce the in loco parentis authority of the *nourriciers,* to provide some space within which the children could get over the initial shock of loneliness that sometimes attended their arrival in the quiet hinterlands of Saint-Pierre, and bond with their adoptive families. But if, after a few days, the children had not settled happily into a particular household, the *colonie*'s general policy was to move them whenever possible—and the abundance of placements meant that such changes could usually be effected without much difficulty. Even in situations where the child's unhappiness arose from loneliness or boredom, *or* from a simple clash of personalities, rather than any maltreatment or neglect per se, the *mairie* saw to it that such children were moved immediately.[76] And if the child was truly inconsolable, the parents could always take the train to Nevers and reclaim him or her.[77] After all, the goal of the municipal *colonie* was to maximize the pleasure that children experienced during their holiday in the Nièvre while minimizing as far as possible the frictions that inevitably arose within the close relationships of which the *colonie* was constructed. Hence, the *mairie* took all complaints from parents and *colons* quite seriously, and contacted the Saint-Pierre office immediately upon receiving the least hint that a child was unhappy with his or her placement.

The Enfants Assistés, for its part, moved quickly to investigate these complaints, but was reluctant to offend the *nourrice* in question by removing children from her care. After all, moving children from one family to another (let alone extracting them from the *colonie* altogether) was not without its risks for the ongoing viability of the organization, for such moves always carried a potential critique of the first *nourrice*'s ways and habits. When requesting such changes, then, the Commission des Colonies was always careful to politely reassure the *nourrice* that the quality of her services was in no way being called into question. Whenever possible, the municipal commission would arrange to send another child to replace the departing one — to make up for the lost income, to be sure, but also to demonstrate the municipality's ongoing confidence in her work: "We realize that Madame Rosette has done nothing wrong and we will send her another, younger girl with our next convoy to make up the number of *pensionnaires* in her charge," wrote Henri Sellier in the case of a young girl being moved due to "irreconcilable differences between the child and her *nourrice*."[78] But as Director Desbruyères brusquely remarked, the risk to peasants' ongoing willingess to work with the *colonie,* and with the Enfants Assistés, remained, for "to move children in such situations is a moral blow to these good people and undermines their authority."[79]

Given the size and duration of the *colonie* (six weeks in the 1920s and early 1930s, extended to eight in 1933, with 300 to 550 children from Suresnes alone each summer after 1929), the number of complaints from children and/or their parents, and the number of interventions to move the deeply unhappy, is strikingly small — 4 out of 181 changed placements in the summer of 1922; 3 out of 160 in the summer of 1923.[80] The percentage of return requests, on the other hand, was consistently quite high, suggesting that by and large, the children who spent their summers in the Nièvre *colonie* were generally satisfied, even happy with their host families.

The Decline of Family Placement:
Sellier's Nièvre *Colonie,* 1935 to 1939

Nearly 500 young Suresnois . . . left on Monday the 25th of July for six weeks in the beautiful countryside of the Nièvre, Cher, and Allier, where they will stock up on pure air and make the most of their vacation time . . . Under the paternal eye of Henri Sellier, *conseiller général* and mayor of Suresnes . . . , the eleven buses . . . set off for the Gare de Lyon . . . where the children . . . then mounted a special train for Nevers . . . The arrival and distribution of the little *colons* to their *nourrices* was a most picturesque spectacle. The donkey carts, cars, and occasional bus that pulled up, by turns, to take each young Suresnois to the farms and nearby villages brought a bustle of activity, a note of life, to this normally quiet spot. *Nourrices* and children, who for six weeks will be reunited as a second family, fondly embrace and make merry.[81]

By the early 1930s, the *colonie* of Suresnes was firmly established in the Nièvre, thanks to Sellier's careful management of the Commission Inter-communale (which was, by this point, in the process of quietly dissolving, as the component members went their separate ways). Relations between the municipality and the office at Saint-Pierre were harmonious and con-fident, strengthened by more than ten years of successful collaboration in the municipal *colonie* — "your most important work," as one director put it — and nourished by the bonds of personal friendship that gradu-ally arose between the men of the municipal Commission des Colonies and the directors at Saint-Pierre with whom they worked so closely.[82] Hence the annual tour of inspection by the Suresnes delegation was also the occasion for long dinners at the Hotel Clouard in Saint-Pierre, fes-tive occasions that extended to the families of these men and which, over time, took on the character of reunions among old friends.[83]

The municipal *colonie* was also, by this time, equally well anchored in the city's growing array of hygienic institutions aimed at guarantee-ing the health and well-being of the rising generation, institutions whose organization and management had devolved almost entirely into the hands of the *assistantes scolaires*.[84] But in the mid-1930s, after some thir-teen years of uninterrupted expansion, during which the *colonie* acquired a widely lauded and solidly institutionalized place on the local landscape, the Nièvre *colonie* began a sudden, and irreversible, decline. Why did an institution in such apparent good health undergo such an abrupt reversal of fortune? Clearly the economic crisis played a role in provoking this decline, for as several *assistantes scolaires* observed, renewed insecurity at work was, by 1935, causing parents to hesitate before sending their chil-dren on holiday: "Living with constant uncertainty about work . . . the conscientious ones prefer not to commit themselves to costs they are not sure of being able to meet."[85] Once the economic crisis had set a down-ward trend in motion, however, other factors intervened to prolong it, factors that emerged over the course of the municipality's determined campaign (1935–38) to reverse this decline. Indeed, from the mid-1930s down to the invasion of May–June 1940, the *mairie* found itself confront-ing a certain resistance to the municipal *colonie,* and to the broader policy within which it was inscribed, that all schoolchildren leave the city dur-ing the summer holiday.

In particular, parents seem to have resented the mounting pressure to send their children away from the city during the *grandes vacances d'été*, a pressure which rose as soon as the annual vacation census began to register a drop in the numbers of schoolchildren leaving the city over the summer. For so long as the *colonie* was expanding (1920 through 1933), and the overall percentage of children spending their summers in the countryside held steady at 74 to 80 percent, the *mairie* exerted scant pressure to raise that participation to 100 percent, apart from the obligation to fill out the annual vacation questionnaire.[86] But when the 1935 questionnaire revealed a sharp drop (to 60 percent) in the proportion of schoolchildren spending their summers in the country, the *mairie* reacted with sharp vigor. Led by Sellier's fervent disciple Louis Boulonnois, the office issued one inquiry after another to its team of *assistantes scolaires,* asking for their informed opinions on the reasons for the decline: "A crisis in resources for the families who wish to take their children with them to the country. If only the parents had holidays with pay!!" wrote one *assistante scolaire* in the spring of 1936 (just weeks before Léon Blum signed the first paid holidays into existence).[87] Several others returned responses that suggested a growing unhappiness with the family placement formula: "Some parents are reluctant to send their children with the c.v. because they don't wish to be separated from their children, nor send them to board with strangers. Others . . . fear that their children won't receive the care they need outside the parental home. For others still, it is the selfish desire not to spend the money."[88] After expending a great deal of time in a vain effort to convince these families that their children's best interests would be served by turning them over to the municipal *colonie* for the summer, the *assistante scolaire* sadly concluded that "it seems to us quite difficult to change these people's minds; but they are, after all, only a minority." And yet, "the percentage of children who are not confided to us for the c.v. seems, to us, to be on the rise."[89]

Armed with the not terribly surprising news that the economic crisis bore some responsibility for the decline (and choosing simply to ignore the reluctance of "some" parents to send their children with the municipal *colonie*), the *mairie* launched an intense promotional campaign in which the parents of school-age children were repeatedly reminded that in order to enjoy good health and proper development, their children required at least four to six, and preferably eight weeks of uninterrupted holiday in the countryside, and that the municipal *colonie* provided this benefit for an extremely modest fee. To those parents who found the annual vacation inquiry "rather indiscreet" from the point of view of family privacy, Louis Boulonnois simply replied, "We seek above all to secure to Suresnes's children the means to leave the city during the school holidays, and we seek to ascertain precisely how many children have already been able to do so."[90] Concerned that the economic crisis was undermining the gains in child health won by recent municipal action in the schools, *colonies,* and dispensaries, the *mairie* was seeking to reinforce a policy that distinguished the child's life-chances from those of his or her parents by ensuring that all school-aged Suresnois had the chance to leave the city each summer. If the parents were able to provide this for their children, then they had a moral obligation to do so, for in the *mairie*'s view, their children's long-term health depended upon their leaving the city each summer during the crucial years of physiological development. If, on the other hand, the family lacked the financial or human resources necessary to provide for their child's holidays, the *mairie* could furnish the child with a ready-made rural family through its municipal *colonie* in the Nièvre.

In the case of parents over whom the *mairie* possessed some leverage — those drawing unemployment benefits or living off the dole — the moral argument was reinforced by a tangible material incentive: so long as the parents were on the dole or drawing unemployment, their school-age children would enjoy free passage to the municipal *colonie:* "The municipality seeks above all to ensure that all children of the unemployed are able to spend their holidays in the countryside without any cost to their parents."[91] Ultimately, the *mairie* sought to awaken in all parents the recognition of their child's right to good health, independent of family circumstances. Since summers in the country formed an indispensable part of that good health, the parents' recognition of their children's rights in this matter would surely lead them to recast their own summer plans before the overarching interest of their children's health. Or so it was hoped. But with the children of the unemployed, endangered at a crucial phase in their development by the privations of poverty, the need was doubly urgent, and the propaganda accordingly fierce: "[The municipality] views as its solemn duty the obligation to ensure that the little ones [of the unemployed] enjoy this opportunity each year. We know that, on this point, we will be supported by all families who are concerned for the health and well-being of their children."[92] In truth, the *mairie* was by no means convinced that the families of the unemployed were moved by an unwavering concern for the health and well-being of their children: on the contrary, these were the families where active intervention was both necessary (due to the negative impact of poverty and hunger on child development) and possible, thanks to the financial leverage which distribution of the dole gave the *mairie* over its beneficiaries. Over the next three years (1935–38), the mayor's office would conduct a strenuous campaign among these families, seeking to realize within this subgroup of the city population its long-term dream to send *all* school-age children to the countryside each summer.[93]

The campaign was rooted in the *mairie*'s long-standing practice of admitting the children of the unemployed into the municipal *colonie "free of charge,* and without budgetary limitation."[94] In June of 1935, the Ministry of Labor moved to assist such local initiatives with Instruction 8511, on the unemployment benefit, which allowed municipalities to hold back the supplementary allocation for dependent children and use it to help defray the cost of sending the child *en colonie.* In other words, the unemployed parents would no longer hang on to the child's allocation while he or she spent two months frolicking in the countryside at municipal expense; henceforth, that allocation would be held back by the *mairie* and put toward defraying the cost of the child's *pension* during the time the child was *en colonie.* This was, on its face, a quite reasonable policy, and one that helped stretch the sadly finite resources of a municipality like Suresnes, whose ambitious programs of social assistance were being sorely tried by the economic crisis. But in a city where the push to send all children to the countryside had become an official hygienic obsession, Instruction 8511 also became the basis for exerting a new kind of leverage against the unemployed: "It must be understood that this instruction is quite general," wrote Louis Boulonnois in June of 1935. "It covers not only those unemployed who, after having signed their children up for the *colonie,* try to extract them, but *all* school-age children of the unemployed, who can no longer claim that they haven't got the means to send their children for six weeks to the countryside."[95]

Instruction 8511 thus placed a new weapon into the hands of the *mairie* and, indeed, transformed the municipality's generous offer of assistance to unemployed parents into the instrument by which those families were pressured to accept: "The Commission Départmentale de Contrôle des Fonds de Chômage has officially confirmed that the municipality is authorized to *require* that all who receive unemployment benefit send their school-age children to the *colonies de vacances.*"[96] Not only were the parents subjected to an ever more harassing campaign to send their children away, but the allocation they received for each schoolchild was to be withheld during the two months of the *colonie.* If the family backed down and sent its child *en colonie,* the allocation would be used toward his or her maintenance in the Nièvre. If not, the payment would simply be withheld from the family in question, a financial arm-twist which, it was hoped, would drive those parents hoping to guard the child's allocation to give up both allocation and child in the interest of the latter's health and well-being.[97]

The designated enforcers of the new municipal policy were the *assistantes scolaires,* who, in late June of 1935, were asked to establish a vacation census among the children of the unemployed "and instruct the families either to sign their children up for the *colonie,* or to present a medicosocial justification for their refusal."[98] Acceptable "medico-social justification" included evidence (in the form of a "certificate of accomodation") that the child was spending at least four weeks outside the city with relatives, friends, or with a private *colonie* (either a Catholic *colonie* or the local Faucons Rouges [Socialist scout] camp). Otherwise the family was asked to provide a medical certificate, signed by a doctor, attesting that the child's health was too frail for such adventures. The census thus became the occasion not only to count up and identify the noncompliant families, but to intervene once more and persuade them to see the error of their ways. For the obstinate minority who persisted in refusing the offer of free passage, the *mairie*'s instruction was clear: "Cancel all complementary allocations for dependents for those unemployed whose excuse has not been formally authorized by the municipality."[99] The late spring census among the children of the unemployed quickly entered into the rituals of municipal administration; each June thereafter, the *assistantes sociales* would receive a memo from the *mairie* reminding them that it was time to "verify . . . that all children of the unemployed receiving benefit are, without exception, signed up for the *colonies de vacances.* Under no circumstances are any allocations to be paid in cash for school-age children during the period of the municipal *colonies de vacances.*"[100]

The results of the initial 1935 census offer some revealing glimpses into the struggle that was brewing between unemployed parents and the crusading bureaucrats of Sellier's Popular-Front-era *mairie* over who would control the summertime activities of Suresnes's schoolchildren. The census lasted a full month, from 12 June until 12 July of 1935. That summer 139 families were called in, 26 of whom gave in and sent their children after all, and 89 of whom furnished evidence of alternative vacation plans, or a valid medical excuse. The remaining 24 families persisted in their refusal, generally offering the most threadbare justifications for their decision. By the end of the inquiry, the *assistantes scolaires* had reason to be proud of their work. In a colonie of 444, 190 were the children of unemployed parents, 71 of whom had been signed up over the course of their June–July census-cum-campaign to send 100 percent of such children away from the city.[101] Some of the shabbier excuses for refusing the *colonie* included "no reason—fear that their child will be bored"; "mother refuses—father prefers to lose the allocation." Less obviously baseless were the brother and sister who had left with the *colonie* in the summer of 1933, and, in the lapidary formula of the census, had "had difficulty and run away." And then there were those who found that the odor of social assistance clung far too closely to the Nièvre *colonie.* So it was with one man, an out-of-work cabinetmaker who, despite his present precarious circumstances, regarded the *colonie* as "beneath his station" and preferred to try sending his children to stay with family in the Allier out of his own thinly lined pockets.[102] Clearly the campaign to send the children of the unemployed away from the city was running up against some stubborn opposition on the part of the families involved, some of which reflected disenchantment with the municipal *colonie,* some of which suggested that not all parents shared the municipality's bottom-line conviction that a summer in the city was incompatible with their child's normal and healthy development.

The place of honor within the category of acceptable justifications was held by those families who had concocted a valid means of extracting their child from the city for the summer: Catholic *colonies,* the Faucons Rouges, a grandmother in the Vosges, or one mother of four who decided to take her children to her uncle's farm in the Eure, where she was to work on the farm in return for food for the entire family.[103] Equally acceptable was the response, in at least four cases, that the child, aged twelve to fourteen, had already begun working and so no longer had two idle months each summer. And of course the municipality was obliged to release the pressure on those parents who had once again found work and were no longer drawing benefits.

Those parents who offered a valid medical excuse, signed by a doctor, generally encountered little opposition. In at least one case, however, the *assistante scolaire* contested the wisdom of the parents' decision to keep their daughter, recovering from a tonsillectomy, close by their side: "Violette Leclercq has just been operated on . . . [and] is terribly fatigued. She

needs to go to the countryside, but her mother does not wish to be separated from her." [104] In Mme Hoyez's view, the child needed her summer
in the country in order to recover both health and strength. But the *assistantes scolaires* did not confine their inquiries to matters of bodily hygiene
alone; in the case of young Robert Cochet, who, happily, was to be leaving
Suresnes with the Catholic *colonie,* the *assistante scolaire* had inscribed
a poignant addendum: "Things are going very badly at his house—his
mother recently attempted suicide." [105]

On 1 August 1935, three weeks after the *assistantes scolaires* had completed their work, those twenty-four families who had proffered feeble
excuses, or persisted in their refusal to send their children on holiday
come what may, received a curt notification that their supplementary
cash allocation for the child(ren) in question was to be withheld: "You
have decided that it is best not to accept this offer, to the serious injury
of your child and without presenting any real justification for this refusal." [106] But as the *mairie* was soon to discover, the policy of pressuring
the most vulnerable families did little to arrest the decline of the municipal *colonie.* Hence, from a peak of 539 in 1933, the number of *colons* had
already fallen back to 433 in 1935. The annual vacation census confirmed
that this decline was inscribed in the larger drop in the percentage of city
children who were getting out to the countryside each summer, which
bottomed out that summer at a mere 60 percent. With the passage of the
1936 law granting two weeks of paid holiday to adult workers, the percentage of children leaving Suresnes for the countryside recovered rather
quickly, returning to 76.5 percent, then 80 percent, by the summers of
1936 and 1937. But the numbers of children in the municipal *colonie* continued to decline: 417 in 1936, 360 in 1937, 335 in 1938, rising slightly to
400 in 1939, amidst the rumors of war. [107]

Throughout these years, the *mairie* never once relaxed in its efforts to
obtain "the maximum good result," that is, to press ever onward toward
the elusive goal of sending 100 percent of the city's children out to the
fields and forests of the French countryside each summer. [108] To this end,
Sellier and his colleagues maintained a steady pressure on all parents
through the annual vacation census. Within this more global policy of all
children to the countryside, the *mairie* pursued with renewed vigor its
specific pressure on those families over whom it exerted some leverage.
Moreover, the net was officially widened in 1936–37 to include not only
the children of the unemployed but also children from families on public welfare, as well as those identified by the school doctors as medically

at risk.[109] All these families were to be threatened with the loss of their children's allocations should they refuse to release them to the municipal *colonie*. Having obtained a means of pressuring directly those families whose children were presumed to be at greatest risk, developmentally, the *mairie* was determined to exercise its powers as fully as possible.

In the course of this process, the *mairie* came gradually to redefine the goal of "all children to the countryside," narrowing it to a policy of "all children to the municipal *colonie*," at least where the children of these disfavored families (unemployed, on the dole, or sickly) were concerned. Hence, in April 1937, the *mairie* reminded the *assistantes scolaires* that "all children of the unemployed must leave Suresnes during the school holiday: (1) *first and foremost by means of the municipal colonies*; (2) secondarily by those programs that are linked to the public authorities and are entirely free of charge."[110] Over the course of its campaign, the *mairie* had come to regard its own *colonie* in the Nièvre as the surest guarantee that these children would get the dose of fresh air, rest, and good food their health demanded.[111]

What are we to make of the *mairie*'s stubborn pursuit of its own *colonie* in the face of a solidifying opposition to both the municipal *colonie* and the increasingly coercive politics of child health within which it was inscribed? If we step back and consider the evolution of policy over the course of the 1930s, one very interesting fact emerges: it seems that the *mairie*'s effort to quantify the success of its policy further underscored the hygienic significance of the *colonie* in the eyes of its municipal directors. As early as November 1932, then, Henri Sellier was urging his *assistantes scolaires* to begin a more systematic collection of data on the summer vacations of all Suresnes schoolchildren, for "it is of the utmost hygienic and social interest that we know how children under the *obligation scolaire* are spending their vacations." Once gathered, such data would permit a more scientific appraisal of the "hygienic consequences" that summers in the country, versus summers in the city, had for the health of individual children.[112] Once in motion, this systematization of recruitment, medical surveillance, and post-*colonie* statistics-gathering seems to have fuelled the *mairie*'s determination to see that *all* children drew the hygienic benefit. This injected a note of rigor into the social policy that was simply not present before the mid-1930s. The municipality's ambitions in this arena thus expanded in tandem with its capacity to monitor the success of its policies.[113] As late as 1939, then, after four years of effort, chipping away (with scant success) at the resistant hard-

core refusers, the *mairie* was still urging the school directors to carry out
the annual vacation census so that the Municipal Social Service could put
the "maximum pressure" on parents, language that leaves little doubt as
to its crusading vision and unwavering purpose.[114]

In the face of the *mairie*'s relentless campaign, how should we interpret the steady decline in the municipal *colonie*? As we have seen, the
economic crisis and the broader, more temporary drop in the numbers
of young Suresnois spending their summers in the country formed the
context for the specific and ongoing decline in the numbers who joined
the municipal *colonie* in the Nièvre, which, over a scant five years (1933–
1938), declined by nearly half. But whence this abrupt and widespread
disaffection from an institution that Antonin Poggioli had in 1931 termed
"a beloved oeuvre of the people"?[115] Was it rooted in the more specific
struggles that arose between citizens and *mairie* during the difficult years
of the crisis, or does it reflect a longer-term trend toward favoring the
educational *colonie*? Clearly the particular conflicts that arose in Suresnes
between the *mairie* and its unemployed citizens played some role in the
popular disaffection with the Nièvre *colonie*. But the responses that the
assistantes scolaires garnered each year in their general vacation census
among the entire school population suggest that alongside the evident
disenchantment with the system of family placement lay a growing interest in holidays organized for group living: "It is too bad that we do not
have collective placements for the girls over age twelve (for the mothers'
peace of mind)," wrote the *assistante scolaire* at the Ecole Edouard Vaillant in the spring of 1936, "nor for all the little children who need special
diets. It would also be preferable for some of the more rambunctious children."[116] "In the first place, the limit of six years of age is far too high,"
replied another *assistante scolaire*. "Why not have them leave from age
four? Secondly, nine families requested collective placements."[117] The
increasingly frequent demand for a *colonie éducative* suggests that parents were making a positive choice at the very moment when the various
secular *colonies* were defining a distinctive place on the pedagogical landscape, organized around the principle of educating the "whole child,"
and not just the intellect. For, by the mid-1930s, with the blossoming of
popular education initiatives under the aegis of Popular Front cultural
politics, the population at large began to hear a new message: that *colonies de vacances* offered a kind of socialization and education that was
both highly desirable and quite complementary to that of the public primary school. The vacation censuses of 1935–39 suggest that at least some

Suresnois had heard the message and come to believe that from a so-cial, hygienic, and educational standpoint, the collective structure could best deliver what children and their families needed from a *colonie de va-cances,* including that pedagogical surplus-value that proponents of the educational *colonie* had been working so hard to develop and define.

This, then, was the era when the institution of *colonies de vacances* moved decisively toward a more pedagogical self-definition, though without shedding entirely its initial hygienic structure and meaning, and, moreover, succeeded in convincing ever-greater numbers of parents that time spent in a collectivity of children was important to the education and social development of their children. As Antoine Prost would later put it, "It is good for children to socialize with children from other families; thus they begin their apprenticeship to social life."[118] An institution that had been founded to meet the multiple needs of poor urban children, notably for clean air and adequate food, had thus staked an important pedagogical claim, one that had been developing from the outset, but which did not achieve full definition until the 1930s, during the extraor-dinary cultural mobilization of the Popular Front. On the strength of this claim the *colonie de vacances* was beginning to spread upward and outward to the children of the middle classes. But the inevitable victim in this movement was the older system of family placement, which died a quiet and largely unmourned death in late 1930s France.[119]

Hence, the tale of Sellier's *colonie* is, ultimately, the story of a failure. For there can be no doubt that, in the end, the people of Suresnes rejected the *colonie chez les paysans* in favor of family vacations, and/or collective, educational *colonies.*

It is all too easy to talk of the totalizing effects of institutions, their seeming will to control all they survey, once the mechanisms are at last in place, and it is tempting to interpret the trajectory of the Suresnes *colonie* in this way. Hence, what began as a municipal offering to the chil-dren of those workers who had no country relatives was gradually impli-cated in a larger and increasingly determined policy of ensuring that all schoolchildren left the city. This was reinforced by the utter unanimity of interwar medicine: fresh air remained the single, most reliable insur-ance against tuberculosis. The problem with this analysis is, of course, that agents and politics give way to the tentacular forces of the institu-tion, that Frankensteinian offspring of the municipal socialism which, in this case, produced it. But the reality in Suresnes is far more complex and interesting, for once the municipality had folded the *colonie* into the larger, school-based structure of hygienic surveillance by the *assistantes sociales,* this gave the *colonie* something it had never had before: an efficient mechanism of on-site recruitment, and a systematic way to evaluate, year by year, the success of the overall public health policy within which the *colonie* was inscribed. This changed the terms of the interaction between individual Suresnois and the *colonie,* but by no means did it crush the two-way nature of this interaction.

Here we see Sellier's politics of extending chances for the young hitting up against a very hard obstacle, which was the resistance of individual families to a social-medical policy designed in the name of their children.[120] And this, in turn, brings out some of the complexities of a municipal institution of child health and welfare that sought to penetrate those urban families rendered fragile by illness, death of a parent, chronic poverty, or the more temporary condition of unemployment. In each of these cases the *mairie* had strong reason to believe that the school-age children might be suffering the effects of malnourishment and overcrowding in the somber, damp, and substandard housing that remained all too prevalent on the landscapes of the interwar *banlieue.* Of course, such dark visions sometimes missed the mark entirely. Thus, a sick child in one family that was dogged by unemployment turned out to be recovering her health in a "well-aired" little house, to the relief of the *assistante scolaire,* who found she could leave the child in good conscience, rather than trying to force her departure *en colonie.* Yet conditions of housing and nutrition remained sufficiently precarious in 1930s Suresnes that the *mairie* and its team of *assistantes scolaires* took the worst-case scenario as a point of departure for their investigations into the summer plans of children from such families.[121]

In this context, it is worth pointing out that critics who attack the "invasion" of social work into the proletarian private sphere in the name of preserving the inviolability of working-class families against state intervention by professional intermediaries forget what Henri Sellier himself never forgot: that the working-class family is not some undifferentiated unity whose collective purity is guaranteed by its victim status in a sharply hierarchical structure of socioeconomic inequality; it is itself a social structure, organized by age and gender, inside which dwell children who may well be victims of neglect, abuse, or exploitation, and who were, in any event, too often underfed in this era of economic crisis.[122] Unlike many a present-day scholar, wistful for the warm and homey features of authentic, interwar popular culture, and for the working-class families who are the central protagonists in this narrative, Sellier was not at all inclined to romanticize the working-class child's family of origin as an unproblematic haven in the heartless world of industrial capitalism. On the contrary: although, like other advocates of family placement, he had a basic faith in the family as an appropriate environment for child development, he was not categorically prone to presume that families of origin, bound by mere ties of blood, constituted a structure that was always adequate to the task of raising children.

Sellier's awareness that the interests of the individual child might be suffering in the parents' pursuit of their own, not necessarily congruent ends, emerges episodically, often indirectly, in both the discourse and practice of the city's interwar politics of childhood; in policy statements regarding the schools and school health services, and, of course, in the municipal *colonie de vacances*. To cite but one example, a widely diffused article on the city's *écoles maternelles* posed the following question by way of underscoring the magnificence of the school buildings and personnel: "And is there not some risk that people will say that such a perfect setting will tend to uproot the child from its family? But of course not—the mother will always remain the mother. But if the mother is not there, *or if by chance she is unworthy, the child will recover at the school something that is like a family.*"[123] The mayor's quite nuanced politics of the family, which never declared itself as such, is perhaps best characterized as pro-family, but not necessarily favoring the family of origin—an apparent paradox whose underlying logic emerges as we dissect the structures of his *colonie* with the Socialist peasants of the Nièvre. This stance produced a singular kind of "pro-family" discourse where the place of the family was occupied both by families of origin and by various familial and tutelary public institutions, which jostled one another uneasily inside a capacious, if unstable category of family/familial institutions. Thus in June of 1936 Henri Sellier could declare in a nationwide radio broadcast that his new Ministry of Health would "place a host of public institutions at the disposal of families, and . . . place the child under their tutelary protection,"[124] for, curious though it may seem in retrospect, a social policy that grasped both family and familial/tutelary institutions in the same categorical embrace resonated widely in 1930s France. Henri Sellier's politics of childhood was thus undergirded by the notion that the municipality (or state) can provide a supplement to, or substitute for, the family of origin, with the central ambiguity "supplement/substitute for" always being left (significantly) open. As we have seen, this politics was nowhere more clearly, or tenaciously, enacted than in the municipal *colonie de vacances.*

Epilogue: Protestant Virgilianism versus the Leftist Ruralism of Suresnes

On 28 August 1939, the primary schoolteachers of the Département de la Seine were called to a meeting by the authority of the prefect. The purpose: to organize a mass evacuation of school-age children from Paris, in view of the impending war with Germany. The prefect's scheme organized the evacuation through the primary schools, asking that teachers accompany the children to rural school buildings, hastily (and incompletely) transformed into shelters, in safe havens such as the Sarthe. Henri Sellier fulminated against the bureaucratic stupidity with which the entire operation unfolded, gathering thousands of schoolchildren and shipping them, willy-nilly, to rural districts that were hardly prepared to receive them:

> The children were more or less adequately lodged in the local households of those charitable souls who agreed to take them in while a few bales of hay were being spread on the floors of the school classrooms, now emptied of their desks, so that the children could eventually sleep therein. There was of course no question of providing sheets and blankets. As far as any sanitary organization was concerned, it was neither thought of nor planned for . . . They spent the day in horrible courtyards that were so dusty that with the first rains they became veritable lakes of mud.[125]

The material defects of the mass evacuation pointed to a deeper lack of understanding on the part of its organizers, "who are, perhaps, excellent pedagogues, but who know nothing about placing and lodging children." As a consequence, they had organized an evacuation that, "rather than reducing to a minimum the child's sense of displacement by placing them in a family context, concerned itself above all with avoiding any such contact."[126] Sellier did not refrain from comparing unfavorably the ill-organized evacuation of September 1939 with his own highly successful evacuation of 1918. The difference, of course, was that Sellier had avoided large-scale solutions, in which children were herded like beasts into collective refuges, and had relied instead on family placement. Why had the government chosen to adopt such a clumsy and unpleasant evacuation procedure when the extensive network of *colonies* by family placement lay before them? "Twenty-five years of experience and the some 30,000 placements that I have arranged in *colonies de vacances* . . . have led me to regard family placement, under the control of experienced officers of the Assistance Publique . . . as the only way to meet the needs of a wintertime evacuation."[127]

The mayor was particularly angry on behalf of the children of Suresnes, whose subjection to the hardships of this evacuation seemed especially unnecessary, for the city had its own *colonie* in the Nièvre.[128] His robust defense of the *colonie* at the moment of the invasion thus summarizes, retrospectively, the place that the *colonie de vacances* held in the hygienic social politics of the aging municipal Socialist. Most interesting, perhaps, is his ongoing defense of the family as the best setting for child development, a defense that put him somewhat at odds with the pedagogical trends of his time. In an era when the *colonie collective* was defining its own distinctive educational mission, Sellier remained convinced that "family placement . . . offers more advantages than collective placement."[129] Moreover, he believed that *colonies de vacances* should have no direct relation to the school, which should serve merely as the convenient site of their organization.[130] Sellier's utter indifference to the possible harvest of added pedagogical value *en colonie,* not to mention his telling silence on the virtues of the peasantry as models of hard work and familial solidarity, suggests that he held no illusions about the moral virtues of the countryside. Virtues it had, to be sure, but these were less moral/pedagogical than physical/hygienic—a relief from the bad air, constant racket, and stressful disciplines that constrained children's lives in a densely inhabited industrial city.[131] In the end, it was the medical discourse that prevailed, shaping the structure and practice of a *colonie* where all activity took place within the households and farms of individual *paysans nourriciers,* and the commission made scant effort to provide any collective pedagogical activity.

In the long run, however, Sellier's Nièvre *colonie* would fail precisely because of the mayor's obdurate refusal to take the pedagogical turn and transform his program into a collective, educational *colonie* of the sort that, from the mid-1930s on, the Suresnes citizenry seemed increasingly to value. In this respect, Suresnes's citizens participated in the broader, nationwide movement away from family placement, and no amount of coercion from the *mairie* could stanch the tide, as the people of Suresnes simply voted with their feet in mounting refusal of Sellier's old-fashioned

colonie. This refusal reminds us of the powerful limits on the municipality's effort to establish the *colonie,* and the social work that surrounded
it, as "total" institutions. For in the end, even the most vulnerable families, financially dependent on unemployment or welfare benefits, were
occasionally prepared to give up their supplementary allocation in order
to keep their children out of the municipal *colonie.* If in some cases this
refusal may have stemmed from a desire simply to resist the *mairie*'s intervention in the raising of their children, those parents who took the opportunity to protest the lack of a "proper" educational *colonie* were clearly
not resisting the notion of municipal intervention per se, but rather demanding that it take a different, more pedagogical form.

The long-run failure of the Nièvre *colonie* also shows us how the protection of childhood, and ideas of child development and hygiene, were
bound up with ideas about nature and the countryside in this era of
steady industrial and urban development. Among other things, this suggests that the right had no monopoly on anxieties over the long-term
significance of this sea-change for the physical health and emotional
equanimity of the nation. On the left, however, the reflection on a disappearing countryside and its relationship to the life of urban France,
constructed through the *colonie de vacances,* occurred without recourse
to any notion of effecting a return to the land; rather, the hope was to
give the child a living link to the land that would remain a resource to
him or her throughout a life of urban labor.

The question "in what did the ruralism of interwar Socialists consist,"
posed earlier in this chapter, might thus be answered in one word: hygiene. That is to say, the vision of the countryside that unveils itself in this
Socialist *colonie* that made the seemingly archaic decision to place its children with peasant families is in a fact a sturdily unromantic and hygienic
one, where the children left the city for reasons of health and physiological development alone. Their placement, in a de-Christianized and
solidly Socialist rural district, was garnished by no Virgilian discourse
about the lessons these children would learn by following the plough, and
without any romantic illusions about said families, who were selected
and surveilled by the two-pronged control of the Enfants Assistés and the
city's Municipal Commission. In this relationship, the peasants emerge
as citizens of the Republic like any others. Neither the salvation nor
the damnation of France, these ordinary French men and women were
drawn into a network of relations with the city, and with modern preventive medicine, via the Enfants Assistés and Suresnes's *colonie* in the

Nièvre. The one corner of this policy that maintained a certain romantic tendency is found in the Socialists' Rousseauean presumption that a "natural" link, both emotional and physical, binds healthy child development to nature and the countryside: "The *colonies de vacances* . . . respond to that aspiration that lies dormant in every child's imagination: to travel, to be transported to an unknown land, a land of dreams, where one enjoys complete freedom from morning to night, to roam through the forest and over the mountains, where he can fill his hands with wild fruit and eat until he is sated." [132] But all these riches were there as a supplement to the city, where it was presumed these children would live out their adult lives.

By the end of World War II, however, the hour of the *colonie* by family placement had well and truly passed. Hence, with the Liberation came the Communist Party's accession to local power, and one of its very first initiatives was to replace the Nièvre *colonie* (badly weakened by the trials of the Occupation) with a collective *colonie* at Bourdelas, in the Haute-Vienne, purchased in the winter of 1947. In the interim, Mayor Paul Pagès cobbled together solutions that mixed group living with family placement in the Mayenne and Manche for the spillover. But the 1946 propaganda for the city's renovated *colonie municipale* leaves little doubt as to the new pedagogical direction being established:

> Armed with the experience of last year and profiting from a longer preparation period, we have been able to better organize the 1946 holidays of our little ones. A boarding facility in the little town of Sable (Sarthe) and three boarding facilities in the town of Aurillac (Cantal) can take in 520 children. Far be it from us to criticize family placement. Last year the peasants of the Mayenne and Manche did a wonderful job taking in the little Suresnois. Nonetheless, it is collective *colonies* that both children and parents prefer, for the latter are thus assured that they are placing their children in the most reliable material and moral conditions. While awaiting the establishment of a permanent *colonie municipale*—a goal that we will realize as soon as circumstances permit—the decision to rent several boarding facilities will allow us to organize collective *colonies* under the direct supervision of municipal directors.

Following the practice established in Communist municipalities over the interwar years, and especially in the Popular Front period, Pagès established the Oeuvre des Vacances Enfantines de Suresnes. But the new administration did not fully cut the ties with Socialist precedent in

Suresnes; on the contrary, Pagès drew on both the ideology of local solidarity and the network of benefactors patiently built up over the course of Henri Sellier's long tenure in the *mairie:*

> We have just established the Oeuvre des Vacances Enfantines de Suresnes, which . . . will allow us to achieve the maximum in this realm.
>
> Regular Society membership cards cost 20 fr.; anyone who wishes to contribute more substantially to the fund established by the city for the Oeuvre des Colonies will receive honorary and benefactor membership cards.
>
> To restore our children to a perfect state of health, to make them forget, physically and morally, the years of privation, this is a goal which brings all Suresnois together. In the orbit of the great Oeuvre de l'Enfance we are sure to find only persons of goodwill who, like us, are concerned with the happiness of our little ones, future of our nation . . . Our *colonie* is open to all the children of Suresnes aged 7 to 14."
>
> signed, Paul Pagès, Mayor [133]

If the future belonged to the *colonie éducative,* traces of its recent ancestor remained in the funding structure and local significance of the *colonie* as a project of municipal solidarity. Henri Sellier did not live to see the transformation, for in November 1943, after two periods of imprisonment under Vichy, then Nazi orders, the ailing mayor passed away. His beloved Nièvre *colonie,* dogged by material difficulties that had mounted without interruption since the fall of 1939, quietly died a few months later, as parents recalled from the Nièvre children who no longer found shelter from the privations of war in a countryside that lay entirely under German occupation.

CHAPTER FIVE

❧ *Les Lendemains Qui Chantent*

SOCIAL MOVEMENTS AND PEDAGOGICAL

INNOVATION IN THE COLONIES DE VACANCES

DURING THE POPULAR FRONT

Popular memory locates the origins of the *colonies* at the time of the Popular Front, 1936–38. Yet as we have seen, the movement traces its roots back to the early 1880s, when private charity and then the public primary schools began sending small groups of poor and undernourished schoolchildren to spend a few weeks restoring their health in the good clean air of the French countryside. By the summer of 1913, over 100,000 children were spending their school holidays on peasant farms or in purpose-built *colonie de vacances* villas in the countryside or by the sea; twenty years later (1932), over 320,000 children would leave the narrow, smoky streets of industrial France each summer to spend their holidays *en colonie.*[1]

On the eve of the Popular Front victory, then, the *colonie de vacances* had already assumed a significant place in the lives of French children, particularly those of the urban popular classes. And yet the tendency of people to link the *colonies* to the Popular Front is not without significance, for these years did constitute an important moment in their development. "Never before had the *colonies de vacances* been so visible in French society," writes Pascal Ory of the years 1936–37.[2] For alongside a sharp increase in the sheer numbers of children sent, the Popular Front years saw a full-scale redirection of the national *colonie* movement away from earlier, hygienic preoccupations toward a more fully pedagogical orientation.[3] Hence, at the very moment when the *colonies* received a nationwide public statute (via their first comprehensive state regulation, issued by Minister of Health Henri Sellier on 18 June 1937) and unprecedented financial assistance, popular education militants turned their energies to the *colonies de vacances,* collaborating with the ministers of health, sport, and education to establish the Centres d'Entraînement aux Méthodes d'Education Actives, or CEMEA: the first pedagogical institute organized to educate the educators in *colonies de vacances.*[4]

Created in the spring of 1937 to organize a more democratic diffusion of cultural activity, the CEMEA immediately set about organizing training programs for *moniteurs* and directors of *colonies.* With its strong leftist and Popular Front orientation, the CEMEA rapidly became the training ground for *moniteurs* across a broad range of secular *colonies:* Socialist, republican, and Communist alike. It thus became the institutional framework within which a host of theories and practices drawn from the scout movement and from the pedagogical work of theorists associated with the international movement for *l'éducation nouvelle* were diffused rapidly throughout the expanding network of *colonies* and *patronages laïques.* The CEMEA's choice of object was no accident, for the *colonies* held great potential as sites of popular education and pedagogical innovation. Here, one could realize an innovative program for the harmonious education of the whole child (versus the narrowly intellectual "bourrage de crâne" of the republican school), grounded in the new, "active" pedagogies of Célestin Freinet, Roger Cousinet, and Maria Montessori, among others.[5] Such methods had been rigorously excluded from the curricula of state-supported normal schools, and so found little echo in the public primary schools of the late Third Republic.[6] Activists thus turned to the *colonies de vacances,* for though often linked to the schools via the *caisses des écoles,* they lay well outside the formal grip of pedagogic tradition in France. By 1946, popular education militant André Lefèvre could justly claim that "over the past few years, the *colonie de vacances* is without a doubt the single French institution that has realized a conclusive educational reform."[7]

It was during the Popular Front, then, that the *colonies de vacances* first laid decisive claim to a distinctive place on the French pedagogical landscape. The timing of this shift should not surprise us, for by the mid-1930s the educational side of the colonies' dual nature as institutions of preventive hygiene and popular education was notably in the ascendant. This shift owed in part to the steadily diminishing urgency of the hygienic motive, as improvements in public health over the 1920s opened space for a more properly pedagogical use of the *colonies.* As tuberculosis slightly loosened its deathly grip on the child population of urban France, then, the repressed educational impulse, hitherto relegated to secondary status in all but the Catholic *colonies,* rose swiftly to the fore.[8] This is not to say that the hygienic aspect disappeared altogether; rather, it was folded into a larger pedagogy of child leisure aimed at the harmonious development of the entire child, an education of both body and mind that was achieved through physical activities that were meant to engage the social, ethical, and rational/strategic aspects of the child's intelligence as well.

This pedagogical turn was further reinforced by the widespread rejection of family placement in interwar France, a rejection whose roots lay less in the perceived inadequacies of peasant hygiene (this complaint would be far more widely aired in the 1940s) than in a broad agreement among organizers that genuine educational action could not happen inside the intimate and hierarchical structures of the family, even an adoptive, part-time family. Rather, such action demanded the neutral and egalitarian structures of the *colonie,* where children lived, learned, and played in a band of peers, watched over and directed by the disinterested force of the *colonie* staff and director.[9] Finally, with the arrival of Léon Blum's Popular Front government, in June of 1936, the *colonies de vacances* found themselves at the heart of a leftist popular education movement that promoted the adoption of the innovative pedagogical strategies proposed by the international movement for a new pedagogy based on active, child-centered methods. Under the aegis of the Popular Front's democratic cultural politics, *colonies* of all stripes would work overtime to develop and define that particular pedagogical surplus-value that only they could deliver during the long months of the summer holiday.

The rise of the educational colonie thus seems almost overdetermined in the 1930s. For even in the most resolutely hygienicist circles of the *colonie de vacances* movement—those doctors and public health specialists gathered in the Comité National des Colonies de Vacances—activists had begun to show a certain interest in the educational side of the *colonies* during the late 1920s.[10] Hence, alongside the traditional subjects generally aired at the Comité's annual congresses—reports on tuberculosis rates, the vaccination of *colons,* or the old debate over collective versus family placement—participants were now offering papers that addressed matters of pedagogy, generally through the oblique lens of "discipline" or "moral education." By the end of the decade, the Comité's reigning experts on these subjects were all recommending that the *colonies de vacances* embrace their tremendous potential as sites of moral education by adopting techniques drawn from the *laïque* wing of the scout movement, the Eclaireurs de France.[11]

On the strength of its claim to function as an educational institution, able to provide a kind of social education that lay outside the scope of the primary school, the *colonie de vacances* began to trickle steadily upward toward the middle classes.[12] This upward trajectory was surely assisted by the *colonies'* steady movement away from their earlier, hygienic orientation, tinged as it was by the taint of social assistance, toward the more "modern" educational *colonie,* whose distinctive pedagogical mission was defined and pursued with especial vigor by popular education militants in the 1930s. The municipalization of *colonies de vacances,* especially pronounced in the interwar *banlieues rouges,* also contributed substantially to this transformation from charitable work of social assistance to official institution of mass education and leisure. Throughout the interwar period, the municipalization of *colonies de vacances* proceeded in tandem with their growing identification as a prime site of popular education. These two, parallel trends further valorized the educational *colonie* by comparison with its humble, hygienic ancestor, as we will see when we turn to the case of Ivry-sur-Seine.

But first we must explore the process by which the *colonies de vacances* completed their transformation from institutions of preventive hygiene to institutions of popular education and mass leisure for the children of the popular classes. Let us begin with the institutions of that transformation, and with the various pedagogies of play that constituted its essence—from the adventures of medieval chivalry that marked the camps and *colonies* of interwar Catholics, to the leftist *républiques enfantines,* organized around the children's participation in the organization of their own "toy republic." For if the ambition to harness children's ludic energies to the business of learning was not the exclusive property of the *colonies de vacances,* it was here that such pedagogies found their fullest expression in France. After all, not only were such techniques excluded from the republican school, but the various youth movements which might have formed an alternative site of application were, apart from the scouts, numerically quite weak in interwar France—at their peak, the communist Pionniers enrolled some 1,000 children (1935), while the Socialist Faucons Rouges briefly soared to 2,000 during the Popular Front, before falling back to some 200 to 400 members at the end of the decade.[13] The pedagogies of the Faucons Rouges and Communist Pionniers thus found their most consistent application in the Socialist and Communist

municipalities of interwar and 1950s France, where adolescent and young
adult *moniteurs* applied the principles of these youth movements in the
colonies and *républiques enfantines* organized for the children of the Paris
red belt.[14]

Pedagogies of Play and the Renewal of
Popular Education in France

At the center of the *colonies'* claim to deliver a distinctive, holistic, and
child-centered education lay the question of children's play, which by the
early twentieth century had become the object of scientific research and
philosophical speculation in both Europe and the United States. In an
era when the modes and activities of child life were drawing sustained
scrutiny from physiologists and psychologists, pedagogues and philosophers, children's play stepped forth as *the* distinctive and defining activity
of childhood. "[It] appears to be the natural mode of child life, the mode
by which the function of childhood is realized," wrote Catholic pedagogue Elia Perroy. "For the game is all at once a means of acquisition [of
particular skills], of adaptation and expression . . . The child plays because
he is a child, and he is a child because he plays.[15] Here, perhaps, lay the key
to understanding that gulf of physiological and cognitive difference that
distinguishes children from adults. Moreover, achieving a better understanding of the function that games play in the psychological and bodily
development of children would surely aid pedagogues in grasping the
process of human development that, properly guided, unfolds to bridge
that gulf of difference.[16]
   The fascination with children's games, with their urge to play, and
with the seriousness and wholehearted engagement with which children
throw themselves into their games gave rise to sustained inquiry into the
principles that organize the visibly distinct ways in which animals, children, and adults play.[17] The systematic observation of children at play, in
turn, enriched considerably a host of scientific research (and speculation)
into the origins and development of human society, organized around the
famous dictum that ontogeny recapitulates phylogeny. For in the games
and ritualized practices of child society, the larger culture saw, or thought
it saw, its own collective progress from savage past to civilized present
recapitulated.[18] But the studies of children playing together also put new
flesh onto the old dream of educating children through games, of captur-

ing that unique energy and engagement that surges forth in children as they play, and harnessing it to the labor of learning. The varied range of "active methods" that emerged from this effort stood at the heart of the movement for an *éducation nouvelle* that blossomed throughout Europe and the United States after the turn of the twentieth century.[19]

The movement to renew education through child-centered and "active" methods found uneven expression across the map: where Britain and the United States sought to apply the new techniques in the classroom, the pedagogical experts of France's Third Republic sternly rejected play-centered pedagogies as incompatible with the work of learning.[20] Yet the rejection of play as a method of intellectual instruction by no means signified a lack of interest in the educative value of games; on the contrary, French pedagogues and philosophers remained convinced of, and fascinated by, the centrality of games to the moral and physiological development of children. The simultaneous valorization of educational play and its exclusion from the primary school placed games and the new pedagogies constructed around them squarely at the heart of a realm that would (by the 1950s) come to be known as the *périscolaire:* institutions like the *patronages* and *colonies de vacances* that stood on the fringes of the republican and parochial schools, and were intended to promote the health, welfare, and education of school-aged children, especially in poorer neighborhoods. By the mid-1930s, then, militants in France's blossoming popular education movement would seize on the *colonie* as *the* privileged terrain of pedagogical experiment. At its center stood that unknown being, "the child," an object of inquiry whose propensity to play constituted the high road to understanding and accessing his or her innermost being. After all, as one Catholic *colonie* director reminded his colleagues, "It is through the game that the child reveals himself as he truly is, with all his qualities and defects: what a marvelous field of *observation* and *action!*"[21] As we will see, this voyage of discovery would reveal not only the child, in all his or her difference from the adult, but the polysemous nature of the words *play* and *game,* as psychopedagogues wrestled with the questions of what it is children learn through play, the role of fantasy (versus reason) in educational play, and where those acts of learning fall on a work-play spectrum that in some theorists' minds was clearly conceived as a continuum.

But how did play-centered pedagogies actually make their way into the interwar *colonies de vacances*? The question may seem naïve, for the connection between play-centered pedagogies and children's summer holidays seems an obvious one. Yet reconstructing the pathways by which these pedagogies first arrived in the *colonies* reveals the particular ideological baggage with which such pedagogies were freighted in interwar France. Largely consigned to the margins of the republican school, play-centered methods were seized upon by educators in Catholic, Socialist, and Communist educational milieux. Now the term *play* turns out to have meant rather different things to Catholic versus Socialist or Communist educators. But all shared a common conviction that games were where children revealed themselves "as they were," unselfconsciously opening a window onto their moral strengths and weaknesses, their innermost hopes and fears. The main site on which these pedagogies first found widespread application were the various scout movements of interwar France. Here young adult troop leaders received a hands-on apprenticeship in the play-centered pedagogies of scouting. Indeed, it is fair to say that the various youth and scout movements in France constituted a veritable hothouse of experimentation in the application of active, child-centered methods to a project of education that lay outside the formal realm of the school. As such, their methods were ideally suited for application in the *colonies de vacances,* and directors of *colonies* began appropriating scout techniques and applying them in their *colonies* from the early 1930s on. Well before the birth of the CEMEA, then, the *colonies* were already building their distinctive pedagogical method through selective borrowing from the scout toolkit.

In many ways, then, the Popular Front creation of the CEMEA represented the culmination of processes that were already in motion. An exploration of the pedagogical turn in the *colonies de vacances* must therefore begin with the notions of play and child development being deployed by the various scout movements in pre–Popular Front France, from the Catholics' Scouts de France and Guides de France, to the *laïque* Eclaireurs and Eclaireuses de France (as well as the confessional, Protestant, and Jewish branches that split off from the original Eclaireur tree), to the several "Red Scout" movements of Socialist and Communist origin. Each of these drew its coherence as a movement from its own distinctive and overarching worldview that linked a particular understanding of human and child nature with a vision of society as it is or as it might be. In each case, pedagogical method formed the bridge that would traverse the gulf between individual nature and a vision of the collectivity. In terms of method and technique, the different forms of scouting shared a great deal with each other, and with the international movement for *éducation nouvelle:* an emphasis on the importance of concrete experience, versus abstract discourse, in children's learning process, and a common conviction that the game constitutes a privileged arena for learning, thanks to its status as spontaneous and universal childhood activity. As such, each particular brand of scouting exerted enormous influence in shaping the dawning pedagogical agendas of interwar *colonies de vacances,* Catholic and republican, Socialist and Communist alike.

The common conviction of the centrality of games directs our attention to another shared element among these politically and ideologically divergent *scoutismes:* their underlying belief that the child's mind is no simple tabula rasa, awaiting external impression (though traces of this associative psychology remain quite visible in the scout pedagogies of experience) but is, rather, hard-wired for certain kinds of knowledge—language acquisition, to be sure, but also an understanding of morality and justice—which will prosper along predictable developmental pathways and express themselves symbolically in children's play. Scout pedagogies of play all sought to render that symbolic expression real, to make of the game a terrain on which the child experienced a real activity, and made real ethical and technical choices in the social context of the *grand jeu à thème.* Hence, what divided scout pedagogies in this era—e.g., whether a particular pedagogue was convinced of the child's fallen nature (the Catholics' Scouts de France) or original innocence ("red" scout heirs to Rousseauean conceptions of human and child nature)—was ultimately a less significant determinant in the shape of interwar scout pedagogy than their common appreciation of children's play as the key to their social and moral development.

Interwar Scouting: A Pedagogy without Pedagogues?

Early one morning in the summer of 1930, a troop of young scouts awoke in the predawn chill that clung to their camp in the mountain valley of Luz-Saint-Sauveur, high in the Pyrennees. With hasty gestures, the boys readied themselves and their camp for a day whose splendid promise announced itself in the first golden fingers of light that reached past the rocky ridges to warm the shadows of their alpine retreat. At the end of breakfast, the scoutmaster assembled them all and bade them to hush their morning chatter. Into the solemn silence, he began to recite from the sixty-fourth strophe of the *Chanson de Roland:*

Roland the Count mounts on his destrier.
Comes then to him comrade Olivier,
And Gerin comes, and brave Count Gerier . . .
"By heaven, I'm with you sirs!"
"And so am I," Walter the Count affirms,
"I'm Roland's man, him am I bound to serve!" . . .
[But] the twelve companions who in the rear-guard wait
Mean to give battle, and none shall say them nay.[22]

Without another word, the troop-chiefs distributed topographical maps, compasses, food supplies, and the envelopes bearing instructions for the conduct of this early medieval crusade. The boys, already divided into opposing teams, loaded their wagons and set forth on an adventure that would stretch out over a full week. The game of knightly valor had begun, with not a word from the outside, as it were, for everyone present was "inside" the game from the start.[23]

Here lay the heart of the Scouts de France's "pedagogy of the imaginary," in which the game became a total context for the boys' lives in the camp.[24] It was a demanding context, one that required each boy to overreach himself as he strove to attain the heroic ideal that, in the scout psychology, lay at the psychic core of each of them. The *grand jeu scout* would (in theory) allow each and every one to externalize his ideal onto a plane that lay midway between internal ideal and external reality—the plane of the scout imaginary, where great games of Christian heroism and medieval chivalry unfolded across the forests and hilltops of 1930s France. The child's own imagination, trained on the externalization and actualization of his own internal heroic ideal, thus became the primary vehicle for a journey of moral and physical progress, organized and overseen by the scoutmasters, who plundered the literature of boyhood adventure, cowboys and indians, and most especially, of religious heroism, seeking themes that would facilitate this process of self-driven education through total engagement in an all-encompassing imaginary world where the rule of the game held unquestioned sway. For the boys and their leaders in the interwar scout movement, "a scout's life is nothing more than a great game, a festival, a perpetual joy."[25]

How did the Scouts de France develop this particular psycho-pedagogy of preadolescent boyhood? In what ways did their specific use of the game link up with other play-centered pedagogies current in interwar France? And how did the specifically scout version influence the peda-

gogical turn in *colonies de vacances* of the mid-1930s? We have already
seen that by the early twentieth century, Catholic *patronages* and *colonies de vacances* had developed an elaborate set of "active methods," built
around games, gymnastics, and theater as a means to realizing their
moral, religious, and educational mission to re-Christianize the children
of the urban working class. Hence, when the English-born scout movement finally made its journey from British shores to French during the
immediate prewar period (1909–11), it would arrive in a context where
games already held pride of place in the battery of Catholic pedagogical
techniques.

Yet the mainstream Church would not be the first to make use of
Baden-Powell's invention; that honor would fall to the social Catholic
activists organized around Marc Sangnier's Sillon. Always on the look-
out for new methods by which to expand and deepen their often thank-
less ministry to the "heathen" working class, those priests who were running *patronages* and *colonies de vacances* in urban working-class districts
turned a hungry eye across the Channel and inspected with great interest Baden-Powell's new techniques for working with young boys and
(somewhat later) girls.[26] By the winter of 1911, a group of priests and Protestant pastors with urban missions to the people had organized the first
troops of the *laïque* Eclaireurs de France, from which the Protestant sections would split off the following spring (May 1912) to form their own
national organization, the Eclaireurs Unionistes de France.[27]

For their enthusiastic reception of techniques of moral education first
grown on Protestant soil, the social Catholic fringe received the hearty
condemnation of the French hierarchy, which, in the decade before the
war, was recoiling ever more sharply from a hated Republic that had,
in a few short years, visited upon them the horrors of disestablishment
and church-state separation. In this inward turn upon itself, the French
hierarchy aligned itself firmly behind Pius IX's condemnation of modern ideas and "rationalism," that deadly faith which animated the enemies of religion. This turn entailed abrupt rejection of Marc Sangnier's
Sillon and social Catholicism more broadly, movements of outreach to a
de-Christianized people which, in this era of retreat into self-defensive
orthodoxy, were tarred by the brush of "tolerance" for the heterodox and
even atheist attitudes encountered in the working-class districts where
such social Catholic activists lived and worked. For as the upholders
of orthodoxy well knew from the bitter experience of the eighteenth
century, "tolerance" in an age when religion was under sustained at-

tack was merely a trojan horse for Freemasonry and the progressive de-Christianization of the faithful. The Sillon's nascent youth movement, the secular Eclaireurs de France, was thus condemned by the French hierarchy as bearing a "suspicious cosmopolitanism," marked as it was by compromise with and accommodation to the secular spirit of the hated Republic.[28] Many dioceses, including that of Paris, went so far as to forbid scouting to all faithful sons of the Church, threatening to refuse communion, and even banish from the Church all who joined in the suspect movement. Catholic scouting as such would only take shape in the aftermath of the war, whose deep sacrifices, levied on the entire population, narrowed appreciably the prewar rift between Catholic France and the nation.[29]

Whether laïque or Catholic, Protestant or Jewish, aimed at boys or girls, the scout movement in France shared and elaborated one key element of the Baden-Powell legacy: that the most effective way to shape a child was to engage his or her imagination in a task of moral and physical self-construction which unfolded inside a story, a story that each one lived over the course of the scout camp.[30] This technique rested on a psychology of the boy-child that saw him as inhabiting a world that was completely distinct from that inhabited by adults: "Boys have a world of their own, a world they create for themselves, and neither the schoolteacher nor his lessons have any place in it. The boys' world has its own calendar of events, its own code and scale of values, its own lingo and its own public opinion."[31] The profound anti-intellectualism of Baden-Powell's vision (which smacks of Thomas Arnold's public school elitism, vaunting the extroverted energy of boy athletes over the neurotic and effeminate child who hunched, pale and anemic, over bookish preoccupations) was immediately toned down in French Catholic educational milieux, where deeply held convictions about a balanced education that addressed "simultaneously" the mind, body, and soul were the fruit of long experience in running schools, patronages, and colonies de vacances.[32] But the foundational precept, that the child inhabits a distinct and inner world, survived the cross-cultural translation and was intensively cultivated by the first generation of French Scout and Guide leaders. "The boy lives a secret life on the margins of real life," wrote scoutmaster Pierre Delsuc in 1930. "And this secret life of his is far more precious to him than our adult reality. Scouting will never make its mark on the boy unless it succeeds in identifying itself with his inner aspirations; identifying its own organization with the inner ideal that the child longs for. In this

fashion, the child's secret life, hitherto purely imaginary, gets exteriorized onto the plane of tangible reality."[33] Unlike the leftist movements
of Pionniers and Faucons Rouges, where adult leaders sought to minimize children's marginality by integrating them more fully into life on
adult terms, the Catholic Scouts made the child's marginal status into the
basis of an alternative pedagogy that unfolded in a parallel universe built
from the riches of the child's imagination: "The surest way to win over
the child's turbulent interior aspect is to seize hold of that intimate circle
[of friends] within which he so readily takes refuge. How should this be
done? Quite simply, we must offer him a structure that so pleases him
that he will identify that structure with his secret life. As a consequence,
the source of all his enthusiasms will become accessible."[34]

This same psychological precept was extended to girls by Guidemovement founder and ideologue Marie Diémer, who adapted scouting to French and female life through the creation of a distinctly female
story, that of Jeannette and the Blue Forest, "that marvelous land which is
woven of dreams—yet also real—where sweet young girls live and enjoy
themselves."[35] In Diémer's foundation tale, the young shepherdess Jeannette (meant to be an ordinary young girl, and yet the reference to that
other, heroic shepherdess Jeanne d'Arc, comes through loud and clear),
is peacefully watching her sheep in a meadow on the edges of the mythic
forest when she spies a merry band of young girls, dancing rounds in the
Blue Forest. Jeannette's progress to join the magic circle in the forest is
marked by obstacles to be overcome (a fatiguing journey, fording rivers,
and the like) and ethical choices at key moments, for example, when her
determination to join the circle of girls dancing in the forest conflicts with
loyalty to her faithful sheepdog, who cannot cross the river on his own,
and whom she refuses to leave behind.[36] Diémer later explained that she
created the Blue Forest for her girls, rather than imitating the Kiplingesque jungle themes so dear to Baden-Powell's imperial heart, because
it constituted a symbolic space that was true to French myth and social
reality: "The Blue Forest . . . truly exists in each of our provinces."[37]

In the Scout/Guide psychology, then, the child was seen as almost pure
interiority, a small being who inhabits a dream world whose ideals cannot
be reconciled with adult reality. In Pierre Delsuc's view, consciousness
of this fact generally drives the child to close inward upon himself, as he
loses hope in all but his inner world, "a new world that he organizes to
fit his dreams, to give them outlets for expression. Like a prisoner in a
dungeon cell, deprived of all contact with the exterior world, the child

escapes in his spirit and roams freely in the delightful gardens of fancy."[38] The scout technique was to reach the child by making that inner dream world an external reality, that is, by constructing the scout experience as one long game in which the child was invested totally.

Scoutmasters were advised to devote some time to setting the stage for this experience, assembling the troop and then spinning them a tale — the Song of Roland, or a band of wild "redskins" attacking the wagons of gold-rush-fevered pioneers — that would serve as a general theme for the great adventure of the imagination that they would live and play together. Then came the crucial step in negotiating the relationship between external reality and the inner lives of boys: the scoutmaster was to explain carefully the rules that would define and govern the game: "*In this fashion, the scoutmaster brings the tale he has just told into the realm of tangible reality.* This achievement, outcome of a rather weak means [storytelling], has no real-world impact. But the boys attribute reality to this adventure of their dreams, and they ready themselves to become heroes."[39] By projecting the story into the three-dimensional spaces of nature, and providing the narrative frame for its unfolding therein, the rules of the game projected the life of individual imagination onto the plane of lived reality.

Scouting thus invited the child to venture forth from his private inner world of fantasy through a pedagogy that rested on externalizing those fantasies onto a plane that lay midway between fantasy and reality. Camped in a wilderness of forest and mountain crag, nature constituted the principle of implacable reality upon which the scoutmasters unleashed their young charges' energies in carefully orchestrated games of heroic exploit: "Offer to him this world of which he dreams. Give him this child-sized universe where he can move about in freedom ... Let us therefore work to identify the boy's secret world with his patrol ... for in this happy society, things are tailored to his level, and his will proves adequate to the task of provoking reactions therein of which he will be proud or ashamed."[40]

Proponents of scouting based their claim to pedagogical efficacy on what they believed was a more accurate appreciation of the social and psychic realities of child life, not only children's urge to play but their tendency to form themselves into small bands. This latter tendency was believed to arise from the child's acute awareness of his own powerlessness: "Feeling more acutely the need to rely on the support of others, the child is more subject to the gregarious, gang instinct than the adult,

hence the interest of the patrol system," wrote Abbé Gaston Courtois in
his 1938 manual, which adapted scout techniques to the rather different settings of *patronage* and *colonie de vacances*.⁴¹ On this child-centered
base was built a structure that harnessed the natural energies and inclinations of children in a project of collective self-construction. The patrol
of six to eight children, with a young leader chosen from among them
by the scoutmaster or *cheftaine* but with the patrol's consent, was thus a
compromise between the military unit (order) and the gangs that arise
spontaneously among children who play together (nature). This patrol
constituted an autonomous unit within a larger hierarchy (patrol, troop,
district group, regional group, etc.) and was expected to devise its own
name, rallying cry, sign, and traditions: "We must conceive of the patrol
as an organized yet free society, and leave it to the greatest extent possible in the hands of the boys who compose it. Aided by the patrol chief,
the scoutmaster's task is, above all, to lead his members to seek after
the good. He is never more clever than at the moment where he sets a
good idea in motion, and then manages to attribute its authorship to
the boys."⁴² The troop thus constituted a sociopolitical order that combined hierarchy (and subtle manipulation on the part of the scoutmaster
to disguise that fact) with more democratic principles of mutual assistance. In the best of circumstances, it was hoped that this combination
would allow for a subtle dynamic between liberty and constraint, self-
education and a more directed apprenticeship, individual action and collective dynamics.⁴³ Within this structure, the scoutmaster or *cheftaine* was
intended to serve less as chief than as teacher and *animateur,* imparting the techniques of topographical orientation, woodcraft, and outdoor
cooking that would be put to the test in the camp, and explicating the
themes of the game within whose rules and narrative logic the great scout
voyage of the imagination would unfold.

Scout movement theorists and practitioners celebrated scouting as a
practical application of the precepts aired by Maria Montessori, Edouard
Claparède, and Ovide Decroly in the movement for an *éducation nouvelle,* not only in its adoption of the child's needs and character as the basis
of instruction (versus some abstract syllabus of knowledge to be imparted
from on high), but in its deployment of games as the core pedagogical
technique: "The supreme usefulness of the game, so well understood by
the Active School . . . has received its full application in Scouting. All
the hidden corners of the adolescent self are exploited therein in order to
construct his full personality: sensory education, technical training, the

instinct for organized groups, and for leadership, obedience to a chief who has been freely recognized, and, finally, the cooperative instinct."[44] The scout method further approached *éducation nouvelle* in its baseline conviction that all children can learn, on condition that they are enlisted as active participants in that process. Without that engagement, the educator ran the risk that the child would simply dig in his heels in stubborn resistance, or simply withdraw into his lonely inner dungeon-cell. The scout solution was to allow this education to begin within the familiar circle of the child's own little community of peers, the patrol.

Finally, scout pedagogy, like *éducation nouvelle,* emphasized the immediate practical application in the camp of the techniques that children spent so many hours learning in their weekly troop meetings. Gathered in the chuch basements that housed many a scout troop, the children passed the long months of winter mastering the arts of map reading, morse code signaling, and tracking through the woods, techniques that a well-designed *jeu à thème* would be sure to demand of its players: "This game will have no end," wrote Pierre Delsuc. "It continues without interruption, with moments that are more or less animated. Every player joins in the direction of the camp and plays an important role therein . . . Thus we give to boys a large sphere of responsibility in managing affairs within their patrol, and, eventually, in the troop as well . . . After all, as Lord Baden-Powell put it, 'boys are best educated through taking on responsibility.' "[45] The scout game thus combined the imaginative lives of children with a real physical landscape of hills and forests, and so offered a concrete space in which the child made his journey of moral progress, with his own imagination as the primary vehicle of that progress. And yet the interwar organization of the Scouts de France around the notion of the child as a pure interiority that can be mobilized only through appeals to the imagination elevated the sensible and imaginary aspect of the child's intelligence at the expense of the rational: "Does [scouting] not take the scouts out of their ordinary, daily preoccupations in order to place them in a new world?" mused Pierre Delsuc. "Does it not present itself as a series of intellectual images that are wholly distinct from the normal range?"[46] After all, the sole tie that bound each individual imagination to the life of the troop was the theme of the game, offered by the scoutmaster. For the boys, at least, this fine thread of imaginative creation would suffice, for as scout psychology would have it, the imaginary world of the game was more real for young boys than reality itself: "Bound up with their imaginative lives, the theme of the game has nothing imaginary about it. On the contrary, the game draws its interest and originality from its own vibrant reality."[47] At times it seemed as if the interwar leaders of the Scouts de France were prepared to abandon altogether the Church's interest in the rational side of human character in favor of this self-construction through imaginary games. It was as if they wished to make of scout pedagogy an absolute counterworld to the insistent rationalism of the secular and republican school, and so isolate these young Christians from the society around them.

The Catholic scouts thus defined a particular approach to child psychology and the pedagogy of games, an approach that is both odd and fascinating, with one foot in modernity (their carefully thought out, child-centered pedagogy that was explicitly linked to the Active School) and the other on some windswept plain of twelfth-century crusader heroics. The secular Eclaireurs and Eclaireuses de France stopped short of such a total investment in the inner imaginative depths of the child, deploying games and developing wilderness skills as a means to an educational end, that of teaching the child to participate actively and constructively in the social and civic life around him. The Protestant Eclaireurs et Eclaireuses Unionistes and the Jewish Eclaireurs et Eclaireuses Israélites also shared this more moderate, civic and socially oriented pedagogy of games. The national commissioner of the Eclaireurs Unionistes, Jacques Guérin-Desjardins, thus vaunted scouting as "a pedagogy of character building, a game," a method that was "a triumph of adaptation to the child."[48] By sharing the child's life in camp or *en colonie,* the scout leader gained a precious "moral ascendancy" over the child. Yet the glue that held it all together was not the imaginative lives of children but the life of the actual "child community of scouts," where the child learned through experience the value and use of his liberty in constructing a functional collective and civic life: "It is only by experiencing the necessity of the law that the adolescent gains an autonomous moral sense," intoned Guérin-Desjardins in the late 1930s.[49]

Here we confront one of scouting's strongest claims to recognition as a pedagogy of child leisure, and that is its efficacy as a technique for building community among children — civic and rational, for the Eclaireurs; mystical, heroic, and backward looking for the Catholic Scouts and Guides de France. On the strength of this claim alone, scout techniques would spread rapidly to *colonies de vacances* from the mid-1920s on, as Catholic and secular *colonies* began hiring young veterans of the scout movement to serve as *moniteurs* and provide a precious *animation* for children who, it was feared, were being left far too much to their own devices with no real, thought-out program of activities.[50] Hence, at the very moment when programs from across the political and ideological spectrum were taking stock of the great educational potential and actual educational deficiency in most of their *colonies,* the first generation of youth to have passed through the scout movement providentially stepped forth, with tested skills in woodcraft, camping, and fireside storytelling that passed easily from one context to another. Eager to provide their programs with greater pedagogical direction and internal social coherence, the directors of *colonies* seized on these skilled young educators, whose stock of songs, crafts, and games provided the *colonie* with a ready-made structure of educational activities that promised to keep the wolf of idleness far from the *colonie* doors.

The Eclaireurs' deployment of the scout pedagogy of games thus plunged less deeply into the imaginative depths of the child. Indeed, the Eclaireurs seem to have based their pedagogic action on a less autistic and asocial conception of the child. Hence, rather than envisioning the child collectivity as an atomistic group of young beings, each locked inside the separate "dungeon" of his or her own imagination, to be drawn out into some kind of social and cooperative life only by the scoutmaster's imaginative intervention (and even then, only to be engaged on the plane of the scout imaginary, rather than actual social reality), the Eclaireurs departed from the premise that the inner lives of children possess a more social and extroverted dimension. The educator was thus best advised to study child society from a more external, sociological standpoint, as Jacques Guérin-Desjardins advised his colleagues at the 1937 international congress of *colonies de vacances:*

> A *colonie de vacances* is, in fact, a child (or adolescent) "community." The young members of this community quickly constitute a society (in the sociological sense of the term), and this juvenile society presents . . . all the characteristics of an adult society: collective states of mind, the spread of a single, predominant way of life, irresistible currents of public opinion, its own scale of values and traditions, "customaries" of what is "allowed" and what is "forbidden" (this has nothing to do with the *colonie*'s official regulation), *élans* and enthusiasms that give rise to action.[51]

The notion that children are not by nature autistic but rather possess a socially oriented dimension allowed the educator to operate on the level of the collectivity, to mobilize his little society through a series of games that did not have to pass through the mythical depths of the child's innermost fantasies in order to be pedagogically effective.

As we shall see, Socialist pedagogues shared the Eclaireurs' interest in the social rather than internal and imaginative capacities of children. Yet where Socialists would use these capacities as the basis for constructing child republics based on self-government, Jacques Guérin-Desjardins hastened to point out that such child communities possess only limited capacity for self-government; the guiding hand of the adult had to be visible and active at all times:

> In the hands of a wise and moral teacher, one who understands *what he* seeks to obtain and *the manner* in which to attain it, this [community] clearly has a tremendous and productive power. On the other hand, it is hard to shake off a worrisome vision: that inexperienced people, who are, perhaps, not always motivated by the search for the child's best interest, might suddenly find themselves at the head of all these forces and incapable of regulating their flow. The myth of the Sorcerer's Apprentice comes irresistibly to mind.[52]

But if Eclaireur technique presupposed a more social, less atomized vision of the child, it nonetheless shared with its more radical Catholic neighbor a conception of pedagogy as a set of actions and structures that work to externalize the moral sense that is both innate and immanent in each child, a moral instinct whose actualization requires both the exterior action of the educator and a collective setting of peers (versus the hierarchical context of the family) in order to be effective: "Teach the child to exteriorize all the good that lies within her," wrote Anne-Marie Wenger-Charpentier in her 1933 manual. "One is shaping the child for the world."[53] As in all pedagogies of play, the emphasis is placed on actions rather than discourse, on the child's experience of those actions, and on the conclusions she or he draws therefrom, for the active methods of *éducation nouvelle* presumed that children internalized the evidence of their own experiences more easily and more naturally than the mere abstractions of moral instruction by the word. Through the activity of play, then, children could externalize the good that lies within even as they internalized the moral lessons delivered by the game. And their education began with the initial act of submitting their own wills to the collective and rule-bound structure of the game.

The entire process of moral education was thus conceived as a spontaneous unfolding of a natural endowment which, like our natural endowment for language, yearns for expression, in this case through play. Moral education through the pedagogy of games thus demanded less an adult imposition of rules than a propitious context—the child collectivity, guidance by a trained educator, the *grand jeu collectif*—within which the child's innate moral sense would unfold via the gradual emergence of a more elaborate notion of justice. The child's inner good simply could not appear of its own accord; there had to be an external stimulus from a trained educator, delivered in the appropriate context, for childhood's innate sense of justice to emerge.

Educating a "New Kind of Man":
From "Red Scouts" to *Colonies Prolétariennes*

In February of 1934, the Socialist journal *l'Aide,* aimed at the young adult *moniteurs* of the Faucons Rouges (Red Falcons) youth movement, proposed to its readers a *grand jeu* with a social theme, designed to mobilize a consciousness of class struggle among the children of the working class:

> On a storm-tossed sea, four derelict ships are battered by the waves. No one is on board; passengers and sailors have all had the time to flee, and as fires rage out of control on board, the ocean blindly hurls the deserted liners about. According to the *Code maritime,* these ocean liners become the property of whichever intrepid team manages to bring them back into port. Two steamers race through the fog hoping to seize the ocean liners whose half-destroyed sirens still send out the occasional wail.

One of the steamers is named *Coop* and belongs to a cooperative of fishermen "who all work doggedly to improve the lot of their families"; the other is called *Standard* and belongs to a powerful shipping company whose ill-paid seamen work like devils in order to fill the coffers of company stockholders: "In the storm, the two steamers approach, their crews, ears to the wind, listening for the moan of the sirens through the thickening fog . . . Slowly they approach—who will conquer the derelict ocean liners?"[54] The two teams took off across the fields in search of the ghostly galleons that were at stake in this maritime struggle, imaginatively transposed onto land.

We are clearly in a very different world from that of the *jeu scout,* despite a certain outward similarity of form. For in transposing the *grand jeu à thème* to the Socialist *république enfantine,* the adult leaders of the

Faucons Rouges (who were known as "aides," in keeping with their over-arching goal of constructing an anti-authoritarian pedagogy) had cre-ated an entirely different kind of game from the woodland adventures of Scout and Eclaireur fame. In part the divergence owes to the different kinds of qualities the "Red Scouts" hoped to stimulate in their charges, values of solidarity and mutual assistance, a love of peace and freedom.[55] But it also rose from the Faucons' very different understanding of child psychology, where the shape of the child's concerns and inner being were understood to derive from external, social forces, rather than inner drives. Here, the Faucons Rouges shared important common ground with the soviet pedagogies of Krupskaya, Lunacharsky, and Pistrak, where adult work with children in the movement groups (Young Pioneers) and in Pistrak's famous Ecole Lepechinsky was shaped by the conviction that it was the child's social milieu, rather than the inner depths of individual fantasy, that shaped his or her inner preoccupations. As Pistrak repeat-edly emphasized, these inner preoccupations were determined "not by the physiological properties of the developing mind but rather by the external phenomena of existence, and above all by the social relations established among men. [Children's] vital preoccupations rise from the milieu, from life, from children's inner reflections upon actual real-world events."[56]

A psycho-pedagogy in which the child's entire personality structure is understood to be driven by social rather than internal principles of development and orientation implies, of course, that there is a direct re-lation between the child's inner concerns and the shape of his or her external surroundings. From this psychological underpinning flowed a distinctly Socialist understanding of the nature and importance of the child's community to his or her emotional well-being and sociopolitical development, for only a proper organization of the surrounding society could free up the child's internal riches, hitherto blocked by the oppres-sive structures of capitalism. This was especially true within the child's own family, where the violence of capitalist exploitation had left a deep imprint on the shape of individual consciousness: "In our exploitative society it is entirely normal that the child himself also be exploited. In-side the vast majority of families, he suffers from the more or less openly admitted tyranny of the parents. Fathers and mothers were raised in an authoritarian world where they had to obey and accept pressure and vio-lence. Having bent to that discipline, they often come to believe that authority is necessary."[57]

Pedgagogical action on the individual thus began with altering the shape and structure of the immediate social milieu (school or *colonie*), and all instruction, games, and activities in children's groups had to be restructured around this fundamental link between individual well-being and the state of the collectivity.[58] This, in turn, demanded a pedagogical approach that was rooted in present-day social realities, rather than heroic dreams of days gone by, for as Faucon aide Roger Foirier remarked, "Our children's groups do not seek to isolate the child from social reality, unlike scouting, which does so through its emphasis on chivalric traditions and tales of the redskins."[59]

The Faucons Rouges' primary pedagogical form was the child's republic itself, a unique self-governing unit in which the experience of the camp was meant to provide a genuine political apprenticeship to the children of the working class. This political apprenticeship-by-experience inside the prefigurative utopia of the children's republic would, in turn, prepare the way for a larger social and political transformation.[60] As with the Scouts and Eclaireurs, the game served as the chosen pedagogical instrument, the medium through which all genuine child understanding was believed to pass. But the "game" was not just the *grand jeu* that animated the summer's activity; it was the life of the camp itself, in this case the child's republic, structured by the forms of direct democracy and by the relationships of comradeship (versus orders from on high), where children and their adult "aides" were placed on a plane of equality. Within these structures unfolded the game of the republic, where working-class children played at an ideal version of their adult life, in the as yet unrealized Socialist utopia.

> We have thus chosen as a pedagogical method a primitive way of life which, for the child, has the value of an object lesson, and which gives him the chance to personally exercise social functions, to cooperate in the common project . . . Our camps are cooperative workshops; they are consumer cooperatives administered by the Faucons themselves and on their own responsibility; they are Socialist communities in which the equal rights of all are recognized . . . where all submit to a freely accepted discipline.[61]

The democratic order of the Faucons Rouges camp was based on the tent community of ten or twelve Faucons and one to two "aides" — young adults of at least eighteen years whose presence was meant to oil a sociopolitical order that rested on the goals and desires of the children: "The children and the adults, whatever their age, whatever their sex, must be placed on a footing of absolute equality. The aide is neither a chief nor a nursemaid, she or he is a comrade, an equal."[62] The aides were there to serve the children's needs, to help them get through whatever problems arose in the course of their self-governing republic, and to serve, above all, as examples; after all, as the journal *l'Aide* never tired of reminding its readers, "the child will inevitably strive to take you as his model."[63] Adult and child thus dwelt together under the broad canvas roof of a single marabout tent, whose perfectly round borders facilitated both the egalitarian sharing of space and responsibilities and a harmonious sociability at the interior of the canvas-bound circle: "Life in the tent . . . combines play with interesting work in such a way as to develop natural initiative and an individual control in all the comrades of the tent. For in this community, one is part of a social milieu, of a concrete form of socialization; one learns to cooperate, to share, to help, to take an interest in the entire group, to adapt oneself and to rise above one's natural egocentrism and move toward the social community."[64]

Each tent had its own internal system of self-government—the "compagnon de tente" and his or her assistant, who were elected by simple majority—and all members participated as well in the larger deliberations of the republic's overall governing structure, the general assembly of children. In principle, this all happened without adult interference, for "our policy is that the Faucons assume an autonomous responsibility for all measures over which they can deliberate and decide, and all things that they are able to realize." In practice, however, the aides stood by, ready to lend a hand with issues or difficulties that might "surpass their understanding."[65] In this way the Faucons Rouges sought to put into practice the pedagogical precept, common to Socialist and Communist children's groups, that children need to exercise genuine autonomy and power in the organization of their everyday and collective life, supported by strategic assistance from their aides as needed. Socialist pedagogue Kurt Loewenstein thus emphasized that Faucon pedagogy "rests on the complete suppression of all authority of a personal nature, which also entails the abolition of all our ordinary prerogatives as adults and property owners."[66]

Loewenstein's linkage of "adults" with "property owners" directs our attention to the Socialist analysis of adult-child relationships in bourgeois society, where adult power over children was cast as the analogue of capitalist power over the proletariat. Although this analysis applied to all adults and all children, it was seen to hold especially true within the confines of the family, where the emotional fact of more intimate and highly charged relationships intertwined with the centuries-old practice of paternal authority as law: "Working-class families are ruled by authority as much as the families of the bourgeois," wrote Georges Monnet in 1933. "The parents are sovereign powers who enjoy the right to demand obedience. Even the child's curiosity is, for the most part, rebuffed; rather than responding to his questions, rather than allowing him to freely express his feelings, parents too often impose a rule of silence and immobility."[67] The inequalities of age (and sex) were thus deeply etched at the heart of even the most politically aware and active proletarian families, creating conditions of political submission for the young people who dwelt therein. Only in extrafamilial communities of peers, unobtrusively assisted by young adult aides, could children find the kind of egalitarian relationships that would allow them to exercise and develop their social and political capacities: "Our children must not remain confined to the context of the family. The child of the family must become the child of society."[68]

Yet the Faucons Rouges were well aware of the crucial affective role that the family played in child development. They thus proposed the smaller community of the marabout in order to help each child make the transition from the closed circle of the family to the freedom of society via an intermediate social form that would allow an "easy socialization of children without forcing an overly rigid separation from the affective and personal community of the family . . . [T]he life of the tent is a real, communal task to which children attach themselves with pleasure."[69] Freeing up the child's energies from the hierarchical oppressions of the family would thus redound to the benefit of both individual children and the larger society. But liberating those energies demanded a renunciation of adult power on the part of the aides, who would henceforth have to content themselves with reasoned persuasion as a means of maintaining some kind of order and sense of purpose in the child-directed republic: "In asking children to consciously assume their rightful responsibilities, we increase their confidence by making them conscious of the fact that their rights and personalities are the equal of ours. We therefore renounce all punishment and rewards, all systems of praise and distinctions."[70]

The role of the aide, then, was a delicate one. If adequately performed, it would assist the children in their political apprenticeship within the community, an apprenticeship whose benefits were reaped through the experience of organizing collectively their everyday life in its concrete forms. In the course of this apprenticeship, the children would gradually come to see and understand their common interests and needs, even as they gained a concrete experience of how to act in common to achieve their ends. The child's inner nature was, after all, a social one, shaped by external circumstances and oriented outward toward the larger society. Consequently, children were perfectly capable of taking the first step toward political organization on their own, that is, they were capable of organizing themselves into groups, especially outside the setting of school.[71] For the Scouts and Eclaireurs, with their more inward-turned vision of the child, no such confidence in the political or protopolitical capacities of children was possible; indeed, Eclaireur Unioniste chief Jacques Guérin-Desjardins went so far as to assert that children were strangers to politics, that a political child was a contradiction in terms: "There is no such thing as children who are Communists, Socialists, republicans, royalists, or fascists; children are strangers to the realities that these words convey."[72] Given this view of the child's nature, politics in the *colonie* could only arrive by indoctrination from above, as adults sought to impose on children the slogans and loyalties that derived from their own political lives. The only solution in keeping with this vision of the child's nature and interests was to ensure that all *colonies* (indeed, all spaces of children's education) be run by a strict neutrality. In the *république enfantine,* however, "politics" was the life of the child community itself, emerging in the moment, and from the experiences and conflicts that self-government generated within the child community: "We must never forget that children are not simply preparing to become members of society; they already are members of society; they already have their problems, their interests, their goals, their ideals; they are already linked to the life of adults, and to all of society."[73] Children were thus a part of life, already involved, and not languishing on its margins in autistic reverie. They were, then, and of necessity, able to organize themselves.

But if children were capable of organizing themselves, they were not able to articulate, on their own, the common interests that made their collectivity into a genuine community, that is, a group of individuals "united by a particular set of interests of which they are conscious and which are dear to their hearts." Encouraging children to make their groups into genuine communities thus required adult assistance at the level of helping children to articulate those interests which would form the real basis of organization. In order to accomplish this, the aide had to live close to the children's community without stepping all over it, to guide the

children without stifling their initiative: "We must allow the older comrade to lend an imperceptible hand in difficult cases, while orienting the
children's different tendencies in the right direction. More precisely, this
means that *we must arouse in the children concerns that are charged with
social meaning, and to enlarge and develop them, while allowing the children
themselves to discover ways to realize them.*"[74]

Even if the aide accomplished the task with appropriate delicacy, however, there was still the danger of having a community in which the forms
of self-government were present and functioning but where the children
participated in form only, where "the soul of the child is missing, and
only a small part of the child is present, a part that has almost nothing in
common with the tasks on which self-government is founded."[75] This is
where the Faucons Rouges took a special interest in the scout technique
of the *grand jeu*. For one of the great claims the scout movement made for
its *grands jeux* was their effectiveness in attaching the child more firmly
to the collectivity through the esprit de corps that was generated by the
game itself. Though critical of the militarist and imperial purposes to
which scouts turned their *grands jeux,* the Faucons Rouges were nonetheless quite taken with the pedagogical charms of the genre, seeing therein
an activity that linked physical action, "so necessary to children," to mental reflection: "We do not claim to have discovered the *grands jeux.* The
scouts have long utilized it, and the technique of the Red Falcon *grand
jeu* is, in most cases, quite close to that of the scouts." But for the Faucons,
this technique was "only a pretext, for our goal is far more ambitious: For
us, it is the theme that counts, more than the technique, it is the moral
value of the *grand jeu* rather than the *grand jeu* itself. And so, in keeping
with the principle that the child should learn something while playing,
the F.R. must be led to reflect on the game afterwards, almost in spite
of himself, so that he will draw forth, almost inadvertently, the moral of
the game just played."[76]

By offering children *grands jeux* with a social theme, such as the "great
game of the derelict ships," the Faucons Rouges sought to draw on the
benefits of the scout game, notably its extraordinary capacity to mobilize
childhood energy and devotion to a cause, while remaining faithful to
the grounding in contemporary social reality that guided Socialist pedagogy. In addition to the obvious physical benefits delivered by a cross-
country run in pursuit of the missing ships, the game offered ample scope
for the children's moral and social education in the obligatory "autocri-
tique" that followed. Here, the aide could expand upon a wide range

of topics raised by the maritime mise-en-scène: "cooperation; the life of sailors, luxury liners, fires on board said luxury liners, icebergs, etc."[77] By transforming the *grand jeu scout* into a game with a social theme, the Faucons Rouges sought to mobilize and channel the *grand jeu*'s capacity to bond individuals to the collectivity (via team spirit), while rejecting the violent and competitive content typical of scout games, where "all methods that lead to victory are permitted—lying and trickery, ambush and violence."[78]

The Faucons Rouges thus relied on the child collectivity as both context for and agent of a new kind of education that would shape an entirely new kind of citizen, an individual who, in Krupskaya's words, "will tackle every problem in a new way . . . [We must create] a new generation whose habits and attitudes toward other people will be totally different from those in the capitalist society. Building socialism does not only mean developing industries, setting up cooperatives or consolidating Soviet rule, though all that is absolutely essential; it also means remolding our psychology, reshaping our relationships."[79] With the republican school lying squarely in the hands of the state (and thus hopelessly out of reach), the community on which the Faucons set their sights was the summer-long camps and *colonies de vacances,* "the most promising pedagogical setting" for the project of transforming humanity.[80] This choice of site, with its ludic aura and fleeting, estival existence, posed acutely the question that is central to any pedagogy that rests its claims on direct, lived experience: precisely what was the relationship between the future Socialist republic of Faucons Rouges dreams and the evanescent "toy republic" being offered to their children each summer? After all, these weren't real, permanent communities, warned Loewenstein, but more like "oases" where reality itself had been "sent on vacation":

> We might call them pedagogical provinces of the sort described by Goethe in "Wilhelm Meister." Perhaps they play the same role for our children as that played by fairy tales and legends in the ideological education of children in times past. We know perfectly well that our children's republics are artificial constructs made possible only by the fact that, by means that are analogous to social assistance, we exclude from our camps everything that is connected to bourgeois and capitalist elements (financing, for example), so that we can extract the children from these influences, to a certain extent.[81]

But in a pedagogy that relied so heavily on experience, what was the true pedagogical value of a child's community—terrain of supposedly "real" social experiences—where reality itself had been "sent on vacation?" Upon further reflection, Loewenstein conceded that the child's republic was less a prefigurative community than a game in much the sense that Karl Groos had used the term—a "pre-exercise" of faculties that will only truly come into play later in life. Real, Socialist society would thus bear a wholly different aspect from life in the child's republic, which was designed simply to give children a taste for "a just and well-ordered social life," so that these words would not remain a mere abstract formula but rather become something the child had lived and experienced in the "primitive community" of the child republic: "In this way the toy republic becomes an impulse toward real socialism, and the [toy] socialism lived in the child republic becomes a powerful sentiment, filled with love and joy in the hearts of our children."[82] In the place of real socialism, then, the children would have their "toy republic" in which to try out skills like cooperation, fraternity, mutual assistance: human capacities that had grown flabby for lack of practice under centuries of capitalist domination, and on whose exercise the Socialist future depended.

In September of 1933, with the rivalries of Third Period hostility still governing relations between Socialist and Communist organizations in Europe, PCF education militants would criticize the Faucons Rouges' "showy children's republic" on precisely these grounds, underscoring the artificial and constructed nature of the so-called political life that unfolded within this hothouse setting: "One of the principal ceremonies in the camp was an election conducted according to all the democratic traditions: posters, electoral meetings, speeches . . . These elections took place in isolation from the real world, and the directors took pains to keep the children inside the framework of this artificial life." The Communists then proposed that, rather than playing at politics, children should be drawn more directly into the real-life struggles of their class: "The solidarity of French and German children of the proletariat, the vital demands of the underfed and ill-clad children of both nations, all this has been forgotten by the designers of the children's republic.[83] But if PCF theory was more internally consistent, favoring a "strict-constructionist" notion of external and adult-centered reality as the indispensable ground of pedagogical action in their *colonies de vacances,* versus the carefully constructed game of child democracy, party educational militants were much less consistent in practice. Communist *colonies* would thus oscillate between pedagogies that linked children's lives in the *colonie* to current sociopolitical realities and fidelity to the form and dynamic of the child's republic, which was adopted in Communist *colonies de vacances* across France in the late 1930s and 1940s.[84]

How, then, does one give the child the experiences she needs in order to become a class-conscious fighter? Is a summertime of political apprenticeship and *grands jeux* with social themes sufficient, or must the child be plunged into the actual struggles that mark the lives of his parents and community?[85] In other words (and more basic still), what are the experiences needed to provide a genuine education in class? How was one to reconcile the child's need to play, the by now banal proposition that play is the high road to the child's soul, the main way he learns the world, with the social reality requirement common to all Socialist pedagogies? If the Faucons Rouges tested one solution — pouring the socialist realist narrative of the derelict ocean liners into the mold of the scout *grand jeu* — Communist schoolteacher Célestin Freinet proposed an entirely different one. His solution resolved the tension between the two poles of socialist education — play and social reality — by collapsing this tension in a wholesale denial of the necessity of play to children's moral and cognitive development: "*The child has no natural need to play; she has only the need to work,* that is, the organic need to use her potential for life in an activity that is both individual and social, that has well-defined aims that are tailored to the size and possibilities of children."[86] Given a choice between real, creative action and a mere game, a healthy child — that is, one that had not been rendered dull and passive by hours of playing with "jeux haschich" (the interwar equivalent of video games) — would not even choose to play but would opt, rather, to engage in a real, productive, creative activity.[87] Though Freinet was eventually forced out of the PCF at the peak of the cold war (1953), his class-conscious tailoring of *éducation nouvelle*'s active methods to meet the needs of children from the popular classes produced techniques that were adopted wholesale in the "red" *colonies* of Communist municipalities, notably the *étude de milieu* but also the school printing press, at which children produced their own, self-edited journals.

The Faucons Rouges' *républiques enfantines* thus provided an imaginative and highly suggestive response to the key question that has always dogged Marxist educators, namely, how does one deliver an education in class to young children, who have no direct experience of labor? For if, as Marx suggested, the alienating experiences of work under capitalism are the primary school of revolution, then working-class children find themselves once again on the margins of that which is central to the adult life of their people. The Faucons Rouges turned this question around, pointing out that working-class children were already suffering acutely, and consciously, the consequences of class difference in the "crippling sense of envy and humiliation, [and] a sense of the injustice of it all" that dogged each and every one of them: "Only in adolescence, after the harsh trials of apprenticeship, does the idea of struggle, and finally of pride in one's class arise."[88] Surely this suffering proved that, even without the experience of factory labor, an understanding of class was already graven in the child's mind and spirit, an understanding that clearly began with the child's broader, everyday experiences in the milieu. Small wonder, then, that Socialist educators proposed an ideal milieu (the child republic) and a set of radically different experiences — self-government, adults who give assistance rather than orders — as a means of intervening at the psychological core of working-class childhood.[89] As Faucon aide Felix Kanitz put it: "We must emphasize the formation of primary sentiments, for children are more easily influenced by sentiment than by reason. This does not mean we should ignore the education of reason in light of sociological facts, but this latter faculty, for psychological reasons, can only develop later, and will thus reinforce the social education of the child's sentiments."[90] Clearly the work of Socialist educators had to pass by the child's emotional and affective life; indeed, this kind of "sentimental education" in class was essential if Socialist teachers were to endow with a sense of combativeness children whose spirits were darkened, beaten down by a sense of class inferiority. For the Socialist future could not be built from the weary and demoralized human material used up by industrial capitalism; only a generation of proud fighters could accomplish the task.[91]

The socialist effort to combine the advantages of scout and soviet pedagogies thus brought into the open the tension that dwells at the heart of any pedagogy of games, and that is the tension between what is out there in social reality and what kind of reality the games of children constitute. But Socialist educators were on the whole eager to apply cutting-edge pedagogical methods in their *colonies,* even though at the same time they were clearly uneasy with the deployment of imaginary objects of speculation in the mental and moral development of children. Perhaps for all their mental gymnastics, Socialist pedagogues never really shed the idea of an inner child developing through play but rather soldered it onto the idea of individual nature being socially determined. The latter was the explicit proposition on which soviet and Socialist pedagogies were based.

But the other, inner-pointed notion of the individual, in which development is an unfolding outward of innate qualities, continued to wind and in out of the Socialist vision, troubling the notion of a fully socially determined individual and producing pedagogies that oscillated between an obdurate refusal of the imagination and a quiet, implicit acceptance of this as a part of child life.

From the myth-laden encampments of the Catholic scouts to the utopian child republics of the Faucons Rouges, France's various scout movements formed the seedbed in which play-centered pedagogies tailored to the life of a child community were first developed and refined. The centrality of these various *scoutismes* to the diffusion of active, play-based methods across a broad swath of *colonies* can be seen from the briefest survey of *colonie* directors in 1930s France, whose search for techniques that might weld swiftly a diverse group of newly arrived individuals into a coherent community led them to adapt a whole range of scout methods—the division of the *colonie* into smaller teams or patrols, the widespread adoption of a *colonie* uniform, and most especially the scout pedagogy of games, crowned by the *grand jeu à thème:* "A well-planned game that is properly launched, then followed by a judicious critique, constitutes an object lesson that the child assimilates all the more easily, for, thanks to his imagination, he has personally lived it," wrote the national director of Catholic *colonies* and *patronages* in 1938.[92] Adopting the scout organization and technique would thus help to bind the child community into a cooperative whole, through the esprit de corps generated over the course of a long and intensively lived *grand jeu,* but also through scouting's homelier, everyday methods, for "games, songs, and crafts . . . help to build a single, collective soul, while developing skills and abilities in the individual child."[93]

The enthusiasm for "red" scout techniques is no less evident on the left, despite the relative weakness of these movements in France. Hence, in 1935, when the Eclaireurs and Scouts de France together enrolled some 80,000 children (and at least 130,000 by 1939), the Socialist and Communist youth movements together assembled no more than 2,000 to 3,000 children at their apogee (1936), before falling back to a few hundred members each on the eve of the Second World War.[94] Yet it was precisely the numerical weakness of the Communist children's groups and Pionniers that led PCF militants to construct its politics of childhood around the *colonies de vacances* in Communist municipalities. After all, "these *colonies,* which sometimes gather considerable numbers of children (Saint Denis sent 2,500 to its *colonies* in 1933), often do an excellent job of political agitation among the children of the locality around the *colonie.*"[95] If the Faucons Rouges and Pionniers never rallied children in huge numbers, their pedagogical ideas and practices would nonetheless shape the *colonies prolétariennes* that were the jewel in the crown of municipal social politics in the Socialist and Communist municipalities of the interwar Paris red belt.

Bringing Culture to the Masses:
The Popular Front and the Creation of the CEMEA

In the aftermath of the Liberation, journalist Juliette Pary looked back ten years to the era of the Popular Front, recalling the atmosphere of almost naïve enthusiasm in which a new generation of popular education militants embarked upon the adventure of bringing culture to the very youngest members of the *classes populaires:* "A bridge was built between grammar and the fourteenth of July, between the pedagogical demand for a living education that makes study into an exciting game, and the social demand for a forty-hour work week, between *éducation nouvelle* and "leisure." After all, the *école nouvelle* is destined not for a few wealthy children, but for the masses!"[96] The chosen site of this pedagogical revolution was the *colonies de vacances;* the instrument of said revolution was to be the CEMEA, created in the winter of 1936–37 under the enthusiastic patronage of key members in Blum's Popular Front cabinet: Jean Zay and Cécile Brunschwicg at the Ministry of Education, Henri Sellier and Suzanne Lacore at the Ministry of Public Health, and Léo Lagrange at the Ministry of Sport and Leisure.

The history of the CEMEA, their constitution as a kind of "anti-normal school" of teams of activists devoted to the broad diffusion of knowledge and culture, links them to the history of the Popular Front itself: a moment that is remembered above all for the explosion of popular hopes in the massive sit-down strikes of May–June 1936, and for the democratic politics of leisure and culture for all that formed an essential part of the Blum government's response to those hopes.[97] Popular Front efforts to democratize both leisure and culture rapidly acquired a halo of myth in public memory, due in no small part to the very romantic and mythologizing terms in which the actors themselves viewed their efforts: "I did

not often leave my ministerial office during the period of my government," recalled Léon Blum in his testimony at Riom (1941), "but each
time that I did, I crossed the huge Paris suburbs and saw the roads covered
by streams of broken-down jalopies, motorbikes, and bicycles-built-for-
two with working-class couples dressed in matching pull-overs . . . All
this gave me the feeling that, through the organization of work and
leisure, I had . . . brought a kind of beauty, a ray of light, into dark and difficult lives . . . that we had not only pried them from the cabaret, [and] . . .
given them the means to enjoy a real, family life, but that we had opened
up a vision of the future and given them hope." [98] Yet the near-millenarian
hopes stirred by Popular Front cultural politics were a vital part of the
movement itself, for there is no denying the force of those utopic energies
that were mobilized under the sign of culture for the masses. Indeed, it
formed a key ingredient in the history of the CEMEA, as founding member Gisèle de Failly reminds us: "The history of the birth of the CEMEA
is also the history of an era, that of 1936, an era of creation and renewal.
Latent social problems revealed themselves and sharply demanded to be
faced, institutions were called into question, youth took a new place, it
became possible to imagine, to invent." [99] For the first time, equalizing
access to health, leisure, and culture was proclaimed an integral aspect
of the government's larger struggle to redress social and economic inequality.

Small wonder that the *colonies de vacances* were targeted as sites of immediate and tangible action. Backed by a 10,000 F grant from Sellier's
Ministry of Health, cofounders Gisèle de Failly (representing the movement Hygiène par l'Exemple) and André Lefèvre, national commissioner of the Eclaireurs de France, issued a general invitation to all popular education activists interested in working with children, inviting them
to participate in the CEMEA's first training practicum, to be held in the
medieval château of Beaurecueil, at the foot of Mont Saint-Victoire, during the 1937 Easter holiday. [100] For the modest fee of 110 F each, plus
the price of their own railway tickets, participants in the practicum at
Beaurecueil would have the chance to exchange ideas and techniques
in the art of "animation" in the *colonies de vacances*. That April, some
sixty educators converged on Beaurecueil, curious to see what the first
CEMEA practicum held in store for them. Ranging from eighteen to fifty-
two years of age, the trainees were drawn largely from public education, alongside a few representatives from the major youth movements—
Scouts, Pionniers, Faucons Rouges—which had all complained of a lack

of trained cadres.[101] Some had a special interest in education and public health, others had a background in some branch of the scout movement, while others, who had worked in *colonies de vacances* before, brought their own tales of pedagogic triumph or woe to the ten-day seminar at Beaurecueil: "One man of fifty-two told us that finally, for the first time, he would be able to speak about the *colonie de vacances* that he had been running for the past fifteen years."[102]

No matter what their backgrounds and professional interests, however, all participants shared a common experience of instruction in the schools of the Republic, and were initially quite taken aback by what awaited them at Beaurecueil: not an amphitheater ringing with the voice of the instructor but rather a collective experience of living and learning within the ancient walls of the château: "You are all interested in the *colonies*," chuckled André Lefèvre in his opening speech to the trainees. "Eh bien, we will all live as if we were in a *colonie de vacances*."[103] For the next ten days, trainees lived the life that the children would live in their *colonies*, following the daily rhythm of collective meals and housekeeping tasks that structured the practical side of life *en colonie*. When the daily round of chores was finished, the trainees turned their attention to a series of hands-on seminars in song, folk dance, music on homemade instruments, and other crafts that were to become standard elements on the syllabus at the educational *colonie*: "In the courtyard, we experimented with the practical application of this principle to theatrical improvisation and the preparation of children's festivals," recalled Juliette Pary, who waxed lyrical on the CEMEA pedagogy of awakening the child's imagination. What a refreshing difference from the rote learning of canonical texts that constituted the republican school's chosen method for instructing the people about artistic and stylistic beauty: "Above all, no texts for grown-ups imposed on the children! No roles learned by heart! No 'canned beauty,' no banalities, no polishing! Let the children's imaginations run freely!"[104]

The same principles were applied in the courses on song, where Pary found the instructor to be engaged in a laudable "resurrection" of the "organic" nature of popular song: "The goal is to teach the *moniteurs* how to teach the children to sing rather than bleat; how to preserve the musical accent of the song and its popular character . . . Our teacher . . . swept away all the little artificial mimicries of the music hall, and when we sang the song of the sower, he asked that we make the actual sower's gesture."[105] By peeling back the layers of "inauthentic" performance diffused through the mechanisms of mass culture, the CEMEA's popular education activists were restoring to the "kids of the big cities" an art of the *chanson populaire* which would plant in their souls a sliver of the "living reality of the people."[106] An enduring link was thus established in the popular education movement between the notional simplicity of children and the simple verities of rural popular culture, which latter had already been designated as the Popular Front's rallying ground for democratic alternatives to the high culture of museum and opera house.

The practice of living collectively and by the rhythms of a real *colonie* was a tactic drawn from the scout's arsenal of scout-chief training techniques, for, like other open-air youth movements (and like many *colonies de vacances,* for that matter), the scouts had long been organizing on-site pre-*colonies* or pre-camps in order to give the newly recruited staff a rapid, hands-on training (often imparted by more experienced staff) in the skills and improvisational agility that their work with the children would demand. Lefèvre and de Failly adopted this tactic in the conviction (common to both *éducation nouvelle* and *scoutisme*) that the sole way for future *moniteurs* to understand the experience of the children who would soon come under their care was to live that experience themselves.[107]

In applying the *éducation nouvelle*'s pedagogy of experience to their own daily lives, the trainees gained a direct experience of collective effort in a common enterprise that harmonized with the Rousseauean conviction of Popular Front youth movements that hiking, camping, and greater proximity to nature were a sure route to restoring simplicity, truth, and greater transparency to social relations: "We lived a simple life, very close to nature, where the human relations were more naked, more real than in everyday life."[108] Moreover, "the continual presence, the fully communal way of life between officials and participants . . . created an atmosphere of utter confidence. This constant, egalitarian contact struck me as the most essential quality of our training."[109] The collective experience of the practicum, which rapidly became the keystone of the CEMEA's original method for educating the educators, fired individual enthusiasm for the pedagogical revolution that was to be waged in the *colonies de vacances* through the CEMEA's popular education project: "We proposed a radical shift in attitude toward children, another conception of childhood which shaped another way of treating them," wrote Gisèle de Failly some forty years later. "Many young people found themselves in this new way of envisioning education and adhered to it with all their hearts, as if it responded to an unconscious need in their being."[110]

Toward the "Best School of Social Life":
Designing the Educational *Colonie*

The CEMEA were thus born of an unlikely encounter between scouting
and *éducation nouvelle,* two movements for pedagogical reform whose
militants, though converging on issues of content (both supported the
use of active, child-centered methods), traveled in largely separate sociopolitical worlds in interwar France. The gulf in *habitus* is well represented in the initial encounter between Giselle de Failly and André Lefèvre in the winter of 1936–37: the well-heeled and well-spoken daughter
of the *grande bourgeoisie,* drawn by political conviction to a life of social
work and educational activism in the militantly secular and largely bourgeois circles of France's still tiny Groupement Français pour une Education Nouvelle (GFEN), and the laconic "Vieux Castor," commissioner
of the Eclaireurs de France, veteran of the *silloniste* Catholic Action and
popular education movements, hailing from very modest petit-bourgeois
and provincial origins. A dedicated individualist, de Failly had always
been put off by the troop mentality of the scouts, by the militarist aspect
of a movement organized through hierarchy and uniforms, and by the
"childishness" of the entire affair, with grown men and women marching
round in khaki shorts and backpacks, singing hiking songs at the top of
their lungs or leading the pack in a game of capture the flag.[111] It took the
urgent prodding of a trusted colleague, Mme Trenel, at the Ministry of
Youth and Sport, to overcome de Failly's initial reluctance: what benefit
could possibly come from an encounter between individuals representing such different social and political tendencies? But as Mme Trenel
well knew, Lefèvre had a long experience training scout *surveillants,* and
had already developed a plan for creating more elaborate and long-term
"education centers." Moreover, scouting in its various incarnations was
already making a powerful, if unsystematically distributed, contribution
to the pedagogical renovation of the *colonies,* thanks to the growing presence of former scouts among *colonie* personnel.

It would seem, then, the initial impetus (and example) for the educational *colonie* came from the scout movement, with its ambition to educate the whole child through a pedagogy that engaged the child's body,
mind, and imagination in the life of the *colonie* or camp conceived as one
long game: "Dramatic games thus feed our imagination and expand our
cultural repertoire," wrote former Eclaireur Raymond Schalow in his

1946 manual *Joues rouges et belle humeur,* which celebrates the pedagogical value of scout techniques in the *colonie de vacances*. "*Les grands jeux à
thème* are by far the favorite occupation of the older [nine- to fourteen-
year-old] children. In the course of such games, you can ask a lot of the
children. [Moreover], these games meet a number of different educational goals, promoting agility, attentiveness, observational skills, judgment, tracking skills, studies of nature, memory, etc." [112] On the basis of
these techniques, the *moniteurs* were to strive to impart a more holistic
education to their young charges than that which was available in public
primary schools during the other ten months of the year: "The *moniteur*
is not at the head of a troop of twenty or twenty-five children in order to
give them an academic instruction; he is there to strengthen the little ones
and to awaken their spirits, to put them in progressively greater possession of the riches that slumber deep within each of them." [113] The scout
cofounders of the CEMEA thus held proudly aloft the banner of Tolstoy's
famous dictum that "the sole method of education is experience, and
its sole criterion, freedom," a pedagogical stance that harmonized easily
with the democratic cultural politics of the Popular Front. [114]

Fruit of the unlikely alliance between *laïque* scouting and *éducation
nouvelle,* the CEMEA would, in a few short months, produce its own distinctive blend of *éducation nouvelle* and the scout pedagogy of games
which was then broadly diffused to the staff in *colonies de vacances* of
all stripes through the institution of the training practicums. The pedagogical renovation that came out of this union breathed new life into the
colonies, preventing their ossification and, indeed, providing one of the
major justifications for their rapid upward spread to the middle classes
in the years following World War II. [115]

The CEMEA thus had a clear pedagogical agenda from the outset, plus
a well-stocked arsenal of techniques in music, games, and gymnastics
drawn from scouting, rural folklore, and the *éducation nouvelle* movement. How did the CEMEA propose to intervene in the existing *colonie*
structure, that hodge-podge of local initiatives, private and public, confessional and secular, in which the *colonie municipale* was coming to hold
pride of place, in terms of sheer numbers? What kind of terrain for intervention did this mélange of *colonies* offer? If the nascent CEMEA had
drafted a pedagogical balance sheet that summarized the existing state
of affairs in Popular Front-era *colonies,* how might such a document have
looked? In other words, how did the CEMEA define its mission in relation
to existing practice?

While the CEMEA never produced any such balance sheet in 1937, CEMEA activist Denis Bordat would, in 1973, offer an affectionate but highly critical summary of the lamentable state of affairs, pedagogically speaking, that he confronted as a *colon* in the mid-1930s in the *colonie* at Les Mathes, that great "health machine" built by the Communist city council for the children of Ivry-sur-Seine:

> In 1936, at the age of thirteen, I was already an old hand at the *colonies de vacances*. Some years earlier, certain of the working-class municipalities in the Paris region had come to realize that it was unwise to leave the *colonies de vacances* in the hands of traditional, charitable foundations. Some cities purchased châteaux that had been more or less abandoned by their original inhabitants, and turned them over to "the workers' children." Others built, and they built in haste for the need was great. They built according to the available models of collective living: the boarding school in the best cases, the hospital or prison in the worst: immense dormitories with a room for the *surveillant* and huge refectories. It was in just such a *colonie* that I found myself each summer, from age seven until my fourteenth birthday.[116]

Rising on the sun-washed shores of the Atlantic coast, just south of La Rochelle (Charente-Maritime), Les Mathes was a showpiece of municipal communism, with its modern hygienic facilities and immense refectory-kitchen, able to feed eight hundred children at a time:

> I can still hear the mayor [Georges Marrane] today . . . [giving] a great, fiery speech before the city's population, assembled in the square before our *mairie de banlieue:* "And we have the most beautiful *colonie* ever built in France. The most beautiful because it rises in the heart of a great forest that stretches down to the sea. The most beautiful because the *colonie* borders on the endless sand beaches of the Coubre lighthouse where your children swim each day." The parents' eyes grew bright with tears, those who had never seen the sea themselves: "The most beautiful because we have built eight dormitories equipped with 100 beds apiece . . . the most beautiful because we have built an immense dining hall with eight hundred seats, etc." I was one of those 800, somewhere in that refectory.[117]

Bordat did not recall a very heavy adult presence, nor were there any trained personnel:

> The word [*moniteur*] did not even exist for us then, nor the term *surveillant*. To watch over this swarming company there were a total of ten, perhaps twelve adults, aside from the women we used to see working in that great

factory of a kitchen. We would see them coming back early each morning in the truck, loaded to the gills with vegetables, sides of meat, or bottles of milk, for the first and cardinal rule was that we had to be WELL-FED; this food was practically sacred.[118]

The adult presence was thus rather minimal in those early days at Les Mathes, and consisted mostly of *permanents* sent on mission from mayor Marrane's entourage at the *mairie:*

> They were all political or trade union militants . . . One might drive the bus that took us on a brief excursion, another might pass through the dormitory morning or night to ensure that everything was OK. A third would monitor proceedings in the dining hall, passing back and forth between the tables, helping the littlest ones find seats, and making sure that the older children helped the younger ones to EAT WELL.[119]

We will have occasion to return to the *colonie* of Les Mathes in the next chapter, where we will place Bordat's evaluation of the *colonie*'s early years in the context of its longer-term development of a pedagogy of working-class life over the period 1935–1955, shaped and delivered by political militants for whom work with the city's children formed the heart of their lives as political and pedagogical activists. For the time being, Bordat's testimony regarding what was hailed by contemporaries as a showplace *colonie* reminds us of the all-important hygienic mission of the *colonie de vacances,* and how that mission had shaped the institution over the first fifty years of its existence. It was a mission that ceded primacy of place only reluctantly in the mid-1930s. Indeed, the hygienic aspect of the *colonie* remained crucial to its function after 1936, as educators assimilated the physical and bodily side of life in the *colonie* to its larger pedagogical ambition of shaping the whole child—mind, body, and soul—in a harmonious development where one aspect was not supposed to flourish at the expense of others.

How would the action of the CEMEA and its colleagues—the secular Union Française des Oeuvres de Vacances Laïques (UFOVAL) and Jeunesse au Plein Air (JPA), the Catholic Union Française des Colonies de Vacances (UFCV) and the Centres de Formation of the Protestant Eclaireurs Unionistes—transform these great "health machines" into educational *colonies*? For one thing, they increased the supply of trained *moniteurs* while spreading the word that a trained staff was essential to an educational *colonie* worthy of the name. For another, they helped transform *colonie* directors' sense of what constituted an adequate staff-child ratio. Finally, they spread widely the techniques of *éducation nouvelle* and *scoutisme,* which, in the case of the CEMEA, were translated into the secular and democratic terms of Popular Front cultural politics. By the mid-1950s, the CEMEA alone would have trained over 16,500 *moniteurs* and *monitrices.*[120]

But in embracing play-centered pedagogies and placing them at the heart of the educational work of the *colonie,* the various training programs, whether leftist and secular or confessional, also embraced the curiously archaic view of children that nestled at the core of such pedagogy, in which education consisted above all in the exteriorization of qualities deemed already present within the child. While this is quite clear in the case of the Catholics' Scouts and Guides de France, it was no less true of the other popular education militants of the CEMEA. Hence, in the aftermath of World War II, the play-centered *pédagogies nouvelles* gradually shed the scaffolding of *scoutisme,* by which they had first entered the *colonie de vacances,* and really came into their own as framing the prime educational activity in the *colonie.*[121] Here, *en colonie,* none doubted that playing constituted an "essential activity" in child development, and that, in the ever more densely urban nation, the *colonie* remained the privileged site for children's play.[122] But by the mid-1950s, a very curious thing had happened: CEMEA militants were declaring that the fund of children's games, as well as the art of playing itself, was beginning to die out, thanks to the decline of that stable, rural culture that had long sustained them: "There are other [games] that the child tradition has had the wisdom to guard and even enrich across the generations. But many of these games, which were still being played twenty years ago, are now disappearing."[123] Though play was meant to be as natural to the child as breathing, generations of urban living were nonetheless threatening to stamp out altogether this "essential activity" through which children "constructed themselves."[124] Lacking the necessary physical space and those dependable and deeply rooted social ties on which rural children's play-groups had been based since time out of mind, urban children were arriving at their *colonies* with no apparent instinct or taste for play: "As soon as you leave them to their own devices, on the beach or the *colonie* grounds, you find that children don't know how to play on their own any more," observed many a despairing *colonie* director in letters to the CEMEA.[125]

It would seem, then, that the tides of urban and industrial development not only menaced people's ties to the land; they also threatened to rupture children's connection to the age-old culture of rural play-groups: those autonomous societies of village children in which members learned not only the rules of the game but the meaning of justice itself, through games regulated by "le peuple enfant" alone, free of adult interference. With the movement toward cities (where, as the authors remind us, the least open space too often bore the placard "No Games Allowed in the Square"), children had lost contact with the ancient "child tradition," and with the rich fund of games preserved and transmitted by that tradition.[126] Refined by generations of use, these games were the ideal instruments of education. Indeed, "nothing could replace them," mourned CEMEA pedagogues André Schmitt and André Boulogne:

> For in them children find opportunities to exercise a host of gestures useful to their development, and at a cadence that is perfectly suited to their physiological capacities. But they also find opportunities make a spontaneous apprenticeship to social relations under irreplaceable conditions. For the rules, transmitted by tradition and respected by all, are never paralyzing. Deliberately, all is not anticipated in order to allow the players scope for individual initiative, and to give to the game its full range of imaginative adaptation to context and circumstance. Improvisation retains a large role, and in this sense, games from the child tradition strongly resemble those spontaneous dramatic games whose importance is well known.[127]

Faced with the prospect of this loss, CEMEA militants declared that the *colonie* must take up the burden of preserving and transmitting the precious patrimony of games from the "child tradition" to the present generation, "not for the pleasure of recovering the activities of the past, but for the sake of their exceptional qualities."[128] Henceforth, *colonies de vacances* were to reconnect children not only with the French countryside but also with the ancient culture of rural children's games, menaced by the ongoing and relentless urbanization of France.

The CEMEA thus rendered explicit yet another, more purely cultural dimension to the powerful chain of associations that imaginatively bound children to their "natural" habitat in the country. Not only was the countryside the best place to restore their little lungs, a site of fresh food and open spaces for free and joyful movement; it was also the site for the renewal of a traditional culture of children's games, victim of modern industrial and urban life. Of course the job would not be easy, for in order to maintain their educational virtues, the games in question had to unfold spontaneously, and without adult interference.[129] The solution, then, was to create conditions within which the *colons* themselves could "spontaneously" recover their lost patrimony: "You must have propitious conditions of freedom and tranquillity in order to give birth to and develop these games. It takes a long time for a game that is based on social relations to develop, with all of its subtle ceremony. The *colonie* remains one of the rare spots where the children of our big cities can still find such conditions."[130] The manual then goes on to provide historic/folkloric background for a whole series of "ancient popular games, still in favor in certain regions of France": *la galoche, le jeu des cerfs, la balle aux pots, la palette,* and *thèque* (a distant cousin of baseball or cricket), complete with carefully diagramed descriptions of the play.[131] By teaching these games to the *moniteurs,* who were no less disconnected from this world of play than their young charges, the CEMEA would help the broken culture of children's games to recover its forgotten heritage.[132] The *colonie de vacances,* privileged site for renewing children's ties to the land, would also reignite the torch of that ancient rural culture of children, preserving and transmitting the actual structure and rules of traditional games while providing that stable base of reliable social bonds on which such games depend.

The pedagogic turn in the *colonies de vacances* was thus shaped by the interwar fascination with children's games, which found its first broad-based institutional expression in the play-centered pedgogies, and especially the *grands jeux à thème,* which flourished across the various branches of the scout movement. From here the fascination with play moved outward across a broad range of *colonies,* assisted by the CEMEA's—and UFCV's—enthusiastic dissemination of these techniques to *patronages* and *colonies de vacances* throughout France. By the mid-1930s, it seemed that everyone was talking about games and education through play. And yet, as we have seen, each invocation of a play-centered pedagogy turned out to mean something quite different in practice. How are we to understand the common insistence on the centrality and efficacy of games to children's learning in early-to-mid-twentieth-century France? Perhaps it is something like the phenomenon that Alain Boureau has called an "énoncé collectif"; in other words, the notion that children learn by doing what comes naturally (play), first aired in scientific circles at the end of the nineteenth century, was seized upon a generation later by parties and groups across the political and ideological spectrum as they searched for ways to organize children's leisure.[133] Certainly, one is struck by the tremendous energy that was expended on all sides in the effort to harness children's urge to play as a means of imparting some kind of moral and political education. More striking yet, this technique was grounded in two precepts whose validity remained uncontested across the political spectrum: (1) that children already contain an innate, though undeveloped, capacity for moral reasoning, and (2) that as they play, children reveal themselves as they truly are. Not surprisingly, this play-centered window on the child's "true" nature would form the basis of the psycho-pedagogical theory and practice on which *colonies de vacances* were organized from the 1930s through the early 1960s. But I would also like to suggest that the broad appeal of play-centered pedagogies found its roots in a conception of play as an activity that describes a space of perfect freedom, where individual actions are spontaneous and unconstrained: an idealized vision of play that found contemporary expression in Jan Huizinga's widely read essay *Homo Ludens*.[134] Could it be that in the modern West, the exercise of such freedom in childhood has come to seem essential to the development of an autonomous moral and political agency in adult life?

CHAPTER SIX

≥ *Municipal Communism and the Politics*

of Childhood

IVRY-SUR-SEINE 1925–1960

In the spring of 1925, just eight years after the Bolsheviks seized power in Russia, the citizens of Ivry-sur-Seine elected their first Communist city council.[1] Nearly sixty years later, Raymond Lagarde still remembered the groundswell of hope and joy released that night, when the Communists broadcast their victory by placing a red lantern in the cupola that perched on the roof of the *mairie:*

> And we told ourselves, my parents and I, that if the Communists won, there would be a red lantern in the campanile. I must tell you that from up on the plateau you looked out over all Ivry. All these buildings did not exist at the time. The plateau, the hillside was still the country. We were climbing down the pathway to the center city when my father cried out to my mother, "The Communists have made it, look! There's the red lantern in the campanile." That same night there was a huge gathering in front of the *mairie* . . . With Marrane and the victors leading the way, the parade headed first to the Place Gambetta before turning back toward Petit-Ivry . . . There must have been ten thousand people there; entire families joined in the parade.[2]

For the next seventy-three years the Communists would dominate local politics in Ivry, holding the *mairie* without interruption down to this day.[3] How did the Communists come to root themselves so rapidly and enduringly in local political affections? The answer to this question lies partly in the power of popular Bolshevism among French workers during the interwar period. For in the aftermath of World War I, as the French working-class movement experienced first reversal, then crushing defeat, the Bolshevik seizure of power in Russia seemed to revivify the old revolutionary-syndicalist dream of a workers' republic.[4]

Such radical visions held special appeal in the working-class cities of the Paris red belt, where a mournful landscape of factory yards and railway lines, dilapidated housing and weed-choked lots underscored the obscure misery to which the industrial proletariat had been consigned. Nowhere was this more evident than in Ivry-sur-Seine, a once-tranquil village of vineyards, quarries, and market-gardens, clustered round the medieval parish church of Saint-Pierre-et-Saint-Paul. Since the mid-1860s, the city had undergone a profound industrial transformation, fed by a continuous stream of rural in-migration that nearly doubled the city's population in a single generation.[5] The rapid and uncontrolled development produced unprecedented levels of urban blight and a swift expansion in radical and Socialist politics, which put down durable local roots at the time of the Paris Commune. It is perhaps not surprising, then, that the nascent Communist Party would score one of its earliest and most important victories some fifty years later here in "Ivry-la-Rouge."

Early-twentieth-century Ivry still bore the traces of its recent rural past. In part this was due to the scale of industrial development: those who climbed up the hillsides and away from the heavily trafficked ports and railway found themselves crossing an urban landscape that was marked by a thick concentration of small to mid-size workshops and factories, interrupted by the occasional large industry but also by gardens, vineyards, and even the occasional dairy farm: "It is a diverse agglomeration of thatch-roofed houses, factories, villas with terraced gardens, here grouped, there standing alone, as if by chance, with no apparent order. Viewed from a distance, it gives the impression of a young colony, half agricultural, half industrial."[6] So wrote Louis Barron in the mid-1880s, as he strolled about making notes and sketches for his guidebook to the environs of Paris. Thirty years later, Ardouin-Dumazet would evoke the "lost village" in elegiac tones, mourning the disappearance of an Ivry "once known for its graceful landscapes, its gardens, its lovely homes. The factories have destroyed this flowering countryside; of the rustic past there remain but a few handsome horticultural establishments for hothouse lilacs and roses."[7]

The citizens of Ivry recall their interwar landscape somewhat differently. In 1982, Lucienne Ballerat spoke fondly of "the lilac hothouses on the hillside running up to the Fort d'Ivry, around which stretched what we called 'the little wood,' where the children went to play"; while René

Guillard remembers chasing wildly after the cattle as they trooped to the slaughterhouse: "As soon as a herd was spotted at the edges of the city all the kids . . . would race down the street after them, shrieking "voilà les boeufs, voilà les boeufs!"[8]

But there is no denying the deep physical misery that marked working-class life in a city whose rapid and uncontrolled growth strained the very limited infrastructures of this lately bucolic spot.[9] Throughout the long winter months, the unpaved tracks and pathways turned to thick-churned mud, while the narrow, four-to-five-story houses that lodged multiple families (in one or two rooms per family) generally lacked all semblance of modern convenience: only 34.5 percent had running water in 1896, and most had no indoor toilet of any kind.[10] In 1921, Dr. Louis Martin described the "savage abandon" of Ivry's most desolate region, the "Zone," which rose along the embankment of the city fortifications, just behind Petit-Ivry:

> A mass . . . of shoddy barracks fashioned from bits of scrap metal, planks, canvas, and packing boxes, veritable rabbit hutches sprouting in the midst of the small enclosed gardens where rag-pickers dwell . . . Ragged children swarm about; the tiny gardens are almost indistinguishable from the great heaps of garbage that surround them. A strong stench rises from this strange land which, at the gates of the most refined city in the world, flaunts the spectacle of a return to barbaric life . . . Tumbling down the hillside to the edges of the Seine, the huts crowd up against each other in the greenery of the gardens. More than once . . . I have crossed through the gates of the city to look at . . . this multitude of ruined houses, half covered with ivy, marking little spots of gray in the vegetable gardens and flowering hedges, the woodlands of the poor. Rising over the valley choked with the smoke of factory chimneys, this mélange of filth and beauty reveals itself in the splendid light of autumn.[11]

Although the Zone was not Ivry (though Petit-Ivry, which abutted the Zone, came perilously close in terms of physical wretchedness), one still gets a vivid sense of the material poverty that shaped and con-strained working-class life on the southeastern edge of Paris. Within these cramped circumstances arose a dense and lively local culture that was centered primarily in the cafés, at the Brasserie des Sports (chez "Zizi"), and above all in the café-restaurant-hotel of Communist militant Hippolyte Marques, where the "Amis du Rire" gathered each week.[12]

Into this rich neighborhood sociability, the newly elected Communist city council proceeded to sink deep roots, proclaiming its intent to administer the city on behalf of its working-class population so that Ivry might become "a pillar of revolutionary strength, an arm in the merciless struggle against capitalism."[13] To this end, mayor Georges Marrane and his deputy mayors pursued an efficacious and highly successful parish-pump politics that combined social assistance with urban renovation, making the city a veritable showpiece of municipal communism.[14] By the mid-1930s, the Communists could point with pride to a solid record of achievement, celebrated in the pages of the *mairie*'s official *Bulletin municipal officiel d'Ivry:* handsome social housing projects for the more than five thousand homeless or shantytown residents, new medical dispensaries and public bath houses in each neighborhood, a public garden on the plateau above the Seine, road-paving, electrification, and repairs to the Lenin Stadium and other local sports facilities.[15]

But it was the children of Ivry who drew the most vigorous and sustained attention, and the city council set to work immediately, distributing benefits in kind through the *caisse des écoles,* and reinforcing the structures of public education with a plan to build at least two new primary schools. At the heart of the *mairie*'s politics of childhood stood the Oeuvre des Vacances Populaires Enfantines (OVPE), sworn to make "child-kings" of the children of Ivry by taking them on long summer holidays by the sea. In so doing, the *mairie* sought to give working-class children a benefit normally reserved to the offspring of the well-to-do: "Through the loving care of the municipality we will give them all that is possible, so that they might blossom within the structures of capitalist society."[16] The Communists were as good as their word; by 1929, the OVPE had purchased a rambling old farm near the village of Les Mathes, on the Atlantic coast. With the labor of several summers, the old farm was gradually transformed into the great *colonie de vacances* of Les Mathes, creating yet another showpiece of municipal communism, designed and built for the working-class children of Ivry.

Built deep in a maritime pine forest near the broad sand beaches of the Coubre, some five hundred kilometers southwest of Paris, Les Mathes has become a site of local memory, as women and men, now well past retirement, recall with pleasure the songs, games, and seemingly unbounded physical freedom that marked their summers "aux Mathes."[17] Equally important, the *colonie* became a site of remarkable pedagogical innovation soon after its founding, in 1929. Indeed, the interwar and postwar years were marked by a series of conscious efforts to organize daily life and activity in the *colonie* so as to foster independent initiative and a robust sense of agency in these young (six- to thirteen-year-old) children. By the late 1940s, the working-class pedagogues of Ivry would have groped their way toward a structure for daily life at Les Mathes that allowed the *colonie* to function as a kind of ideal children's republic: a mirror of the mother city yet also the site where a future, utopian order might be imagined, even lived, if only briefly, during the summer holiday.

The Communist city council thus sought to anchor its support in a social politics of childhood that centered on providing a real summer holiday for the city's youngest citizens. It was a way to build the Socialist future here and now, for in the practical, and increasingly political, experience of collective life in the *colonie de vacances,* the souls and bodies of Ivry's children might be prepared for the better world they would surely inherit: a world freed from the grim round of poverty and back-breaking labor that shaped the lives of their parents and older siblings. But the *colonie de vacances* was also a way to bind parents' loyalties to the Communist municipality, bringing them directly into the communal project, organized on behalf of their children. In so doing, the men and women of city hall sought to wind the Communist administration through the daily lives and most intimate familial concerns of the people of Ivry.[18]

From *Cure d'Air* to a Cure of Souls:
Catholic *Colonies de Vacances* in Ivry, 1912–1940

But if Ivry's Communists were eventually to produce the most spectacular results, the real pioneers here were the Catholics, who had begun organizing *colonies de vacances* some thirteen years before the Communists took office.[19] The Catholic *colonies* grew directly out of the neighborhood *patronages,* where the abbé and his assistants had gradually developed a pedagogical method that took an active approach to learning, alternating periods of instruction (notably catechism) with games, theater, songs, and informal "chats."[20] These "active methods" were quite naturally extended and adapted to the *colonies de vacances,* which were themselves merely holiday extensions of the life of the *patronage.* If we examine comparatively the competing programs of Catholic and municipal *colonies de vacances* in "Ivry-la-Rouge," we can see that the two institutions developed through a kind of competitive dialogue with one another. For if the Catholics competed with the Communists over the same clientele, they also provided an important model of effective intervention in the collective life of children on holiday, setting a pedagogical example that strongly influenced the form and direction of later, Communist initiatives at Les Mathes.

Just before the First World War, Abbé Garin organized the city's first *colonie de vacances* at La Belle Etoile, a rambling country house in the tiny hamlet of Chevron (Savoie), near the mountain village where the abbé himself had been born. From the summer of 1912 until the early 1930s, La Belle Etoile received, on average, sixty to seventy-five boys and sixty to seventy-five girls each summer (boys and girls were always sent separately, as first one sex, then the other, had the run of the place for four to six weeks apiece).[21] "How many delicate constitutions have restored themselves here!" wrote Garin in 1929. "How many threatened lungs, armed with the pure air of our Alps, have successfully fought back against tuberculosis, that terrible scourge of Ivry's youth."[22] Along with the *colonies* organized by the neighboring parishes of Petit-Ivry and Ivry-Port, the Catholics of Ivry were sending at least 350 children to the countryside each summer. In the 1920s, this put them at the forefront of the local *colonie* movement, ahead of both republicans and Communists in terms of the sheer numbers sent.[23] But in 1932 the Catholics lost La Belle Etoile; henceforth, the organization of the Catholic *colonies* would depend on the goodwill and generosity of wealthy parishioners willing to lend their country homes for six weeks each summer.[24] The abbé thus located a sprawling convent in the rural bourg of St-Flour (Cantal), where the Sisters of Charity of Saint-Vincent-de-Paul welcomed the young girls of Ivry each summer. For the boys, he found a wealthy patron willing to open the doors of his family château, "Sauveboeuf," for six weeks each summer.

The fragility of the Catholic endeavor, so heavily dependent upon the charity and goodwill of the more fortunate faithful, is reflected in the statistics: after 1932, at precisely the moment when the Communist *colonie* was experiencing a real "take-off," the number of young Ivryens sent on Catholic vacations fell to about 250. This condition of financial dependency (and uncertainty) increased when, in 1929, the Communist town council canceled the already tiny municipal subsidy to the Catholic *colonies*.[25] Lacking any public funding whatsoever, the Catholic *colonies*

relied entirely upon charity and voluntarism, plus the obligatory contribution paid by the family of each young *colon*.[26]

The Catholics' recurrent financial woes point to the powerful anticleri-
calism of the era, part of the ongoing struggle between an increasingly
embattled Catholic minority and the rest of the nation. Nowhere was this
struggle more vigorously pursued than in "Ivry-la-Rouge" where anticlerical sentiment crossed party lines, and predated the election of the
Communists by some fifty years.[27] By their own account, the priests of
the city's three parishes were regularly subjected to abuse at the hands of
Ivry's "pagan" children each time they stepped out onto the streets of the
working-class city.[28] It was not uncommon for Catholic processions to
become the occasion of great street fights, but as Jean Millet recalls, the
Catholic-*laïque* struggle was pursued with especial fervor in the school-
yards of the "red" city:

> At school it was the war of the rings. We had rings graven with crosses, and
> the Communists, too, had rings, carved with the hammer and sickle . . .
> Every day the priest waited for us at the school gates, where we told him
> what the teacher had taught us, and he then corrected that which he judged
> to be false . . . What marked me, throughout this entire period (1936–38),
> was the fact that, kid though I was, I had to declare my colors. I was a Chris-
> tian in a red working-class district. It was obvious, it was written in my
> every act.[29]

Children were thus centrally implicated in the political and ideological battles that set Catholic against Communist in interwar Ivry. Small
wonder, then, that local parish literature, including (and perhaps especially) the literature aimed at children, was marked by a vehemence that
occasionally bordered on paranoia: "ATTENTION AUX CAMARADES de vacances," tolled Abbé des Graviers in solemn warning to the boys of the
patronage at the beginning of each summer.[30] The girls, for their part,
were treated to an elaboration of similar themes intended to reinforce
a strong Catholic identity in the face of blandishments from competing Communist child and youth organizations: "It is not enough to say
you are proud to be a Christian, so long as the others are quite proud
to declare themselves pagan and 'emancipated,'" warned Abbé Soutif.
"Wouldn't it be smarter to try an approach that blends a dash of the Scout
spirit with a soupçon of JOCiste élan?"[31] Behind the annual summertime adjurations to the boys and girls of the *patronages* loomed the larger

understanding that "we are in Ivry, in a country where the struggle for and against God is ardent. We must always be on our guard."[32] It was in this spirit of militant Catholic defense that the parish *colonies de vacances* unfolded in interwar Ivry.

In organizing the collective life of children on vacation in the countryside, the Catholics pursued a clear line: reinforce the Catholic working-class family while seeking to counter the powerful influence of the street. In addition, there was the missionary hope that the child saved might help re-Christianize the fallen families of Ivry, that each might become a little conduit by which these atheist and uprooted families might someday return to the fold. The children who went were recruited each year from the *patronages* and parish schools, institutions where the religious education of children was pursued with great zeal and dedication.[33] The "educational mission" continued in the *colonie,* under circumstances that allowed for an encounter between pupil and teacher that was at once more relaxed and informal, yet far more intensive as well. The child was, after all, a captive audience for a minimum of three weeks.

It was their pointed focus on educating the child in this context that had distinguished Catholic *colonies* from their very origins. Unlike the *dames d'oeuvres* of Protestant charity, who preached "freedom" for children during the school holidays, or the schoolteachers of the republican *colonies scolaires,* who sought to combine a very light regime of study with long hours of recreation and repose, the organizers of Catholic *colonies de vacances* took an activist approach to learning in the *colonie,* which, in their view, offered a unique context for an intensive religious formation: "In the *colonie,* all things are in fact educational . . . provided there is a real educator about," intoned Abbé Lorenzo during the summer 1936 recruitment drive for the parish *colonie.*[34]

Catholic pedagogues set great store by their innovative "méthodes actives," and had long scorned the pedagogical passivity of the secular *colonies,* "where they strive above all to fatten the child, or leave the child too much to his own devices."[35] An alternating succession of prayer and hikes, work and play, thus shaped the collective lives of Catholic children on holiday. During the first twenty years of their existence (1912–32), the boys' and girls' *colonies* of Ivry, though organized separately, followed remarkably similar routines. Rising at seven each morning, the children would kneel at their bedside and begin the day with a brief prayer. After their morning *toilette,* the entire company would troop to the chapel for mass. Only then did they return to the refectory for a rapid breakfast of bread and café-au-lait. The rest of the morning was generally spent inside the *colonie* or close by on the grounds, engaged in some combination of housekeeping, writing letters home, games, and, for the girls, sewing and crocheting.

If we look comparatively at the recital of the morning's activities in the boys' and girls' *colonies,* an interesting and significant pattern of gender distinction emerges, for if the daily cycle of housekeeping tasks in the *colonie* involved children of both sexes, the recreation that followed these chores bore the clear mark of gender distinction. Hence, the boys' *colonie* no less than the girls' rested on the principle that the children (especially the older ones) would each take a turn in serving at table or clearing up afterwards, in sweeping out the dormitories or peeling vegetables for dinner. Making a virtue of necessity, the directors celebrated the contribution that this collective "school of housekeeping" made to the *colonie*'s larger educational goal of rendering *colons* of both sexes more "attentive, obliging, open, [and] well brought-up."[36] Yet the evidence suggests that the girls were spending considerably more time at these tasks than boys, and performing a wider range of domestic chores. To cite but one example, on the periodic days of rest that the children took from their strenuous round of long hikes, the boys truly rested (or more likely played on the *colonie* grounds), while the girls spent these afternoons washing the *colonie* laundry in a nearby stream: "It is so charming to watch the littlest girls running through the water while the older ones soap and scrub energetically on their knees. Their tongues work just as busily as their hands, for to be a truly good laundress, the tongue must wag as swiftly as the arms scrub."[37] On a more day-to-day basis, the gymnastic exercise and quiet, interior games that feature so prominently in the morning activities of boys were replaced, in the girls' *colonie,* by a few hours of handwork each day. Crochet-hooks or needles in hand, the girls would sit quietly, outside on the grass if the weather was fine, fingers flying under the watchful eye of the *directrice.*

While the boys played games, then, the girls engaged in housekeeping tasks and manual activities intended to refine their skills as future housewives. The insistence on providing manual training for girls sprang from traditional notions of what constituted an appropriate and useful education for working-class children. Such notions also governed the instruction offered in the *patronage des garçons,* where courses in industrial drawing and manual training in traditional crafts featured prominently on the weekly list of activities. In the *colonie des garçons,* however, this tra-

ditional conception of popular education was clearly being abandoned in
favor of more modern, "active" methods, organized around games and
the developing pedagogical conviction that playing was the fundamental activity in children's lives, and crucial to their social, physiological,
and cognitive development. The sexual division of recreation in the two
colonies—work/manual training for girls, games and outdoor sports for
boys—thus points to a deeper divergence in the understanding of what
constituted proper educational activities for the two sexes, a divergence
that would only harden with the spread of the scout movement and its
particular version of play-centered pedagogy to the *colonies des garçons*
of the 1930s.

After lunch the *colons* generally set off on a promenade into the surrounding countryside: "The little woods, the scenic villages, the fresh
orchards make for a marvelous vacation," assured Abbé Garin (who
should have known, since Belle Etoile was his childhood home, and the
woman who oversaw the *colonie* was none other than his own sister).[38]
The region was, moreover, blessed with a number of religious and historical sites which provided worthy goals for the children's daily hikes,
a panorama of sites whose historical interest and natural beauty would
nourish the minds and spirits of Ivry's young Catholics, even as their
lungs drew in the sharp, dry air of the Savoie.[39] These hikes could easily
last for five or six hours, and the girls and boys generally carried their
afternoon snack along with them, to be enjoyed in the welcome shade
of a spruce grove on the long road home. Upon returning from the day's
excursion, the children might pay a visit to the chapel, to salute the holy
sacrament. Then came dinner, which was usually followed by a chat with
the abbé. This latter ended with a prayer, and the entire *colonie* filed off
to bed by 9:30, or sometimes ten o'clock. Once or twice in the course of
the summer holiday, this rhythm would be broken by a longer excursion
of two to three days, with the children departing by bus for the more
distant sights of Geneva, Lake Leman, Lausanne, or Chamonix.

This collective life, deemed "familial" by the priests, seminarians, and
bonnes soeurs who organized it, allowed children to experience a thoroughly Christian education in the course of their normal lives *en colonie*.
Daily religious exercises were integral to the round of games and hikes,
ordering the flow of time and lending all activity in the *colonie* a powerful
Christian significance. Further, the structure of life in the *colonie* allowed
the staff to intervene not only in matters spiritual, but in more basic and
banal dimensions of life as well, dimensions where the working-class

child's education was often sadly deficient. But however tightly linked to the *colonie*'s more spiritual purpose, the lessons in comportment and orderliness were, ultimately, no more than a means to a spiritual end whose realization demanded a complete rupture with the corrupt milieu of the Paris red belt: "The essential task for us is to educate Catholics . . . One must never mix those who lack faith with those who believe, for this difference cuts infinitely deeper than that which separates aristocrat from bourgeois or proletarian."[40]

These, then, were the rhythms that guided the lives of both girls and boys in the Catholic *colonies* of Ivry-sur-Seine for the first twenty years of their existence. With the exception of the morning "recreation"—sewing for girls, games for the boys—and the heavier burden of household tasks borne by the female *colons,* the guiding structure of prayer and recreation, housekeeping and daily promenades was remarkably similar in both *colonies.* But in the summer of 1932, all semblance of parallel structure between the two *colonies* gave way, as the boys' *colonie* turned to the wholesale adoption of scout pedagogical techniques while the girls' *colonie* continued to operate along the old lines.

The occasion for this abrupt divergence was the loss of Belle Etoile, which forced both *colonies* on a southwestward migration. Now, merely shifting headquarters did not necessarily entail any departure from the well-worn routines that had governed the two *colonies* since prewar days. And in the case of the girls, no such rupture ensued. Hence, the transplantation of their *colonie* to the small bourg of Saint-Flour placed the girls under the watchful eyes of the aging Sisters of Charity of Saint-Vincent-de-Paul. But the change in scenery did not disrupt the inherited structures of the *colonie,* whose leisure aspect was still grounded in long afternoon promenades, with the occasional overnight trip by bus to liven things up. Yet it was quite another matter for the boys' *colonie,* where the departure to the château de Sauveboeuf coincided with (and perhaps provoked) an abrupt break with the pedagogic structure that had shaped their summers at Belle Etoile. Hence, from the summer of 1932 on, the *colonie* at Sauveboeuf evolved quite rapidly, taking on board a host of new activities, drawn directly from scout pedagogical techniques. Faced with the *grand jeu,* centerpiece of the Scouts' "pedagogy of the imaginary," the daily promenade receded steadily in importance; henceforth, the long summer afternoons would be filled with a range of *grands jeux*— mock battles, games of hunting and tracking through the woods, capture the flag—whose educational benefits were lauded by Abbé des Graviers:

"Our young and even our older *colons* are completely enthralled by the tracking game through the woods. It is, moreover, a very educational game, for it calls on the sense of initiative and observation, and demands that the team captain lead his men ably, dividing the tasks among them so that no time is lost. Finally, it is a team game where all strive toward a common good."[41]

The *colonie*'s longstanding educational mission was thus reoriented around the scout pedagogy of the *grand jeu.* Here, the abbé and his colleagues were merely following a pedagogical turn that was being taken in *patronages* and *colonies* across Catholic France in the 1930s. For in adapting scout educational techniques to the boys' *colonie,* the directors of Catholic *colonies* were quite self-consciously bringing to children (especially boys) the benefits of modern pedagogical technique. Quick to perceive the importance of play in shaping the imaginative, social, and cognitive worlds of children, interwar Catholic educators were building a coherent educational strategy around the wholehearted devotion with which children threw themselves into their play. Within this elaborate "pedagogy of the imaginary," games involving teams and competition were presumed to foster cooperation, obedience, and a sense of adventure in the child: "It's a game, but it's also a lesson in valor, in the sacrifice of one's own preference, of one's own personal game, for the common interest."[42]

But if play was the high road to the child's soul, let alone his or her inner development, then why were girls presumed to need less such stimulation? Why were they left to the tender, and traditional mercies of the crochet-hook and the needle? And did this sexual division of "recreation" — work for girls, adventure for boys — invariably reign supreme in Catholic *colonies de vacances*? A quick glance at the nearby Socialist city of Suresnes, where the young girls of the *patronage* of the Rosary (Notre-Dame-de-la-Salette) passed a vigorous three weeks in Bologne in the summer of 1913, ascending the riverside cliffs with the aid of a pick ax, answers the question with a resounding no.[43] The Suresnes *colonie*'s prewar turn toward a more active outdoorsmanship for girls foreshadowed the tremendous progress that gymnastics, organized sports, and *guidisme* would make among Catholic girls in the 1930s. Indeed, the parish of Saint-Pierre-et-Saint-Paul boasted its own small but lively troop of Guides who, from the winter of 1932–33, were organizing woodland day trips in the parks around Paris, punctuated by periodic overnight campouts on the property of wealthy do-gooders like the comtesse de Cha-

bannes, whose ancestral lands at Neauphle-les-Vieux became the site of
the Ivry Guides' inaugural camp-out, over the long Pentecost weekend
of 1933.

Cheftaine Travert's report of their activities that weekend underscores
the Guides' faithful adherence to the spirit and method of scout pedagogy, in which outdoor religious devotions and *grands jeux* held pride
of place. The girls first pitched their tents under the spreading branches
of a large spruce wood: "Breathing in their lovely scent, the silence broken only by the chirping of birds, we found ourselves living life in its
most simple and restorative guise." At the *cheftaine*'s whistle, the camp
rose bright and early each day, offered a small prayer of thanks, and
then gathered for half an hour's gymnastic exercise. After their morning *toilette,* the Guides trooped off to morning mass in the villa's church:
"United by prayer and the fervent communion among us, our hearts all
beat as one." At this point it was time for the inevitable housekeeping
chores in the camp, which were attacked with "energy and joy," perhaps
because the outdoor setting rendered these tasks a mite more interesting,
or perhaps because Guide ideology enjoined them to undertake each task
"with a smile." At noon, the girls would tuck into their lunch, savoring
the flavor of a wood-fire-cooked meal, then stretch out under the trees
for a nap on the grass. The afternoons were filled with *grands jeux* and
excursions in the district, which were "interspersed by our study circles,"
carried over from the life of the *patronage.* Twilight brought the flag-
lowering ceremony, followed by dinner and a campfire. The girls would
sing and dance around the fire, and as it began to burn low, the chaplain
would speak a few words. The girls then sang to Jesus "to watch over us
all," and as the fire at last burned out, a great silence fell, and all filed
quietly to their tents. On the final night of the Pentecost weekend, the
camp ended with the girls linking hands: "Bound together in a chain
of love, we sang our magnificent Chant des Adieux." Thus fortified by
their open-air retreat, the girls sallied forth into the world "to live by our
beautiful scout ideal."[44]

From the outset, Abbé Garin lent his active support to the Guides of
Ivry—and this raises the question why such techniques were never applied in the girls' *colonie,* when, by the late 1930s, they were reaching
boys (and some girls) in Catholic *colonies* all across France. The answer
lies partly in the structure of the *colonie des filles* itself, which was shaped
and constrained by the site of its relocation: a rural convent whose aging
population was probably not up to the gymnastic and woodland feats of

guidisme. In other working-class parishes, notably Suresnes, the presence of young, Guide-trained *cheftaines* in the *colonies des filles* allowed for that measure of adventure and physical prowess that convent-based *colonies* simply could not provide. But if the Guides provided a framework for girls' vigorous and autonomous outdoor adventuring, the organization was nonetheless reluctant to part entirely from conventional images of Catholic femininity. Torn between the siren song of the scout adventure and demonstrations of fidelity to the parental hearth as the girl's only true mission in life, the Guides lurched between declarations of loyalty to home and the desire for adventure abroad. This ambivalence was built in to the Guide structure from the top down, where the top was constituted by the regular parish hierarchy. Hence, when the abbé welcomed the new troop in January of 1933, his words reflected the widespread uncertainty of parents and church hierarchy about whether the Guides would promote an undue "virilization" of young girls. Indeed, his "welcome" seemed primarily intended to reassure those anxious parents who feared that the Guides would simply tear their daughters from the parental home. He thus closed his remarks by neatly demonstrating that *guidisme* actually fit very comfortably into traditional Catholic doctrine on the sexes — though equally human, and subject to the same laws of the flesh, girls and boys, women and men are consecrated to distinct and complementary ways of life in their everyday existence: "It is for this reason that there are no 'girl scouts' but rather the Guides of France! It's an entirely different thing! Same spirit, same law, to be sure, but the practical applications are completely distinct." He developed the point by going so far as to deny the Guides' evident outdoors and athletic orientation, claiming theirs was a purely domestic and within-the-household application of scout principles: " 'Guidisme' remains prudently feminine: it prepares girls neither for a life of adventure nor of exploration. It does not build athletes! The 'Guide's' primary obligation begins at home, with the table to be set and mother to be helped. To have a 'Guide' at your house is to have a jewel . . . of docility and open good cheer!"[45]

As the life stories gathered in the collection *Scoutisme féminin et promotion féminine 1920–1990* make clear, the abbé was kidding himself here, for the activities of the Guides inevitably took them other places besides the family hearthstone.[46] In the company of peers, girls periodically escaped the narrow structures of home and parental (especially maternal) control. Together, they discovered games, woodcraft activities, and new ways of thinking about spirituality and religious devotion within the framework of camp: "Gathered for the open-air mass in a semicircle around the priest, and not merely relegated to the back of the church, we no longer 'go' to mass, we participate in it," wrote one enthusiastic young Guide.[47] Indeed, had the abbé simply stopped to read the Guides' reports on their camping trips or day-long sorties to the nearby park at Vincennes, he would surely have trimmed his sails a bit. And yet the contradictory pull between outdoor adventure and fidelity to Catholic ideals of girlhood and womanhood was no mere figment of the abbé's imagination; it cut right through the Guides' enthusiastic accounts of their own activities and identity: "Like their brother Scouts, the [Guides] are preparing themselves for life, seeking, under the guidance of their *cheftaines,* to improve, harden, and masculinize themselves, while remaining devotedly, cheerfully, and courageously at the hearthstone," wrote *cheftaine* Travert of her troop in the fall of 1932, just months before the girls left their homes for a weekend of woodland adventure.[48]

"To Make Child-Kings of the Children of Ivry"

If the Catholics were the pioneers in developing Ivry's earliest *colonies de vacances,* it was the Communists who profited from the model in organizing their own *colonie* at Les Mathes. They did not tarry long in launching this endeavor; in the summer of 1925, not two months after their victory, the Communist *mairie* organized the OVPE as a separate and charitable venture.[49] Six comrades from the OVPE board (all of whom sat on the city council) then set off for a six-week holiday by the sea with ninety-two young girls and boys in tow.[50] Their destination: a declassified military fort in the small fishing village of Saint-Vaast-la-Hougue, on the northeastern coast, near Belgium.

The report in the city's *Bulletin municipal* stresses the wonder and joy that seeing the ocean inspired in the children, these children who were so different from "that other, privileged youth who . . . each year contemplate the same beauties at Deauville or Nice, depending on the whims of their parents."[51] The report then outlines the activities in a typical day: the children got up at 6:30 A.M., washed, had breakfast, then played on the beach and swam until 11:00, when they broke for lunch. This meal was followed by a long afternoon nap, lasting till 2:30 P.M., at which time the children returned to the beach for more games and swimming, and a snack of bread and chocolate, taken on the sandy shore at 4 P.M.

Dinner followed soon after, at 6:00; by 8:30 or 9 p.m., all were meant to be in their beds and sleeping. The report also provides a typical day's menu, for the quality (read: much meat) and amount of food consumed by the children formed a central theme in the Communist publicity for the municipal *colonie*.

Over the next two years, the comrades of the ovpe would continue to run their *colonie* in this fashion, taking over two hundred children to declassified forts on the Ile de Ré and the Ile d'Oléron: "I remember it well," recalls Marius Prunières. "I was ten and we were lodged in the barracks for the guards of the nearby prison [where the condemned awaited transport to the forced labor camps of Guyanne and Cayenne]. From our rooms you could still see the prisoners on the other side of the moat. With some ingenuity, we fashioned 'fishing lines' of knotted ropes, in order to gather blackberries from the [dry] moat."[52] But the military authorities soon got wind of the fact that their old barracks were being used to house children from a "red" *banlieue*. At the end of the summer of 1928, the army closed its doors to the young Ivryens.

During the six months that followed, the ovpe scoured the cheaper regions of the Atlantic coast, searching the Vendée and Charente-Maritime in hope of finding land for a *colonie de vacances* of their own. By the summer of 1929, the comrades had located, purchased, and refurbished an old farm near Royan, thirteen hectares of pines and a large kitchen garden just five kilometers from the sea. Over the next several years, the volunteer labor of local, *charentais* Communists and Ivryens combined with substantial injections of municipal cash to replace the crumbling barns with five brand new dorms, able to accommodate 100 children apiece, and a refectory-kitchen with the capacity to feed 800 at a time. The number of children sent rose spectacularly during the 1930s, from 230 (summer 1928) to more than 500 in 1934, before topping 600 in the late 1930s. By 1950, one third of Ivry's schoolchildren were spending their summers at Les Mathes.[53]

The departure for Les Mathes rapidly became an annual event, a municipal festival celebrating the Communist *mairie*'s special concern for the "petits gosses" of Ivry. Thus each year, on a Sunday afternoon in July, the children would assemble on the broad sandy ground in front of the city hall, to say their good-byes amidst an enormous throng of parents and well-wishers (some ten thousand citizens turned out for this event in the summer of 1948).[54] The children would then parade down the main street to the railway station, accompanied by a blaring fanfare from the

All the photographs in this section are courtesy
of the Archives Municipales d'Ivry-sur-Seine.

(*Above*) Along the docks of the Seine in fin-de-siècle Ivry.
(*Below*) The industrial city at the turn of the twentieth century:
the rue du Grand Gord (now rue Louis Bertrand).

The Petits Ivryens à la Campagne, assembled for departure
in front of the *mairie,* summer 1923.

The less orderly and more festive departure for the
municipal *colonie communiste* at Les Mathes, summer 1935.
(*Below*) The arrival, mid-1930s. Having arrived from
Paris on the 5 A.M. train into Arvert, the children begin
their summer holiday with a five-kilometer hike across
the peninsula to Les Mathes.

The *colonie* at Les Mathes, principal building (*above*),
and refectory (*below*), mid-1930s.

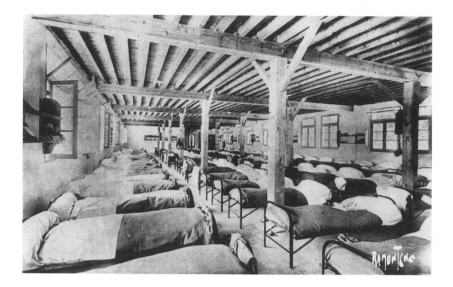

Dormitory at the *colonie* at Les Mathes, mid-1930s. The mattresses were stuffed with straw, "which was good, it was more hygienic," recalled former *colon* Vital Marques.
(*Below*) In the pine forest that surrounded the *colonie,*
summer 1930.

At low tide on the great sand beach of the Coubre, 1929 or 1930.
(*Below*) In a clearing in the *colonie* forest, the *colons* build a human
pyramid under the watchful eye of the gymnastic instructor
(behind the group and off to the left), summer 1930.

A picnic on the grass marks the annual, mid-August visit of the parents to the Ivry *colonie*, mid-1930s. In the right foreground stands a car flying a hammer-and-sickle-blazoned banner from its hood.

Poster advertising the city's annual kermesse
"for the benefit of the Vacances Populaires
Enfantines," June 1937.

The annual kermesse,
June 1934: Maurice
Thorez (head of the
French Communist Party
and deputy for the canton)
addresses the crowd,
surrounded by a host of
strapping young *colons,*
whose glowing good
health broadcasts the
virtues of the municipal
colonie.

(*Below*) A group of older, adolescent *colons* display their gymnastic prowess at the annual *colonie* fête, 15 August 1946. The banner behind them is emblazoned with Maurice Thorez's famous phrase: "Childhood, our sweetest hope."

A human (child) star welcomes the parents to the annual
colonie fête, 15 August 1947
(*Below*) *Monitrice* Raymonde Laluque and her *équipe,*
summer 1948.

Moniteur Roger Debrieux and his *équipe,* summer 1948.
(*Below*) Bearing the tricolor sashes that mark their office,
the municipal council of the child's republic of "Villanous"
solemnly poses for an official photo, summer 1949.

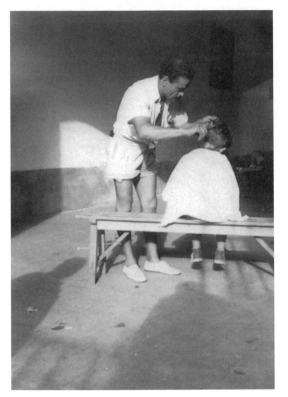

Even in the midst of the mass that arrived each summer at Les Mathes, there were moments of individual attention; here, prompted by the search for the redoubtable louse. Late 1950s. (*Below*) The Ivry *mairie,* decorated for a cold-war kermesse with watchwords from the Movement for Peace: "Children need peace as flowers need the sun." Ca. 1950.

Fundraising poster for the *laïque colonies* of the
Jeunesse au Plein Air, early 1950s.
Private collection of the author.

city's marching band. Any tears or anxiety brought on by the departure would fade rapidly in the shouts and excitement of the trip—or so reassured one reporter from *Le Travailleur:* "During the trip from Ivry to the Montparnasse station we sang revolutionary songs. Our watchwords, free Thaelmann and the soviets everywhere, resonated warmly with the workers whom we met along the way."[55]

Like their Catholic counterparts, the Communists clearly saw their *colonie* as a privileged site for the political education of children. But in the early days (1928–34), logistical and material questions dominated, pressing matters of pedagogy to the margins: How was the *mairie* to finance a full reconstruction of the *colonie*'s extensive, and sadly dilapidated, grounds; or find sufficient funds to send all young Ivryens for free, if need be?[56] And how might they muster the human resources to organize and watch over so many children? Discussions of education and child psychology are thus largely absent from the minutes of OVPE meetings before the late 1930s. Vital Marques remembers the extraordinary freedom that marked his summers *en colonie* during the early days at Les Mathes, when some dozen or so adults looked after the four to five hundred children who arrived each summer:

> The staff consisted of a few deputies and administrators, and the organization left much to be desired. Nonetheless I can tell you we were never bored. We drove them crazy! To deal with us for an entire month, now that took some courage. Some of the deputies weren't even paid, especially those who worked in factories. They took a month without pay. Often they stayed two or three months with us . . . We accustomed ourselves quite rapidly to this great *colonie*. Aside from the broad sand beaches, the most striking and beautiful aspect was the great forest that surrounded the *colonie*. We would hike dozens of kilometers there each day, singing revolutionary songs that we had learned at the *patro [municipal],* for the *colonie* was not fenced off; the space belonged to us. Only one place was off-limits, an old wine cellar with huge vats for pressing the grapes. It was dangerous for us kids.[57]

The few accounts that we have from this period all mention the spontaneous formation of small groups among the children, gangs that seem to have had a certain coherence, permanence, even, if we are to judge by the fact that they were known by the names of their leaders: "Left to our own initiative, we formed little bands of kids who were usually about the same age," recalled Denis Bordat:

Sometimes they were mixed and other times not, depending on the moment; bands of ten to fifteen kids with their chiefs and their pecking-orders,
gangs that were sometimes rivals and at other times allied . . . Each year I
fought Pergaud's *War of the Buttons* at least a hundred times, building and
destroying huts that gradually became fortresses over the two months of
vacation . . . [These were] real forts with their own defenses, their weapons
that had to be made, their own stocks of munitions, their particular treasures that were collected on hunting trips of all sorts . . . It was the gray
and green lizards, and the little snakes and vipers, who paid the price here.
For these treasures had to be preserved in boxes and cages, little improvised
zoos that had to be defended against the inevitable raids of an opposing
gang . . . Often one member had to keep watch at noon, and so miss his
lunch. Given the huge number of kids, his absence from the refectory could
scarcely be noticed.[58]

As Marques reminds us, the snakes and lizards did not remain confined
to the boxes of these makeshift zoos — plenty found their way down other
children's shirts, and into the capacious pockets of mischievous *colons* like
Vital's brother, "La Terreur," who carried a ready supply of these unhappy reptiles in his pockets, so that he could later make handsome little
displays on the tables of the *moniteurs* and service people.

The self-designed amusements of the undersurveilled Ivryens extended well beyond the realms of war games and teasing: during the
obligatory post-lunch nap, for example, the children would spread their
straw mats in an immense clearing and put on impromptu entertain-
ment, singing popular songs and dancing for each other. "One of our
games was choosing the 'queen of the charleston.' The *moniteurs* would
start us off and we would continue, transforming the game as we went."[59]
And of course the fun did not necessarily end when the lights went out:
one night, "Jacques's gang" sneaked out of the dormitory to a neighboring dairy farm, where they led all thirty cows from their stalls and took
them to a clearing for a vast nighttime corrida.[60]

But the collective life of children held its terrors as well: "Imagine the
arrival," writes Denis Bordat:

Lost in a context too vast for a child of seven to comprehend. The anguished
search for the toilet . . . too afraid to ask where "the place" is and, after
finding it by accident, discovering that the doors do not close, or that the
automatic flushing mechanism will soak you if you happen to walk in at the
wrong moment. Discovering collective showers at an age when I no longer
bathed in front of my mother. I didn't even know what a shower was, for at

home we used a basin in the kitchen sink. The terror of being naked in front
of fifty other kids . . . The terrifying sound of adult voices, cutting through
the noise and crying: "wash yourselves, soap yourselves, rinse yourselves,
dry yourselves, dress yourselves." And the bed wetting . . . I had never wet
my bed, but each morning a good dozen of the hundred kids in the dorm
would have wet their sheets, "les pisseux" as they were known. At night, I
could hardly sleep, gripped by the fear that this might happen to me . . . and
one night it happened . . . the accident, an absurd dream. . . . I could not fall
back asleep that night. At daybreak I got up before the others and made my
bed oh-so-tightly with the soiled sheets. When the monsieur came by, close
past my bed, as he did each morning, he said "oh that's very good, your bed
is very well made today, bravo!"[61]

At this stage, with no real pedagogical agenda, and a ratio of staff to
children that permitted nothing more than the most basic surveillance
(perhaps ten or twelve *permanentes* were sent to look after some three
to four hundred children in the early 1930s), games and activities at Les
Mathes show no clear gender division. Because the *colonie* was mixed
from the outset, with the only segregation occurring in the sleeping and
collective shower arrangements (the girls slept on the lower floor, boys
on the higher), boys and girls played together at some moments, separately at others, with no guiding principle other than their own friendship preferences. As we will see, the pedagogical guidelines that the OVPE
gradually developed for the *colonie* were built on the basis of a gender-
mixed child society in which complete equality of the sexes formed but
one of the utopian principles that was to be lived in the summer-long
child's republic.

In June of 1930, the OVPE at last defined its first rule for the *colonie,*
twenty-three regulations addressed to the "comrades surveillants" in the
hope that this might introduce some order into the chaotic little world
of Les Mathes. These rules—which made no reference to any boy-girl
distinctions—reflected the OVPE's concern for hygiene, order, and a constant surveillance of the children, for the organizers lived in dread of
accidents, especially swimming-related accidents (children drowning, or
being swept out to sea). They also sought to define clear and hierarchical
lines of authority converging on the *colonie*'s single director. Thus each
moniteur was put in charge of eighty children, which meant seeing that
hands got washed before meals, that the dorms were kept clean and in
order, that clothes were laundered and properly redistributed each week
(a small administrative nightmare), that heads were checked regularly

for lice. And under no circumstances were the *moniteurs* to argue in front of the children; all disputes were to be referred to the director.[62] The rule then outlined a typical day in the *colonie,* an action-packed agenda that competed with the exhausting schedules designed by the Catholics: not a moment was left unfilled, and nothing was left to chance, nor to the tastes and preferences of children. The abhorred entity (unstructured time) was thus crammed to the gills with a relentless round of meals, games, hikes, and collective exercises (gymnastics, human pyramids, folk dancing), with the climactic daily sea bath crowning each afternoon.[63] This, too, was a highly structured event, in part because of the fear that someone might drown (no one ever did), but also because of the near-mythic healing powers attributed to the good salt air and brief dips in the ocean. Each afternoon, the *moniteurs* would take their young charges on a five-kilometer hike through the woods and down to the sandy shores. The *moniteurs* would then wade in waist deep and link hands, forming a human chain that held the children in the calm shallows near the shore. Every fifteen to twenty minutes the whistle would sound and one group would come out to dry off while another ran in to splash and paddle about. On the return hike, the children would take their afternoon snack of bread and chocolate under the pines of the Clapet forest.

One *moniteur,* Lucien Laborie, recalls the ill effects that standing an hour or more in the chill Atlantic waters exerted on his young system: "There were eight hundred kids who swam in relays, eighty kids at a time . . . [so] we *moniteurs* each spent a good two hours in the water. The kids would splash us, in order to show their sympathy. After several hours, I would emerge, quite blue with cold." In the midst of his own discomfort, though, Laborie was struck, and quite moved, by the sight of these children, making contact with the ocean for the first time:

> The discovery of the sea by these kids, most of whom were seeing it for the first time: now that was ecstasy. The fine sand beach that ran on for miles, the calm waters, the little dunes breaking up the endless, flat stretches of sand; the kids were delighted. I saw kids who were quite drunk with plea-sure, who, when they first caught sight of the sea stood utterly still for a few seconds before hurling themselves forward to plunge their heads re-peatedly into the water, and even into the sand. They were bursting with joy . . . they had no idea the sea could be all that.[64]

In all of these activities girls took a vigorous and visible part, as tes-tified in the photographs of sports and games at Les Mathes, published each year in the *Bulletin municipal officiel:* "Crossing the Finish-line in the Girls' 250 Meter Race," "*Vaillantes* and *Vaillants* Out Camping," or "Games on the Lawn," with little girls scrambling madly in a kind of three-legged race up a grassy slope on the *colonie* grounds.[65] In addition, the directors organized numerous matches of *ballon prisonnier* and handball that pitted girls against boys in vigorously contested matches in which the girls, often as not, emerged the victors.[66] Ivry had a lively tradition of women's sports that extended back to the formation of the women's section of the Socialist Union Sportive du Travail d'Ivry (USTI) in the aftermath of World War I: "We were utterly absorbed in the club," recalled Mme Clerville. "I threw shot-put . . . the javelin, and the discus. My sisters and I also played basketball. We were three times the champions of France."[67] Local Communists seized on this tradition, expanding the range and number of female sports associations and celebrating women's athleticism as a direct and valuable means of enhancing their autonomy and sense of self-worth and self-reliance: "she will gain moral qualities that will stand her in good stead in hard times," wrote the editors of the *Bulletin municipal:* "endurance, energy, will power, and a certain sense of independence, thanks to which she will no longer think of herself as man's inferior."[68] Small wonder that this veritable cult of women's sports should have found such powerful expression in the municipal *colonie.*

The question of discipline raised by the 1930 regulations directs our attention to the issue of adult-child relationships in the *colonies de vacances.* What kind of relationships did the OVPE hope to foster in the *colonie* at Les Mathes? The general guideline put forth here adjured that *moniteurs* be firm, but never brutal or rigid. This principle sat easily with the popular leftist notion that children were "a beginning," adults in a process of becoming, as opposed to a diminished incarnation of adult life. As such, they should never be driven by blows and punishments.[69] The vision of a firm yet flexible authority also informed the notion, first developed in the mid-1930s, that the holiday should be organized through mutual discussion and agreement between adults and children, rather than by one-way impositions of authority. Children should thus be consulted in these matters, "treated not as pawns but as young comrades."[70]

During the Popular Front and postwar periods, that is, from 1934 until the early 1950s, this democratic concept of the adult-child relation became a central pillar in a Communist pedagogical practice that strove to foster an active, "grassroots" political agency among the *colons* by creating institutions of children's self-government within the *colonie*. In constructing their own pedagogy of child leisure, Ivry's Communists drew from several sources, including an abundant leftist and soviet pedagogical literature that underscored the urgent need to overturn patriarchal authority (the familial analogue of capitalist power) by granting children both autonomy and power: "It is necessary to find a form of organization which is governed by neither individual egoism nor by the herd spirit; one that stimulates the highest form of activity and of solidarity," wrote Communist pedagogue Edwin Hoernlé in 1924: "This organization is the free, self-administered and self-legislative children's group . . . [A] new relation between adults and children is developing, not in the homes of the proletariat but in the children's groups . . . Inside them the life is that of a completely free community."[71] But they also drew from a fund of ideas that resonated strikingly with Catholic views on the importance of collective organization among children, where children's natural urge to play could be oriented so as "to stimulate those qualities, those faculties and feelings which correspond to our conception of humanity."[72] Within the structures of the Communist *colonie,* then, children's play became a kind of apprenticeship to adult life, as Socialist visions of a "just and well-ordered social life" became a "living reality," incarnated in the "primitive community of the child's republic."[73]

Hence, like the Catholics, Communist pedagogues also saw the urge to play as distinctive to children, the activity that qualitatively separates the child's way of being from the adult's. The crucial difference lay in how each group chose to mobilize this fact within a pedagogy of child leisure. The Catholics thus strove to unleash the social and ethical energies of children within pseudofamilial hierarchies of religious affiliation, to build generationally ordered brotherhoods and sisterhoods of robust Catholic conviction in a militantly secular society. The Communists, by contrast, ordered their young troops along more horizontal and democratic lines, locating these smaller groupings within the more overtly political structures of a child's republic that was explicitly intended to nourish political awareness and a spirit of activism among the adults of tomorrow as they chased about hunting snakes and lizards in the wooded hills around Les Mathes.

Both Catholic and Communist pedagogues thus strove to direct the spontaneous activity of children, in particular their urge to play, toward the development of a resilient autonomy. To that end, they sought to make of their *colonies* alternative child societies, intended to shape self-activating yet nonegotistical individuals who could militate effectively in the hostile world of the present toward the realization of a future, utopian society, be it a society of Socialists or a community of the faithful. But where the Catholic *colonies* practiced rigorous gender-segregation, the *colonie* at Les Mathes adhered firmly to the principle of *mixité,* intended to overcome bourgeois falsity in gender relations ("le monde du flirt bourgeois") but also to arrive at a more complete and egalitarian integration of girls and women into the public world of civic life and politics.[74] As we shall see, the structures of the child's republic of "Villanous" at Les Mathes were arranged with just such egalitarian visions in mind.

But the process of endowing their children with a resilient autonomy could not proceed without contradiction, for in late 1920s France, and especially during the so-called Third Period (1928–34), such pedagogical ideals ran up against the increasingly harsh realpolitik of a revolutionary party in a world where revolution had failed to spread beyond the borders of the Soviet Union. In this context, the democratic goals of the party were increasingly displaced into that misty realm of After-the-Revolution in favor of a present-day politics of discipline and struggle in defense of an embattled Soviet regime. In pedagogical realms this generated an unresolved tension between those who clung to the dream of children's self-administration and those who felt the need for a more heavy-handed intervention and guidance of children's activity along politically correct lines. The wish to foster a resilient autonomy among the *colons* thus battled with the urge to channel the children's energies into precisely defined political molds. This produced an uneasy oscillation in the Communist *colonie,* with the "free, self-administered and self-legislative" children's groups being used, by turns, as structures of genuine self-administration, or, alternatively, as functional groups in which peer pressure could be employed to encourage the less zealous to fall into line.[75]

In the Communist *colonies de vacances,* the pedagogical-political organization by children's groups was most fully realized in the aftermath of the Second World War, during the era of "leftist humanism" within the PCF. But it had its roots in the everyday experiences of children and *moniteurs* at Les Mathes during the 1930s. Hence, in the summer of 1934, the *Bulletin municipal* boasted that Les Mathes was distinguished from "other, bourgeois *colonies*" by its pedagogical method: "We thus teach children to organize for themselves. They form various committees, each of which has its own function: the hygiene committee, the games committee, the disciplinary committee, etc. The older children are put in charge of groups of ten kids each, under the supervision of the adult staff, in order to organize hikes, meals, life in the dormitories."[76] This suborganization in troops of ten was no doubt a creative (or perhaps desperate) response to the lizard-filled wildness of the early days at Les Mathes. But there is no mistaking the Communists' sincere concern with the very poignant question that lay at the heart of their enterprise, namely, how does one nurture the resilience and autonomy of working-class children, growing up in the hostile indifference of bourgeois society? "As he plays in the streets, the marketplace, in shops, even at home, the proletarian child senses the structures of the bourgeois world from a very early age, with its privileges for the owning class and its disadvantages for the dispossessed," wrote Kurt Loewenstein in 1933. "The inequality between classes reveals itself quite early in the life of a working-class child and offers him a very limited role in society. We must therefore vanquish this sense of inferiority and replace it with pride in belonging to the working class by showing the child that he can accomplish something serious and important."[77]

The developing practice of self-government in the *colonie* thus hints at a pedagogical solution to the latent contradiction in Marx's theory between his conceptualization of the proletariat as an exploited mass, destined to triumph, Spartacuslike, over its oppressors, and his vision of industrial workers as the pioneers of a new society, freed from the dominance of capital. The pedagogy of rendering children responsible for themselves resolved the tension by recasting it across the lifespan of a single generation, providing a passage that moved one from vision A (mass of exploited slaves) to vision B (the proud heirs to a world transformed) via a clear developmental and educational process. Moreover, it is important to recall that these children, being shaped for the collectivity of the future, were an entirely new subject of pedagogic treatment, not only because they issued from a working-class (rather than bourgeois) milieu, but also because they constituted the human material from which that future society was to be constructed. Communist pedagogues thus sought to shape the child in such a way that she or he would be an appropriate point of departure for the new society, and a vital first step in its realization. Unlike previous, "bourgeois" pedagogues, who focused on integrating the child into an existing society, Communist educators worked to shape a child who could be both heir to and architect of the dawning Socialist utopia.[78] The children of the Paris red belt thus found themselves at the heart of the social transformation, and the life of the world to come.

From as early as 1930, the OVPE sought to lay the foundation for such an education by building an informal pedagogic "chat" into the *moniteurs'* weekly routine. Each week, a different *moniteur* took charge of leading the session, and the lion's share of the discussion was devoted to careful explications of working-class life and labor, pitched to a child's level of understanding (by which they meant using lots of concrete examples). Traces of this policy are scattered through the boxes of the OVPE archives, moldering in the basement of Ivry's city hall: collective notebooks kept by dormitory troops each bearing the names of various proletarian occupations (the Butchers, the Blacksmiths, the Coal-Face Sorters) whose study formed a part of the group's collective project over the long summer months. This might be carried out by a direct "étude du milieu," in which the *colons* would visit a lighthouse, port, farm, or factory in order to describe what they saw there, and to speak with the workers and peasants about their daily life and labor: "We entered a tiny room where two women were threading oyster shells along a wire," wrote the boys from the Blacksmiths' troop after a day spent exploring the oyster park at Marennes: "The women told us that their métier is difficult because they must invest so much hard labor before they can sell their oysters. Moreover, they earn practically nothing."[79] The results were then assembled in team journals, whose painstakingly printed pages, enhanced by pasted-in photos and vivid crayon sketches, record the collective work of the group. In the summer of 1951, for example, the Equipe des Trieuses ("Sorters at the Coal-Face" — girls aged thirteen to fourteen) wrote to the *centre d'initiative* at Montceau-les-Mines for further information on the archaic occupation for which their troop had been named. In reply, they received a series of prewar postcard photographs showing the *trieuses* at their arduous labors. The photos form an eloquent frontispiece to the poem through which the girls learned about the harsh lives of women workers in the nation's recent industrial past:

Les Trieuses

They have blackened hands and broken nails
these women from the black country in the mining center,
who, throughout the live-long day, see the world through
    dust-shrouded eyes.

The grey coal to be sorted arrives at an infernal rate
And when the day is over they must return to their homes,
must feed the husband and two little boys
who down in the mineshaft have lost the sunlight altogether
It's a brutal life.
They give up their sleep, and then their lives, in order to sort the coal.
But soon a great cry will rise up to the sky
An end to all fighting; misery, cease to haunt us!
Now the sun will shine bright on the land
An end to the bitter rhythm!
The coal will arrive without the painful toil of men and women.[80]

Such conscious fostering of a politicized class awareness could happen in a variety of settings at Les Mathes: while out hiking with the *moniteur;* on the beach at Ronce-les-Bains (where, in the summer of 1949, a group of children, bearing aloft a red hat inscribed with the words "Socialisme, avenir du monde," circulated the Stockholm Appeal among the bourgeois bathers); at the *colonie*'s Saturday night film festival, where films like *Le Foulard Rouge* would later form the object of critical review in the girls' collective journal. One cannot help but be struck by the central role of song and poetry in shaping this education; just two weeks before they recorded the poetic tale of the *trieuses,* the Equipe des Trieuses had learned the song of Henri Martin and Raymonde Dien, sung to the tune of "Colombe vole, vole oiseaux."[81] If the pedagogical approach sought to stir the girls' interest by appealing to their particular, presumably girlish preoccupations — the fate of women workers at the coal-face, the romantic tale of Raymonde Dien's loyalty to the brave Henri Martin — the pedagogic goal was always to enliven a vigorous sense of class, rather than gender/feminist identity. For in the child's republic at Les Mathes, the interests and concerns of girls were understood to be enfolded entirely within the larger, class-conscious politics that structured the *colonie.*

From the mid-1930s onward, then, the adult staff at Les Mathes focused increasingly on democratizing the relations of power that obtain between adult and child. Staff and *moniteurs* thus organized the *colonie* on the principle of equalizing the adult-child relation, replacing hierarchy and orders from above with relations of consultation and friendship that acknowledged the child's need for both guidance and autonomy and power: "Moral authority needs no whistles, no slaps to the head or other punishments to sustain itself," wrote Venise Gosnat at the end of his first summer directing the child's republic at Les Mathes: "Love for the child, the constant endeavor to understand the sentiments that move him, and great confidence in him; these will suffice."[82] These relations were gradually institutionalized in a set of explicitly political forms whereby, in the immediate postwar era, the 700 to 900 children of Ivry could organize, collectively and on their own initiative, the long summers at Les Mathes.[83] This "constitution" consisted of a series of committees (hygiene, games, discipline), crowned by the municipal council of Les Mathes, elected each summer by universal childhood suffrage, with half the seats reserved to the girls.[84]

A full-blown child's republic, organized in conscious imitation of the local government in Ivry, thus rose anew each summer in the pine forests of the Charente-Maritime. Some sense of the form that this political apprenticeship took in the immediate postwar years can be gleaned from the records of the general assembly, a weekly meeting of the entire *colonie* each Sunday morning that was led by the *colonie*'s municipal council:

> Thus the second deputy took the floor: "Comrades, it is my conviction that when we go to the Co-op [the *colonie*'s child-operated candy store], each of us should purchase a few bonbons for the young comrades who have no money to buy things with. Are you with me?" (unanimous YES). A third deputy then took the floor: "My dear comrades, there are flowers in the woods and meadows, there are vases on our tables [in the refectory]. The municipal council believes that we children are not insensitive to the beauties of nature; we are sure that the *colons* are ready to show their appreciation by filling these vases each day with flowers from the fields." (applause, Bravo! Bravo!)

The enthusiasm waned abruptly when a member of the hygiene committee rose to propose a more stringent exam for head lice, but said committee then regained ground when one of its youngest members spoke her mind on the vexed subject of bed wetting: "Some kids are peeing in their beds. It smells bad and they shouldn't do it! (Bravo, kiddo, Bravo!)" And it was determined that the sheets of the "pisseux" would be washed each day.[85]

The pedagogy of working-class life also found its way into these meetings, for instance, on the day when the young mayor of Les Mathes rose to scold his fellow *colons* for having stolen the pine sap buckets off the trees in the forest: "My dear comrades, we've been informed that a forest guard came by to complain to the *colonie* because someone has been pulling the *godets à résine* from the pine trees in the woods. If it is our own *colons* who are responsible for this, then that is very bad. For those who harvest the pine sap are workers, like our own parents; they must earn their living." [86] For the young citizens of the republic of Les Mathes, the collective life of children, "playing" together on vacation, was not only an apprenticeship to adult life; it was an apprenticeship to a life of political engagement as well, a world in which everyday affairs were imbued with political meaning and choice: "We always believed that the *colonie* should not exist in isolation from the rest of society, that it should be closely linked to the issues of everyday life, and especially to working-class life in Ivry," Lucien Laborie later remarked. "Our principle was never to impose, but rather to discuss." [87]

The End of the République Enfantine de Villanous:
Cold War Politics and the Reinscription of the Line Separating
Politics from Culture

In the summer of 1998, Lucien Laborie spoke at some length about his experiences working with the children of Ivry, first as *moniteur,* then director of Les Mathes. In the course of this conversation, a very interesting fact emerged: in 1951, after two summers as a *moniteur* at Les Mathes, Laborie decided to join the Communist Party:

> Although I had lived among militants all my life in Ivry, it was working at the *colo des Mathes* that led me to join the party . . . I was invited to work at the *colonie* in 1949, and that experience triggered my decision, because I saw then what the Communists had done [for the children] . . . I threw myself wholeheartedly into the life of the OVPE, the kermesse for the benefit of the *colonie,* the tombola. Every Sunday morning we stood in the marketplace and sold tickets [for the tombola]. It was this militant activity on behalf of the *amicale des moniteurs,* and the children of Ivry, that broadened my horizons.[88]

Laborie was not alone in his political conversion; the records of Ivry's *amicale des moniteurs* list a dedicated core of some twenty or more young women and men (about one quarter to one third of the *colonie* staff in any given summer) moved to party activism by their experiences working with the children at Les Mathes: "In those days working with the *colonie* formed a part of their life as militants," recalled Denis Bordat: "It was intimately bound up with their political engagement."[89] The heady atmosphere of fervent political engagement that animated the *colonie* at Les Mathes in those years was clearly nourished by the broad hopes raised by the Liberation, and their subsequent eclipse in the early years of the cold war. But as the cold war heated up, the *colonies* of the *banlieues rouges* were to find themselves called to account by the State Secretariat for Sport and Youth, which in the summer of 1951 leveled accusations of "undermining the moral freedom of children" against a whole host of red *colonies,* Ivry among them.[90] When the dust had settled, the child's republic of Villanous, and the larger idea that children might be treated as political beings, were all hastily put aside by municipalities that sought to protect their social policy achievements from being dismantled altogether by a newly hostile regime.

The first shots in this battle were fired by the secretariat, which in the spring of 1951 denied to Ivry the customary state subvention for its 1950 *colonie,* claiming that the children had not enjoyed as much "freedom of thought" as was "desirable," and that "the educational activities practiced therein were inspired by a political ideology." From the secretariat's point of view, it was simply not acceptable for *colonies,* which constituted a kind of "extension" of the school, to fail to respect the principle of neutrality imposed on public school teachers.[91] Mayor Marrane returned a vehement letter of protest in which he underscored first of all the broad recruitment of *moniteurs* at Les Mathes, which included several "practicing Catholics" and one young seminarian preparing for the priesthood.[92] More importantly, he argued that the *colonies* were in no sense a part of the centralized system of public education. Rather, they were organized under private auspices, by religious orders and *oeuvres de vacances.* Even the *colonies scolaires,* organized under the aegis of the *caisses des écoles,* could not be considered a part of the republican school per se, and in no way constituted its "extension."[93] The secretariat was therefore utterly mistaken in its assertion that municipal *colonies* should strictly avoid all activity that smacked of politics.[94] After all, Catholic *colonies* had long practiced an overt policy of religious education and open proselytizing; were not Communist voters—taxpayers who had duly elected their Communist *mairie*—entitled to the same right, that is, to a *colonie* that preached their vision of the world?[95]

Marrane's argument against the *laïque* conception of public space as ideologically neutral space made pointed (if oblique) reference to the re-

cently revived debate over state funding for Catholic schools (the Marie
and Barangé laws, finally passed in September of 1951), underscoring
the blatant unfairness of a regime that tolerated the Catholic breach of
neutrality even as it threatened to shut down the Communist one. But
the ears of the secretariat remained closed to such logic, and in July of
1951, the director of the secretariat went so far as to threaten to close
down, "by force, if necessary," those *colonies* that persisted in an openly
political organization.[96] This time, the director pointed the finger at specific aspects of the pedagogic structure at Les Mathes, whose "activities unfolded around political themes and slogans." Hence, "the songs,
games, and decoration of the halls were all inspired by a single orientation, [while] the children's troops . . . were given names like 'Maurice
Thorez'; 'Raymonde Dien'; 'Mao-Tsé-Toung,' etc. The *moniteurs* were
instructed on such topics as the atomic bomb, the war in Korea, etc."[97]
Even if no parents had ever complained about the blatant politicization
of their children, the breach of *laïcité* was plainly evident.

   In the changed political circumstances of the early 1950s, with the
Communists excluded (since May 1947) from the government and the
Catholic Mouvement Républicain Populaire (MRP) playing an increasingly central role in holding together fragile parliamentary majorities,
the laws granting state support to Catholic schools passed without difficulty. At that same moment, the *colonies communistes* found themselves
deprived of all state financial support. The timing could hardly have
been worse, for as wages continued to lag behind prices, workers' purchasing power fell to an all-time low. The hygienic need for municipal
colonies was thus more urgent than ever, for it was the children who suffered most seriously from the drastic decline in working-class incomes,
as PCF councillor Pierrette Petitot pointed out during that same summer
of 1951. The consequences were all too visible in the pinched, pale faces
of these children, a majority of whom were seriously malnourished, a
consequence not only of the war but of the "deplorable impact that the
low standard of living in working-class families is having on the health
of their children."[98] Despite the loss of state funds, then, the PCF took
firm steps to ensure the preservation of its *colonies,* starting with a sharp
call to order issued to the Communist municipalities in late August of
1951, just days after the secretariat's threats of imminent closure arrived
on mayoral desks across the *banlieue rouge.*[99]

   The PCF's August 1951 report opened with a reminder to its readers
that parents who sent their children to Communist *colonies* were not

always political fellow-travelers, and might, therefore, object to the political education being given therein. Moreover, the report went on to suggest that the practice of treating children as political beings might in fact be pedagogically unsound: "The concern with 'doing politics' above all (and without sufficient prior reflection) leads to unfortunate errors while giving a certain pretext to the reactionary maneuvering of the Ministry of Youth and Sport. *It is a mistake to regard the child as a small adult* who can simply take the latter's place."[100]

If it was a strategic error to use children for certain kinds of "propaganda," such as selling *l'Huma-Dimanche* in the streets on Sundays (for this simply put off the very people whom the PCF sought to convince), the real problem was more fundamental. Having children "do politics" in the *colonie* was not the same as giving them a real education that would allow them to develop into ethically aware and politically active adults: "Displaying HUMANITE in the *colonie* allows some people to avoid the *long, exacting, and patient work of education, adapted to the child,* that the directors and *moniteurs* must accomplish!" scolded PCF reporters Waldeck l'Huillier and H. Jambon. Hence "the thoughtless and overfrequent repetition of slogans conceals a refusal to study the children who are confided to us, to study their reflexes, to satisfy their need to learn and their curiosity, to awaken their minds and guide their first discoveries about life and society, to give them a civic education in keeping with our Communist morality."[101]

Given the hostile political environment, one is tempted to read this pedagogical critique as a purely tactical maneuver: the PCF was advising its municipal *colonies* to back away from the pedagogy of treating children as responsible agents in their own right not because the practice had been found wanting but because the state was threatening to close down their *colonies* altogether. At the same time it is striking to see how quickly party officials rediscovered the very criticisms they had leveled twenty years earlier against the Socialist *républiques enfantines* of the Faucons Rouges, rehabilitating their old objections to the artificial "game" of politics that the Faucons generated inside the artificial atmosphere of their summer-long children's republics.[102] More interesting yet is the rapidity with which the party's pre–Popular Front uneasiness with the pedagogy of play and its problematic relation to social reality resurfaced. Was it right, the PCF reporters asked, that a child of fourteen, having spent his summer in the dorm of the "Black Sea Sailors," should laughingly refer to his "summer on the Black Sea," with no real sense of the gravity of the affair, nor even any clear idea of when the mutiny actually took place? Closer to home still, "Can one play . . . at 'Libération' or 'Maquis' without a serious preparation, and without putting into the game those elements that can be truly 'played' and understood by children?" While the authors readily conceded that many young militants had received just such a political apprenticeship in countless *colonies rouges* across the nation, they nonetheless maintained that what was called for at this time was not children "doing politics" but a better "orientation" of pedagogical directors and *moniteurs,* so that the adolescents who emerged from those *colonies* might engage in more age-appropriate activism within the centralized structures of the party organization. The authors thus concluded that "while relying heavily on their elected officials, the militants who run the *colonies* will give us thousands of young activists for the UJRF and UJFF." [103]

Perhaps, then, the pedagogical call to order, which may also have allowed a reining in of those *colonies municipales* that had grown too independent in their political/pedagogical aims, was not so distasteful to PCF officialdom after all. [104] What is clear, however, is that from the fall of 1951 forward, the pedagogical directors of the red *colonies* executed a sudden about-face, burying all traces of the children's republics and repeatedly advising their staff that the locus of instruction had shifted from having children "do" politics to waging the cultural battle against those trashy American comics and films that "train the child to become a 'killer' rather than a human being": "All these magazines imported from America focus on gangsterism, the super man, colonialism, racism, and develop in the child the instincts of a killer, the wish to be the strongest, in order to brutalize him and better prepare him for war. These lubricious magazines and reviews highlight sex and scenes of rape, which gives rise to vice in the child and, by the same token, to all kinds of sexual problems." [105] Since it was hopeless to try and convince profit-hungry booksellers to stop peddling such stuff, the only solution was to confront these "rotten comics" head-on in the *colonie* by explaining to children the difference between this degenerate literature and healthy magazines like the PCF comic book *Vaillant.* [106]

The turn from "doing politics" to controlling the cultural ambiance in the *colonie* was characterized by militants as a shift away from "political" to "educational" *colonies.* Directors were thus advised to avoid such classic practices as naming the tents and dormitories for those militants "beloved by the working class" and to focus instead on developing the children's "sense of the beautiful, and of work." Through this more diffuse, "moral" education, children would come to understand what it means to be a human being who is fully conscious of his or her rights and duties.[107] Henceforth, then, education at Les Mathes was to be a "civic education in keeping with our communist morality," and pedagogical staff were urged to turn their energies to creating the kind of cultural ambiance within which young children would learn to shun the bad (trashy films and comics that promoted the values of "pin-ups and cowboys") and embrace the good (*Vaillant*). At the same time, the *colonie* would no longer set forth any overarching political framework within which to locate these cultural choices regarding how to use their vacation leisure.[108] Rather, this latter was to flow from the person of the *moniteur,* who now more than ever had to embody the political virtues that were no longer incarnated in the pedagogical structure of the *colonie:* "The *moniteur* . . . must not shut himself off in utter 'neutrality,'" concluded Ivry's *amicale des moniteurs,* "for given current social problems, he has a moral obligation to react":

> He must not regard the *colonie* as existing in isolation from the rest of the world, for the *colonie* situates itself at the cutting edge of education. He must speak to the children of their parents' daily worries; he must explain to them the life that actually awaits them, the laborious struggle that stretches before them. He must therefore let them know that in the current situation, they are accountable . . . In acting this way, he places the children on the alert and makes them conscious that life is made not only of dreams, illusions of gangsterism, etc., etc., but that its principal factors are: Love, Work, and Peace." [109]

If the "orientation" of the *colonie* was no longer a matter of "banners and slogans," but above all a matter of "heartfelt conviction" on the part of the *moniteur,* who must henceforth set the example in his own person, it was more urgent than ever to recruit *moniteurs* from the milieu, and preferably militants from the factories.[110] From the mid-1950s, annual reports from the *amicale* regularly bemoaned the growing presence of CEMEA-trained students and teachers, at the expense of the soughtafter "worker-cadres": those "politically conscious and informed militants who will allow us to sow the seeds of future militants among the youth, and [to shape] workers who are ready for the struggle." [111] For politics and pedagogy now had to meet in the person of the individual *moniteur,* who, in the words of Ivry militant Pierre Feltz, must at all times

be "with his children" even as he always felt himself "to be a militant."
While it was a relatively simple matter to do as the CEMEA did, and train
young women and men in the technical aspects of the work (hygiene,
games, songs), it was quite another business altogether to make of each
moniteur a "militant on behalf of childhood, one who leads his games
with all his heart, who understands the 'colo' in light of humanity's social and political problems . . . , and who is fully engaged in the struggle
for peace and the construction of a new society."[112]

The frequent references in all this literature to the struggle for peace
and the Movement for Peace—a PCF watchword since the onset of the
cold war—suggests that political education was, in fact, to continue in
the red *colonies,* but without fanfare and banners, in the more intimate
setting of "moral education" as it unfolded in informal chats between
moniteurs and their *colons.* Hence, as the political activity of children receded in importance, the militancy of individual *moniteurs,* and the role
of the *amicale* in nurturing and promoting that engagement, grew ever
more pronounced. For the 1951 turn from "political" to "educational"
colonies implied a more delicate "cultural" strategy in which the individual *moniteur* had to embody the very political virtues that had been
banned from the public life of the *colonie.* At the same time the PCF
warned its mayors against granting too much autonomy to their *amicales des moniteurs,* which should, under no circumstances, be allowed
to "transform themselves into syndicates."[113] Through a healthy dose of
democratic centralism, the PCF would see its municipal *colonies* through
the crisis of 1951.

Thus, in the autumn of 1951, Communist pedagogues in Ivry, and in
red *colonies* all across France, reinscribed the line between culture and
politics that had been effaced by the broadly democratic politicization
of culture and popular education in Popular Front and post-Liberation
France. Henceforth, all explicitly political language at Les Mathes would
be confined to the half-day ceremony commemorating the Liberation
each 26 August.[114] In the summer of 1952, then, the children's republic
of Villanous was, interestingly enough, replaced by an extensive experiment in organized *mixité* among the adolescent *campeurs* and *colons,* with
mixed sports, dramatic games, and a series of three-day, co-ed camping
trips under a nervously watchful surveillance: "It was essential to banish
all hint of promiscuity," recalled Lucien Laborie of that first summer of
organized *mixité:* "We had them marching in segregated columns two
hundred meters apart."[115]

Children's Play as Their "Apprenticeship to Life":
Politics and Pedagogy in the *Colonies Communistes*

"When I think back on our approach in the *colonie* in those days, I wonder if we didn't take things a bit too far," mused Lucien Laborie in 1981:
"During those excursions to Ronce-les-Bains (a rather bourgeois resort)
they marched with a red hat on which was inscribed 'socialism, future of
the world.' They had local youth signing the Stockholm Appeal [against
the Bomb]." On the other hand, "we never forced those young people to
sign the Appeal, and during one of those marches, a woman from Ronce-
les-Bains angrily mocked *monitrice* Yvonne Zellner, saying: 'you would
do better to darn the kids' socks instead of . . .'"[116] The retired director of Les Mathes hastened to point out that the "children" in question
here were in fact adolescents aged fourteen to sixteen, young people who
in his words "were fairly brimming over with politics; it was part and
parcel of the time they were living through."[117] In this they approached
closely their *moniteurs,* for whom the politics of the Liberation and cold
war (Movement for Peace, the Defense of Childhood) were matters of
immediate and daily engagement—in the politics of the PCF, to be sure,
but also in the daily lives of the children in the *colonie,* for one could not
really separate the former from the latter.

Nonetheless, Laborie found himself wondering whether this particular, Communist effort at popular education had, in the end, amounted to
nothing more than yet another instance of education as a top-down imposition of norms and discipline. His reflection invites us once again to
consider the links between the pedagogy of working-class life developed
at Les Mathes and the larger, social politics of working-class childhood
within which the Communist *colonie* was inscribed. How is one to understand a social politics of working-class childhood elaborated by a party
that sought to root itself in the hearts of the local electorate by a conscious
strategy of improving the lives of working-class children? Throughout
this book I have argued that visions of education as simply inculcating
some kind of discipline, whether emanating from the republican state
or from the Comintern, do not begin to capture the complexity of what
was actually going on in the various *colonies de vacances,* where the pedagogical practices being developed and deployed to organize the collective
life of children on holiday were organized around a very rich and complex concept of play. Children's play was thus understood as defining and

occurring within an intermediate area of experience, a domain between
the child's inner world of fantasy and the implacable realities of the external world. Within this transitional space, each child plays in order to
work out what it means to be an individual who acts in the world.

In the case of the *colonies,* these notions of agency were worked out
in relation to the peers and *moniteurs* with whom the child interacted.[118]
Hence the staff in these *colonies* (in particular the young *moniteurs*)
understood themselves to be both witnesses to and participants in a
process of development that they could not directly control. As Lucien
Laborie reminds us, this was equally true in the Communist *colonies,* notwithstanding their episodic ambivalence regarding the pedagogy of play:

> For me, pedagogy entails knowing how to make use of what arises in the
> moment, to take advantage of those opportunities that the child will accept,
> and to never refuse those opportunities created by the child himself. For
> me, pedagogy is at work in a whole host of things. For instance, to show a
> child how to handle a knife in one way and not another; one could regard
> this as simply a matter of good conduct, but it is also and above all a way to
> show the child how to make use of his hands in one way and not another . . .
> [And so] the child comes to see that it is in his own best interest to behave
> in this way; that he enriches his life, and acquires new skills.[119]

As one reads through the records of the *amicale des moniteurs,* one sees
how the various political projects of even so hierarchical and centrally
directed an organization as the French Communist Party—the worker-
peasant alliances of the Popular Front, or the "struggle for peace" movement of the cold war era—existed in a complex and changing relation to
more nuanced pedagogies of children's play that arose in the leftist and
working-class *colonies de vacances.* It is precisely this perception of the
colonies' mission, where the staff participate in (and perhaps assist) the
child's self-construction as an agent through various forms of play, that
cannot be grasped by a formula that views education as mere indoctrination. For if play was conceptualized as the intermediate space in which
the child learns what it means to act, one cannot simply reduce the educational projects of the *colonie de vacances* to a kind of Foucauldian disciplinary structure (despite the often explicit political ordering of these
colonies); the notions of child development that all parties were working
with were simply too complex.

And yet these pedagogical initiatives could not proceed without
contradiction, for the entire Communist project was marked from the

outset by conflicting views of the relationship between the agency of individual activists, the demands of the collective will, and the larger, dialectical framework of history. Within the Communist *colonies de vacances,* these tensions found homelier expression in the collective life of children on holiday, whose adult organizers were caught between the temptation to impose a more centralized discipline and the desire to foster a resilient autonomy and spirit of initiative among working-class children. This contradictory pull mirrors a constant, larger tension that cross-cut the PCF in these tumultuous years, over the relationship between the autonomy of local actors in relation to the party's centralized and increasingly hierarchical control. This tension was particularly marked during the "Third Period" (1928–34), when the demand that all grassroots activities submit to the control of the party sat in uneasy relation to the desire to shape and educate future militants who could take responsibility for themselves and seize opportunities for political action within bourgeois and capitalist society. It is a tension that marked and shaped the collective life of children as it unfolded in the Communist *colonies* of interwar and 1950s France.

Finally, what does the comparative study of the *colonies catholiques* and the Communist *colonie municipale* in Ivry tell us about the relationship between the gender-neutral discourses on working-class childhood produced by the *colonies de vacances* and the often quite gendered practices that shaped everyday life within those *colonies*? Is it enough to say, as has Anna Davin, that the term *childhood* "denied difference," suffocating beneath its universalist pretensions the differences and inequalities that distinguished materially the lives of working-class boys and girls? [120] Or is it perhaps more useful to nuance this singular assessment by considering the consequences for girls of the differently gendered pedagogical orders established by the Catholic and Communist *colonies* of interwar and postwar Ivry? The Catholic policy of segregating the sexes from an early age thus dovetailed with an ideology that openly upheld traditional gender divisions in the name of a functional complementarity within a family whose underlying structure of female subordination was so familiar as to remain unspoken. The result was the separate and unequal education that girls and boys received in their respective *colonies*. Hence, at a moment when pedagogues of all stripes (but Catholics leading the way here) were celebrating child's play as the central and defining act of child life, girls in Catholic *colonies* were often spending their recreational hours in housekeeping tasks and handwork. Where boys' *colonies* swiftly adopted the scout pedagogy of the imaginary, sending their young charges racing through field and forest on games of chivalry and mock war, the girls were often left behind to sew quietly in the company of the good sisters, broken up by the daily promenade to visit the local shrines and *calvaires*. Even in the *colonies* organized by Guides *cheftaines* rather than provincial nuns, Catholic girls confronted a most ambivalent brand of scouting, poised uneasily between the call to adventure and the fear that too much sport and independent activity would "virilize" the girls beyond all hope of recall to home and family.

But was it any better in the Communist *colonie*? What kind of education for girls did this Communist *mixité* deliver? Was it a mere coexistence of separate "others"? Or was it a singular alignment of both sexes behind an implicitly boy-centered definition of the child, with the girls assimilated to the model but occasionally diverging from it or falling behind? In truth, this seems to have fluctuated over the life of the *colonie* at Les Mathes, depending on the circumstances. Hence, at the outset, the absence of all pedagogic structure left the children largely to their own devices, a condition which, by the few accounts we have from this period (1929–33), produced a combination of mixed and segregated games and forms of child sociability. But with the arrival of more clearly defined educational goals and methods, and of the additional staff needed to implement them, the *colonie* developed its class-conscious pedagogy of rendering children responsible for themselves in a *colonie* that was recast as a toy republic. Here, children of both sexes were meant to participate equally in playing at the life of engaged militancy and political responsibility that awaited them in the factories and neighborhood associations of the mother-city, Ivry-la-Rouge.

There can be no doubt that this public structure of full and equal participation in the life of the child's republic at Les Mathes encouraged a vigorous engagement of both sexes in the sports, games, and political life of the *colonie*. But the politics of equal public participation did not always suffice to bring girls and boys together on fully equal terms. Thus in December of 1952, *monitrice* Renée Laborie noted that a disquieting sexual division of play had arisen in the manual workshops at Les Mathes, as the range of activities pursued by girls narrowed alarmingly. She urged her colleagues to join her in a vigorous countermeasure: "We must ensure a greater variety in the girls' activities; they can't simply confine themselves to knitting, sewing, and weaving."[121] But lacking any clear criticism of the sexual division of labor within the family, the *moniteurs* of

Ivry were singularly ill-equipped to draw out the conclusions of observations like Renée Laborie's. For if the party had once boasted feminist
theorists like Alexandra Kollontai, who had cogently explored the particular problems women faced as a result of the sexual division of labor
within the working-class family, such analysis had been resolutely shut
down with Stalin's turn to an increasingly natalist family politics, rooted
in a traditional, patriarchal notion of the family. The post-Liberation
PCF, loyal both to Stalin and to the industrial and demographic reconstruction of France, did not produce any feminist novelties on this front.
On the contrary, the defense of the family became a central aspect of
postwar PCF policy.[122] All that was left to women and girls, then, was
an analysis that located their equality in the public sphere only, leaving
untouched the domestic division of labor, and those sexual divisions of
play that, developmentally speaking, seemed to underwrite them. And
yet the *colonie*'s militant (if somewhat puritanical) *mixité* seems at the
very least to have created the conditions under which an awareness of
particular gender inequities could emerge among the *moniteurs*. Hence,
even in the very darkest years of PCF pro-natalism, Renée Laborie could
be troubled by a sexual division of play that, while utterly in line with the
conventional family values that underpinned the party's gender politics,
sat uneasily with the egalitarian promise of life inside the *colonie* at Les
Mathes.

The concern with play and the free exercise of imagination as a means
of learning to act in the world thus stood at the heart of pedagogical reflection across the political spectrum, animating both theory and practice
in the *colonies* of Catholics and republicans, Socialists and Communists.
This common concern lends a fundamental unity to the comparative
study of the *colonie de vacances,* for with the fin-de-siècle rejection of the
play-centered, kindergarten model of early childhood education in favor
of the more "propaedeutic" model incarnated in the *école maternelle,* the
colonies became the prime site for the elaboration of pedagogies of play
in early-twentieth-century France.[123] But it also directs our attention to a
larger debate on the relationship between adult agency and a particular
understanding of children's freedom. For nestled within these pedagogies of play lies a conception of human freedom and moral agency whose
gradual unfolding reveals an unexpected and ludic ground to modern
Western notions of agency. This conception rests on a particular vision
of the child's "freedom" that consists not in the absence of adult tute-
lage/control but rather in the absence of adult responsibility. It is a free-

dom that is conceived retrospectively, in the adult's nostalgic recollections of his or her own childhood as the time when one's imagination roamed freely. And it is a freedom that harmonizes with broader discourses on childhood found in fin-de-siècle writings all across Europe (pedagogical, but also biographical and autobiographical), discourses that suggest that this particular vision of childhood's freedom has acquired a profound weight and significance in modern Western culture. Indeed, this freedom forms the implicit basis for adult agency, insofar as it defines the developmental pathway by which the ethical and political agency of the adult is achieved. Its absence or curtailment (for instance by a premature initiation into factory labor) thus signals a real and poignant loss, a thwarting or deformation of human development that, in the modern imagination, can never be made up later on. The profoundly gendered forms of children's play in twentieth-century *colonies de vacances* remind us that behind the seemingly neutral and falsely universal notion of "the child" stood boys and girls whose distinct and unequal pathways to adulthood, forged in the thickets of play, would produce adults in whom, to no one's surprise, moral and political agency would take clearly gendered forms.

✍ *Epilogue*

Children belong to the Republic before they belong to their parents.

—Danton, Speech before the Convention, 13 August 1793

With the end of World War II, the *colonie de vacances* finally came into its own as a mass institution in France, serving the needs of both working-class and middle-class children for fresh air, good food (which was much needed across the classes during the years of restrictions), and that special kind of social education that children gained by leaving the narrow circle of family and school and spending four to six weeks in these summertime children's collectives. Thanks to their unique structure—a child community, extracted from the city and let loose on the beaches and hillsides of rural France (though always in the company of trained educators)—the *colonies* provided children with that "incomparable school of social education that is life in a collectivity."[1] Far from their familiar milieux and routines, thrown together with others of their same age, girls and boys found that they had to call on hitherto untapped inner resources, to rely on themselves more fully and in new ways if they were to get along in this novel setting. Moreover, the diverse body of children who arrived each summer found that the differences that might in other contexts divide them were temporarily submerged in the collective structures of the *colonie,* which presented each of them with a common challenge. In this way, education in the child's collectivity had the effect of bringing forth the individual strengths and qualities of each child, for, as Philippe Rey-Herme put it, "one's own merit, innate or acquired, is, in the last resort, decisive." In a well-structured and intelligently run *colonie,* then, "differences of wealth, or in the parents' social standing—even of race or nationality—count for very little in comparison with one's personal richness . . . the social being no longer counts for very much, and only the individual remains."[2]

Educators and parents in postwar France thus remained faithful to the

Durkheimian precept that real education of the individual begins out-side the family, with the introduction of the child into the larger society. Parents in particular thus valued the *colonie* for the apprenticeship in initiative and autonomy it afforded its young clientele, who emerged from this *école des loisirs* more independent, extroverted, and resource-ful.[3] Equally vital, the *colonie* met the needs of working mothers, who had always constituted a significant percentage of the French labor force, while responding to a broader sense that children should not be left to hang about in the streets during school holidays but rather should be taken in hand by trained *moniteurs*.[4]

By the mid-twentieth century, then, the *colonie de vacances* had traveled a long road, from philanthropic program at the end of the nineteenth cen-tury to a truly national social service that, by the late 1940s, was delivering health and educational benefits across an increasingly broad swath of the child population. From 420,000 children in 1936, the *colonies* expanded (after their sharp decline during the Occupation) to embrace 700,000 by 1947, reaching 880,000 the following summer. In the mid-1950s, the 1 mil-lion mark was passed, and by 1962, 1,350,000 children were spending four to six weeks "en colo" each summer.[5] As we have seen, this expan-sion was characterized by a long-term shift from hygienic to educational *colonies* over the course of the interwar period. Yet it is important to re-call that this shift entailed less a jettisoning of previous hygienic concerns than a shift in emphasis, a greater weighting of the "educational" part-ner in that indissoluble couple "education/hygiene." For ultimately one finds that the stress on body or mind as locus of action shifts continu-ously in the discourse on the *colonie* (and indeed, on child development in general), moving about in such a way that the educational/hygienic distinction becomes almost untenable: you feed the body to reach the mind, you train the mind to care for the body, you use sport and games to hone the moral sense, and elevate that "innate" sense of justice. After all, in a creature who is still growing, the inseparableness of mind and body is especially evident. *Colonies de vacances* thus continued to bridge the mind-body divide through a practice that placed personal hygiene and sports/gymnastics at the heart of a broader program of child-centered instruction, intended to increase individual children's self-reliance and autonomy from adult and familial supervision.

But the ability of *colonies* to reach up the social ladder and transform the holidays of middle-class children as well sprang not only from their parents' demand for a social education of their children; it was, crucially, enabled by the traditions of republican solidarity in which secular *colo-nies* were rooted. As the history of the *colonies de vacances* illustrates, this tradition contained a potential for far-reaching social assistance, orga-nized around the republican primary school and linked to the child's status as a future citizen of the Republic. We have seen how this poten-tial was most fully developed in Socialist and Communist municipalities, which used it to create local anticipations of the social republic in the here and now. Yet it also resonates quite clearly in the earliest pronounce-ments of Third Republican legislators as they built up and expanded the *caisses des écoles,* established to provide material assistance to schoolchil-dren "not by charity, but through republican solidarity." In the minds of republican legislators, this was a form of assistance that citizens could accept "without hesitation or displays of false deference," for it was orga-nized through the horizontal ties of republican solidarity.[6] Linked to the potential citizen status of children, and their obligation to attend primary school, the *caisses* reached out to children as future citizens of France, assuring to those children whose families were hamstrung by want the material means to fulfill their *obligation scolaire,* condition of their future activity as full, adult citizens and mothers of citizens.

The tradition of republican solidarity was implicitly extended to em-brace privately funded and confessional *colonies* as well, via the laws and regulations that, from 1937 forward, stipulated a uniform, national regu-lation of the hygienic and pedagogic conditions inside each *colonie de vacances* that opened inside France. Financed by the *département,* the mu-nicipality, the *caisses des écoles,* and, after 1945, by the *comités d'entreprises,* France's *laïque colonies* flourished in the penumbra of the republican school, in the domain of the *périscolaire.*[7] This fact alone lent them a uni-versal valence that allowed the institution to transcend its original audi-ence, circumscribed by poverty and ill-health, and deliver its educational surplus-value to all French schoolchildren.[8] In their steady, trickle-up movement toward children of the middle class, then, the *colonies* offer a prime instance of the process whereby the welfare state has come together in France—a development that proceeded less by top-down impositions than through the central state's gradual adoption and expansion of al-ready developed private and local initiatives.

The rooting of French *colonies* in the traditions of republican solidarity also permits us to revisit from a rather different vantage point the much discussed (but by no means exhausted) comparison between the social politics and social visions that underpinned a liberal state like Britain versus those of republican France. Hence, when we look across the Channel to see what kinds of initiatives formed the British equivalent of the *colonies,* we find that such initiatives remained confined to the narrow realm of private charity. Stepping back to scrutinize the wider terrain of social assistance surrounding British primary schools, we find that turn-of-the-century efforts to establish something so basic as a school meals program ran into the principled opposition of powerful private interests, notably the Charity Organisation Society (cos), which argued that any such systematic assistance could only undermine the willingness of parents to feed their own children. Rather than assisting such children, the state would do better to leave them malnourished and pale, a constant reminder at the heart of poor families that they, too, had obligations to fulfill. Public provision of school meals could only "remove the spur to exertion and self-restraint, which the spectacle of his child's hunger must be to any man in whom the feelings of natural kindness are not entirely dead," argued the experts at the cos.[9] Even in those instances where feckless parents simply let their children starve, "it is better, in the interests of the community, to allow in such cases the sins of the parents to be visited on their children rather than to impair the solidarity of the family and run the risk of permanently demoralizing large numbers of the population by the offer of free meals to their children."[10] While the Education Act of 1906 finally made provision for the establishment of school cafeterias in the public (board) schools, resistance to state interference with parental responsibility remained strong, and cities like Bradford, which instituted a municipal meals program well before the 1906 act, remained the exception.[11]

Exploring comparatively the shift from the laboring child to the schooled child, common to Western societies at the end of the nineteenth and turn of the twentieth centuries—a shift in which the *colonies de vacances* were centrally implicated—thus allows us to consider from a new angle the very different structures that undergirded liberal states, founded on the notional autonomy of families and the child's enclosure therein, and the republican form, in which the state established a direct relation to the child as a potential citizen.[12] In the former case, policymakers treated parenting as a purely natural function: a social duty that sprang unproblematically from the biological fact of having produced offspring and whose effective conduct rested on the moral fiber of individual parents. British policies thus aimed to spur manifestly defective parents to greater efforts while, more broadly, seeking to maintain

the parents (and especially fathers) as mediators in the relationship between child and state. Children were thus left to the collective fate of
the family that had produced them. In Republican France, by contrast,
policymakers seem to have turned rather precociously to a more social
conception of parenting, grounded in the perception of the child as a
potential citizen and in the legal framework that upheld that vision: the
obligation scolaire, to be sure, but also the 1889 law on morally abandoned
children, as well as the Assistance Publique's entire structure of orphan
placement, which maintained these children as wards of the state even
as they were confided to the care of peasant families.[13] Within this political and legal framework, such publicly funded supplements to parental
care as municipal crèches or *colonie de vacances,* grounded in the rights
and needs of children as future citizens of the Republic, struck no one
as constituting an untoward interference with the private functioning of
the family.

In 1991 Jean Houssaye, retired director of the State Secretariat of Youth,
remarked with puzzled sadness that the *colonie de vacances* had lately
acquired the "superannuated charm of a yellowed postcard" that one
gazes upon nostalgically, as the now-archaic strains of Pierre Perret's
"Les jolies colonies" rise softly in the background. In a sense, the answer
to his puzzlement was all too obvious: with the arrival of prosperity in
the households of ordinary French families, and the extension of longer
vacations to working adults, 78 percent of French children were, by the
early to mid- 1980s, spending their holidays in the company of their parents.[14] The "Trente glorieuses" of 1945–1975, during which the *colonies
de vacances* enjoyed their greatest and most far-reaching popularity, had
finished, ironically, by delivering to the households of France a level of
income that would allow individualist models of consumption to trump
the collective pleasures of an institution that was rooted in the solidarities
of an earlier era.

But had not something vital been lost in the headlong rush toward the
family vacation? After all, the same surveys that showed a majority of
children leaving on vacation with their parents also revealed a youthful
lumpen proletariat, dwelling at the heart of those one in five families
who could not afford to leave on vacation at all.[15] With the gradual decline of the *colonies de vacances* after 1968, it was precisely these children
who stood to lose the most. Indeed, as defenders of the *colonies* pointed
out, the ever-quickening pace of urban development placed city children,

and especially poor city children, at an ever greater risk: "Firstly because they are the most vulnerable and fragile; because they, too, like the adults around them, suffer the aggressions of a life that is ever more dehuman-ized; because they suffer the consequences when overburdened adults have no time to give them either the care or attention they need; because the city, the neighborhood, the apartment house are not built for them. The spaces grow ever smaller, constraining all opportunity for move-ment, expression, and communication."[16] Worse, despite the gap that remained between the relatively short vacations of adults (three to four weeks in this period) and children's long summer holiday from school, municipalities were, by the late 1970s, devoting less time and person-nel to providing structured leisure activities for local children. "The use of this free time poses social problems which we can no longer ignore," grimly reminded Socialist educator Robert Penin in 1977.[17] But private and public institutions were by this time providing only a partial response to the problem, in the form of *centres aérées, maisons pour tous,* and other part-time solutions based not in the countryside but in the urban neigh-borhoods where the children lived, or on the suburban outskirts of those cities.[18]

With the *colonie de vacances* no longer a national priority, nor a mu-nicipal one, French children are being reabsorbed into their families and into the fabric of city life. And, as the Secretariat of Youth acknowledged in 1973, the more supple formula of the peri-urban *centres de vacances,* visited on a daily rather than month-long basis, does not begin to provide what the *colonies* offer, for "attending a neighborhood recreation center can never offer children the change of scene and the encounter with na-ture." Gone, too, is the opportunity for the experience of life in a child's collectivity, for the collective life children find in these recreation centers is "pretty close to that which the child experiences throughout the rest of the year. It's kind of like a 'Wednesday half-holiday throughout the year.' "[19]

People I talked with who had been brought up in the *patronages* and *colonies* of working-class and red *banlieues* during the 1940s, 1950s, 1960s and 1970s spoke regretfully of the recent decline in these public insti-tutions of child leisure, and attributed all kinds of present-day social problems, especially violence in the *collèges,* to the disappearance of this extrafamilial guidance provided by the city's young adult *animateurs.*[20] Moreover, those parents who do send their children *en colonie* (generally with the *comités d'entreprises,* which represent the cheapest alternative) continue to appreciate the *colonie* as "a means of preparing the child for his future, adult life, and so for life in society." While parents sometimes adduce the particular skills acquired therein as evidence of its pedagogical efficacy, the *colonie*'s real educational benefit continues to be seen as a social one, for the *colonie* remains "a site of confrontations and exchanges necessary to understanding one's relationship to the world and to other people."[21]

It would seem that *colonies de vacances* have retained parents' esteem as institutions of social education. How, then, are we to explain the steady decline in their usage since the late 1960s, a decline that, since the mid-1980s, has become quite precipitous?[22] A SOFRES survey from 1982–83 suggested that in the prosperous post-1968 economy, marked by lengthier vacations for all, families are no longer forced to send their children *en colonie* simply to keep them off the streets. Torn between an atmosphere of "ambient familialism" and their desire to give their children the educational advantage, parents are opting less and less for the collective, educational approach in favor of the individualist and familial one.[23] And this, in turn, suggests that the economic transformations of the postwar period have been accompanied by a gradual shift away from the kinds of values and structures that sustained the *colonies* from the 1880s through the 1970s. Thus, Mark Lilla has suggested that for many French people, 1968 marked "the triumph of a new social ideal of individualism, and the snapping of the last attachments of solidarity binding French society together. The family, the Church, the republican schools, even the Communist Party suffered a crisis of legitimacy, from which they have not recovered, in the name of the individual's right to self-determination, a right that has become the sole measure of social legitimacy." While individual self-determination is a concept so familiar to Americans as to appear almost banal, Lilla points out that it is a new idea in Europe "and it makes the French particularly uneasy."[24] One can see how this shift in values has played itself out in the *colonies de vacances,* which already in the 1960s were turning to smaller-scale and more individually tailored forms of organization and activity. But the larger sea-change in economy, culture, and values had already begun to gnaw away at the kinds of social solidarity that republican France has sustained since the late nineteenth century, and on which the *colonies* depended. Despite numerous efforts to individualize the *colonie* structure, the numbers of children sent have continued the decline first registered in the late 1960s.

The rise and fall of the *colonies de vacances* thus reveals important as-

pects of France's recent history as experienced by working- and middle-
class people, and allows us to talk in more profound ways about the social and cultural impact of the economic transformation since 1945: the
end of rural France, clearly, but also the end of a kind of public solidarity, rooted in political values and forms of sociability that the arrival
of unprecedented prosperity inside the households of ordinary folk has
steadily undermined. The decline of the *colonies de vacances* may thus
mark the end of a period in recent French history where democratic
and individualist practices were combined with and sustained by certain
forms of solidarity that were underwritten by the republican state in its
local and national incarnations.

NOTES

Preface

1 To cite but one example, a recent issue of *Le Monde* ran a front-page article whose title, "La jolie colonie de Matignon, dans la Vallée blanche," made droll reference to an impromptu ski weekend taken by Lionel Jospin and his cabinet. *Le Monde,* 14–15 Mar. 1998, 1.

Introduction

1 This was in 1924. Interview with Raymond Lagarde, Archives Municipales d'Ivry-sur-Seine (hereafter A.M. d'Ivry), Association pour l'histoire d'Ivry, interview 50, 7 Jan. 1982, 1–3. These interviews were conducted in 1980–82 by the Association pour l'histoire d'Ivry under the direction of Fernand Leriche, a retired schoolteacher and Parti communiste français (PCF) militant.

2 Hence, aside from the work of former minister of youth and sport Jean Houssaye, devoted to analyzing the recent decline of the *colonies,* the sole historical work is Philippe-Alexandre Rey-Herme's two-volume study, a purely institutional survey that covers the early years (1880–1936) and ends before the Popular Front. See Philippe-Alexandre Rey-Herme, *Les Colonies de vacances: Origines et premiers développements* (Paris: privately published by the author, 1954); and Rey-Herme, *Les Colonies de vacances en France, 1906–1936: L'Institution et ses problèmes* (Paris: Fleurus, 1961). See also Jean Houssaye, *Le Livre des colos: Histoire et évolution des centres de vacances pour enfants* (Paris: La Documentation Française, 1989); and Houssaye, *Un Avenir pour les colonies de vacances* (Paris: Editions Ouvrières, 1977); and Houssaye, *Aujourd'hui les centres de vacances* (Vigneux: Editions Matrices, 1991).

3 *Bulletin municipal officiel d'Ivry-sur-Seine* 23 (Mar. 1930): 34. The newspaper identified the *colonie* as the keystone in the Communist city hall's politics of "improving the future of working-class childhood."

4 A.M. d'Ivry, brochure 359, *Les Petits ivryens à la campagne* (Ivry, 1936), 184; and *Les Petits ivryens à la campagne* (Ivry, 1924), 9.

5 *Bulletin municipal officiel d'Ivry-sur-Seine* 23 (Mar. 1930): 34, and ibid. (Aug.–Sept. 1931): 20.

6 Louis Vuillemin, *Pour l'avenir de la race: Colonies scolaires et camps de vacances. Guide pratique pour leur organisation et leur fonctionnement* (Paris: Charles-Lavauzelles, 1927), 25.

7   Alain Vulbeau, *Le Gouvernement des enfants* (Paris: Desclée-Brouwer, 1993), 109–10 and 115.

8   On the question of working-class food practices in mid-twentieth-century France, see Paul-Henry Chombart de Lauwe's fascinating study *La Vie quotidienne des familles ouvrières: Recherches sur les comportements sociaux de consommation* (Paris: CNRS, 1956).

9   *Vous et vos enfants* (supplement to the *Bulletin paroissal d'Ivry-Centre*), "Le jeu," Feb. 1938, 7.

10 Robert Penin, "Les Colonies de vacances," *Ecole et socialisme* 7 (July 1977): 17.

11 Moreover, this silence cannot ultimately be attributed simply to the possibility that in this discourse, "child" functioned as a "universal placeholder," analogous to the term *man,* for the sex of the child was sometimes given, other times not. A lot of ambiguity surrounded that not; sometimes it meant just boys, other times *mixité,* and there are times when it's just not clear whether one sex or both is being spoken of. (I refer here to Luce Irigaray's famous assertion that "the subject is always inscribed as masculine, even when it would pose itself as universal or neuter: man. Yet man is not neuter, but sexed." Luce Irigaray, *Ethique de la différence sexuelle* [Paris: Editions de Minuit, 1984], 14.)

12 "M.C.," response to a questionnaire regarding *colonies mixtes,* circulated at the Congrès régional at Beauvais, 1930, cited in Rey-Herme, *Les Colonies de vacances en France, 1906–1936,* 366–67.

13 Ibid., 366. Indeed, what the girls were presumed to gain from contact with the boys is arguably more important—a deeper, more human set of qualities (frankness and simplicity) than the mere bodily cleanliness that girls were thought to impart to their brothers. One woman director agreed that the boy-girl encounter produced a kind of gender-crossing in the characters of the sexes, but found that the "virilization" of girls that resulted was most heartily to be avoided: "In playing together with the boys, the girls risk overtaxing themselves and losing their charm and feminine qualities in the masculine hurly-burly"—another response that reposes implicitly on the conviction that, far from being natural and spontaneous, masculine and feminine characters are fragile constructs of human culture. "Mme R.," ibid., 365. Louis Vuillemin, on the other hand, believed that in *colonies mixtes,* the girls exercised a "civilizing" influence over the more "turbulent" boys, lending an element of "gaiety, kindness, goodness, and grace" to their games and creating a general atmosphere of "sweet harmony" in the *colonie* that could only redound to its benefit. Vuillemin, *Pour l'avenir de la race,* 45.

14 Anonymous response to questionnaire, cited in Rey-Herme, *Les Colonies de vacances en France, 1906–1936,* 367.

15 Indeed, the dense personal networks that these colonies created, link-

ing peasant village to working-class city via a continuous circulation of money, children, health, and welfare *surveillants,* may allow us to further explore what Yves Lequin has called "the long survival of rural values in the working-class cities of France." Yves Lequin, "L'espace ouvrier: Le regard géographique," *Historiens et géographes* 350 (Oct. 1995): 235.

CHAPTER I Repairing the Body, Restoring the Soul

1 Louis François Portiez, *Des Voyages: De leur utilité dans l'éducation* (Paris: Imprimerie Nationale, n.d.), 2–3. Philippe Rey-Herme notes that Portiez presented this project to the convention on 20 Messidor of the Year II, that is, in August 1794. Philippe-Alexandre Rey-Herme, *Les Colonies de vacances: Origines et premiers développements* (Paris, 1954), 20. Louis Portiez (1765–1810) was a student of law who had left his native Beauvais to study in Paris in the late 1780s. Militant republican and avid reader of "Jean-Jacques," Portiez threw himself into the hurly-burly of events during that first revolutionary summer of 1789, and was among the crowd that stormed the Bastille on 14 July. His uncompromising republicanism later won him a seat in the convention, as deputy from the Oise. There he voted unhesitatingly for the king's execution (January 1793), and then turned to questions of culture and education in the young Republic. His views on education combine the conviction that culture and republican virtue are linked with the Rousseauean notion that "all education should happen through action." *Des Voyages,* 3. See also L. Portiez, *Sur l'instruction publique* (Paris: Imprimerie Nationale, n.d.).

2 I say "men" because Portiez's speech continues in terms that leave little doubt as to the gender of these young citizens, in whom patriotic and warrior virtues were to meet with a stalwart republicanism, reinforced by their open-air voyage of discovery. *Des Voyages,* 2–3.

3 Ibid., 4.

4 Ibid., 7.

5 Ibid., 5.

6 Ibid., 7. Portiez makes no bones about the importance of the journey itself, not only for its salutary "uprooting" effect, which (in theory) opened students to observing and understanding the laws and customs of other societies, but also in order to extract youth from the deadly grip of paternal power: "How much useful instruction an intelligent leader can impart to these young men who are, for the first time, traveling far from the paternal household." Ibid., 3–4.

7 Ibid., 16.

8 Ibid., 24.

9 Ibid., 25.

10 See Antoine Prost, *Histoire de l'enseignement en France, 1800–1967* (Paris: Armand Colin, 1968), 21–69, for a discussion of this reform, which affected secondary schools only. Primary schools would receive no comparable centralized statute before the Guizot law of 1833.

11 E. Porcher, "Voyages de vacances," *Revue pédagogique,* June 1880.

12 Ibid., 31. Rey-Herme notes that Porcher was explicitly inspired by Portiez's revolutionary dream. See Philippe-Alexandre Rey-Herme, *La Colonie de vacances hier et aujourd'hui* (Paris: Editions Cap, 1955), 20.

13 E. Porcher, "Voyages d'instruction des Ecoles Supérieures Municipales: L'Ecole Turgot au Havre en 1877," *Revue pédagogique,* Mar. 1878.

14 Article 15 of the law of 10 April 1867 (Victor Duruy), which recommended the creation of these charitable funds, stipulates: "The *caisse des écoles* is intended to help poor children in the public schools. It reduces the parents' burden . . . distributes aid in food, clothing, shoes, and sometimes, in case of accident or sickness, monetary aid as well." Cited in Rey-Herme, *Les Colonies de vacances: Origines,* 54. The law of 23 March 1882 required that each commune establish a *caisse* in order to promote regular school attendance. The *caisses* were supported by a combination of municipal funding, subventions from the *département* and the state, annual membership dues paid by those who administered the *caisses,* charitable contributions, funds raised by public subscription, and any monies that could be raised by leasing local school buildings. See Jean Chardavoine, "La Caisse des Ecoles," *L'Information municipale* 12 (Dec. 1937): 8. It was from these *caisses* that municipal *colonies* would draw an important part of their funding.

15 His report was delivered on 25 January 1887.

16 V. Brouet, "Les Colonies scolaires de la ville de Paris," *Revue pédagogique,* 15 Jan. 1902, esp. 15.

17 The fifteenth arrondissement was the sole remaining hold-out. By the turn of the twentieth century all twenty arrondissements had organized *colonies scolaires* for both girls and boys.

18 Dick May, *Revue philanthropique,* June 1897, cited in L'Oeuvre de Trois Semaines, *Rapport pour l'été 1897* (Saint-Maur: Imprimerie J. Lievens, 1898), 12. On the rather remarkable career of socialist-feminist writer Dick May (pseudonym of Jeanne Weill), see Christophe Prochasson, "Dick May et le social," in Collette Chambelland, ed., *Le Musée social en son temps* (Paris: Presses de l'Ecole Normale Supérieure, 1998), 43–58.

19 Théodore and Suzanne Lorriaux, *Notice sur L'Oeuvre de Trois Semaines après 25 années d'existence* (Paris: Rasquin, 1906), 3–4.

20 Ibid. The three girls were lodged with "a good country widow" who undoubtedly needed the cash. Philippe-Alexandre Rey-Herme notes that Théodore Lorriaux's 1880 lecture tour in the United States constituted a second wellspring for the Lorriaux initiative, for it was during this trip

that the pastor became acquainted with the work of his American colleague William Parsons, who placed needy young urban Protestants with rural families of the faith each summer in hopes that such trips might reinforce both soul and body. Rey-Herme, *Les Colonies de vacances: Origines,* 169.

21 Suzanne Lorriaux, *Oeuvre de Trois Semaines, Rapport, 1892* (Paris: J. Lievens, 1893), 2.

22 At least two hundred women gathered each day to mend clothing in the program's workshop. In addition, young girls were trained in a series of traditional women's trades—sewing, artificial flowers, lingerie—in the adjoining "school-workshop."

23 Mme de Pressensé, cited in Rey-Herme, *Les Colonies de vacances: Origines,* 186.

24 Indeed, the Chaussée de Maine had used the Oeuvre de Trois Semaines as intermediary for its first *colonie* (summer 1882), choosing some twenty children who then joined the Lorriaux's *colonie* in the Loire.

25 Hence in 1883 Cottinet was quite unaware of the work of Lorriaux and Mme de Pressensé; the structural similarity in the *colonies* is owing to their derivation from the single, common source in Zurich.

26 Wilhelm Bion, *Les Résultats des colonies de vacances* (Zurich, 1900), cited in Rey-Herme, *Les Colonies de vacances: Origines,* 212.

27 Ibid. The 1907 etymology of the term *colonie de vacances* is to be found in the *Trésor de la langue française,* vol. 5 (Paris: Editions du C.N.R.S., 1977), 1060.

28 Delassaux became director of the Oeuvre de Chaussée de Maine in 1898. Quoted in Arthur Delpy, *Les Oeuvres de colonies de vacances* (Paris, 1903)—extraits de la *Revue philanthropique,* 10 June 1903 and 10 July 1903, 41. The peasant hosts were generally termed *nourrices, familles nourricières,* or *gardeuses.*

29 Ibid., 41.

30 Mme d'Eichtal and her husband had already taken an active interest in the nascent *colonie de vacances* movement, going so far as to place a part of the family property at the Lorriaux's disposal in the summer of 1882.

31 Figures from Lorriaux, *Oeuvre de Trois Semaines, Rapport, 1892,* 2; and Oeuvre de Trois Semaines, *Rapport, 1897,* 30–31. See also Eugène Plantet and Arthur Delpy, *Les Colonies de vacances: Organisation et fonctionnement* (Paris: Hachette, 1910), 45.

32 Théodore and Suzanne Lorriaux, *Notice,* 9.

33 Ibid., 9.

34 Suzanne Lorriaux, *L'Oeuvre de Trois Semaines, Rapport* (Paris, 1882–83, cited in Rey-Herme, *Les Colonies de vacances: Origines,* 172. Dated 1 December 1882, this report took the form of a letter to all who took an interest in the program.

35 Mlle Alice Delassaux, *directrice* of the Chaussée de Maine, speaking at the 22 April 1903 session of the Société Internationale pour l'étude des questions d'assistance, the proceedings of which were reprinted in A. Delpy, *Les Oeuvres,* 16–17.

36 Suzanne Lorriaux, *L'Oeuvre de Trois Semaines, Rapport* (Paris, 1882–83), cited in Rey-Herme, *Les Colonies de vacances: Origines,* 172. In its early days, the Oeuvre de Trois Semaines recruited exclusively through Protestant charities, and so conserved a strong confessional profile. By the late 1880s, however, the program shifted to a stance of religious neutrality, and sent children from Catholic, Jewish, and secular households as well. Plantet and Delpy, *Les Colonies de vacances,* 44.

37 The Oeuvre de Trois Semaines was in no sense of the term a *colonie scolaire;* rather, its organization was "familial," which meant that it recruited its *colons* through the networks of Protestant charities in Paris, and not through the primary schools. The program thus sent people of all ages on the three-week "cure d'air," from children as young as three to apprentices and young workers of both sexes aged sixteen to twenty. As time went on, it even sent a few exhausted mothers of "familles nombreuses" to spend a few weeks resting up with their entire brood.

38 Théodore and Suzanne Lorriaux, *Notice,* 9.

39 The program's formula was three weeks in the countryside and four weeks at the sea, on the theory that the journey to the coast took longer.

40 Théodore and Suzanne Lorriaux, *Notice,* 17.

41 While the Oeuvre de Trois Semaines has left no archival trace beyond 1914, the Chaussée de Maine continued well into the interwar period (the last report I found was for the summer of 1938), and was regarded by many as the "most important program of its type (family placement) in France." Rey-Herme, *La Colonie de vacances hier et aujourd'hui,* 15. On 9 September 1890, President Sadie Carnot recognized the Chaussée de Maine as an "oeuvre d'utilité publique." Several years later, the Trois Semaines received comparable recognition.

42 "Les Colonies de vacances," *La Vie heureuse,* July 1903, 140. For the children of provincial cities such as Lyon or St-Etienne, placement with the local peasantry could run as little as fifty centimes per day per child. Delpy, *Les Oeuvres,* 38.

43 M. Lefort, cited in ibid., 38.

44 Alice Delassaux, cited in ibid., 38.

45 Ibid., 38. Clearly, these rules imply that children were placed on fairly prosperous farms. Pastor Comte maintained a one-cow minimum, and preferred at least three, not only to ensure that the children drank milk regularly, but because the number of cows was a visible marker that the family enjoyed a minimal level of comfort, and suggested that the *colons* harbored therein would not become cash-cows for a family too poor to

feed them properly. Louis Comte, *L'Oeuvre des Enfants à la Montagne* (Saint-Etienne: Relèvement social, 1902).

46 Oeuvre de la Chaussée de Maine, *Rapport, 1905,* 14.

47 Taken from clause 5 of Comte's "Recommandation aux Parents Nourriciers," reprinted in Rey-Herme, *Les Colonies de vacances: Origines,* 320–21.

48 Delpy, *Les Oeuvres,* 17.

49 "Les Colonies de vacances," *La Vie heureuse,* 1903, 140.

50 Comte, cited in Planter and Delpy, *Les Colonies de vacances,* 94.

51 Comte, cited in ibid., 94.

52 Alice Delassaux, cited in Delpy, *Les Oeuvres,* 38.

53 Ibid. Mlle Delassaux pursued the analogy in a discussion of Comte's Lyon-based Les Petits Enfants à la Montagne, which placed an entirely different population, the children of industrial workers, in this case the miners of St-Etienne's notoriously wretched "Soleil-noir" district, with the very poor peasants of the Jura: "The miners' children are far poorer than our little Parisians; they are used to a much harder life, and I think that they adapt quite well to life with the mountain folk, where the food consists largely of chestnuts, milk, yogurt, and cheese. We could never give such things to our little Parisians, who are, after all, accustomed to their steaks and chops, but for the children of Saint-Etienne, it works very well." Ibid., 39. Earlier, Mlle Delassaux had referred to the Chaussée de Maine's clientele as comprising "children from all the arrondissements of Paris and from the industrial suburbs." Ibid., 15.

54 The *colonies de vacances* had a role to play here as well, functioning occasionally as brokers in the permanent placement of urban children as apprentices or domestic servants on peasant farms. Alice Delassaux referred to these definitive placements as a kind of culmination of that "initiation to the life of the fields" that the *colonie chez les paysans* vouchsafed to its *colons:* "There are even some *colons* who, after having spent a summer in the country, are seized by the ardent desire to return, to live and work there forever. This program has already been able to satisfy this wish in several cases." Cited in Delpy, *Les Oeuvres,* 17. I found concrete, if scanty, evidence of such placements in the municipal *colonie* of Suresnes, which placed local children with the Nièvre peasantry over the period 1919–45. This suggests that while such reverse migrations did sometimes result from children's placement in a *colonie chez les paysans,* they were comparatively rare, and loomed far larger in the pro-*colonie* propaganda (especially in the immediate pre- and post–World War I eras) than in the everyday lives of working-class children.

55 Louis Comte, *L'Oeuvre des Enfants.* Comte further notes that with children spread across more than six hundred families, he'd only had to effect about twelve transfers for filthiness of the home or poor (moral) example set by the peasants.

56 Ibid.

57 Ibid. Jean Houssaye notes that *surveillants* generally included the children of local peasant families in their collective *animation* of the *colonie* (games, songs, excursions). Jean Houssaye, *Le Livre des colos: Histoire et évolution des centres de vacances pour enfants* (Paris: La Documentation Française, 1989).

58 Delpy, *Les Oeuvres,* 16. The notion of liberty being vaunted here clearly implies that it is in the private sphere, rather than in the realm of public affairs, that a truly good and virtuous life can unfold.

59 Comte, cited in Plantet and Delpy, *Les Colonies de vacances,* 93.

60 *Rapport de la Clef des Champs de Limoges,* cited in Plantet and Delpy, *Les Colonies de vacances,* 95.

61 Anna Lampérière, cited in Rey-Herme, *Les Colonies de vacances: Origines,* 197.

62 Wilhelm Bion, *Les Colonies de vacances: Mémoire historique et statistique* (Paris: Delgrave, 1887), 21.

63 Marie Dutoit, *Madame de Pressensé: Sa vie* (Paris: Fischbacher, 1904), 132.

64 She would soon part ways with Mâlon over the Socialists' acceptance of violent revolution, for "Mme de Pressensé could envision the Revolution only in terms of Love." Cited in Rey-Herme, *Les Colonies de vacances: Origines,* 182.

65 Oeuvre de la Chaussée de Maine, *Rapport, 1905,* 19. Mme de Pressensé extended her vision of cross-class solidarity to the children of the bourgeoisie, who were invited to contribute to the *oeuvre de vacances populaires* through their subscriptions to the children's journal *St. Nicholas.* Edmond Cottinet later organized a parallel program of mutual aid among children through some of the city's wealthier lycées, hoping thus to build solidarity among children who would later "mingle behind the flag," when they performed their military service. E. Cottinet, *La Colonie scolaire du IXe arrondissement, rapport, 1884* (Paris: Imprimerie Chaix, 1885), 3–4.

66 In her discussion of post–World War II family placement in the Ardèche, Dominique Dessertine speaks of the long tradition of taking in urban orphans that bound the peasantry in poorer regions to the city's most underprivileged children in "networks of solidarity . . . among the poor." Dominique Dessertine, *La Société lyonnaise pour la sauvetage de l'enfance* (Toulouse: Erès, 1990), 179.

67 For a classic statement of the necessarily public and nonfamilial nature of education, see Emile Durkheim, *L'Éducation morale* (Paris: Félix Alcan, 1925).

68 These were after-school day-care programs, pioneered by the Catholic Church in the mid-nineteenth century. They were open on Thursday and Saturday afternoons, and provided games and, in the case of Catholic programs, preparation for first communion as well. On the origins and de-

velopment of Catholic youth programs, see Max Turmann, *Au Sortir de l'école: Les patronages* (Paris: Lecoffre, 1901); Gerard Cholvy, *Patronage: Ghetto ou vivier?* (Paris: Nouvelle cité, 1987); and Cholvy, *Histoire des organisations et mouvements chrétiens de jeunesse en France, XIXe–XXe siècles* (Paris: Editions du Cerf, 1999).

69 E. Cottinet, *La Colonie scolaire du IXe arrondissement,* Report to the *Caisse des Ecoles* (Paris: Imprimerie Chaix, 1883).

70 The criteria of selection are reproduced (in the represented voice of Cottinet himself) in Francisque Sarcey's preface to Wilhelm Bion, "Les Colonies de vacances." Bion wrote his report at the request of Ferdinand Buisson, director of primary education, and it is addressed explicitly to the "people of France, who have always shown themselves to be open and alive to humanitarian ideas and works, and whose ardent affection for children is known far and wide." Bion, "Les Colonies de vacances," 25.

71 E. Cottinet, *Les Colonies de vacances en France et à l'étranger,* Mémoires du Musée Pédagogique, 2d series, part 47 (Paris, 1889), 575.

72 Francisque Sarcey, preface to Wilhelm Bion, "Les Colonies de vacances," 6–7.

73 Ibid., 8.

74 Ibid., 7–8.

75 Dr. Hutinel compared Grancher's findings among this fairly prosperous population with a group clearly less favored by fortune, the orphans and "morally abandoned" children of the Département de la Seine who had been placed on peasant farms by the Assistance Publique's division of Enfants Assistés. The good doctor found that under 1 percent (15 out of some 18,000 examined) had similar lesions; their "tubercular roots" had been "regenerated" by the fresh country air. Grancher's study is cited in Houssaye, *Le Livre des colos,* 29. Professor Landouzy is cited in Delpy, *Les Oeuvres,* 19. Hutinel's study is cited in Dr. Emile Ciuciu, *Préservation de l'enfance par le grand air* (Paris: Thèse en médecine, 1908), 15.

76 Cited in Emile Cheysson's preface to Louis Delpérier, *Les Colonies de vacances* (Paris: La Librairie Victor J. Gabalda et Cie., 1908), xv. The *Congrès Nationale des Colonies de Vacances* of 1923 cites Grancher's results as 14 percent of schoolboys and 17 percent of schoolgirls. By the turn of the century, the *colonie de vacances* had become the weapon of choice in the struggle against tuberculosis precisely because it reinforced the health of children at risk. If sanatoria could "at great cost and struggle" cure the occasional tubercular child, the *colonies de vacances* "prevented children from becoming tubercular." R. de Felice, "L'Oeuvre des colonies de vacances," *L'Idéal du foyer: Revue littéraire, artistique, économique et sociale de la famille,* 1 May 1903, 127.

77 "Les Colonies de vacances à Paris," *Revue pédagogique,* 15 June 1887, 513–14. Reprint of Cottinet's speech at the Musée pédagogique, 26 May 1887.

78 E. Cottinet, *Les Colonies de vacances de la ville de Paris en 1887* (Paris: Delgrave, 1888), 6. Some families took advantage of the annual slowdown to head out to the countryside and work the harvest, either for wages or (in the case of families returning to their village of origin) some combination of wages and upkeep. See Serge Grafteaux, *Mémé Santerre* (Paris: Editions du Jour, 1975) for one account of this seasonal alternation of rural and industrial labor.

79 "Les Colonies de vacances à Paris," *Revue pédagogique,* 15 June 1887, 513–14.

80 Until the Paris city council voted official support to the *colonies scolaires* (June 1887), the *caisses* could make no special contribution to the *colonies* over and above their ordinary per-student subvention. Cottinet thus used his philanthropic contacts to raise money privately for those first *colonies scolaires* (1883–86). Once the Paris city council had approved the *colonies scolaires, caisses* were free (and indeed encouraged) to support the venture, to which the city council added an annual municipal subvention.

81 Cottinet, *La Colonie scolaire, 1883,* 7.

82 Ibid., 9.

83 Ibid., 6; and Cottinet, *La Colonie scolaire du IXe arrondissement, rapport, 1885* (Paris: Imprimerie Chaix, 1886).

84 Cottinet, *Les Colonies de vacances, 1887,* 6.

85 Cottinet, *La Colonie scolaire, 1883,* 11–12.

86 Ibid., 6.

87 Cottinet, *Instruction sur la formation et le fonctionnement des colonies de vacances* (Paris: Imprimerie Chaix, 1887). The normal school-leaving age was thirteen, though it was possible to take the exam at twelve, an option that children from poor families often exercised, so that they might begin to work right away.

88 Extract from the journal of Antoinette Fauconnier, reproduced in E. Cottinet, *La Colonie scolaire, 1884,* 9. *Colons* of both sexes were expected to keep a journal while *en colonie* and to spend an hour each day writing in it.

89 Ibid., 9. Cottinet's expectation that the children might dance together that afternoon is not so strange when one recalls that at the time (mid-1880s) *bals d'enfants* were a common affair. See Rey-Herme, *Les Colonies de vacances: Origines,* 224.

90 Ibid., 12.

91 Ibid., 13.

92 "Les Colonies de vacances à Paris," *Revue pédagogique,* 15 June 1887, 513.

93 Ibid., 515. Here, Cottinet populates his rural idyll with figures from La Fontaine's *Fables,* which every French schoolchild would have known by heart.

94 This was the founding meeting for the Comité Parisien des Colonies

de Vacances. Other signatories to the public appeal that was launched that day in support of the *colonies* included Octave Gréard, M. le Royer (president of the Senate), and M. Floquet (president of the Chamber of Deputies). Ibid., 516. Hovelacque was a staunch republican and militant advocate of secularism in the public primary schools, which he urged the council to purge of all "unauthorized" clerical personnel from as early as 1878. Soon after this organizational meeting at the Musée Pédagogique, the Paris city council began granting the *colonies scolaires* an annual subvention, which by 1902 exceeded 200,000 F. (The individual *caisses* were by this time contributing a grand total of 94,000 F to the venture.) V. Brouet, "Les Colonies scolaires," 16.

95 Cottinet, *Les Colonies de vacances, 1887,* 34. Fifteen years later, school inspector Brouet wryly observed that the toothbrush remained an "unfamiliar object whose use is generally unknown." V. Brouet, "Les Colonies scolaires," 18. Cottinet outlined the ideal trousseau in his report to the Oeuvre des Colonies de Vacances on Paris's *colonies scolaires* in 1887: "A suitcase—a pair of hiking shoes—a pair of regular shoes—a canvas hat with a neck-covering—4 shirts—4 towels—6 handkerchiefs—a warm cloak or sweater—a light cloak or sweater—a clothes' brush—shoe-brush and polish—toothbrush—a comb and hairbrush. We would also add to this list two wool vests, a bar of soap, and a big sponge." Cottinet admitted that in only one arrondissement (out of twenty) did the *colons* actually turn up at the departure with a full trousseau; in all the other *colonies scolaires* that summer, the (women) directors were at their wits' end over the shabby and incomplete state of the children's trousseaux, the very worn state of the children's clothing, and the great quantity of mending that, as a consequence, landed in their laps. The ultimate solution, of course, lay with the *caisses des écoles,* who filled the gap by purchasing and distributing shoes, and by organizing committees of women ("so competent in such matters") to oversee the assemblage of the trousseaux before the departure and complete them with items sewn and knit by their own hands. Ibid., 33–34.

96 Cottinet, *La Colonie scolaire, 1884,* 10.

97 Cottinet, *Instruction,* 3. The definition goes on to specify the limits of this brief *cure d'air:* "The *colonies* do not accept sick children. They are not a reward. Their object is a rest cure, aided by natural exercise in the country, and by cleanliness, good food, and happiness." Ibid., 3.

98 Ibid., 13.

99 Cottinet, *Les Colonies de vacances, 1887,* 33–34.

100 Report on the *colonies* of the second arrondissement, cited in Cottinet, *Les Colonies de vacances, 1887,* 13.

101 Ibid., 17 and 27.

102 Cottinet, *La Colonie scolaire, 1884,* 10–11.

103 This according to M. Lécart's laconic notes on the field trips made by the *colonie des garçons* at Chaumont that summer — some fifteen in the space of three weeks. Cottinet, *La Colonie scolaire, 1884,* 31–32. At this stage, long hikes constituted the primary activity *en colonie,* far outweighing the importance of games, whose pedagogic interest and value were less widely recognized in nineteenth-century France, relative to their great popularity in the twentieth century.

104 Ibid., 10–11. As Arthur Delpy later remarked, the central pedagogical tactic in the *colonies scolaires* was to "observe [nature], and link science to life." Delpy, *Les Oeuvres,* 5.

105 Cottinet, *La Colonie scolaire, 1883,* 15.

106 Cottinet, *La Colonie scolaire, 1884,* 18–19. Journal of G. Laurens, twelve years old.

107 Ibid., 19. Journal of Régine Orner, twelve years old.

108 Cottinet's report on the *colonies scolaires* in 1889 pursues the theme of girlish domesticity, as he recounts with relish the *colonies* of the fourteenth and twentieth arrondissements, where the boys and girls shared the same lodgings, in villas by the sea at Berck-sur-Mer and Trilport. Housed with the boys in the same *colonie,* the young girls "took it upon themselves" to see to the boys' mending: "Little junior housewives, women workers at the age of ten, often incapable of repairing their own clothes, since their mothers try and spare them the chore, we saw them turn their ingenuity to the torn shirts and shorts of *messieurs les gamins* and then return them in a decent state. Happy those schoolmistresses who accepted this touching chore on the girls' behalf, and then helped them carry it out with honor!" E. Cottinet and A. Cahen, *Les Colonies de vacances de la ville de Paris en 1888 et 1889* (Paris: Hachette, 1890), 9.

109 Cottinet, *La Colonie scolaire, 1884,* 13.

110 Ibid., 25. Journal of Gabrielle Lachaud, ten years old.

111 Ibid., 28. Journal of Marthe Savantré, thirteen years old.

112 Cottinet, *La Colonie scolaire, 1885,* 10, emphasis original. Journal of an unnamed young girl.

113 Cottinet, *La Colonie scolaire, 1884,* 20.

114 Ibid., 20.

115 Ibid., 24.

116 Cottinet, *La Colonie scolaire, 1885,* 12.

117 Cottinet, *La Colonie scolaire, 1883,* 11; and Cottinet, *Instruction,* 18, emphasis original.

118 Cottinet, *La Colonie scolaire, 1884,* 12. Emphasis original. Cottinet also sought to impart a solid grasp of the geography of the sites visited by requiring that the *colons* illustrate their journals with hand-drawn maps detailing the itinerary of the previous day's promenade. The benefits of this exercise were multiple, for sketching maps demanded that the child con-

ceptualize, then represent the territorial space traversed, exercising a combination of mental and manual skills close to those of industrial drawing
and so crucial to skilled and artisanal labors of all sorts, from dressmak-
ing to wood and metalworking. But the lesson had its patriotic implications as well, given the eastern location of Cottinet's first *colonies scolaires:*
"Our boys crossed the Bussang pass that separated them from unhappy
Alsace, and their journals show traces of the emotion that seized them at
the sight of Prussian uniforms. Their school museum, too, holds samples
of earth, rocks, and plants that they carried back from their pilgrimage . . .
Besides a few good pounds worth of additional flesh, bone, and muscle,
they brought back with them to Paris a hatred of the conqueror and a
real understanding of the *idea of boundaries.*" Ibid., 17 and 14. Emphasis
original.
119 Cottinet, *Instruction,* 18.
120 Henri Martin, "Les Colonies scolaires en France et à l'étranger," review of
W. Bion, *Die Ferienkolonien und Werwandte Bestrebungen auf dem Giebete
der kinder-Gesundheitspflege,* Zurich, 1901, in *Revue pédagogique,* July 1903.
121 Cottinet, *La Colonie scolaire, 1884,* 24. Journal of Marthe Savantré, age
thirteen.
122 Ibid., 25. The rather smug tone of these reports, standing proudly on the
hind legs of urban sophistication, owes perhaps to the age of the authors
concerned, who were, on average, twelve years old.
123 Cottinet, *La Colonie scolaire, 1884,* 26.
124 Ibid., 26.
125 Cottinet, *Les Colonies de vacances, 1887,* 30. Herein lay the virtues of *colonisation chez les paysans,* in Bion's original sense of the term.
126 Ibid., 31.
127 Ibid.
128 Cottinet, *La Colonie scolaire, 1884,* 27.
129 Cottinet, *Instruction,* 17.
130 Ibid., 17; and Cottinet and Cahen, *Les Colonies de vacances, 1888 et 1889,* 8.
131 Cottinet, *Instruction,* 18.
132 The comment that one did not recognize one's own child, so greatly transformed, physically and in demeanor, by the weeks spent *en colonie,* swiftly
became a basic trope of *colonie de vacances* propaganda, as much resorted
to by Protestant charity as republican schoolteachers: "Imagine, Madame,
I did not recognize my own daughter, she is so fresh and tanned. When
she left, she weighed 40 pounds, and now she weighs 46½." Chaussée de
Maine, *Rapport, 1905,* 16–17. Cottinet, too, delighted in closing his annual reports with tales of parents, wide-eyed and incredulous as they collect their transformed offspring: "The good people could not believe their
eyes. 'Is that our daughter? She's bigger than her brother! . . . she's stronger
than her mother!' That's the kind of thing you hear." Cottinet, *La Colonie*

scolaire, 1883, 16. This kind of language would be laid on with an equally thick brush in interwar leftist municipalities, which sought to root their claims to govern for the people in the brightened, healthy faces of the city's smallest and poorest citizens.

133   See, for example, the extensive hygienic data—height, weight, thoracic perimeter, red blood cell-count—painstakingly recorded for each of Paris's twenty arrondissements in Cottinet, *Les Colonies de vacances, 1887* (Paris, 1888). The summary data for all ten *colonies* in 1884 includes the observation that "just like last year, the girls grew faster than the boys. Doubtless less well-fed in their families, the girls catch up faster on holiday." (The remark that the least well-fed fill out the fastest *en colonie* also turns up in Delpy, *Les Oeuvres* as well.) "Moreover, they are older and they hike less." (The boys were ten to eleven, the girls twelve to thirteen). See Cottinet, *La Colonie scolaire, 1884,* 36; Cottinet, *La Colonie scolaire, 1885,* 26–27. During the first several years, teachers proved singularly inept at the collection and interpretation of this data. One teacher's inexpert wielding of the yardstick produced the improbable statistic that her girls had grown, on average, 8 cm. during the four weeks *en colonie,* while another reported with horror that her group had actually shrunk over the holiday (it turned out she had measured her group shod at the departure and barefoot at the return). On these various misadventures with the yardstick, see Cottinet, *La Colonie scolaire, 1884;* and *La Colonie scolaire, 1885.*

134   Taken from one of Lécart's medical charts, reproduced in Cottinet, *La Colonie scolaire, 1885,* 18–19. Cottinet compiled this sample chart by combining a host of maladies and observations drawn from various individual cases recorded by M. Lécart.

135   E. Cottinet, *Les Colonies de vacances en France et à l'étranger,* Mémoires du Musée Pédagogique, 2d series, part 47 (Paris, 1889), 577.

136   "Les Colonies de vacances," *La Vie heureuse,* July 1903, 139.

137   Cottinet, *Les Colonies de vacances en France et à l'étranger,* 589.

138   Philip Nord makes a similar point when he notes that neo-Lamarckianism gave the men of the Third Republic an extraordinary faith in the power of education: "Pedagogy was elevated, in Letourneau's phrase, to the first of the sciences, for it did not only illuminate the path of human progress but had the potential to deliver humankind an evolutionary push forward." Philip Nord, *The Republican Moment* (Cambridge: Harvard University Press, 1995), 43. Nord goes on to quote Paul Broca, who observed that "not only does education make a man superior . . . it even has the power of raising him above himself, of enlarging his brain, of perfecting its shape." Ibid., 43.

139   Cottinet, *Les Colonies de vacances, 1889,* 577.

140   Cottinet, speech before the Comité Parisien des Colonies de Vacances, 11 July 1887; cited in Rey-Herme, *Les Colonies de vacances: Origines,* 238.

141 Cottinet, *Les Colonies de vacances en France et à l'étranger,* 588.

142 "Les Colonies de vacances à Paris," *Revue pédagogique,* 15 June 1887, 515.

143 By 1901, the *maître/colon* ratio had reached an average of one *maître* for every twenty *colons* in the Paris *colonies scolaires.* Rey-Herme, *Les Colonies de vacances: Origines,* 422.

144 Cottinet, *Les Colonies de vacances en France et à l'étranger;* and Cottinet and Cahen, *Les Colonies de vacances, 1889 et 1899,* 3–4, which gives the 1888 total as 869. The 1889 report did not break down by sex.

145 Delpy, *Les Oeuvres,* 13. There is some ambiguity on the question of initiative here — the *colonie* could be a way for the school/municipality to extract the child from its own family or, alternatively, for a family to rid itself of one child too many. In either case the *colonie* was overstepping the bounds, transforming a work of social assistance into a full-time substitute for the family.

146 *Compte rendu de la 17e assemblée générale de la Caisse des Ecoles du VIIIe arrondissement: Colonie et voyages scolaires de 1889.*

147 *Registre de la Caisse des Ecoles du VIe arrondissement,* cited in Rey-Herme, *Les Colonies de vacances: Origines,* 405.

148 Letter from the head of the second arrondissement to the prefect of the Seine, 18 November 1892, cited in Rey-Herme, *Les Colonies de vacances: Origines,* 421–22.

149 *La Colonie scolaire de Mandres-sur-Vair en 1889* (Paris, 1889).

150 Mandres was a small château in the Vosges, surrounded by two hectares of park land, which former mayor Duval-Pihet donated to the eleventh arrondissement's *caisse des écoles* in 1888. Possession of the property allowed the *caisse* to send increasingly large numbers of children *en colonie,* from 200 (sent in two groups of 100) during that first summer of 1889, reaching 1,000 (sent in four groups of 200) by the summer of 1901. Rey-Herme, *Les Colonies de vacances: Origines,* 418.

151 François Ponsard, "Une Colonie scolaire," *Le Temps,* 15 Aug. 1905. The ministerial visit was scheduled to coincide with the annual *fête de la colonie,* when parents were invited to spend the day at Mandres and be entertained by the gymnastic and choral performances of their offspring. The streets and neighborhoods cited — Popincourt, Folie-Méricourt — were old artisan districts known for their poverty and political radicalism during the great urban insurrections of 1789–1871; indeed, their names were synonymous with urban poverty.

152 *La Colonie scolaire du Ve arrondissement,* report to the *caisse des écoles,* 1892 (Paris, 1893). The extract is taken from the child's journal.

153 The Société's international dimension was in fact far less developed than its national one. Hence, while discussion embraced statistics and descriptions of various programs in Russia, England, and the rest of continental Europe, delegates to the conference seem to have been drawn from French

programs alone, with the *colonies scolaires* being especially well represented. The conference extended over two sessions, held a month apart, and the proceedings were published in full in *La Révue philanthropique,* 10 June 1903 and 10 July 1903. (In each case, the proceedings consisted of a lengthy report by Arthur Delpy of the *caisse des écoles* for the eighth arrondissement, followed by intense and, at times, vituperative discussion.) Delpy then reprinted the whole proceedings under his own name: Arthur Delpy, *Les Oeuvres de colonies de vacances* (Paris, 1903). All citations are drawn from this version.

154 Ibid., 39. Even the relatively spartan accommodations of the *colonies scolaires* were bound to seem luxurious to children who dwelt for most of the year in "poor, cramped rooms that serve at once as kitchen, dining room, and bedroom." Unnamed schoolmistress, cited in V. Brouet, "Les Colonies scolaires," 23.

155 Delpy, *Les Oeuvres,* 37. The overall rates of expenditure for *colonies de vacances* over the summer of 1913 underscore the relative cheapness of family placement: L'Oeuvre de Trois Semaines: 80,005 F; the Chaussée de Maine: 194,651 F; the Caisses des Ecoles Parisiennes: 430,156 F. Cited in Rey-Herme, *Les Colonies de vacances en France, 1906-1936: L'Institution et ses problèmes* (Paris: Editions Fleurus, 1961), 41–42.

156 Delpy, *Les Oeuvres,* 14. At this time the selection of children rested with a special committee composed of members of the *caisse des écoles,* assisted by medical inspectors. V. Brouet, "Les Colonies scolaires," 17. Up through the end of World War I, children went uninsured on their summer holiday, their fathers having signed a paper absolving the municipality of all responsibility in case of accident or sickness. This would change in the aftermath of the war.

157 Delpy, *Les Oeuvres,* 14.

158 Ibid., 14–15.

159 Ibid., 15. At the Congrès National des Colonies de Vacances, held three years later (1906) in Bordeaux, the debate between family placement and collective living raged furiously once again. See Rey-Herme, *Les Colonies de vacances: Origines,* 478.

160 Delpy, *Les Oeuvres,* 17.

161 Dr. Noir, *Application rationnelle du système des colonies* (Paris, 1905), cited in Plantet and Delpy, *Les Colonies de vacances,* 96.

162 Delpérier, *Les Colonies de vacances,* 119.

163 Noir, cited in Plantet and Delpy, *Les Colonies de vacances,* 96.

164 Unnamed *surveillant* quoted in Dr. Beauvisage, "Les Oeuvres d'assistance scolaire et les colonies de vacances de la région lyonnaise," *Congrès de l'Association Française pour le Développement des Sciences* (Lyon, 1906).

165 M. Delarasse, in Delpy, *Les Oeuvres,* 18.

166 Dr. Beauvisage, in ibid., 26.

167 Letter from the mayor of the second arrondissement to the prefect of the Seine, 18 Nov. 1892, cited in Rey-Herme, *Les Colonies de vacances: Origines*, 423.

168 J. Houssaye, *Le Livre des colos*, 59.

169 Chaussée de Maine, *Rapport, 1905*, 18.

170 This fact emerged in the course of an especially interesting discussion of funding and the problem of parents who could well afford to send their children on holiday and yet chose to send them free of charge to the school *colonie*, in other words treating as a universal benefit of citizenship (like the primary school) what the directors of the *caisses* all agreed was a program of social assistance. The ambiguity of the *colonie scolaire* stemmed from the fact that it was linked to the primary school, as opposed to an institution of social welfare, pure and simple (such as the municipal welfare offices). The directors all agreed that the solution lay in demanding a contribution from those families who could pay, rather than in eliminating their children altogether. Delpy, *Les Oeuvres*, 35.

171 Dr. Georges Dequidt, "Colonies de vacances," *Air et soleil*, July–Sept. 1928, 7–8. This was the official publication of the Comité National des Colonies de Vacances.

172 Hence, while the youth of both sexes (aged thirteen to sixteen) remained most numerous in field, shop, and factory, their younger siblings now found themselves, by law, warming the benches of the *école primaire*. The advent of the republican school thus forced an abrupt recasting of adult-child relations, creating a divide in social experience between school-aged children and their elders, while creating new lines of sociability among children of different families by gathering them into horizontally ordered, age-stratified groups. See Colin Heywood, *Childhood in Nineteenth-Century France: Work, Health, and Education among the "Classes Populaires"* (Cambridge: Cambridge University Press, 1988), and Antoine Prost and Gérard Vincent, eds., *Histoire de la vie privée*, vol. 5 (Paris: Seuil, 1987). While the school-leaving age was raised from thirteen to fourteen under the Popular Front, 95 percent of French children were still leaving school at thirteen in the early 1940s, most in order to go to work. See Sarah Fishman, "Youth in Vichy France: The Juvenile Crime Wave and Its Implications," in Sarah Fishman et al., eds., *France at War: Vichy and the Historians* (London: Berg, 2000), 210.

173 Cottinet, *La Colonie scolaire, 1885*, 23.

CHAPTER 2   Toward a Pedagogy of Child Leisure

1   See Jean Houssaye, *Le Livre des colos: Histoire et évolution des centres de vacances pour enfants* (Paris: La Documentation Française, 1989), 37, for statistics on the number of programs, and Philippe-Alexandre Rey-Herme, *Les Colonies de vacances: Origines et premiers développements* (Paris: published privately by the author, 1954), 486, for the number of children sent in 1906.

2   Comte thus hoped that a national federation might press more successfully for collective train-fare reductions for the *colonies*. In addition, he envisioned the federation functioning as a kind of clearinghouse for the study of particular issues—pedagogical, hygienic, legal—that organizing a *colonie* might raise. This is precisely the function that its successor organization, the Comité National des Colonies de Vacances, would serve during the interwar period.

3   Rey-Herme, *Les Colonies de vacances: Origines,* 485. Of this early "laïcité ouverte," Gérard Cholvy remarks that it was that "liberal protestantism, which is practically detached from all Christian dogma, that had the greatest affinity with secular and republican ideology." Gérard Cholvy and Yves-Marie Hilaire, *Histoire religieuse de la France contemporaine,* vol. 2, *1880–1930* (Toulouse: Privat, 1987), 48.

4   Especially in the Assumptionist paper *La Croix,* which howled for the head of the innocent captain.

5   On the Dreyfus Affair, see Jean-Denis Bredin, *L'Affaire* (Paris: Fayard, 1991); and Maurice Larkin, *Church and State after the Dreyfus Affair* (London: Macmillan, 1974).

6   Maurice Allard (a Blanquiste, and arguably the most avid "mangeur de curés" in the Chamber), speaking out against the Church before the Chamber of Deputies, 10 April 1905, quoted in Cholvy and Hilaire, *Histoire religieuse,* 105.

7   There were representatives from six Catholic programs present that day. It would take another national meeting, four years hence, before any kind of working federation could be established at the national level. See Rey-Herme, *Les Colonies de vacances: Origines,* 485.

8   Hence, in 1913, the Catholic Union Nationale des Colonies de Vacances (UNCV, founded in 1912, under the leadership of Abbé Gosselin) included ten non-Catholic programs (nine neutral and one Jewish) alongside the core membership of 161 Catholic programs, while Abbé Vallier, impelled by the militant desire to assure an active Catholic presence in nonconfessional circles, remained an honored guest at the national congresses of Comte's nonconfessional Fédération Nationale (transformed in 1923 into the Comité National de Colonies de Vacances and Oeuvres

de Plein Air [CNCV]). The separation of the Catholic UNCV and the secular organizations continues to this day. Joseph Lavarenne, *Un Pionnier, une initiative: Le père Vallier et la Colonie de Verrières* (Lyon: Editions du Sud-Est, 1953), 64–65. Statistics on UNCV membership can be found in G. Cholvy, *Histoire des organisations et mouvements chrétiens de jeunesse en France, XIXe-XXe siècle* (Paris: Editions du Cerf, 1999), 165.

9   In most French cities, this process had already begun some ten years earlier, under the aegis of local authorities. See Philip Nord, *The Republican Moment* (Cambridge: Harvard University Press, 1995), and Max Turmann, *Au Sortir de l'école: Les patronages* (Paris: Lecoffre, 1901). On the separation, see Jean-Marie Mayeur, *La Question laïque, XIXe-XXe siècle* (Paris: Fayard, 1997); Cholvy and Hilaire, *Histoire religieuse;* Jacques Le Goff and René Rémond, eds., *Histoire de la France religieuse,* vol. 4 (Paris: Seuil, 1992); Antoine Prost, *Histoire de l'enseignement en France, 1800–1967* (Paris: Armand Colin, 1968), esp. chaps. 8–12. Many of these teachers shed their clerical garb, armed themselves with the elementary teaching certificate, and returned in secular incarnation to finish out their careers.

10 I have adopted Cholvy and Hilaire's very useful distinction between the *laïcité ouverte* of the 1880s and the more hard-line *laïcisme militant* of the early twentieth century. Cholvy and Hilaire, *Histoire religieuse.*

11 Cholvy and Hilaire, *Histoire religieuse,* 103–4. In the end, some forty thousand women left the convent in the wake of Combes's law, and one third of the nation's private Catholic schools were closed between 1902 and 1905. (Le Goff and Rémond, *Histoire de la France réligieuse,* 52.) One gets a sense of the scope of Combes's action when one recalls that in 1902 nearly one quarter of the nation's children were enrolled in Catholic schools. See Larkin, *Church and State,* 2; and Larkin, *Religion, Politics, and Preferment in France since 1890* (Cambridge: Cambridge University Press, 1995), pt. 1.

12 The phrase is taken from Tertullian, and is quoted by Michel Lagrée in the title of his article "Exilés dans leur patrie (1880–1920)," in François Lebrun, ed., *Histoire des catholiques en France du XVIe siècle à nos jours* (Toulouse: Privat, 1980), 407–53.

13 Cholvy, *Histoire des organisations,* 50.

14 Turmann, *Au Sortir,* 74. Emphasis original. Turmann was a professor at the Collège Libre des Sciences Sociales. In 1896, M. E. Védie, vice president of the Commission des Patronages, reminded the membership during the annual "journée des Patronages" that their job was to take each child of ten who crossed the doorstep of the patronage for the first time and make of him a good worker, and a good Christian: "But this is not all, Messieurs, for this child will also become a citizen of the great French nation, he will be called to cast into the electoral urns a vote that will have the same weight as yours. He must therefore understand his duties to society and his superiors, and also his rights—everything that is called civic and

social education—and we will have failed in our task if, by cowardice or excessive prudence, we do not teach him how to exercise this liberty for his own benefit and that of others." Cited in Turmann, *Au Sortir,* 275.

15 See Cholvy, *Histoire des organisations,* chap. 3, for a fuller discussion of the Church's reaction to the secularization.

16 François Veuillot, "Autour d'un patronage," *L'Univers,* 15 Apr. 1897, 1. Note Kérivan's transfer of nature imagery to the *patronage,* achieved via tropes of sunlight, fresh air, and children moving freely through nature, even when that "nature" was a closed courtyard in the dense, industrial Maison-Blanche district. *L'Univers* was the journal that reflected papal policy most faithfully in the 1890s. Its circulation was, however, quite limited—under 20,000 copies sold daily, versus the 180,000 copies of *La Croix* sold off the newsstands each day. Larkin, *Church and State,* 67.

17 Félix Kérivan, "Le patronage de jeudi," *Bulletin de la Commission des Patronages,* cited in Turmann, *Au Sortir,* 226–27.

18 Turmann, *Au Sortir,* 38 and 205. Geneviève Pujol gives a slightly higher figure for 1900: 4,168 Catholic *patronages* (2,351 for boys and 1,817 for girls) and 1,276 secular ones. Geneviève Pujol, *Le Métier d'animateur* (Toulouse: Privat, 1978), 17.

19 Cholvy, *Histoire des organisations,* 103.

20 Turmann, *Au Sortir,* 135.

21 René Michaud, *J'avais vingt ans: Un jeune ouvrier au début du siècle* (Paris: Syros, 1983), 36.

22 A. de Ségur, "Un patronage entre ciel et terre," *L'Univers,* 28 June 1896.

23 R. Michaud, *J'avais vingt ans,* 36.

24 Turmann, *Au Sortir,* 134, quoting Abbé Schaeffer, director of the *patronage des filles* of St. Joseph de Plaisance (fourteenth arrondissement), one of the largest *patronages* for girls in Paris at the time.

25 Turmann, *Au Sortir,* 127.

26 Ibid., 72–73.

27 Cholvy and Hilaire, *Histoire religieuse,* 113.

28 The phrase for the subheading comes from "La formation littéraire dans les patronages," *La Vie au patronage, édition des garçons,* Jan. 1914, 10.

29 Abbé Schaeffer (Patronage des Filles de St. Joseph de Plaisance), quoted in Turmann, *Au Sortir,* 132.

30 Ibid., 134.

31 "Le Patronage des vacances," *Bulletin mensuelle, Notre-Dame-de-la-Salette* (Suresnes), Sept. 1910, 8. The article implies that the *patronage des vacances* was mixed, or at least that the girls' *patro* had joined forces with the boys' for the midsummer festival.

32 Abbé Vallier, quoted in Rey-Herme, *Les Colonies de vacances: Origines,* 355–56. For a discussion of early modern Jesuit pedagogies that used games and theater to educational ends, see François de Dain-

ville, *L'Éducation des jésuites, XVIe–XVIIIe siècles* (Paris: Les Editions de Minuit, 1978), pt. 5, "L'Éducation par le jeu."

33   "La Bataille de Garches (15 septembre 1910)," *Bulletin mensuelle, Notre-Dame-de-la-Salette* (Suresnes), Oct. 1910, 3–4.

34   Christian Guérin, *L'Utopie: Scouts de France* (Paris: Fayard, 1997).

35   From a detailed description of the organization of the girls' *patronage* at St. Joseph de Plaisance, found in Turmann, *Au Sortir,* 381.

36   Turmann, *Au Sortir,* 380–81. Emphasis original.

37   Ibid., 379.

38   Ibid., 382.

39   Ibid., 383. The monthly bulletin *La Vie au patronage* was aimed at the directors of *patronages,* and featured at least one, and often two, short plays purpose-written by the editors for children to perform in the *patronages.* The passion for theatrical production in the *patronages* peaked in the immediate prewar years, giving way, after 1918, to the growing interest in scouting, camping, and woodcraft.

40   Félix Kérivan, editor of *Le Patronage,* July 1899, cited in Cholvy, *Histoire des organisations,* 100.

41   *Bulletin mensuelle, Notre-Dame-de-la-Salette* (Suresnes), July 1912, 7.

42   Ibid., Sept. 1912, 7. Abbé Foucher was clearly steeped in the fin-de-siècle Catholic ideology of the artisanal craft as socioeconomic anchor for the youth of the working classes, who, if they trained in the parish shoe-making shop, would "acquire a trade that would allow them to work at home, and even ease the family budget by repairing their worn shoe-leather." Ibid. See also Félix Kérivan, "Une journée de dimanche au patronage Saint-Gervais," *Bulletin de la Commission des Patronages,* cited in Turmann, *Au Sortir,* 222; and A. de Ségur, "Un patronage entre ciel et terre," *L'Univers,* 28 June 1896.

43   de Pitray, *Nouvelles du Patronage Olier,* Mar. 1898.

44   Ibid. In August 1899, Abbé de Pitray, whose Olier *patronage* was open only to children from the public schools, elaborated on the scope of social Catholic outreach to these "de-Christianized" children: "Many [Catholics] speak ill of these children, but I defend them . . . I believe it is possible to effect a broader rapprochement in which those who do not share our beliefs have their place in a greater brotherhood that Christ would not condemn." de Pitray, *Nouvelles du Patronage Olier,* Aug. 1899.

45   As the *patronages* were swamped by school-age recruits in the wake of public school secularization, adolescent boys began to avoid what had become, in their view, a program for young children. Directors of *patronages* were distressed by the drop in adolescent attendance, and made no bones about the fact that the growing focus on sports was a direct response to this problem of retaining young males after they had made their first communion and had left school for the adult world of shop and factory.

46   Cholvy and Hilaire, *Histoire religieuse,* 165. In 1913 the FGSPF boasted over 150,000 members.

47   Quoted in Cholvy, *Histoire des organisations,* 161. See also Pierre Gaussin, who defended the turn to sports in terms of discipleship, noting that "while large calves and a broad chest aren't everything," a healthy body was the condition of an active and "productive" religious engagement. Pierre Gaussin, "Que peut-on attendre des patronages?" *La Vie au patronage,* 15 Feb. 1912, 71.

48   Abbé J. Aubert, speaking at the *journée diocésaine* of the *patronages des garçons,* Paris, 1920, quoted in Cholvy, *Histoire des organisations,* 161.

49   Abbé Gaston Courtois, *Orientations actuelles de nos Oeuvres de Jeunesse,* doc. n. 43, Union des Oeuvres Ouvrières Catholiques, supplement to *l'Union* of December 1931. Courtois was national director of the Oeuvres de la Jeunesse and participated in the direction of Les Coeurs Vaillants, which published a children's journal (under the same name) that was distributed through the *patronages.*

50   Félix Kérivan, "Le patronage de jeudi," cited in Turmann, *Au Sortir,* 230.

51   Abbé Charles Vallier, "Un Congrès de patronages tenu par des enfants," pt. 2, *La Vie au patronage,* 15 Feb. 1914, 78. The congress took place at the Verrières *colonie* and brought together about one hundred boys from the Lyonnais region aged 10 to 14.

52   Abbé Henry Bruneau, "L'Oeuvre des Saines Vacances (Douvaine)," *Bulletin de l'Association des Anciens Elèves de Saint-Sulpice,* 1902.

53   de Pitray, *Nouvelles du Patronage Olier,* June 1897.

54   Bruneau, "L'Oeuvre des Saines Vacances." Bruneau concludes by pointing out that children from better-off families did not need the *patronage;* it was necessary only for children from working-class families, for, as one of his colleagues remarked, "The people, apart from a few rare instances, no longer know how to raise their children." E.P., "Comment organiser une colonie de vacances," *Bulletin de l'Association des Anciens Elèves de l'Ecole de Saint-Sulpice,* Aug. 1905.

55   de Pitray, *Nouvelles du Patronage Olier,* Aug. 1899. The abbé was in fact describing the atmosphere of his newly organized "Colonie Edouard," which was an extension of the Olier *patronage,* "a little *patronage* born of the larger one," as de Pitray put it in his *Nouvelles du Patronage Olier* of October 1903.

56   de Pitray, *Nouvelles du Patronage Olier,* Mar. 1898.

57   Abbé Schaeffer, describing the girls' *patronage* at St. Joseph de Plaisance. Cited in Turmann, *Au Sortir,* 379. One might imagine that such a "maternalist" structure granted the girls' *patronages* a greater measure of autonomy vis-à-vis the Church hierarchy. Yet the *directrice*'s authority was ultimately shaped and limited by the higher (if also more distant) authority of the priest or chaplain in charge of the program. As the priest's

"natural intermediary," she gave the girls "practical advice," while leaving matters of piety—catechism, confession, services, sermons—in priestly hands. Turmann, *Au Sortir,* 380. The abbé goes on to note that ideally the *directrice* should live in the *patronage* itself, or at least in the neighborhood, so that she might always be available to the girls. Ibid., 383–84.

58 Bruneau, "L'Oeuvre des Saines Vacances."

59 Michaud, *J'avais vingt ans,* 39.

60 Abbé Schaeffer, cited in Turmann, *Au Sortir,* 134; and F. Kérivan, "Un patronage de jeudi," cited in Turmann, *Au Sortir,* 228. Kérivan edited *Le Patronage,* the national organ of the FGSPF, which was founded in 1898 (the journal began publication five years later).

61 de Pitray, *Nouvelles du Patronage Olier,* Mar. 1898.

62 Abbé Boyreau, "Le Courrier de Notre Dame du Rosaire," May 1897, quoted in Turmann, *Au Sortir,* 236–40. Emphasis original.

63 The patronage St-Joseph-de-Plaisance welcomed girls from pre-catechism classes right up till the eve of marriage. Turmann, *Au Sortir,* 132.

64 Edouard Petit, *Premier rapport,* published in the *Journal officiel,* 11 Aug. 1896, 4601. (Part 2 came out the following summer, on 29 July 1897).

65 Léon Bourgeois, president of the Ligue d'Enseignement and former prime minister of the Republic (1895–96), speaking before the league's annual congress at Rouen in 1896. Cited in Turmann, *Au Sortir,* 151–52. Solidarism, which historian J. E. S. Hayward termed "the official social philosophy of the French Third Republic," is in many ways the secular analogue of social Catholic doctrine. Both philosophies deny the inevitability of class conflict and stress instead the construction of cooperative and collaborative relations among classes. Presumptions of vertical class order underpin both doctrines, with a chain of reciprocal obligations linking lower to higher. In the secular, solidarist version, these mutual obligations are envisioned as part of an original social contract. See J. E. S. Hayward, "The Official Social Philosophy of the French Third Republic: Leon Bourgeois and Solidarism," *International Review of Social History* 6 (1961): 19–48.

66 G. Cholvy, *Le Patronage: Ghetto ou vivier?* (Paris: Nouvelle Cité, 1988), notes that secular *patronages* seem rarely to have worked very well. At the time of the Paris Exposition (1900), when the Catholic Church boasted over 3,500 *patronages* in France, the *laïcs* had opened a mere 800. Most of these were opened in regions where Catholic *patronages* were especially numerous and thriving: the Nord and Pas-de-Calais (209), the Seine (88), the Marne (39), the Gironde (41), Seine-Maritime (44), and the Aude (65), suggesting that Petit and Bourgeois sought to compete directly with the Catholics on this novel terrain. Edouard Petit's 1905 speech before an audience in Biarritz leaves no doubt on the matter: "Even if all the parochial schools were closed tomorrow, the battle would still not be won, for the

Catholic *patronages* would still be standing, and I am more afraid of ten *patronages* than of one hundred parochial schools." Cited in Cholvy, *Histoire des organisations,* 103.

67   Abbé Lorette, "Oeuvre des Saines Vacances," *Bulletin de l'Association des Anciens Elèves de Saint-Sulpice,* 1903.

68   E.P., "Comment organiser une colonie de vacances," *Bulletin de l'Association des Anciens Elèves de l'Ecole de Saint-Sulpice,* Aug. 1905.

69   The statistic comes from Philippe-Alexandre Rey-Herme, *La Colonie de vacances hier et aujourd'hui* (Paris: Editions Cap, 1955), 36.

70   Bruneau, "L'Oeuvre des Saines Vacances." See also G. Jarosson, "Oeuvres des Saines Vacances, notes complémentaires," *Bulletin de l'Association des Anciens Elèves de Saint-Sulpice,* 1903.

71   *Rapport général sur les conférences et les oeuvres de la Société de Saint-Vincent-de-Paul* (Paris, 1904), 34.

72   Rey-Herme, *La Colonie de vacances hier et aujourd'hui,* 38.

73   Unnamed *colon* at the Edouard *colonie,* summer 1898 or 1899, cited in Rey-Herme, *Les Colonies de vacances: Origines,* 334. De Pitray named the *colonie* for his recently deceased friend Edouard Tafoureau, with whom he had spent the previous summer at Bourdiou.

74   The presence of two "grand-mères"—Mme de Pitray and Mme Saint Claire Deville, president of the Dames de Saint-Sulpice—as well as a houseful of servants, must surely have helped with the material organization of life in the Edouard *colonie.*

75   Rey-Herme, *Les Colonies de vacances: Origines,* 333.

76   De Pitray, *Nouvelles du Patronage Olier,* Aug. 1899.

77   "Lettre de M. Culty, réponse de M. Calon," manuscript found in the archives of the Société Saint-Vincent-de-Paul, cited in Rey-Herme, *Les Colonies de vacances: Origines,* 365.

78   De Pitray, *Nouvelles du Patronage Olier,* Aug. 1903.

79   Ibid.

80   Bruneau, "L'Oeuvre des Saines Vacances."

81   Bruneau, "L'Oeuvre des Saines Vacances."

82   Ibid.

83   Dr. Beauvisage, "Modes de placement," in *Congrès national des Colonies de Vacances,* ed. F. Gibon (Paris, 1910), p. 80. Emphasis original.

84   Abbé C. Vallier, "Une Colonie de vacances dirigée par des séminaristes" (Lyon, 1904).

85   Unnamed priest cited in M. Turmann, *L'Education populaire, les oeuvres complémentaires de l'école en 1900* (Paris: Lecoffre, 1904), 178–79. The programs in question were the "Vacances à la Campagne" of Lyon and Saint-Etienne, organized by the Société de Saint-Vincent-de-Paul in the summer of 1903. At first, these *colonies* mixed family placement with placement in a series of collectives founded in rural convents and Catholic

schools. But as the number of children rose, the percentage of family placements dropped steadily; where such placements had accounted for fully
half the *colonie* in the summer of 1904 (114 out of 238 children), placement
in peasant homes dropped off rapidly thereafter, reaching one in five in
1906 (100 out of 500 children sent) before disappearing altogether over the
next couple of years. "Rapport lu à l'Assemblée Générale de Lyon, le 9 déc.
1904," *Bulletin de la Société Saint-Vincent-de-Paul* 676 (Apr. 1905); and "Les
colonies de vacances de Saint-Etienne: Rapport du Comité," *Bulletin de
la Société Saint-Vincent-de-Paul* 697 (Jan. 1907).

86 Abbé Vallier, cited in Turmann, *L'Education populaire,* 171. Emphasis
original.

87 See Rey-Herme, *Les Colonies de vacances: Origines;* and Delpy and Plantet,
Les Colonies de vacances.

88 Rey-Herme, *La Colonie de vacances hier et aujourd'hui,* 45.

89 Bruneau, "L'Oeuvre des Saines Vacances." Emphasis original.

90 Ibid. I speak of the child in the masculine pronoun only because the *colonies* under discussion here were unquestionably male. As we will see, a
similar pedagogy was enacted in the *colonies des filles* by the *directrices* and
secularized (sort of) *bonnes soeurs.*

91 Ibid. and *Bulletin mensuelle,* Suresnes, Sept. 1909, 5. "René" was the
(doubtless fictive) child-author of the periodic "Lettre de la Colonie" published each summer in the *Bulletin mensuelle.* Whether the author of this
passage was a *colon* or the abbé himself matters little for our purposes
here: either author gives us an unvarnished look at the pseudofamilial network on which the Catholic "psycho-pedagogy" of child leisure rested.
Abbé Bruneau underscored the psychological importance of that bedside
moment *en colonie,* the vulnerability and openness of the child as he's
falling asleep: "We all recall the tender little words and, sometimes, the
gentle reproaches that our mothers spoke each night as they came to kiss
us good night."

92 E.P., "Comment organiser une colonie de vacances."

93 Douvaine, *Règlement,* article 3, reprinted in Rey-Herme, *Les Colonies de
vacances: Origines,* 392–98.

94 Douvaine, *Circulaire aux parents,* clauses 1 and 2, reprinted in Rey-Herme,
Les Colonies de vacances: Origines, 399–400 (emphasis original). At the
same time that the directors sought to place themselves in the moral position of parents vis-à-vis the *colons,* they also emphasized that the actual,
biological parents should maintain an interest in the fate of their children
by participating in the cost of sending them to the *colonie:* "We must require this if we wish to prevent them from losing the habit of upholding
their first duty," warned "E.P." in his 1905 pamphlet "Comment organiser
une colonie de vacances."

95 Bruneau, "L'Oeuvre des Saines Vacances."

96 Abbé Evrard, "Le Personnel des colonies de vacances," *Congrès national des colonies de vacances catholiques* (Limoges, 1911), 159–70.

97 Evrard, "Le Personnel," 159–70.

98 Abbé Laroppe, *Dans la vallée de Celles: Souvenir d'une colonie de vacances* (Paris: Bloud, 1911).

99 From the brochure *Colonie de vacances du petit séminaire de Poitiers à Brétignolles,* 1911, cited in Rey-Herme, *Les Colonies de vacances en France, 1906–1936: L'institution et ses problèmes* (Paris: Fleurus, 1961), 214.

100 *Colonie de vacances du petit séminaire de Poitiers,* cited in Rey-Herme, *Les Colonies de vacances en France, 1906–1936,* 214.

101 See Jean-Noël Luc, *L'Invention du jeune enfant au XIXe siècle: De la salle d'asile à l'école maternelle* (Paris: Belin, 1997).

102 Bruneau, "L'Oeuvre des Saines Vacances."

103 Ibid.

104 Lavarenne, *Un Pionnier,* 69.

105 Ibid.

106 Vallier, cited in Turmann, *L'Education populaire,* 172.

107 Vallier, letter to Max Turmann, cited in Turmann, *L'Education populaire,* 173.

108 Lavarenne, *Un Pionnier,* 87.

109 Ibid., 83–84.

110 Ibid., 80.

111 E.P., "Comment organiser une colonie de vacances."

112 Report of the thirty-ninth general assembly, *caisse des écoles,* eighth arrondissement (Paris, 1911), 49.

113 Lavarenne, *Un Pionnier,* 146. Vallier was quite consistent in his inclination toward toughness in matters of the body. When a child complained of a stomach ache, for example, his counsel was always one of prudent suspicion in the face of children's "abundant imagination." If having a stomach ache got you a few little privileges, like a sweet, hot *tisane* from the *colonie* nurse, well then, the child would "sincerely feel" that queasiness of which he complained. But replace the sweet tea with a more bitter brew, and see how quickly the entire company is suddenly cured. Ibid., 147.

114 Ibid., 166.

115 "Les Colonies des vacances de Saint-Etienne: Rapport du Comité," *Bulletin de la Société de Saint-Vincent-de-Paul* 697 (Jan. 1907).

116 C. Vallier, "Une Colonie de vacances dirigée par des séminaristes." Catholics scornfully labeled the hygienic programs of their secular competitors as "colonies d'engraissement," which I have liberally translated as "food-farms."

117 The *patronages,* too, had to rely on students and seminarians in their *colonies* for the simple reason that the confrères who staffed them during the

school year either could not leave the *patronage* for that long (remember all the children who *didn't* leave town *en colonie*), or else took off on summer vacations of their own. For those who felt the *patronage/colonie* drew its strength from lay confrères, the turn toward young priests was an unhappy development: "The Oeuvre des Saines Vacances has been invaded by clericalism," wailed Abbé Lorette in 1903 (though he later admitted that this turn might raise the level of "true piety" among the *colons*). Lorette, "Oeuvre des Saines Vacances."

118 Vallier, "Une Colonie de vacances dirigée par des séminaristes."

119 Lavarenne, *Un Pionnier,* 85–86.

120 Vallier, "Une Colonie de vacances dirigée par des séminaristes."

121 Turmann, *L'Education populaire,* 175.

122 Vallier, "Une Colonie de vacances dirigée par des séminaristes."

123 Ibid.

124 Cholvy, *Histoire des organisations,* 103 and 240.

125 Marie-Thérèse Cheroutre, "Albertine Duhamel," in Geneviève Poujol and Madeleine Romer, eds., *Dictionnaire biographique des militants, XIXe–XXe siècles: De l'éducation populaire à l'action sociale* (Paris: Harmattan, 1996), 125. Duhamel entered St-Odile's when she became an orphan, at the age of fourteen. She emerged two years later and, "practically at the gates of the convent," married her father's childhood friend M. Duhamel.

126 "Rapport à l'Assemblée Générale de Lyon, 9 déc. 1904," *Bulletin de la Société de Saint-Vincent-de-Paul* 676 (Apr. 1905).

127 Ibid.

128 Ibid.

129 "Souvenirs de Vacances," *Bulletin mensuel, Notre-Dame-de-la-Salette,* Suresnes, Sept. 1913, 3.

130 Ibid.

131 Alison Lurie, "Not for Muggles," *New York Review of Books,* 16 Dec. 1999, 6–8.

132 Hence in 1955, CEMEA cofounder Gisèle de Failly warned *moniteurs* against displaying an "excessive sentimentality" with the children: "It is especially tempting to be sentimental with the little ones; they are adorable and sweet, and their words and facial expressions enchant us and make us feel tenderly toward them. We long to take them in our arms and prattle away in baby-talk to them. But we must not abuse this pleasure, lest we work against our proper function which, let us not forget, is to help the child to grow up." Gisèle de Failly, *Le Moniteur, la monitrice* (Paris: Editions du Scarabée, 1956), 31–32.

133 Carolyn Steedman argues that in England, over the period 1780–1930, ideas about childhood became a vehicle for expressing notions of subjectivity and interiority. Childhood thus became the history of each indi-

vidual self, of his or her physiological and cognitive unfolding. As we reach adulthood, that past becomes only partly retrievable, but it remains within us, our core identity (an idea that Freud would make much of when he named this childhood, now lost in partial and fragmented memories, our unconscious mind). Steedman thus writes of a broadly shared assumption that there was "a *bildung,* a wholeness in interiority that will figure itself forth from inside to outside." And it was this belief that came to rest on the figure of the child in nineteenth-century England. Carolyn Steedman, *Strange Dislocations: Childhood and the Idea of Human Interiority, 1780–1930* (Cambridge: Harvard University Press, 1993), 15.

CHAPTER 3   Family Placement in a Socialist Mode

1   Dr. Landouzy, quoted by M. Delarasse in Arthur Delpy, *Les Oeuvres de vacances* (Paris, 1903), 18.

2   One need only glance through the pages of *Air et soleil,* official organ of the nonconfessional Comité National des Colonies de Vacances, or read through the reports at the Comité's periodic national congresses, to appreciate the natalist and nationalist turn that *colonie de vacances* propaganda took in the aftermath of World War I.

3   Archives Municipales de Suresnes (hereafter A.M. de Suresnes), section L, Commissions Scolaires, folder 361 (Colonies de vacances, 1915 à 1918), Victor Diederich, Emile Taque, and Eugène Michel, "Oeuvre des Colonies de Vacances," 1 June 1916. Mayor Diederich was president of the municipal *colonie;* Taque and Michel, who served on Diederich's municipal council, were secretary and vice-president, respectively.

4   Roger-Henri Guerrand observes that the crisis of national health at the end of the war placed the "défense sanitaire" on the same plane as the "défense nationale." Roger-Henri Guerrand, "Sellier et le service social," in Katherine Burlen, ed., *La Banlieue oasis: Henri Sellier et les cités-jardins* (Vincennes: Presses Universitaires de Vincennes, 1989), 124. As Rey-Herme points out, this implied a very local financing of *colonies* as well, with the central state contributing only indirectly, e.g., through its support of the "Pupilles de la Nation" (children whose fathers had been killed in the war), for whom the state picked up the bill. But direct subventions to the *colonies* were scant, and came most often from municipal coffers, or occasionally departmental ones. Between 1914 and 1936, *colonies* subsisted largely on the basis of charitable gifts, municipal funds (including the *caisses des écoles*), and contributions from the parents, though these latter were often symbolic sums, generally covering less than one third of the cost of sending their child. See Rey-Herme, *Les Colonies de vacances*

en France de 1906–1936: L'Institution et ses problèmes (Paris: Fleurus, 1961), 41–76.

5 This is not to say that the Chaussée de Maine and Oeuvre de Trois Semaines disappeared, or even diminished in size; on the contrary, both continued to flourish throughout the interwar period and even into the postwar years. But their relative weight diminished sharply after 1918, as municipalities and (later) industry ceased using them as intermediaries and began to organize their own *colonies.*

6 A.M. de Suresnes, D670, dossier 1931, Antonin Poggioli, "Les Colonies de vacances," Report to the Fédération Nationale des Municipalités Socialistes, 28 Apr. 1931, 2.

7 Ibid.

8 Martine Delahaye, *Les Enfants du Mont-Valérien* (Ardèche: Lienhart, 1997), 51. Delahaye gathered her interviews while working in an old-age home in Suresnes in the early to mid-1990s.

9 Cited in Marie-Geneviève Dezès, "L'Évolution urbaine à Bobigny, Ivry, Suresnes: Quelques repères statistiques," in Burlen, *La Banlieue oasis,* 238.

10 Journalist Eugène Gibon thus reported that out of the 20,000 Suresnois over the age of ten counted in the 1932 census, more than 18,000 were rural migrants. Eugène Gibon, "Les Enfants au soleil!," *Le Suresnois,* 28 July 1934, 1.

11 Delahaye, *Les Enfants du Mont-Valérien,* 46–47.

12 Martine Cochard, "La Politique éducative d'une muncipalité pendant l'entre-deux-guerres: Suresnes, 1919–1939" (Mémoire de maîtrise, Université de Paris V, 1983), pt. 1.

13 The city thus expanded by 68 percent over the period 1919–1936. Marie-Geneviève Dezès, "L'Évolution urbaine," in Burlen, *La Banlieue oasis,* 238.

14 O. Seron, *Histoire de Suresnes* (Suresnes: published privately by the author, 1926), 398, notes that in 1925, 1,400 families (that is, 2,700 people) lived in furnished rooms and boardinghouses "for lack of real housing." See also M. Cochard, "La Politique éducative."

15 Paul Rabinow notes that Sellier was "arguably the major figure in French urbanism during this period." Paul Rabinow, *French Modern: Norms and Forms of the Social Environment* (Cambridge: MIT Press, 1989), 261.

16 Interview with Georges Goblot, published in Municipalité de Suresnes, *Il y a cinquante ans . . . Henri Sellier installait la première municipalité à direction socialiste à Suresnes, 1919–1969* (Saint-Ouen: Imprimerie Maubert, 1970), 52. Goblot had served as Sellier's secretary since 1912. He later (1929) founded the local municipal newspaper, *Le Suresnois,* which local historian Michel Guillot termed a "vehicle for Sellier's thought." Michel Guillot, "Bio-bibliographie d'Henri Sellier," in Burlen, *La Banlieue oasis,* 296.

17   The phrase "pivot du réformisme français" is taken from Patrick Fridenson and Madeleine Rébérioux, "Albert Thomas, pivot du réformisme français," *Le Mouvement social* 87 (1974).

18   Although inscribed into the Paris bar in 1907, Sellier never actually pleaded a case.

19   Madeleine Rébérioux, "Un Milieu socialiste à la veille de la Grande guerre: Henri Sellier et le reformisme d'Albert Thomas," cited in Burlen, *La Banlieue oasis,* 28–29.

20   In 1906, he was elected general secretary of the Bourse du Travail in Puteaux, and in 1913, he was named secretary of the Syndicat des Employés de Commerce.

21   Vaillant founded the Comité Révolutionnaire Centrale on 1 January 1881, which in 1898 was renamed the Parti Socialiste Révolutionnaire. Elected to the municipal councils of both Vierzon and Paris in 1884, Vaillant opted for the latter, and served until 1893. See Jean Maitron, *Dictionnaire biographique du mouvement ouvrier français,* 2d series, vol. 9 (Paris: Editions Ouvrières, 1971), 254.

22   Henri Sellier, speech of 26 May 1926, cited in *Il y a cinquante ans,* 2. Vaillant was from Vierzon, some twenty miles northwest of Bourges. Maurice Dommanget, *Edouard Vaillant: Un Grand socialist, 1840-1915* (Mayenne: Floch, 1956), 266.

23   Edouard Vaillant speaking before the fifth Congrès Socialiste Internationale, Paris, 23–27 September 1900, quoted in Dommanget, *Edouard Vaillant,* 128. See also Adrien Veber, *Le Socialisme municipal* (Paris: V. Giard and E. Brière, 1908).

24   Henri Sellier, "Le 'citoyen' Vaillant," *Le Populaire,* 29 Jan. 1940, cited in Dommanget, *Edouard Vaillant,* 136.

25   Henri Sellier, speech of 26 May 1926, cited in *Il y a cinquante ans,* 2. The Musée Social grouped mostly Le Playist and solidarist reformers. Claude Pennetier argues that Sellier's pragmatic "esprit réalisateur" did not operate at the expense of his revolutionary vision but rather in harmony with it, while Rémi Lefebvre takes a more critical view of Sellier's collaboration with the reformists of the Musée Social. Claude Pennetier, "Henri Charles Sellier," in Jean Maitron, *Dictionnaire biographique du mouvement ouvrier français,* 4th series, vol. 41 (Paris: Editions ouvrières, 1992), 219–25, and Rémi Lefebvre, "Le Socialisme saisi par l'institution municipale," *Recherche socialiste* 6 (Mar. 1999): 9–25.

26   Henri Sellier, *Le Parti socialiste et l'action communale* (Paris: La vie communale, 1925), 13.

27   Maurice Halbwachs, *La Classe ouvrière et les niveaux de vie: Recherches sur la hiérarchie des besoins dans les sociétés industrielles contemporaines* (Paris: Alcan, 1912); and Halbwachs, *La Politique foncière des municipalités* (Paris: Librairie du Parti Socialiste, 1908).

28 Henri Sellier, *Les Banlieues urbaines et la réorganisation administrative du Département de la Seine* (Paris: Imprimerie nationale, 1917).

29 Henri Sellier, cited in Katherine Burlen, "Sciences du logement et gestion sociale des populations," in Burlen, *La Banlieue oasis,* 103. Clearly this conception of the city as relief or refuge from work owes more to Durkheimian sociology than to Marxist political economy, for Durkheim defined alienation in terms of an opposition between human society and physical matter. The alienation of workers from human society was thus the inevitable consequence of industrial labor, which, in Durkheim's view, demands that workers leave human society and orient themselves toward physical matter (wood, metal, cotton), whose transformation into usable goods constitutes the heart of industrial labor. This orientation toward matter inevitably distorts workers' representations of themselves and others, for these representations are always mediated by the physical matter with which they work. Work in the highly taylorized factories of modern industry merely exacerbated this problem because of the way in which the scientific organization of work (assembly lines and fragmented tasks) further decomposed the social relations of labor. Only through a return to the intense socio-cultural life of the city could these women and men recover social health and a more balanced, socially rooted set of perceptions and representations. See Maurice Halbwachs, *Classes sociales et morphologie* (Paris: Editions de Minuit, 1972). See also Burlen, "Sciences du logement," in Burlen, *La Banlieue oasis,* 283, n. 35.

30 There was, clearly, an element of prefigurative living in the notion of *solidarité sociale,* but it was, in itself, insufficient (and in no way intended) to actually reshape human nature or interactions, any more than municipal socialism itself was seen as adequate to the task of "putting an end to the regime of capitalist exploitation." Antonin Poggioli, "Rapport de l'Union des Municipalités Socialistes de la Seine," *56e Congrès administratif de la Fédération de la Seine du Parti socialiste,* 26–27 Oct. 1935, 131. See also Henri Sellier, *Le Socialisme et l'action municipale* (Paris: La vie communale, 1934).

31 The term "participatory urbanism" comes from Katherine Burlen, "Henri Sellier et la doctrine de Suresnes," in Yves Cohen and Rémi Baudouï, eds., *Les Chantiers de la paix sociale, 1900-1940* (Fontenay-Saint-Cloud: Editions de l'Ecole Normale Supérieure, 1996), 270.

32 Henri Sellier, *Programme municipal pour les élections de 1935* (Paris: Union des élus municipaux socialistes, 1935), 19.

33 Sellier, cited in Rabinow, *French Modern,* 335.

34 Henri Sellier, *Programme municipal pour les élections de 1935.* See also Burlen, "Henri Sellier," in Cohen and Baudouï, *Les Chantiers de la paix sociale,* 269.

35 Delahaye, *Les Enfants du Mont-Valérien,* 46–47.

36 To name but a few of his many affiliations. For the full list, see René
    Sordes, *Histoire de Suresnes* (Alençon: Imprimerie Corbière et Jugain,
    1965), 527–28.

37 *Urbanisme,* special issue on Suresnes, January 1935, 1. Martine Cochard
    notes that 75 percent of the interwar population belonged to the class of
    skilled workers: factory workers, foremen, technicians, office employees,
    lower-level cadres, and women and men employed in the growing tertiary
    sector. Martine Cochard, "De l'éducation à la formation professionnelle:
    Le cas de Suresnes, 1919–1939," in Burlen, *La Banlieue oasis,* 212. See also
    Cochard, "La Politique éducative," 12.

38 Delahaye, *Les Enfants du Mont-Valérien,* 81.

39 Martine Cochard notes that 985 children were using the lunchrooms in
    1937–38. Cochard, "La Politique éducative," 24–25.

40 Delahaye, *Les Enfants du Mont-Valérien,* 82.

41 The upper divisions consisted of one or two years of postprimary school-
    ing given to young teenagers within the four walls of the primary school
    and supervised by the school principal. The courses mixed repetition of
    material covered in the higher grades of primary school with preparation
    for what were termed "upper primary schools" (EPS), which were housed
    in their own buildings and lasted for a minimum of three years. Together,
    these offerings constituted the main form of secondary education avail-
    able in poor and working-class districts, constructing a narrow pathway
    of limited upward mobility that allowed bright children from the *classes
    populaires* to move into jobs requiring some higher and technical educa-
    tion: supervisory and even lower management positions in factories, office
    work (secretarial or accounting), or jobs in the lower echelons of the public
    service, such as primary schoolteacher, postal clerk, etc. Sellier put sub-
    stantial municipal resources behind expanding the range of courses avail-
    able to teenagers of both sexes, and constructed two upper primary schools
    (one for boys, the other for girls) in the course of his vast program of mu-
    nicipal reconstruction.

42 By 1931, 40 percent of the city's two-to-six-year-olds were enrolled in the
    city's four nursery schools. Cochard, "La Politique éducative," 211.

43 Instruction in the nursery school was thus based on the techniques of
    Montessori and Decroly, while the elementary classes (ages 7 to 13) were
    organized around a range of *pédagogies nouvelles,* notably the organization
    of school work in groups (versus the competitive individualism of main-
    stream schooling in France), frequent school trips, and Freinet's school
    printing press. Cochard, "De l'éducation à la formation professionnelle,"
    in Burlen, *La Banlieue oasis,* 214. Open-air schools for frail and tuber-
    cular or pretubercular children represented the cutting edge of interwar
    hygiene and pedagogy, and Sellier took pains to organize open-air classes
    in all the city schools from the very start of his administration, in 1920.

44 Suresnes thus spent 32.16 percent in 1932, 35.9 percent in 1936, and 36.2
    percent in 1937 on education and *oeuvres d'enfance,* as compared with 18 to
    22 percent in Levallois-Perret, 14 to 18 percent in Saint-Denis, 13 to 14 per-
    cent in Boulogne-Billancourt, and a mere 7 to 8 percent in the bourgeois
    suburb of Neuilly over the same period. Jean-Paul Brunet, *Un Demi-siècle
    de gestion municipale à Saint-Denis-la-Rouge* (Paris, 1981), 15. Martine Co-
    chard adds child-oriented expenditures budgeted under "hygiene" and
    "assistance"—the crèches, dispensaries, and centers for infant hygiene—
    to come up with a figure of at least 40 percent of the 1937 budget devoted to
    oeuvres d'enfance. Cochard, "La Politique éducative," 17. She further esti-
    mates that the child population of Suresnes (ages 0 to 14) rose by 90 percent
    over the interwar period, which meant the city had need of roughly twice
    the classroom space and facilities available in 1920. Ibid., 12–13. The high
    levels of spending went largely for building maintenance, salaries for non-
    teaching staff, and the purchase of classroom furniture and equipment.
    Jean-Paul Brunet points out that Saint-Denis consecrated a substantial
    share of the educational budget to social services dispensed through the
    school (lunchrooms, *colonies de vacances,* the *caisse des écoles*): 17.5 per-
    cent in 1931, rising to 34.1 percent in 1936–37 (depths of the Depression),
    whereas these provisions, though by no means neglected in Suresnes, con-
    sumed a much smaller portion of the education budget: 5.7 percent in
    1931 and 6.3 percent in 1936–37, respectively. Brunet, *Un Demi-siècle,* 15.
45 Mme Maudry and M. Dussert, "Henri Sellier et l'éducation," *Il y a cin-
    quante ans.*
46 Unnamed right-wing sourpuss, quoted in Robert Pontillon, "Le Créateur
    du Suresnes moderne," *Il y a cinquante ans,* 6.
47 Cited in Cochard, "La Politique éducative," 21.
48 Henri Sellier, "Le Parti socialiste et l'action communale," 37.
49 Burlen, "Henri Sellier," in Cohen and Badoui, *Les Chantiers de la paix
    sociale,* 281.
50 Boulonnois was a schoolteacher who had taught in the Suresnes primary
    schools since 1911. He was named bureau chief in 1921, at which point
    he left teaching in order to consecrate himself fully to the job. His wife
    was a member of the municipal team of social workers. Boulonnois, who
    was eventually named *secrétaire général de la mairie,* gradually became a
    kind of right-hand man to Sellier, a devoted apostle who systematized
    Sellier's municipal socialist vision into the "Suresnes doctrine" (so-called
    by Boulonnois himself), in which he professed a kind of mystical faith. See
    Louis Boulonnois, *La Municipalité en service social: L'Oeuvre de M. Henri
    Sellier à Suresnes* (Paris: Berger-Levrault, 1938). Boulonnois's zealous faith
    in this systematized social hygiene produced a kind of rigidity in applica-
    tion which led Yvonne Knibiehler to name him "le Saint Just du service
    social." Yvonne Knibiehler, "Socialisme et service social: L'action d'Henri

Sellier, Maire de Suresnes, Ministre du Front Populaire," *Sociologie du Sud-Est* 28–29 (Apr.–Sept. 1982): 119.

51 Louis Boulonnois, "Histoire et systématique des fonctions de l'assistance scolaire," *Journées médico-sociales de l'enfance d'âge scolaire,* 4–6 Apr. 1935, 204.

52 By 1925, there were already six *assistantes,* in addition to the visiting nurses; by 1939, the office boasted fourteen *assistantes sociales.* On the strategy of deploying the *assistantes* geographically, see Dr. R-H Hazemann, "Assistantes familiales ou infirmières scolaires?" *Hygiène par l'exemple,* July–Aug. 1928, 183–87.

53 Boulonnois, "Histoire et systématique," 205.

54 Cited in Cochard, "La Politique éducative," 27.

55 *Mémoire de la service social à Suresnes,* n.d., probably from the mid-1930s, quoted in Cochard, "La Politique éducative," 27–28.

56 Hazemann notes that Suresnes piloted the system of *polyvalentes,* which was later picked up and deployed in other cities. Hazemann, *Le Mouvement sanitaire,* January 1928, 15–21.

57 Boulonnois, "Histoire et systématique," 209.

58 See Luc Boltanski, *Prime éducation et morale de classe* (Paris: Mouton, 1969), for a discussion of the collaboration of medicine and "l'institution scolaire" in early-twentieth-century France. Jacques Donzelot, too, has observed the central role that the universal and compulsory primary school has played in dispensing medical and hygienic assistance in France. See Jacques Donzelot, *La Police des familles* (Paris: Editions de Minuit, 1977).

59 Indeed, Katherine Burlen observes that the dialogic structure that was meant to underpin "participatory urbanism" never really got off the ground. Burlen, "Henri Sellier," in Cohen and Baudouï, *Les Chantiers de la paix sociale.*

60 The 1935 electoral program thus emphasized that public health and social assistance were "intimately linked," and were exercised not only in the interests of individual recipients but in the "common interest of all the commune's inhabitants" in a "collective protection" of public health. Sellier, *Programme municipale pour les élections de 1935,* 59.

61 The medical metaphors are genuine. Katherine Burlen remarks that Sellier strove to "do politics like an administrative doctor." Katherine Burlen, "Henri Sellier," in Geneviève Poujol and Madeleine Romer, eds., *Dictionnaire biographique des militants, XIX–XXe siècles: De l'éducation populaire à l'action culturelle* (Paris: Harmattan, 1996), 346. Sellier himself wrote of the urgent need to block the spread of tuberculosis by a complete program of preventive public health, guided by the information gathered in the social assistants' home visits. See Henri Sellier, *Le Crise du logement et l'intervention publique en matière d'habitation populaire dans l'agglomération parisienne* (Paris: OPHBM, 1921).

62 Knibiehler, "Socialisme et service social," 119.

63 Sellier, quoted in Burlen, "Henri Sellier," in Cohen and Baudouï, *Les Chantiers de la paix sociale,* 274.

64 On the deficiencies of the "repressive hypothesis," see Marcel Gauchet's illuminating introduction to Gladys Swain, *Dialogue avec l'insensé,* in which the author speaks of his experience in Foucault's seminar on Pierre Rivière: "In this undertaking by the psychiatrists, we wished only to see the expression of a 'strategy of power,' the will to make a 'medical appropriation,' or to put it more mundanely, a form of professional self-assertion through the conquest of a domain of expertise. That these factors may all have played a role in the affair does not mean that the essence of the matter does not lie elsewhere." Marcel Gauchet, introduction to Gladys Swain, *Dialogue avec l'insensé: A la recherche d'une autre histoire de la folie* (Paris: Gallimard, 1994), xlviii.

65 Robert Nye, *Crime, Madness, and Politics in Modern France: The Medical Concept of National Decline* (Princeton: Princeton University Press, 1984).

66 The use of terms like "preserving the race" thus draw our attention to the ways that broader fears of national degeneration at the turn of the century were shaping the bodily and biological ground of a socialist vision, in which physical well-being constituted the essential basis of effective social and political action. For parallel developments in Britain (grounded in the medical research of Edouard Séguin), see Carolyn Steedman, *Childhood, Culture, and Class in Britain: Margaret McMillan, 1860–1931* (New Brunswick: Rutgers University Press, 1990).

67 Henri Sellier, quoted in Burlen, "Henri Sellier," in Cohen and Baudouï, *Les Chantiers de la paix sociale,* 276.

68 A.M. de Suresnes, D670, dossier 1937, Emile Gérard, "Rapport sur les Colonies de Vacances," *10e Conférence Nationale des Municipalités Socialistes,* 11–13 Sept. 1937, 3.

69 L. Rouget, "De l'éducation physique," *Bulletin de la ruche,* 1.1 (10 Mar. 1914): 8.

70 A.M. de Suresnes, D49, *Registre des déliberations du conseil municipal,* meeting of 31 May 1920, 469. The city council organized its various commissions in keeping with the notion of participatory urbanism, inviting members of local associations to serve alongside delegates from the city council. The Commission de l'Enseignement et de l'Éducation Populaire thus assembled six municipal councilors, along with delegates from the public schools, representatives from neighborhood sports and musical societies, and representatives from each of the "associations postscolaires." A.M. de Suresnes, D49, *Registre des déliberations du conseil municipal,* meeting of 9 June 1920, 369.

71 In the theory of direct management, the commune manages directly any service that is deemed of public interest, using methods of management

adopted from the private sector. On the importance of direct management to the early-twentieth-century conception of municipal socialism
in France, see Patrizia Dogliani, "La Théorie de la régie directe: Edgar
Milhaud et Henri Sellier," in Burlen, *La Banlieue oasis,* 37–45.

72 At the turn of the century, the working-class cities of Asnières, Cour-
bevoie, Clichy, Clamart, Pantin, and Montrouge all used the Chaussée de
Maine to organize their *colonies scolaires.* See Oeuvre de la Chaussée de
Maine, *Rapport, 1905,* Paris, 1906, 18.

73 Dr. P. F. Armand-Delille and Dr. Ch. Lestocquoy, "Le Placement familial
permanent dans la campagne," *Congrès National des colonies de vacances
et oeuvres de plein air* (St-Etienne, 1925), 133–34. Family placement thus
favored the archaic, polycultural peasant family that was fast disappearing in early-twentieth-century France. The regions excluded for family
placement were often quite acceptable for *colonies collectives;* for instance
Catholic *colonies* often preferred the Norman and Breton coasts because
of the number of religious sites and calvaries, and the piety of the local
population, which was felt to provide a hospitable atmosphere. Hence,
during the 1920s, *colonies collectives* tended to settle by the ocean, while
colonies by family placement continued to favor the rural regions of central
France. See Corinne Hubert, "Demain on part en colo . . . Les premières
colonies de vacances de l'actuel Val-de-Marne sous la IIIe République"
(Mémoire de maîtrise, Université de Paris VIII, 1986), 46–47.

74 Louis Conlombant, *Manuel du surveillant (à lire et à méditer avant le dé-
part et à relire pendant le séjour)* (Paris: Oeuvre parisienne des Enfants à la
Montagne, 1931), 3.

75 Ibid., 4.

76 Ibid., 12. While it is difficult to imagine that peasant smallholders were
much interested in whatever agrarian wisdom these urban schoolteachers
proffered, Conlombant's dedication to the project of reinforcing urban-
rural ties in this fashion is quite striking, and by no means an isolated phenomenon among directors of *colonies de vacances,* as even the most casual
glance at the minutes from interwar congresses of the Comité National
des Colonies de Vacances reveals.

77 Les Enfants à la Montagne, first organized in 1906, took schoolchildren
aged five to twelve and placed them in the Cantal for forty-five days. (Conlombant felt children over twelve were too old for family placement, that
they got bored, made mischief, or ran away, and he preferred to send them
with *colonies collectives.*) In 1929, the program began organizing vacations
specially for the children of families that were originally from the region.
Between 1906 and 1925 it sent a total of 9,134 children to the Cantal, and
in 1930 alone, sent 620. Ibid., 32. Conlombant's program was still going
strong in the early-to-mid-1950s, but by this time directors were rather defensive about their pedagogically obsolete structure (which they justified

by citing a collective animation of the *colonie* based on up-to-the-minute pedagogical techniques drawn from the CEMEA). Ibid., 16. See also Louis Conlombant, "Placement familial dans les colonies de vacances," *Revue médico-sociale et de protection de l'enfance* 6, no. 4 (1938).

78 Conlombant, *Manuel du surveillant,* 10.

79 Oeuvre de la Chaussée de Maine, *Rapport, Année 1918–1919,* Paris, 1919.

80 Until 1907, when the newly unified socialist party (SFIO) organized a local branch, radical republicans freely termed themselves socialist, though the term had little practical political significance.

81 Figures on the first *colonies* are taken from Sordes, *Histoire de Suresnes,* 479. From the outset (1904), the city council provided a subvention of 4,000 F each year for the *colonie.* Information on the budget is drawn from A.M. de Suresnes, *Registre des délibérations,* D49, 43–44, and from wartime reports of the city's Oeuvre des Vacances Scolaires, found in A.M. de Suresnes, section L, Commissions scolaires, folder 361, *colonies de vacances,* 1915–18.

82 Seron, *Suresnes autrefois et aujourd'hui,* 380. See also Christian Betron, "Acteur de l'histoire locale à Suresnes," in *La Banlieue en fête: De la marginalité urbaine à l'identité culturelle* (Paris, 1988): esp. 116.

83 Germain Bazin, "La Rosière de Suresnes et le prix de vertu," *Bulletin de la société historique et artistique de Suresnes,* 7 (1936): 34.

84 The Catholic *patronages* of the Rosary (girls), and of Notre Dame des Victoires (boys), founded just after the Separation, in 1907–8, were followed swiftly by Mayor Diederich's zealously secular *patronage municipale,* which, from 1909 on, assured that children, released from school every Thursday afternoon, could run and play in a spot that was safe from the dangers of the street, and from the preachings of the local curé.

85 The regulations of the Chaussée de Maine thus stipulated that the program admit children "irrespective of religion." L'Oeuvre de la Chaussée de Maine, *Rapport, 1918–1919,* 13.

86 Rationing was introduced by the spring of 1915, and the shortage of staples, especially bread, grew truly acute by 1917. See Jean-Jacques Becker, *Les Français dans la grande guerre* (Paris: Laffont, 1980). In 1915, the municipal council responded to the increasing demand by according the *colonie* a 2,000 F supplementary credit to cover rising costs, for the council predicted (correctly) that the war would raise "considerably" the demand for the *colonie.* A.M. de Suresnes, *Registre des délibérations,* D49, 22.

87 Figures drawn from A.M. de Suresnes, *Registre des délibérations,* D49, 173, and A.M. de Suresnes, section L, Commissions scolaires, folder 361, *colonies de vacances,* 1915–1918. In the summer of 1919, 184 children left with mayor Diederich's last, Chaussée-de-Maine-brokered *colonie.* A.M. de Suresnes, R 26, dossier 1919.

88 The commission was a subset of the city council's educational commis-

sion, and was staffed by several of its most prominent members, notably republican (and Protestant) deputy Alexandre Joyeux (1873–1941). Joyeux was the scion of an old Suresnes family, a republican who served under Diederich and was then reelected in 1919 as a part of the republican "Bloc des intérêts communs." According to René Sordes, Joyeux rapidly became Sellier's faithful disciple, which judgment is confirmed by the fact that in 1921 he became one of Sellier's deputy mayors. Joyeux was placed on the commission of education and codirected the Socialist administration's newly revamped municipal Commission des Colonies de Vacances from 1921 forward. "Nécrologie, Alexandre Joyeux," *Bulletin de la société historique et artistique de Suresnes* 10 (1939–1950): 186; and Sordes, *Histoire de Suresnes,* 525.

89 A.M. de Suresnes, section L, Commissions scolaires, folder 361, Colonies de Vacances, 1915–18, Brochure: Ville de Suresnes, "Oeuvre de Vacances Scolaire," 15 June 1915. On the "orphans of the nation," see Olivier Faron, *Les Enfants du deuil: Orphelins et pupilles de la nation de la première guerre mondiale (1914–1941)* (Paris: Editions de la Découverte, 2001).

90 Ibid. At the end of the war, the national office of the Pupilles de la Nation would shoulder the financial burden of maintaining France's many war orphans, which maintenance always and explicitly included a summer in the local *colonie.* Suresnes had over three hundred such orphans, some 10 percent of whom spent their summers in the Nièvre *colonie.*

91 A.M. de Suresnes, Registre des Déliberations, D49, "Rapport de Monsieur Michel sur la visite de Monsieurs Amiel et Michel à la Colonie de Vacances, 1915," 3 Dec. 1915, 43–44. Forty-nine girls and sixty-one boys participated in the 1915 *colonie,* at a cost of 5,630 F, which was supplied by three sources: the city (1,385 F), donations (2,195 F), and the personnel of the Arsenal at Puteaux (1,749 F). See A.M. de Suresnes, section L, Commissions scolaires, folder 361, Colonies de Vacances, 1915–18, Brochure: Ville de Suresnes, "Oeuvre des Colonies de vacances," 10 June 1916.

92 "Les Enfants au soleil!," *Le Suresnois,* 28 July 1934, 1. Sellier had been deputy mayor in Puteaux since 1912, and when the mayor, Lucien Voilin, was mobilized, Sellier seems to have taken on his duties.

93 Ibid., 1.

94 Family placement thus remained quite widespread in the Paris suburbs until the late 1920s, with Socialist and Communist municipalities practicing both forms. (Collective living became a matter of principle with PCF pedagogues only in the mid-1930s.) Only the Catholics and the *colonies scolaires* of Paris were rigorously collective from the outset. I found not a single instance where a center or right-wing republican administration chose to organize a municipal *colonie de vacances*; after all, their political claim to fame rested on spending as few tax dollars as possible. Center and right-wing municipalities thus left such matters in the hands of private

charity, the Catholic Church, and/or the local *caisse des écoles*. See Jacques Girault, ed., *Ouvriers en banlieue, XIXe–XXe siècle* (Paris: Éditions ouvrières, 1998).

95 It was the peasant *nourrices* themselves who initiated the relationship by applying for orphans at the local agency of the Enfants Assistés. The director then vetted the requests and added all suitable applicants to his pool of potential *nourrices*.

96 "Les Enfants au soleil!," 1. See also "La Colonie de vacances des enfants de Suresnes," *Urbanisme,* Jan. 1935, 55–56. The Enfants Assistés was first organized as a separate wing of the Assistance Publique during the Second Republic, in 1848. It was not until the turn of the twentieth century that the Enfants Assistés launched a systematic policy of provincial placements for Parisian foundlings (who numbered some two thousand children per year by the end of the 1920s). The majority of provincial offices (twenty-three out of thirty-two) were opened in the provinces of central France, and eight of the thirty-two in the Nièvre alone. A.M. de Suresnes, 21 Q 3, Administration Générale de l'Assistance Publique, *Les Enfants assistés pupilles de la Département de la Seine,* Ecole d'Alembert, Montévrain, n.d. (ca. 1930), xxvi and 25.

97 A.M. de Suresnes, D669, Union Amicale des Maires de la Seine, "Procès verbal de l'Assemblée générale du 1er Décembre 1939," 4 (Henri Sellier speaking); and H36, Henri Sellier, "Note pour M. le Directeur de l'Enseignement," esp. p. 2.

98 A.M. de Suresnes, D670, dossier 1931, Antonin Poggioli, "Les Colonies de vacances," report to the Fédération Nationale des Municipalités Socialistes, 28 Apr. 1931, 2–3, emphasis original.

99 The total fell to 417 (1936), then 360 (1937), before bottoming out in 1938 at 335. In 1939, the numbers rose again, to 400, probably due to rumors of war and the wish to get one's children out of harm's way. A.M. de Suresnes, 26R, dossiers 1921–31, and 27R, dossiers 1932–39, for statistics on the *colonie* each year.

100 See the electoral programs of 1919, 1925, 1929, and 1935, reproduced in Boulonnois, *La Municipalité en service social,* 110–23. See also A.M. de Suresnes, 29R, for the dossiers of vacation questionnaires from the primary schools that formed the backbone of the campaign to get children out of the city each summer.

101 A.M. de Suresnes, 26R, dossier 1921, Service des Colonies de Vacances, "Aux mères de famille!" 2.

102 The memos to the school principals and *assistantes scolaires* stress the hygienic and "social" importance of the annual vacation census, whose results would shed light on the "conditions in which children subject to the *obligation scolaire* spend their holidays." A.M. de Suresnes, 29R, memo to the school principals and the *assistantes scolaires,* 26 Nov. 1932. Louis Bou-

lonnois's memo to the *assistantes scolaires,* dated 19 May 1936, suggests that the city first started gathering systematic data on schoolchildren's holidays in 1930–31, although the earliest survey results preserved in the archive date from 1932. A.M. de Suresnes, 29R, memo from Louis Boulonnois to the *assistantes scolaires,* "Vous avez été invitées le 27 avril à réfléchir . . . ," 19 May 1936.

103   A.M. de Suresnes, 29R, "Statistique de vacances, 1932," gives the following figures: out of a total school-age population of 2,490, 1,839 (i.e., 73 percent) had left Suresnes for about six weeks in the summer of 1932. 553 of these children left in the company of their parents, many of whom must have traveled back to the village of origin, and a further 882 were sent off by themselves to stay with relatives and friends in the *pays natal.* Official records show that 469 children left that summer with the municipal *colonie* (although the 1932 "Statistique" lists only 424), and 70 with the Catholic "colonies de placement collectif." Although the article makes no explicit reference to the city's Catholic *colonies,* the patronages of the Rosary (girls) and Our Lady of Victory (boys) continued to send children to the Haute-Savoie, the Vosges, the Landes, and the Norman and Breton countrysides throughout the interwar period, with about thirty to forty children in each *colonie.* See *Bulletin mensuel, Eglise de Suresnes,* June 1920, 7; and ibid., Nov. 1925, 9.

104   The author goes on to note that the children's trousseaux would be "discreetly" completed should any items be lacking. "La colonie de vacances des enfants de Suresnes," 56.

105   Anonymous working-class child, presumably (though not necessarily) female, remembering her childhood just before the Great War. Delahaye, *Les Enfants du Mont-Valérien,* 29.

106   Ibid., 33.

107   A.M. de Suresnes, D49, *Registre des délibérations du conseil municipal,* meeting of 9 Jan. 1920.

108   A.M. de Suresnes, 26R, dossier 1921, letter of 1 May 1921 from Sellier, Joyeux, Piquet, and Valette to their "Chers Concitoyens," seeking donations for the municipal *colonie.* The letter reminds us of the tremendous financial difficulties confronting a municipality that was launching multiple social programs simultaneously and along a broad front in the midst of the severe economic downturn that followed the demobilization and reconversion of the war economy in France.

109   A.M. de Suresnes, 26R, dossier 1920, "Etat récapitulatif des sommes reçues comme dons pour les colonies de vacances," lists local associations (the "Gaieté Suresnoise," the fire brigade, the Anciens Elèves, the war veterans' league (Union Nationale des Combattants), local businesses, and a large number of individuals (including Sellier himself) as contributors to the municipal *colonie.* Within two years, local industry would become the

single most important contributor, in terms of sheer financial weight, even as individuals and associations continued to contribute smaller sums.

110 A.M. de Suresnes, D50, *Registre des déliberations du conseil municipal,* meeting of 30 July 1920.

111 A.M. de Suresnes, 26R, dossier 1920, letter from Coty to Sellier, 12 Oct. 1920.

112 Ibid.

113 A.M. de Suresnes, 26R, dossier 1922, Ville de Suresnes, Service des Colonies de Vacances, Henri Sellier to his "Chers Concitoyens," n.d., 2. This was his annual fundraising letter. In the early 1920s, about one third of the cost of *colonie,* i.e., 1 F per day per child, came from the subvention granted since 1915 by the departmental Conseil Général. In July of 1927, the subvention was raised to 2 F per day per child. See A.M. de Suresnes, 29R, dossier "Subventions," "Note sur les modalités d'intervention du Département en faveur des communes pour l'organisation des colonies de vacances," June 1930.

114 A.M. de Suresnes, 26R, dossier 1926, Ville de Suresnes, "Colonie de Vacances pour 1926," and dossier 1922, Ville de Suresnes, Colonie de Vacances en 1922, "Avis Aux Familles," 1. The 1926 announcement "Colonie de Vacances pour 1926" is the first document to mention the active participation of *assistantes* and *infirmières scolaires* in organizing the *colonie.*

115

Year	Total number of colons	Free	Some financial assistance	Total number aided
1928	283	111	47	158
1930	295	101	55	156
1932	469	266	105	371
1933	539	250	150	400
1935	433	211	175	386
1936	417	230	164	394
1939	400	129	185	314

A large number of the free admissions in 1935 and 1936 were the children of the unemployed. The reduced numbers sent and high rates of financial aid overall reflect the impact of the economic crisis, which was most severely felt in the mid-1930s. Those who were granted reduced rates generally paid up to about half their child's pension. In 1930, for example, 55 children were admitted to the *colonie* at reduced rates, 42 of whom paid from 10 to 50 percent of the 250 F pension. The remaining 13 paid 60 to 80 percent (150–200 F) of the 250 F pension. A.M. de Suresnes, 29R, dossier

"Subventions," memo from the mayor's office, "L'envoi à titre gratuit ou à tarif réduit de certains enfants . . . ," 19 Nov. 1930. Table constructed from data gathered in the A.M. de Suresnes, 26R, dossier 1928, and 27R, dossiers 1933, 1934, 1935, 1936, and 1939. See also 29R, dossier "Subventions," memo from the mayor's office, "L'envoi à titre gratuit ou à tarif réduit de certains enfants . . . ," 19 Nov. 1930; and "Tableau des Tarifs d'admissions aux Colonies de Vacances, 1932."

116   There are notable variations in the reported numbers of children sent each year, depending on the source consulted. I decided to use figures taken directly from the papers of the municipal Commission des Colonies de Vacances, which include detailed budgets, as well as the records from the annual meeting at which fee reductions for the needy majority of *colons* were established. The nature of these documents, in particular their connection to the all-important matter of municipal budgets, suggests the figures given therein for each summer's *colonie* are probably the most reliable.

117   A.M. de Suresnes, 26R, dossier 1921, letter of 7 April 1921 from Lucien Voilin (mayor of Puteaux) to Depuyset [*sic*], and dossier 1923, letter of 23 July 1923 from Birckel (Dépuiset's successor, who directed the Saint-Pierre office for one year — 1923) to Henri Sellier, p. 1, in which Birckel speaks of Sellier's legitimate desire to group his *colons* "in the smallest sector possible." Each provincial office of the Enfants Assistés covered a district of about fifteen to twenty kilometers around the town where the agency stood. The agency's "territory" thus comprised a unit of land that corresponded roughly to the arrondissement (it was slightly smaller): Administration Générale de l'Assistance Publique, *Les Enfants assistés*, 61.

118   A.M. de Suresnes, 26R, dossier 1923, letter of 23 July 1923 from Birckel, 1.

119   A.M. de Suresnes, 26R, dossier 1921, letter from Sellier to Voilin, May 1921.

120   A.M. de Suresnes, 26R, dossier 1921, letter from Sellier to Voilin, 26 July 1921. Sellier goes on to point out that the agency would henceforth allow no more than four municipal delegates per locality for a period of no longer than forty-eight hours. These visits had to be arranged two weeks in advance so that the director of the service at Saint-Pierre could accompany the municipal delegation on its tour; there would be no more impromptu dropping in on the *nourrices*.

121   A.M. de Suresnes, 26R, dossier 1921, letter from Dépuiset to Sellier, 13 June 1921, 1–2.

122   A.M. de Suresnes, 26R, dossier 1921, letter of 3 May 1921, from Sellier to Voilin.

123   A.M. de Suresnes, 26R, dossier 1921, letter from Dépuiset to Sellier, 6 Sept. 1921.

124   The precipitating factor in the break-up seems to have been Sellier's unwillingness to continue indefinitely a structure that placed sole respon-

sibility for more than one thousand children of different communes, industries, and trade unions on his shoulders only. Suresnes stayed with the Enfants Assistés, but others were unable to continue with them in the absence of Sellier's patronage. In 1933, for example, the Travailleurs Municipaux went back to Conlombant's Oeuvre des Enfants à la Montagne, which they had been using until they joined Sellier's consortium in the early 1920s.

125 The 1923 consortium thus included *colonies* from Puteaux (380 children), Boulogne (350), Suresnes (150), Bezons (80), and the Travailleurs Municipaux—a grand total of 1,140. A.M. de Suresnes, 26R, dossier 1923, letter from Sellier to Birckel, 4 July 1923.

126 A.M. de Suresnes, 26R, dossier 1921, letter from Dépuiset to Sellier, 3 Feb. 1921, 1. Boulogne-Billancourt was in fact a single municipality at the time.

127 Ibid. There were a total of 21 problem cases out of 128 children sent that year.

CHAPTER 4   Inside the Nièvre *Colonie,* 1923–1939

1 The bourgs and villages included Langeron, Luthenay-Uxeloup, Marssur-Allier, Mornay-sur-Allier, Neuville-le-Decize, Saint-Parize-le-Châtel, Saint-Pierre-le-Moûtier, Villeneuve-sur-Allier, and Chatenaysur-Imbert. A.M. de Suresnes, 26R, dossier 1922, "Statistique numérique des journées de présence des enfants de Suresnes envoyés à la campagne pendant la durée des vacances." In lean years, when drought dried up the vegetables in the *nourrices'* gardens, the *colonie* was extended westward to Azay-le-Vif and on into the Cher, near Saincoins.

2 A.M. de Suresnes, 26R, dossier 1923, letter of 23 July 1923 from Birckel to Sellier, 1–2. Sellier asked that the young Suresnois be placed by preference in the Cher, his own native *département.* 26R, dossier 1923, Sellier to Birckel, 4 July 1923.

3 Ernest Blin, "La Population dans le Canton de Saint-Pierre-le-Moûtier" (Paris: Editions de la Revue du Centre, 1929), 3. Blin was also a "correspondent" for the Ministry of Public Instruction.

4 Ibid., 7–8.

5 Ibid., 8–9.

6 Ibid. Mars and Azy were the most seriously depopulated villages, and contained only farmers and forest workers. Chatenay and St-Parize were both slightly larger bourgs, with shopkeepers and artisans in addition to the farming population.

7 See letter from Henri Sellier to the director of the center at Saint-Pierre, 9 July 1920, requesting placements for the young Suresnois. Found in A.M. de Suresnes, 26R, dossier 1920. The curve straightened out in the worst

342 NOTES TO CHAPTER 4

years of the economic crisis, 1935–36, when nearly half the children were sent for free and another 40 percent received financial assistance. In 1935 and 1936, only 10.8 percent and 17 percent, respectively, paid full pension. (27R, dossier 1935, Commission des Colonies, 1935; and dossier 1936, Commission des Colonies, 1936.) We can judge the extent of the monetary sacrifice being asked of working-class parents thanks to a dossier of requests for financial assistance with the fees for the *colonie*. Each request includes the parents' earnings for a two-month period in the spring/summer of 1924, and helps to put that year's *pension* of 150 F into perspective. One wood and metal worker (male) earned 2,703 F over the eight-week period from 10 May to 4 July, while another male (autoworker at Saurer) earned a total of 1,652 F in two months. One young woman who worked in a dyeworks earned 733 F over eight weeks, while a driller (male) at Dion Auto had earned 1,532 F over the last four *quinzaines*. Still another woman who worked in a metals and electrical appliances shop earned 676 F for two months' work. Paying full price at the *colonie* would have thus demanded a full two weeks' wages from the woman metalworker, and over half the two weeks' salary paid to a semiskilled man (driller) in the automobile industry. Clearly, paying the full *pension* represented a considerable sacrifice for all but the most highly paid and skilled workers, especially if they had more than one child to send *en colonie*. A.M. de Suresnes, 26R, dossier 1924, file of requests for financial assistance.

8   A.M. de Suresnes, 26R, dossier 1923, Colonies de Vacances, 1923, Commission of 22 May 1923. By the late 1920s, the *assistantes scolaires* in each primary school were handling the entire recruitment for the *colonie,* assembling the medical records and nominative lists with the children's preferences regarding their placement, on which the Commission des Colonies and Enfants Assistés would base their work. See A.M. de Suresnes, 26R, dossier 1929, memo from Henri Sellier to the *assistantes scolaires,* "Colonies de vacances 1929," 22 May 1929.

9   See, for example, A.M. de Suresnes, 26R, dossier 1931, letter of 11 April 1931 from Mme Gabillet to the Municipal Commission des Colonies de Vacances; or the letter from Mme Feullit to the Municipal Commission, n.d.

10 The *colonie* was thus formally open to all children aged six to thirteen, and most of the *colons* were aged eight to twelve. In 1923, for example, 17 out of 172 *colons* were aged seven, 22 were aged thirteen (these constituted the outer age limits that particular year), with the remaining 133 clustered in the eight to twelve range. A.M. de Suresnes, 26R, dossier 1923, Colonies de Vacances, 1923, Commission des Colonies, 22 May 1923. In 1937, responding to parental demand, the commission extended the lower limit downward to age five, provided the child was accompanied by an older sibling. The upper age limit was never a barrier to admission, but

served more as a guideline for the target population judged in most need of the *colonie* for their correct physiological development. But adolescent workers of both sexes (as high as age seventeen) occasionally requested a placement in the *colonie* during their own, brief holidays. See, for example, A.M. de Suresnes, 27R, dossier 1933, Joyeux to Mme Bernadat-Lhéritier, 30 May 1933, requesting that she take in a sixteen-year-old boy, now working in a pharmacy, who had spent all his childhood summers in the Nièvre *colonie*. Each year the commission received three to five such requests (which were always granted), for young workers generally did not have much vacation time at their disposal—a few feast days at best—before the 1936 law granted everyone two weeks' paid vacation. Moreover, the *colonie* constituted a very cheap holiday—just over 7 F per day in 1933—and therefore was well within the reach of most apprentices.

11   A.M. de Suresnes, 26R, dossier 1921, "Chers Concitoyens," fund-raising letter from Henri Sellier, P. Valette, A. Joyeux, and Piquet to the citizens of Suresnes, 1 May 1921, 2.

12   A.M. de Suresnes, 26R, dossier 1921, Service des Colonies de Vacances, "Aux mères de famille!," 1.

13   See, for example, A.M. de Suresnes, 26R, dossier 1923, Mlle Hardy (*assistante sociale*), "Rapport sur Mme Marchand remariée à Leroy," 31 May 1923. The Marchand family had five children, four of whom were teenagers already at work, but whose wages were quite low; the father worked in the foundry at the Arsenal at Puteaux. Mme Marchand requested financial aid in order to send her youngest daughter back to the *colonie* that summer, to stay with her same *nourrice*.

14   A.M. de Suresnes, 27R, Henri Sellier and Alexandre Joyeux, instruction to parents, "Votre enfant étant admis à participer aux Colonies de Vacances . . . ," 13 June 1935.

15   A.M. de Suresnes, 26R, dossier 1921, letters from Sellier to his fellow mayors in the Commission Intercommunale, 16 July 1921 and 1 July 1921.

16   Sellier and Joyeux, instruction to parents, "Votre enfant étant admis . . . ," 2.

17   A.M. de Suresnes, 26R, dossier 1927, letter from Mme Derosiers to an unnamed *assistante scolaire*, n.d.

18   A.M. de Suresnes, 26R, dossier 1928, letter from Ernest Blin to Alexandre Joyeux, 17 Oct. 1928, 1. See also 26R, dossier 1928, letter from Alexandre Joyeux to Ernest Blin (director of the St-Pierre Service des Enfants Assistés from 1924 to 1932), 19 July 1928: "We are most embarrassed about the incontinent ones," wrote Alexandre Joyeux to Ernest Blin in July of 1928. "I gather all the mothers in order to bring them face to face with the problem and beg them not to forget to add a protective sheet to their child's trousseau."

19   The trousseau included a cape or coat and hat, a change of clothing, a sweater, two pairs of clogs or shoes "in good condition," a pair of san-

dals or *espadrilles,* and "le linge nécessaire," that is: three shirts, three pairs of pants (or three skirts), three school smocks, three pairs of socks, three hankies, and three bath towels. Finally, the child had to have a kit that included a large-toothed comb, a fine-toothed comb (to aid in the endless combat against head lice), a bar of soap, toothbrush, shoe polish, and stamps and envelopes for the children's letters home. A.M. de Suresnes, 26R, dossier 1927, "Composition du Trousseau," 3 June 1925.

20 Sellier and Joyeux, instruction to parents, "Votre enfant étant admis . . . ," 13 June 1935, 2.

21 A.M. de Suresnes, 26R, dossier 1923, Colonies de Vacances, 1923, "Rapport des Délégués MM. Valette, Falguerette et Legeay Conseillers Municipaux relatif à la visite générale des enfants," 16 Sept. 1923.

22 Administration Générale de l'Assistance Publique, *Les enfants assistés,* 60.

23 Ibid., 61. For nearly a century, the Enfants Assistés had provided peasant wives in these districts with a steady source of cash income that doubtless helped ensure the longer-term survival of these increasingly marginal farms in an era of protracted agrarian crisis and price collapse on international agricultural markets.

24 Ibid., 63.

25 Ibid., 68.

26 Ibid., 73.

27 I found only one mention in the entire archive of children being taken to mass, in a letter from Madeleine Pichard to her mother. A.M. de Suresnes, 27R, dossier 1935, Madeleine Pichard to Mme Raymond Pichard, Aug. 1935, enclosed in a letter from Mme Pichard to Henri Sellier, 16 Aug. 1935.

28 A.M. de Suresnes, 26R, dossier 1928, letter from Ernest Blin to Henri Sellier (forwarded to M. Hoyez of the Commission des Colonies), 16 Aug. 1928, 1–2.

29 A.M. de Suresnes, 27R, dossier 1933, Mme Yolly-Firmini to the Municipal Commission des Colonies, 16 July 1933, 1–2. Dominique Dessertine notes that taking in orphans from the Enfants Assistés played an important role in the household economy of women in regions like the early-twentieth-century Nièvre, where there was little industrial work for women and agriculture had become steadily more male with the shift from subsistence polyculture to large-scale cattle raising. Dominique Dessertine, *La Société lyonnaise pour la sauvetage de l'enfance* (Toulouse: Erès, 1990), 179–80.

30 I found only one case in which a *nourrice,* one Mme Deville, put three in a bed, and it was the children who complained (in part because one of the three was a bed wetter.) A.M. de Suresnes, 26R, dossier 1928, 8 Oct. 1928, A. Joyeux to E. Blin.

31 A.M. de Suresnes, 27R, dossier 1934, Service des Enfants Assistés de la Seine, "Colonies Scolaires," brochure addressed to potential host families.

Of course, not all *nourrices* shared the feminine predilection, and one Mme Vachez, who wanted five or six *colons,* was of the opinion that having all boys was definitely the easiest. A.M. de Suresnes, 27R, dossier 1936, letter from Mme Vachez to A. Joyeux.

32 A.M. de Suresnes, 26R, dossier 1928, letter from Blin to Sellier regarding complaints from the parents and children of the Thomson-Houston *colonie,* paragraph on the Plateaux children, 18 Nov. 1928.

33 The remaining forty were ultimately placed with other families. A.M. de Suresnes, 26R, dossier 1921, letter from the Assistance Publique to Henri Sellier, 16 July 1921. Signature unreadable, but it was probably from Dépuiset. The widespread abstention of *nourriciers* from the *colonie* in 1921 was no doubt the fallout from the two difficult summers of 1919–20.

34 Rey-Herme, *Les Colonies de vacances, 1906–1936,* 198.

35 A.M. de Suresnes, 26R, dossier 1931, letter from Mme Vachez of Saint-Parize-le-Châtel to an unidentified family in Suresnes, 23 June 1931, 1.

36 A.M. de Suresnes, 26R, dossier 1921, letter from Dépuiset to Sellier, 27 June 1921, 1–2.

37 In 1920, then, *nourrices* received 75 F for boys under seven, 85 F for boys aged seven to ten, and 95 F for boys over ten (at the time, the *colonie* accepted children aged five to thirteen); girls under seven brought 65 F, girls seven to ten 75 F, and girls over ten, 85 F. A.M. de Suresnes, 26R, dossier 1922, Dépuiset, "Colonie des Enfants des Ecoles de Boulogne-sur-Seine, Puteaux et Suresnes." See also 26R, dossier 1921, memo from Sellier to his fellow mayors in the intercommunal consortium regarding the organization of the 1921 *colonie,* 1 July 1921.

38 "La Colonie de vacances des enfants de Suresnes," *Urbanisme* (Jan. 1935), 56.

39 Louis Conlombant, *Manuel du surveillant,* 16. The sole reference I found to any kind of collective animation came at the end of a memo to Ernest Blin from Alexandre Joyeux, in which the latter mentioned that he would be carrying the "film of the *colonie*" with him to Saint-Pierre when he made his annual inspection tour, on Sunday, 2 August 1931. Joyeux planned to show the film twice that day, to groups of *colons* and *nourrices* in Saint-Pierre and then in the village of Mornay. In order to round out the two sessions, Joyeux planned a short play at the end of each screening. A.M. de Suresnes, 26R, dossier 1931, memo from Joyeux to Blin, 11 July 1931, 2.

40 Hence, permanent placement of urban children on rural farms—a goal that was occasionally broadcast in national conferences of the Comité National des Colonies de Vacances—played no role in the ideological orientation of the Suresnes *colonie.* Indeed, I found only one case over twenty years in which a Suresnes family requested that their son, already on holiday with the *colonie,* be placed permanently on a nearby farm—"or wher-

ever you judge it best to place him." A.M. de Suresnes, 26R, dossier 1929, letter from Vernel Manescax to Alexandre Joyeux, 27 July 1929. On the other hand, people sometimes prolonged their children's stay in the *colonie* if it suited the family's needs. See A.M. de Suresnes, 26R, dossier 1929, Percheron to Jubier, 1 Sept. 1929. The Percheron family enclosed a letter to their young son expressing the hope that he was happy to stay on with the Jubier family, enjoining him to be good, and attaching a 5 F bill so that the boy could buy himself some sweets.

41 "Rapport des Délégués MM. Valette, Falguerette et Legeay," 1.

42 A.M. de Suresnes, 26R, dossier 1921, letter from Dépuiset to Sellier, 27 June 1921, 2.

43 A.M. de Suresnes, 26R, dossier 1921, memo from Sellier to his fellow mayors in the intercommunal consortium, 1 July 1921, 1–2.

44 A.M. de Suresnes, 26R, dossier 1928, letter from Joyeux to Blin, 8 Oct. 1928.

45 A.M. de Suresnes, 26R, dossier 1928, letter from Blin to Sellier, 18 Nov. 1928.

46 A.M. de Suresnes, 26R, dossier 1923, letter of 23 July 1923 from Birckel to Sellier, 2.

47 "Rapport des délégués MM. Valette, Falguerrette et Legeay."

48 Conlombant, *Manuel du surveillant,* 7. Etienne Guillard underscored this point at the 1937 international congress of *colonies de vacances,* stressing that one way to guarantee that peasant *nourrices* were motivated solely by love of children was to ensure that the *pension* paid out to the *nourrices* "never gave them the means to realize a profit" from their young guests. Etienne Guillard, "Les Conditions d'efficacité du placement familial," *Congrès internationale des colonies de vacances* (Paris: 1937), 78.

49 A.M. de Suresnes, 26R, dossier 1928, Blin to Joyeux, 30 July 1928, 1–2. Emphasis original.

50 A.M. de Suresnes, 27R, dossier 1931, Blin to Joyeux, 28 June 1931, 1–2.

51 Eugène Gibon, "Retour des colonies de vacances," *Le Suresnois,* 17 Sept. 1932, 2.

52 A.M. de Suresnes, 26R, dossier 1930, Commune de Suresnes, Colonies de Vacances, "Instruction pour les Parents." The agency at Saint-Pierre, too, had an interest in brokering all contact between parents and *nourriciers,* fearing that the latter might try to raise their income by going behind the backs of the Enfants Assistés and directly "blackmailing" parents for more money. The agency was clearly trying to maintain a close, bureaucratic control over the *paysans nourriciers'* levels of remuneration, so that nothing resembling a free market would break out in the business of child rearing. See A.M. de Suresnes, 27R, dossier 1936, Desbruyères to Joyeux, 9 Sept. 1936, especially the paragraphs regarding the Saint-Georges girls, placed with Mme Jaquet (Mornay), 2.

53 A.M. de Suresnes, 26R, dossier 1930, Commune de Suresnes, Colonies de Vacances, "Instruction pour les Parents."

54 See, for example, the case of Jacqueline Schellenberg and Angèle Curtenaz, lodged with the Brérard family in Mars-sur-Allier. While there was no evidence (or claim by the girls) that they were being mistreated, the girls were unhappy in the country and sobbed daily that they wanted to go home. When M. Schellenberg tried to visit in hopes of sorting things out, he was outraged to learn that he had no right to do so. M. Schellenberg was furious and demanded that the mayor "use his power" to move the children to another household if there was still time to do so, or to "give the necessary orders" so that he could go up and fetch them home himself. A.M. de Suresnes, 26R, dossier 1930, H. Schellenberg to Henri Sellier, 12 Aug. 1930; and letter from Jean Brérard to M. et Mme Schellenberg, 8 Aug. 1930.

55 A.M. de Suresnes, 26R, dossier 1930, Commune de Suresnes, Colonies de Vacances, "Instructions pour les Enfants," 2–3.

56 Ibid.

57 A.M. de Suresnes, 26R, dossier 1930, Commune de Suresnes, Colonies de Vacances, "Instructions pour les Nourriciers," 4.

58 "Rapport des Délégués MM. Valette, Falguerette et Legeay," 1.

59 Conlombant, *Manuel du surveillant,* 25.

60 A.M. de Suresnes, 27R, dossier 1935, letter from Madeleine Pichard to her mother, undated but probably written in mid-August, p. 2. The letter was folded into a dossier that included a similar letter addressed to her father. No sooner did they receive these disturbing missives than the parents forwarded the whole to Alexandre Joyeux, along with a letter asking that he make a "discreet inquiry" into the children's situation on the Dupont farm, particularly the claim that they had been struck. Their letter arrived in Suresnes the next morning, and Joyeux forwarded the entire file immediately to his friend Desbruyères and asked that he investigate the claim. Desbruyères presumably received the file the next day, for he set out to visit Mme Dupont the following morning. The swift responses in Suresnes and Saint-Pierre suggest the seriousness with which claims of physical abuse were taken, and the speed with which complaints were investigated.

61 A.M. de Suresnes, 27R, dossier 1935, letter from Joyeux to Desbruyères, 17 Aug. 1935. Joyeux asks his "friend and colleague" to look into the affair "with your customary discretion" and determine if there was any basis to Madeleine's complaint. There was no overt reference to the children's claim that they had been struck; Joyeux's letter confines itself to a discussion of how much work could reasonably be asked of the *colons.*

62 A.M. de Suresnes, 27R, dossier 1935, letter from Joyeux to Desbruyères, 17 Aug. 1935.

63 A.M. de Suresnes, 27R, dossier 1935, Desbruyères to Joyeux, 19 Aug. 1935. He moved the children to another farm in the same commune of Langeron.

64 Ibid.

65 A.M. de Suresnes, 27R, dossier 1935, letter from Denise and Zitite Chollet to their mother and grandmother, Aug. 1935.

66 A.M. de Suresnes, 27R, dossier 1935, Joyeux to Desbruyères, 29 Aug. 1935.

67 Ibid.

68 A.M. de Suresnes, 27R, dossier 1935, Desbruyères to Joyeux, 3 Sept. 1935, 1.

69 Ibid., 1–2.

70 Ibid., 2. On the morning of his visit, Desbruyères was treated to an exhibition of the good *nourrice*'s excellent care, as the children were given a thorough (and "inhabitual") wash, and then fed an excellent dinner of rabbit, mushrooms, nuts, salad, and fruit. "I could not imagine any reason to move these children." And yet not all complaints of sexual misconduct or abuse met with such suspicion. In 1943, when the Nièvre *colonie* had become a year-round refuge for several hundred young Suresnois whose parents wished them to escape the pinch of urban food shortage and the dangers of bombardment, seven-year-old Yvette Caron was the victim of an attempted rape at the hands of the farmer who had taken her in. The city's *assistantes scolaires,* detached on permanent mission to the *colonie,* assured the child's rapid transfer to another lodging. Two years later, when the city disposed of a combination of collective and family placements in Normandy, Mayor Paul Pagès was careful to ensure that the child be moved from a family placement into the collective *colonie* "not because she is unhappy with the people who have taken her in, but because this young girl was the object of an attempted rape by the farmer who had taken her in in 1943 . . . [E]ver since her mother cannot bear the thought that the child be placed on a farm." A.M. de Suresnes, 28R, letter from Paul Pagès to M. Guedou, Directeur, Colonie de vacances de Suresnes, Château de Loges Marchis, Saint-Hilaire du Harcouet, 17 July 1945; and Paul Pagès to Mesdames les Assistantes Scolaires, Colonie de vacances de Suresnes, Château de Loges Marchis, Saint-Hilaire du Harcouet, 17 July 1945, 1.

71 A.M. de Suresnes, 27R, dossier 1933, Joyeux to Desbruyères on the Rachou children, lodged with Mme Marnier, at Gentilhomme, in Azay-le-Vif, 26 Aug. 1933.

72 Hence we have the case of six children (at least), all placed on the same farm, who participated in a collective complaint against their *père nourricier,* whom they roundly condemned as a "bad man" who hit them for "getting into mischief" while his wife "wept" and tried to protect them. Interestingly enough, the children sent their complaint directly to Joyeux, rather than to one of their parents. A.M. de Suresnes, 26R, dossier

1928, R. Schoub et al. to Alexandre Joyeux, "Le fermier est un méchant homme . . . ," 2 Sept. 1928.

73   A.M. de Suresnes, 27R, dossier 1935, Joyeux to Desbruyères, 17 Aug. 1935.

74   There were four or five such letters in a dossier of twenty to twenty-five complaints over the entire interwar period.

75   A.M. de Suresnes, 26R, dossier 1928, Resumé de vacances, Ecole des Garçons Voltaire, cours moyen, 2eme terme (the boy was therefore about ten years old). It was his first summer with the *colonie,* and he had been placed for six weeks on a farm near St-Parize.

76   A.M. de Suresnes, 27R, dossier 1939, letter from Henri Sellier to the Saint-Pierre office regarding *nourrice* Rosette and the child Arlette Monière, 27 Sept. 1939.

77   See, for example, A.M. de Suresnes, 26R, dossier 1932, letter from the deputy mayor to Mme Joseph Richard of Saint-Parize-le-Châtel, 6 Aug. 1932, informing *nourrice* Richard that the Hoppeler parents would be arriving in two days to reclaim their son. While the parents recognized that Mme Richard had done an excellent job, the boy was bored and unhappy, and the parents had decided it was best to take him home. Mme Richard would of course be paid for the time that young Hoppeler had stayed in her care, and was to understand that the decision to allow the child to return to Suresnes contained no implied criticism of her skills as *nourrice.*

78   A.M. de Suresnes, 27R, dossier 1939, letter from Henri Sellier to the Saint-Pierre office regarding *nourrice* Rosette and the child Arlette Monière, 27 Sept. 1939.

79   A.M. de Suresnes, 27R, dossier 1935, letter from Desbruyères to Joyeux on the resolution of the case of the Richard children, 19 Aug. 1935.

80   A.M. de Suresnes, 26R, dossier 1922, Valette, Bardy, and Joyeux, "Rapport de la Délégation aux Colonies de Vacances 2 au 6 Septembre 1922 inclus," 7 Sept. 1922; and 26R, dossier 1923, Colonies de Vacances, 1923, "Rapport des Délégués MM. Valette, Falguerette et Legeay Conseillers Municipaux relatif à la visite générale des enfants," 16 Sept. 1923.

81   Eugène Gibon, "Nos enfants aux colonies de vacances," *Le Suresnois,* 6 Aug. 1932, 1.

82   A.M. de Suresnes, 26R, dossier 1929, letter from Ernest Blin to Alexandre Joyeux, 7 May 1929, 2.

83   A.M. de Suresnes, 27R, dossier 1932, letter from Joyeux organizing the "déjeuner amicale" for Ernest Blin, 29 Sept. 1932. See also 26R, dossier 1925, Ernest Blin to Alexandre Joyeux, 7 Dec. 1925; and dossier 1929, Ernest Blin to Alexandre Joyeux, 7 May 1929; Ernest Blin to Alexandre Joyeux, 17 July 1929; and Ernest Blin to Alexandre Joyeux, 17 Oct. 1929.

84   See, for example, A.M. de Suresnes, 27R, dossier 1933, "Affaire Gigant," which illustrates the central implication of the *assistante scolaire* in managing the fate of a thirteen-year-old *colon,* Marie Gigant, who was caught

stealing while *en colonie* at Saint-Amand (Cher). When the child was brought before the judge, it was the *assistante scolaire,* and not her own parents, who handled the matter.

85   A.M. de Suresnes, 29R, dossier 1936, Ville de Suresnes, Mairie de Suresnes, memo to the *assistantes scolaires,* "Vous avez été invitées le 27 Avril à réfléchir . . . ," 19 May 1936, response from unnamed *assistante scolaire,* written in the margins.

86   See A.M. de Suresnes, 29R, dossier 1932, memo from Sellier to the *assistantes scolaires,* 26 Nov. 1932. Since the early 1920s, the *mairie* had encouraged schoolteachers to set a kind of "how I spent my summer vacation" essay at the return to school in October, so that they could have some way of knowing whether the children who left with the municipal *colonie* were satisfied with their experience or not. Only in 1930–31 did the *mairie* begin systematically collecting data via a single questionnaire distributed by the *assistantes scolaires* to each child and his or her family. Each year's inquiry posed the same questions: how many children left the city the previous summer, in whose company, and for how many weeks? The *assistantes scolaires* then examined the results in light of each child's longer-term health profile as recorded in the medical record. See also A.M. de Suresnes, 29R, dossier 1937, "Chronique Municipale — Les Vacances de nos Enfants," 18 Jan. 1937.

87   A.M. de Suresnes, 29R, dossier 1936, Ville de Suresnes, Mairie de Suresnes, memo to the *assistantes scolaires,* "La statistique dressée sur l'emploi des vacances scolaires 1935 . . . ," 27 Apr. 1936, response from unnamed *assistante scolaire,* written in the margins.

88   A.M. de Suresnes, 29R, dossier 1936, report from the *assistante scolaire* at the Ecole Jean Macé, "Au sujet des statistiques sur les vacances scolaires," 18 May 1936. A small note attached to the *statistique* notes that the average number of children leaving on holiday had remained "about the same," at just over 75 percent since 1933, when the *assistantes scolaires* at Jean Macé had begun keeping records.

89   Ibid.

90   A.M. de Suresnes, 29R, dossier 1937, letter from Louis Boulonnois to M. Galbois justifying the *mairie*'s annual vacation census, 8 Nov. 1937; and 29R, dossier 1937, response from the parents of Guy Bousquet to the 1937 vacation inquiry, 30 Jan. 1938. Boulonnois' justification of the *mairie*'s policy was a form letter that was sent out to smooth the ruffled feathers of parents who felt their family's privacy was being violated by the inquiry.

91   A.M. de Suresnes, 27R, dossier 1935, letter from Henri Sellier to each unemployed drawing benefit who had school-aged children, "Le Municipalité attache le plus grand prix . . . ," 26 June 1935. In the case of those children who benefited from the special regime offered by the Open-Air School, the *mairie* exerted a purely moral pressure, with none of

the strong-arming visible in the case of the unemployed. Rather, Sellier simply pointed out that their child's demonstrably fragile health would suffer if she or he did not enjoy at least four weeks holiday in the country; moreover, "the municipal *colonie* guarantees the child an eight-week stay." A.M. de Suresnes, 27R, dossier 1937, letter from Sellier and L. Desbrousses, Médecin Inspecteur, to the parents of children in the Ecole de Plein Air, 5 May 1937.

92   "Le Municipalité attache le plus grand prix . . . ," 26 June 1935.

93   Boulonnois was acting on Sellier's behalf, since the latter was at this point largely taken up with his duties at the head of the newly created Ministry of Health. But the mayor's signature on key documents shows he approved of the policy, and was clearly responsible for setting its general direction in 1935, the first summer it was applied.

94   Emphasis original. A.M. de Suresnes, 27R, dossier 1935, letter of 27 May 1935, from mayor's office to Marcel Martin, director of the Caisse Interdépartementale des Assurances Sociales de Seine et Seine et Oise. By 1937, the normal daily allocation was 4 F per day for each child under sixteen who wasn't working. If that child left *en colonie,* the allocation was raised by 1.50 F, and a total of 5.50 F per day went to meeting the cost of the child's *pension* (the remaining 2–3 F of *pension* presumably came from municipal coffers). The subvention came from the Ministry of Labor and the *département* of the Seine, as provided for in the Ministry of Labor's decree of 28 July 1937.

95   A.M. de Suresnes, 27R, dossier 1935, memo of 20 June 1935 from the mayor's office (signed by Boulonnois). Ministerial Instruction 8511 is dated 15 June 1935.

96   A.M. de Suresnes, 27R, dossier 1935, memo from Henri Sellier to the *assistantes scolaires,* 24 June 1936, confirming the practice set in place the previous summer. My emphasis.

97   The *assistante scolaire* at Payret-Dortail thus wrote scathingly to the *mairie* of "those unemployed who refuse to send their children just so they can keep the allocation." A.M. de Suresnes, 29R, dossier 1936, memo from the mayor's office to the *assistantes scolaires,* "Vous avez été invitées le 27 Avril à réfléchir . . . ," 19 May 1936. Reply from Payret-Dortail.

98   Memo of 20 June 1935 from the mayor's office (signed Boulonnois). Boulonnois also asked the *assistantes* to "keep him informed" of everything they learned.

99   Ibid.

100 A.M. de Suresnes, 27R, dossier 1935, memo from Henri Sellier to the *assistantes scolaires,* 24 June 1936. Thus did Sellier remind his *assistantes scolaires* that it was up to them to enforce the policy the municipality had set in place the previous summer.

101 A.M. de Suresnes, 27R, dossier 1935, memo from the *assistantes scolaires,*

"Enfants des chômeurs," 7 July 1935. (The 1935 dossier gives both 444 and 433 as the total number of children sent that year.)

102 A.M. de Suresnes, 27R, dossier 1935, memo from the *assistantes scolaires,* "Noms des parents qui n'envoient pas leurs enfants," 11 July 1935. One young girl who would be fourteen in September wiggled out by claiming "female trouble," which vague formulation was accepted as "bon." Finally, one family withdrew their two sons after learning that the family with whom they had been placed the previous summer had no room this summer. Ibid.

103 Memo from the *assistantes scolaires,* "Noms des parents qui n'envoient pas leurs enfants"; Sellier, "Le Municipalité attache le plus grand prix . . . ," 26 June 1935, reply from an unemployed parent, scrawled in the margins (signature unreadable); and memo from *assistante scolaire* Hoyez, "Colonies de Vacances, Rappel des chômeurs," 2 (n.d. but attached to another report, from *assistante scolaire* Girard, dated 1 July 1935).

104 Memo from *assistante scolaire* Hoyez, "Colonies de Vacances, Rappel des chômeurs," 1.

105 Memo from the *assistantes scolaires,* "Noms des parents quin' envoient pas leurs enfants."

106 A.M. de Suresnes, 27R, dossier 1935, memo from mayor's office to recalcitrant unemployed, 1 Aug. 1935.

107 1936 dossier also gives 323 as the total number that left that summer. The discrepancy in total figures reported (417 versus 323) undoubtedly reflects the struggles around sending the children of the unemployed, which were especially acute that summer. A.M. de Suresnes, 27R, dossier 1936, Commission des Colonies; dossier 1937, commission of 22 May; dossier 1938, commission of 25 June; dossier 1939, Commission des Colonies.

108 A.M. de Suresnes, 29R, dossier 1937, memo from the mayor's office to school directors and *assistantes scolaires,* 9 Apr. 1937. The memo goes on to recount official disappointment with the results of the October 1936 vacation census, which showed that 76.5 percent had left the city that summer. This was a significant rise from the 60 percent of 1935; nonetheless, "far too few schoolchildren" were leaving Suresnes during the summer holiday. Ibid.

109 A.M. de Suresnes, 27R, dossier 1937, memo of 9 Apr. 1937 from the *mairie* to all school principals, *assistantes scolaires,* and *assistantes sociales* dealing with the unemployed, or with clients at the municipal welfare office.

110 Ibid., my emphasis.

111 A.M. de Suresnes, 27R, dossier 1938, memo from the prefect of the Seine to the mayors, "Envoi des enfants des chômeurs en colonies de vacances pour 1938," 19 July 1938. The Ministry of Labor Decree of 28 July 1937, which gave the subvention to help send free of charge all children of the unemployed, was still in effect in 1938. The prefect shows some ambiva-

lence over the policy of pressuring unemployed heads of households, but he upheld it nonetheless in the name of the children who were suffering the consequences of their parents' misfortune.

112 A.M. de Suresnes, 29R, dossier 1932, memo from Sellier to the *assistantes scolaires,* 26 Nov. 1932.

113 Hence in the winter of 1938, when the proportion of children leaving the city for the country had fully recovered to its pre-crisis level of 80 percent, the *mairie* was no longer content with such returns but urged its *assistantes scolaires* to still greater efforts, aiming ever toward 100 percent. A.M. de Suresnes, 29R, dossier 1938, memo from the mayor's office to the *assistantes scolaires,* 17 Jan. 1938.

114 A.M. de Suresnes, 29R, dossier 1939, memo from the mayor's office to the primary school principals, n.d., but the attached responses from the *assistantes scolaires,* dated August 1939, suggest that the memo was issued earlier that same summer.

115 A.M. de Suresnes, D670, dossier 1931, Antonin Poggioli, "Les colonies de vacances," report to the Fédération Nationale des Municipalités Socialistes, 28 Apr. 1931, 1.

116 A.M. de Suresnes, 29R, dossier 1936, memo from the mayor's office to the *assistantes scolaires,* 27 Apr. 1936.

117 A.M. de Suresnes, 29R, dossier 1936, reply to memo of 27 April 1936, from the mayor's office to the *assistantes scolaires,* 15 May 1936. The age limit was in fact lowered the following summer to five, on the condition that these young ones were accompanied by older siblings.

118 Antoine Prost, *Histoire de la vie privée,* vol. 5 (Paris: Seuil, 1987), 84.

119 While family placement enjoyed a brief wartime revival in the guise of *colonies de refuge,* the only such *colonies* to survive the Liberation were the Chaussée de Maine and Conlombant's Oeuvre des Enfants à la Montagne. Dr. Raymond Schalow's postwar manual *Joues rouges et belle humeur* reminds us that for the organizers of *colonies* in the 1940s, wartime *colonies chez les paysans* had been nothing more than a "last resort" in response to the extreme privations imposed by the Occupation. This had prolonged the life of an institution (family placement) that, in his view, could not continue, given the growing gap between rural and urban standards of hygiene. To the *moniteur* who found him or herself forced to organize such a *colonie* in the still-uncertain postwar period of ongoing restrictions, when food remained hard to come by and *colonies chez les paysans* remained—alas—necessary, Schalow offered scant consolation: the job would be a "delicate" one, given the peasants' "particularly defective" hygiene and the "rural slums" in which many of them dwelt. Under such circumstances, the *moniteur*'s "revulsion" at the mud, dung heaps, and general squalor of rural life was quite understandable in view of "the filth of the villages, result of contact with the beasts and their

excrement . . . [T]he farmer . . . wades through the mud of the fields
and village roads. His work thus leaves him perpetually filthy." Raymond
Schalow, *Joues rouges et belle humeur* (Paris: Editions des Eclaireurs de
France, 1946), 134.

120 Of course plenty of families remained faithful to the municipal *colonie,*
which was a precious resource for working mothers in particular. See, for
example, A.M. de Suresnes, 27R, dossier 1935, letter from Mlle Gabrielle
Bécue to M. Joyeux, 4 Aug. 1935. Mlle Bécue was a nickel-plater at the
Unic factory in Puteaux, where she earned the mediocre salary of 700 F
per month. She was almost certainly a single mother, and relied on the
colonie to look after her sickly daughter, Claire, once school let out in the
summer. (Her letter stresses that she chose the *colonie* for her daughter
precisely because of its strict "medical surveillance," which, she hoped,
would build up the ailing child.) But in late July of 1935, Claire fell ill
while *en colonie,* and Joyeux proposed to send her back to Suresnes to recu-
perate with her mother. Mlle Bécue refused absolutely, pointing out that
the city had taken on a responsibility for the sickly child, and was now
trying to "escape all responsibility" and dump the problem back in the
overwhelmed mother's lap. Gabrielle Bécue thus took the municipality's
hygienic and social claims for its *colonie* quite seriously, and asked that
Joyeux place Claire in the hospital at Saint-Pierre, rather than bringing
her back to the city, which would "compromise definitively" the child's re-
covery. Hoist with his own petard, Joyeux conceded the point and placed
Claire in the hospital later that month. See 27R, dossier 1935, Joyeux to
Desbruyères, 29 Aug. 1935.

121 A.M. de Suresnes, 27R, dossier 1935, memo from unnamed *assistante
scolaire* (signature unreadable), "Colonies de Vacances, Rappel des chômeurs," n.d. but attached to another report (from *assistante scolaire* Girard)
dated 1 July 1935.

122 Apart from the point about chronic undernourishment, this clearly ap-
plies equally to the better-defended families of the bourgeoisie, to whose
foyers the *assistantes scolaires* rarely gained (or sought) access in this
period. See Jacques Donzelot, *La Police des familles* (Paris: Editions de
Minuit, 1977), for an especially clear presentation of the notion that social
work constituted an attack on the masculinity of the proletarian father,
mounted by the bourgeois social worker and her craven ally from within,
the working-class wife. Thus, while the coercive policy of sending the children of the unemployed *en colonie* might seem to be an instance of that
"ambivalent social investigation" of which Donzelot speaks, situated at
the crossroads of "repression" and "assistance," a closer look reveals that
the policy showed its repressive aspect most sternly to parents, while the
assistance was channeled directly to the children. It is, therefore, "ambiva-

lent" only if one regards the family as a single entity whose interests are internally consistent and undifferentiated.

123   "La Colonie de vacances des enfants de Suresnes," 38, my emphasis.

124   Radio broadcast of 6 June 1936, announcing the social politics of his new Ministry of Health, quoted in Burlen, "Henri Sellier," in Cohen and Baudouï, *Les Chantiers de la paix sociale,* 276.

125   A.M. de Suresnes, H36, Henri Sellier, "Note pour M. le Directeur de l'Enseignement," 7 Sept. 1939, 3–4.

126   Ibid., 1, 4.

127   Ibid., 6–7.

128   Sellier, speech of 13 June 1940, cited in Sordes, *Histoire de Suresnes,* 576.

129   A.M. de Suresnes, 27R, dossier, 1937, Sellier to the prefect of the Seine, 3 Nov. 1937. Not that Sellier objected to vacations organized around political/pedagogical goals; on the contrary, from 1933, when the Faucons Rouges organized their first troops in Suresnes, Sellier granted the Socialist organizers of summertime "républiques enfantines" substantial financial aid and the moral support of the *mairie* as well. A.M. de Suresnes, 27R, dossier 1933, letter from Roger Foirier to Henri Sellier, 18 June 1933, and dossier 1935, letter from Germaine Fauchère to Henri Sellier, 19 Sept. 1935, and Louis Boulonnois, "Sur la reclamation . . . des Faucons Rouges," 8 Oct. 1935.

130   "Les Colonies de vacances, dont l'organisation actuelle n'est que le complément, doivent être considérées comme n'ayant aucune rapport direct avec l'école." A.M. de Suresnes, H36, Henri Sellier, "Note pour M. le Directeur de l'Enseignement," 7 Sept. 1939, 1.

131   This, although municipal Socialists clearly believed that hygiene itself contained a moral element, that is, that bodily health was the essential ground of human action, and of a politically conscious proletarian vigor. This was nowhere more essential than in the period of child development, where poor housing and scant food could render children crabby or listless. Children from working-class milieux thus had fewer "faults and vices" than "illnesses," wrote Dr. J. Godard in 1933. "If you rebuild their bodies . . . and cure their hereditary defects with judicious therapies, you will see the so-called defects lessen. Apathy, laziness, indolence or irritability, irrational tempers, and restless movement will all disappear." J. Godard, "Croissance et développement physique de l'enfant," *L'Aide: Bulletin mensuel des Amis de l'Enfance Ouvrière de France,* 1 Feb. 1934, 19.

132   Poggioli, "Les Colonies de vacances," 1.

133   A.M. de Suresnes, large folio, unnumbered, containing posters from the 1940s, "L'Oeuvre des Colonies de Vacances," n.d. but clearly printed in the spring of 1946.

CHAPTER 5   Les Lendemains Qui Chantent

1   Jean Houssaye, *Le Livre des colos: Histoire et évolution des centres de va-*
    cances pour enfants (Paris: La Documentation Française, 1989), 37 and 39.
    Houssaye's *Un Avenir pour les colonies de vacances* cites a figure of 110,000 to
    120,000 for 1913 (45,000 girls and 70,000 boys). Jean Houssaye, *Un Avenir*
    pour les colonies de vacances (Paris: Editions ouvrières, 1977), 15. Although
    the war put a dent in these figures, the number of *colons* rose once again,
    to 130,000 in 1921. From 170,000 in 1926, the *colonies* continued to expand,
    reaching over 200,000 by 1929, 300,000 in 1931, and 420,000 in 1936. The
    average stay was forty days, and most *colonies* were of middle size, taking
    in some sixty to seventy children at a time. After dropping back a second
    time during World War II, the number of colons soared after the Lib-
    eration, reaching 880,000 by 1948, and topping 1 million by the mid-1950s
    (ibid., 19). Although post-1945 growth in the *colonies* is doubtless linked to
    the post-1942 baby boom, the considerable expansion of the interwar years
    looks all the more impressive when one recalls the pervasive demographic
    decline in these years: though the child population was dwindling, an in-
    creasingly large percentage of this shrinking population was spending its
    summers *en colonie.*

2   Pascal Ory, *La Belle illusion: Culture et politique sous le signe du Front Popu-*
    laire, 1935–1938 (Paris: Plon, 1994), 68.

3   420,000 in the summer of 1936, and over 620,000 left the following sum-
    mer, thanks to the assiduous efforts of the new, Socialist minister of sports
    and leisure, Léo Lagrange. By 1939, nearly 700,000 children were spend-
    ing eight weeks each summer in *colonies de vacances.* Houssaye, *Le Livre*
    des colos, 37 and 39.

4   On the 1937 regulation, see Hélène Dreux, *Les Colonies de vacances à place-*
    ment collectif, thèse de médicine (Paris: A. Legrand, 1938); and Dr. H.
    Cambéssèdes and J. Boyer, *Hygiène des institutions de plein air* (Paris: J.-B.
    Baillière et fils, 1945). The Sellier-Lacore decree of 18 May 1937 created de-
    partmental *comités de surveillance des colonies,* each of which had to include
    at least three representatives from primary education and four from the
    health field (two doctors and two delegates from the Assistance Publique).
    All departmental subventions to *colonies* had to be approved by these *co-*
    mités. Detailed ministerial instructions were attached to the decree de-
    fining minimum hygienic conditions and adequate medical surveillance.
    The law of 17 June 1938 extended state protection to all school-age chil-
    dren in *colonies,* including those in family placements, and Pascal Ory has
    called it "the first official text establishing a state mission regarding the
    programs of leisure for youth" (Ory, *La Belle illusion,* 766).

5   See M. J. Roumajon, "Le Rôle des colonies de vacances dans la formation

intellectuelle de la jeunesse," *Congrès international des colonies de vacances,* Paris, 1937, 35–41.

6   In 1937, the general secretary of the Eclaireurs (scouts), Théo Koeppé, thus noted that "the active methods have not yet penetrated French pedagogical habits, and very few instructors know how to use them." Théo Koeppé, "La Formation des cadres dans les colonies de vacances," *Congrès international des colonies de vacances,* Paris, 1937, 50.

7   André Lefevre, introduction to Dr. Raymond M. Schalow, *Joues rouges et belle humeur* (Paris: Editions des Eclaireurs de France, 1946), 1.

8   Dominique Dessertine and Olivier Faure, *La Maladie entre libéralisme et solidarités: 1850–1940* (Paris: Mutualité française, 1994), note that between 1920 and 1940, tuberculosis rates in France fell by half.

9   Durkheim and Alain are two of the most eloquent proponents of the notion that education requires a neutral setting outside the family where the child is among equals and under the tutelage of a disinterested teacher, whose concern with the child's success is purely professional (versus the inevitable engagement of parental pride in the success or failure of the child to grasp some idea or technique immediately). Alain, *Propos sur l'éducation* (Reider, Paris, 1932); and Emile Durkheim, *L'Éducation morale* (Paris: Alcan, 1925). On the eve of World War I, Louis Delpérier invoked this same argument in support of *colonies* by collective, versus family, placement. Louis Delpérier, *Les Colonies de vacances* (Paris: J. Gabalda, 1908).

10 The Comité National des Colonies de Vacances was the interwar successor to Louis Comte's Fédération Nationale des Colonies de Vacances.

11 See Raoul Vimard, "Le surveillant idéal," in *Congrès national des colonies de vacances et d'oeuvres de plein air,* Saint-Etienne, 17–19 Apr. (Paris, 1925), 205–9. Also E. Sautter, "Le travail de l'éducation morale dans les colonies de vacances," and Commandant Fabre, "Allocution," both in the *Congrès national des colonies de vacances et d'oeuvres de plein air,* Reims, 22–24 Apr. 1927 (Paris, 1927), 189–97 and 60–61. Commandant Fabre had directed fourteen *colonies* over the period 1920–27. See also Fabre, "La discipline dans les colonies de vacances et oeuvres de plein air," *Congrès national des colonies de vacances et d'oeuvres de plein air,* Pau, 5 7 Apr. 1929 (Paris, 1929), 161–66.

12 See Jacques Guérin-DesJardins, director of the "Centre de Formation des Moniteurs" (Eclaireurs de France), "Le Rôle éducatif des colonies de vacances," in *Congrès internationale des colonies de vacances,* Paris, 1937, esp. 25.

13 Ory, *La Belle illusion,* 770 and 772. As compared with 12,000 Eclaireurs and 60,000 Scouts de France in 1935. Ibid., 775, 773. By 1939, there would be 100,000 Scouts de France, 20,000 Eclaireurs, and 10,000 Eclaireurs Unionistes. Rémi Fabre, "Les Mouvements de jeunesse dans la France de l'entre-deux-guerres," *Le Mouvement social,* July–Sept. 1994, 11.

14 At the Liberation, the PCF transformed the Pionniers into the Vaillants and the Vaillantes, a move which social Catholic activists resented in the extreme, as their very successful organizations for children of the popular classes, created during the 1930s, were titled Coeurs Vaillants (boys) and Ames Vaillantes (girls).

15 Elia Perroy, "Le Jeu et les jeux," *Educateurs,* Jan.–Feb. 1949, 50. See also Jean-Yves Château, *Le Jeu de l'enfant après 3 ans, sa nature, sa discipline, introduction à la pédagogie* (Paris: Vrin, 1946).

16 By the turn of the twentieth century, Europe and North America had produced an enormous scientific literature on this subject, nearly all of which treated childhood development as the natural unfolding of a preordained, teleological process.

17 See Karl Groos, *Les Jeux des animaux* (Paris: Alcan, 1902); and Groos, *The Play of Man* (New York: D. Appleton, 1901).

18 The classic example of this kind of reasoning is to be found in Granville Stanley Hall, "Recreation and Reversion," *Pedagogical Seminary,* 1915, 510–20.

19 Christian Guérin thus notes the temporal coincidence in the publication of Baden-Powell's *Scouting for Boys,* Montessori's *Psychologie de l'enfant et pédagogie expérimentale,* and Claparède's *Pédagogie scientifique,* all of which appeared in 1908. Christian Guérin, *L'Utopie: Scouts de France: Histoire d'une identité collective, catholique et sociale, 1920–1995* (Paris: Fayard, 1997), 50.

20 Even in the *écoles maternelles,* educators set aside the Froebelian model of a play-centered "child's garden" in favor of a more propaedeutic approach, in which games alternated with periods of formal instruction in reading, counting, and writing, with the whole being conceived as preparation for the more rigorous disciplines of primary school. See Jean-Noël Luc, *L'Invention du jeune enfant au XIXe siècle: De la salle d'asile à l'école maternelle* (Paris: Belin, 1997). See also Alain, *Propos sur l'éducation,* for an eloquent exposition of the republican and *laïque* position on the function of the school as an institution that, purpose-built for the education of children, mediates between family and society. In the course of developing his argument about the incapacity of the family to educate its children (due to the power of its emotional ties, and of parental pride, which provides no neutral space within which the child can err), Alain specifies the nature of the work accomplished within the school, which is neither work as adults know it (since it is not conducted under the constraints of the market), but neither is it play, being linked to the serious business of growing up and leaving one's childish amusements behind.

21 *Revue des patronages,* Jan. 1914. More recently, Jean Houssaye described the training practicum by which *moniteurs* prepared for their role in the

colonies as an "apprenticeship" in understanding who and "what" the child is. Jean Houssaye, *Aujourd'hui les centres de vacances* (Vigneux: Editions Matrice, 1991), 74.

22 Transcription of strophe 64 from Léon Gautier, trans., *Le Chanson de Roland* (Tours: Alfred Mame et Fils, 1897), 78, cited in Guérin, *L'Utopie: Scouts de France,* 166–67. Guérin notes that the scoutmaster revised Gautier's text somewhat in order to make it more accessible to his scouts (most, if not all of whom had doubtless encountered this poem already in the schoolroom, as a part of the national cultural *patrimoine* to be learned by heart).

23 The tale of the scout camp at Luz-Saint-Sauveur is taken from the case of "Jean M.," a fictional composite constructed by Christian Guérin from a host of *témoignages* from participants in the interwar scout movement in Paris. Guérin, *L'Utopie: Scouts de France,* 166–67.

24 The term is from Guérin, *L'Utopie: Scouts de France.*

25 Réginald Héret, *La Loi scoute: Commentaire d'après saint Thomas d'Aquin* (Paris: Spès, 1929), 74.

26 Guérin, *L'Utopie: Scouts de France,* 58–60.

27 The Eclaireurs Unionistes were linked to the Reformed (Calvinist) Church in France without being dependent upon it (unlike the Catholic Scouts de France, which was entirely bound up with the hierarchy), and promised to "awaken" the child's spirituality on the basis of "Christian principles." The Eclaireurs de France, by contrast, grounded itself in a *laïque* "civic morality" which respected the liberty of consciousness and religious expression among its members. This is not the crusading secularism of Gisèle de Failly or the Ligue d'Enseignement, but rather a pluralist secularism in the spirit of the early Third Republic, in which the religious spirit is recognized as a part of the human being and allowed to develop as it will. The female branch (Eclaireuses) was organized in 1921.

28 Indeed, in the use of those signals, animal cries, and totems so dear to Baden-Powell's heart, the upholders of orthodoxy detected the nefarious influence of Freemasonry. See Paul Copin-Albincelli, "La Question des boy-scouts ou éclaireurs en France," *La Renaissance française,* 1913. A former mason of the eighteenth degree, Copin-Albincelli was especially well placed to lead the campaign against scouting as Freemasonry in sheep's clothing.

29 See Stéphane Audoin-Rouzeau and Annette Becker, *La Grande guerre: 1914–1918* (Paris: Gallimard, 1998); and Annette Becker, *La Guerre et la foi: De la mort à la mémoire, 1914–1930* (Paris: A. Colin, 1994).

30 I have liberally translated here Guide chief Marie Diémer's characterization of scout method as she presented it in the journal *La Cheftaine,* a pedagogical journal for Guide troop leaders: "The best way to prepare

little girls and boys to be good guides and scouts is to have them live a beautiful story." Marie Diémer, "Pourquoi j'ai écrit le livre de la Forêt bleu," *La Cheftaine,* Apr. 1936.

31 Baden-Powell, quoted in Henri Bouchet, *Le Scoutisme et l'individualité* (Paris: Alcan, 1933), 182.

32 Ibid., 11.

33 Pierre Delsuc, *Plein jeu* (Fonteny-sous-Bois: Editions de l'Orme Rond, 1985), 19.

34 Ibid., 25.

35 Anne-Marie Wenger-Charpentier, *La Cheftaine des jeannettes (Dans la Forêt bleue)* (Paris: Spès, 1933), 11. The author goes on to identify the child's imaginary world as superior to the adult one, and closer to "the Truth": "Children, whether boys or girls, always live in a marvelous reality that is quite superior to ours, and doubtless closer to the Truth, for it contains much more Beauty and Joy. This is why life is so sweet to them." Ibid., 16. Wenger-Charpentier's identification of the child's inner world with "innate" moral instincts and greater proximity to Truth entails an idealization of childhood's superior moral quality that is rarely seen in the French context.

36 Marie Diémer, *Le Livre de la forêt bleue* (Montreuil-sous-Bois: Imprimerie de la Seine, 1933).

37 Marie Diémer, "Pourquoi j'ai écrit le livre de la Forêt bleu." Diémer was raised Protestant, converted to Catholicism in the early 1920s, and made her promise as one of the first *cheftaine guides* in 1923–24. She drew on her enormous biblical culture to construct child-sized saints' lives for the Guide movement and its cadet branch, the Jeannettes.

38 Delsuc, *Plein jeu,* 23. There is an interesting parallel here with Piaget's notion of the young child (up to age six or seven) as caught up in his own autistic and inner reality, which cedes only gradually to the real world of cause and effect, and rational argument. See Jean Piaget, *Le Langage et la pensée de l'enfant: Etudes sur la logique de l'enfant* (Paris: Denoël, 1984), and Piaget, *La Construction du réel chez l'enfant* (Paris: Delachaux et Niestlé, 1996). In his episcopal benediction at the 1935 Journées Nationales des Scouts, Mgr. Bruno de Solages offered a rather extreme statement of this notion of the child as given over to his or her interior and imaginative life: "From his internal perspective, the life that his imagination produces is more important than the other. It is not a life on the margins of real life; rather, this imaginary life is his reality." Bruno de Solages, *Philosophie du Scoutisme,* report of the Journées Nationales, 1934, Feb. 1935, n. 120, 163–64.

39 Delsuc, *Plein jeu,* 14.

40 Ibid., 25–26.

41 Abbé Gaston Courtois, *Pour "réussir" auprès des enfants: Quelques con-*

seils de pédagogie pratique (Paris: J. Ruckert, 1938), 41–42. The abbé goes on to note that children are especially susceptible to "crowd psychology." Ibid., 42.

42 Delsuc, *Plein jeu,* 26.

43 Guérin, *L'Utopie: Scouts de France,* 53–54.

44 Henri Bouchet, *Le Scoutisme: Bases psychologiques. Méthodes et rites* (Paris: Alcan, 1933), 47. The active school was a part of the new education movement. See also André Sevin, *Vers une éducation nouvelle: Réflexions sur le scoutisme* (Paris: G. Enault, 1930).

45 Delsuc, *Plein jeu,* 26–27.

46 Ibid., 15.

47 Ibid., 15. Abbé Gaston Courtois also stressed the "prodigious" power of the child's imagination; indeed, "his imagination precedes his will . . . hence the importance of the stories, themes, and myths we choose." Courtois, *Pour "réussir" auprès des enfants,* 43–44.

48 Jacques Guérin Desjardins, entry on *scoutisme* for the interwar *Encyclopédie française,* cited in Françoise Mayeur, *Histoire générale de l'enseignement et de l'éducation en France* (Paris: G-V Labat, 1981), 3: 599.

49 Ibid., 599.

50 Jacques Guérin-Desjardins, "Le rôle éducatif des Colonies de Vacances," *Congrès international des colonies de vacances,* Paris, 1937, 25.

51 Ibid., 24.

52 Ibid., 24, emphasis original.

53 Wenger-Charpentier, *La Cheftaine des jeannettes,* 45–46.

54 "Grands jeux," *L'Aide: Bulletin mensuel des Amis de l'Enfance Ouvrière de France,* 1 Feb. 1934, 31.

55 Martin Gleisner, "Comment transformer les grands jeux en jeux collectifs (1)," *L'Aide: Bulletin mensuel des Amis de l'Enfance Ouvrière de France,* Mar. 1937, 2–4. For a suggestive comparison with "red" summer camps in the United States, see Paul C. Mishler, *Raising Reds: The Young Pioneers, Radical Summer Camps, and Communist Political Culture in the United States* (New York: Columbia University Press, 1999).

56 Pistrak, *Les Problèmes fondamentaux de l'école du travail* (Paris: Desclée de Brouwer, 1973), 26, 160.

57 Berthold Friedl, "La conscience de classe chez l'enfant," *L'Educateur prolétarien,* 10 Dec. 1935, 112.

58 Russian psychologist Lev Vygotsky provided key theoretical underpinning for this psycho-pedagogical stance. See Lev Vygotsky, *Pensée et langage* (Paris: La Dispute, 1997).

59 Roger Foirier, cited in Guy Viel's untitled report of the 10 November 1935 meeting of the Cercle National des Aides at the Mutualité, in Paris, *L'Aide: Bulletin mensuel des Amis de l'Enfance Ouvrière de France,* Dec. 1935, 8–9, 8.

60 See Kurt Loewenstein, "Pédagogie Socialiste (Cours des Aides, 7 nov.

1933)," *L'Aide: Bulletin mensuel des Amis de l'Enfance Ouvrière de France,* 1 Dec. 1933.

61 "Self-government aux camps," *L'Aide: Bulletin des Amis de l'Enfance Ouvrière de France,* June–July 1938, 13. The Faucons Rouges followed Pistrak in distinguishing self-government in Socialist schools and *colonies de vacances* from models of self-government tried out in various bourgeois settings, the most famous of which was William Reuben George's child's republic for young orphans and juvenile delinquents in late-nineteenth-century New York. In the latter case the constitution and laws were handed down from on high, and the youthful delegates of adult authority were there simply to help the teacher or administrator maintain his authority. The child thus became an instrument of adult authority, rather than part of a child-run order. See Pistrak, *Les Problèmes fondamentaux,* 129–30.

62 Dr. Lion, "Egalité et supériorité," *L'Aide: Bulletin des Amis de l'Enfance Ouvrière de France,* June 1937. Like the Jeunesses Communistes, the Faucons Rouges preferred using adolescents and young adults as aides, for as PCF militant Léa Bourreau remarked, youth are "closer" to children, can win their confidence more easily, and thus can get them to work effectively without exercising an "overly tight control." Léa Bourreau, "Le Travail parmi les enfants," *Cahiers de bolchevisme,* Nov. 1926, 2061.

63 Georges Monnet, "Notre tâche," (Cours des Aides, 7 nov. 1933)," *L'Aide: Bulletin mensuel des Amis de l'Enfance Ouvrière de France,* 1 Dec. 1933, 9.

64 "Notre Tente," *L'Aide: Bulletin mensuel des Amis de l'Enfance Ouvrière de France,* Mar. 1935, 5.

65 "Self-government aux camps," 15.

66 Loewenstein, "Pédagogie Socialiste," 3. This was the first such training course organized by the newly hatched Faucons Rouges in France.

67 Georges Monnet, "Notre tâche," 7.

68 "Pédagogie et psychologie de la Tente," *L'Aide: Bulletin mensuel des Amis de l'Enfance Ouvrière de France,* Apr. 1936, 6.

69 Ibid., 7. See also Loewenstein, "Pédagogie Socialiste," esp. p. 3.

70 Loewenstein, "Pédagogie Socialiste," 3.

71 Pistrak, *Les Problèmes fondamentaux,* 163.

72 Guérin-Desjardins, "Le Rôle éducatif," 26–27.

73 Pistrak, *Les Problèmes fondamentaux,* 29.

74 Ibid., 134–35, 137–38, 138 (my emphasis).

75 Ibid., 136.

76 "Grands jeux," 30. Note the eternal appeal of painless, unconscious learning, once again vaunted. The Faucons Rouges also took great pains to distinguish their "red" scouting from "the ordinary scouting" of the Scouts and Eclaireurs. (See "Camp de Pâques [autocritique]," *L'Aide: Bulletin mensuel des Amis de l'Enfance Ouvrière de France,* June 1935, 12–13.)

77 Ibid.

78 Martin Gleisner, "Comment transformer les grands jeux en jeux collec-
    tifs," 2. Here the Faucons Rouges sought to follow Krupskaya's warning
    that games, though "a very important factor in uniting children," had to
    be chosen carefully; "for some games hamper the development of collec-
    tivist instincts, divide children instead of uniting them." Krupskaya, "The
    Young Pioneer Movement as a Pedagogical Problem," cited in Krupskaya,
    On Education (Moscow, 1957), 120.

79 Krupskaya, "Four Lines of Work among Young Pioneers" (speech at the
    Seventh Congress of the Young Communist League, 21 March 1926),"
    reprinted in Krupskaya, *On Education,* 112–13.

80 Monnet, "Notre tâche," 8.

81 Loewenstein, cited in ibid., 9.

82 Ibid. The term *pre-exercise* is found in Karl Groos, *Les Jeux des animaux*
    (Paris: Alcan, 1902).

83 "Les Organisations d'enfants. II — La presse enfantine et les organisations
    prolétariennes d'enfants," *Cahiers de contre-enseignement prolétarien,* Sept.
    1933, 8.

84 In fact, as Eric Bimbi points out, PCF educational politics over the interwar
    period wavered constantly between these two poles of reforming educa-
    tional practice within the Republic (i.e., before the Revolution), and so
    creating the equivalent of Loewenstein's "pedagogical oases," or pursuing
    the more combative (and negative) politics of the "école de classe," which
    rejected the idea that education in a class society could ever be neutral.
    In the latter case, the pedagogue's job becomes the largely negative act of
    countereducation, that is, unmasking the bourgeois lies that are the daily
    diet in the republican primary school classroom. Though clearly a product
    of the post-1920 Socialist-Communist split, these two poles of educational
    politics in interwar France also corresponded quite closely to the prewar
    debate between the *ouvriériste* anarcho-syndicalism of the Guesdistes and
    the Jaurèsiens' more heterodox notion of a "social republic." Moreover,
    they constitute two currents of thought that in fact coexisted across the
    interwar life of the party. See Eric Bimbi, "Le PCF et l'enseignement à
    l'école primaire de 1921 au milieu des années 1930" (Mémoire de maîtrise,
    Université de Paris I, 1991).

85 This is precisely what PCF education militant Léa Bourreau meant when
    she suggested that militants should "draw proletarian children into the
    class struggle, and so elevate their class consciousness." Bourreau, "Le tra-
    vail parmi les enfants."

86 Célestin Freinet, *L'Education du travail,* reprinted in Célestin Freinet,
    Oeuvres pédagogiques, ed. Madeleine Freinet (Paris: Seuil, 1994), 1: 157,
    emphasis original. Freinet goes on to say that this work must respond to
    one of the most "urgent tendencies" in children of that age, that is, their

need to feel powerful, "to surpass themselves and others, to bring home victories, both large and small, to dominate someone or something."

87 The term "jeu haschich" is taken from Freinet's sustained argument against the "pedagogical mystique" of educational play, in Célestin Freinet, "La vraie place du jeu en éducation," *L'Educateur,* 1 Mar. 1940, 173–75. Freinet's working-class pedagogy recast the old *ouvriériste* insistence on proletarian political and cultural autonomy in terms of a quasi-Heideggerian vision of working-class culture, which took the archaic culture of the rural poor as the point of reference for building an authentic and culturally autonomous proletarian education. For Freinet, then, the distinction was not between fact and fantasy but rather between healthy (authentically popular) versus alienating (bourgeois and mass-market) works of the imagination: "All those marvels that have a solid rooting in the children's subconscious, which emerge as the mysterious expression of some ancestral fate, can harmoniously assist in the child's education and development. But we must sternly reject all the ingenious, and often abracadabra-ish schemes of those neurotic scribblers for whom fantasy is nothing more than a game with words and phrases, with no human consequences." Freinet, *L'Education du travail,* and Freinet, "Des lectures pour nos enfants?" *L'Educateur prolétarien,* Dec. 1932, 131–36., esp. 135–36, where he recommends drawing on the "ancient ancestral cultural fund" of legends and tales that constitute the "only popular elements that the children of our public schools can really absorb." In these "folkloric monuments" the people will find their "sturdy popular roots that can still resist the most elaborate instruments of brainwashing and enslavement."

88 "Revue de Presse," review of Georgette Guegen-Dreyfus, *Tu seras ouvrier,* in *L'Aide: Bulletin mensuel des Amis de l'Enfance Ouvrière,* May 1935, 14. See also Berthold Friedl's fascinating survey of class consciousness among children of the Paris *banlieue,* based on an inquiry conducted with 150 children in a *colonie de vacances* of the *banlieue sud.* Berthold Friedl, "La conscience de classe chez l'enfant," part 1, *L'Educateur prolétarien,* 10 Dec. 1935, 112–15, and part 2, 25 Dec. 1935, 137–38: "The proletarian child's development is intimately bound up with his social class. The economic base of this class is his base, its social framework gives form to his social being, and its ideology creates the atmosphere to which the child's psychic life attaches itself." Ibid., 112.

89 Krupskaya, "Le Mouvement Jeune Pionnier," 8 Apr. 1927, reprinted in Krupskaya, *De l'Éducation: Recueil d'articles (1920–1937)* (Moscow, 1958).

90 Felix Kanitz, "Lutteurs de l'avenir," in *Les Faucons Rouges, pratiques et méthodes,* Documents de l'Action populaire, Oct. 1933, cited in Rey-Herme, *Les Colonies de vacances en France, 1906–1936,* 336.

91 "The children of the working class must become courageous fighters, the ingenious and tenacious architects of the new society. In order to ac-

complish this task, we need a working class that loves liberty and solidarity, that is conscious and proud of its power and its mission." "Cours
de Loewenstein," *L'Aide: Bulletin mensuel des Amis de l'Enfance Ouvrière
de France,* 1 Dec. 1933 and Jan. 1934. Cited in Rey-Herme, *Les Colonies de
vacances en France, 1906–1936,* 334.

92 Courtois, *Pour "réussir" auprès des enfants,* 103. The critical commentary
(auto-critique) of the game after its conclusion was also drawn from the
scout arsenal. See Delsuc, *Plein jeu.*

93 Ibid., 50.

94 Ory, *La Belle illusion,* 770 and 772; and Fabre, "Les mouvements de jeunesse," 11.

95 "Les organisations d'enfants. II," 32. The article stresses the importance of
imparting a strictly "workerist" education to proletarian children, in the
prewar tradition of working-class cultural autonomy (*ouvriérisme*). This
confirms what the structure of social and cultural politics in the interwar
Communist municipalities suggests, namely, that the social and cultural
politics of the PCF maintained an important current of *ouvriérisme* that
links back directly to prewar traditions. See also Marc Riglet, "L'Ecole
et la Révolution: Aspects du discours révolutionnaire sur l'école pendant
l'entre-deux-guerres," *Revue française de la science politique* 3 (June 1978):
488–507.

96 Juliette Pary, "14 Juillet," in Pary, *L'Amour des camarades* (Lille: Victor
Michon, 1948), 40. Pary's comment reminds us of the *éducation nouvelle*'s
very popular valence in France, where such methods were excluded from
mainstream, republican curricula. Pary joined in the first CEMEA training
practicum at Beaurecueil as a participant-observer, in order to prepare a
series of articles on the popular education movement for the journal *Marianne.* She was especially well chosen for the task, for in 1935 Pary had
directed a *colonie* for children from an unnamed *banlieue parisienne* — a
tale whose high and low points are recounted with great relish in Juliette
Pary, *Mes 126 gosses* (Paris: Flammarion, 1938).

97 Ory terms the CEMEA one of the "pillars" of Popular Front "cultural democratization." Ory, *La Belle illusion,* 767.

98 Léon Blum, cited in Louis Bodin and Jean Touchard, *Front populaire 1936*
(Paris: Armand Colin, 1985), 141. Jacques Soustelle captured the mille-
narian hopes surrounding the Popular Front's democratization of culture:
"Parallel to the great popular and social movement of the Popular Front,
or rather forming merely one aspect of it, a vast cultural movement is unfolding in France. Its motto could be this: open up the gates of culture.
Break down the barriers which surround, like a beautiful park forbidden to the poor, a culture reserved to a privileged élite." Jacques Soustelle, *Vendredi,* 26 June 1936, cited in Bodin et Touchard, *Front populaire
1936,* 135.

99   Gisèle de Failly, "Grandir," in Denis Bordat, *Les C.E.M.E.A., qu'est-ce que c'est?* (Paris: Maspéro, 1976), 19–20.

100 Beaurecueil was the site of scout *camp-école,* a wolf-cub camp (scouts under the age of twelve), and a scout-chief training center. Gisèle de Failly began her career in public health, and in the early to mid-1930s had served as "chargée de la coordination des éléments du service social" in Sellier's *mairie.* In January of 1936, she left Suresnes for a post with L'Hygiène par l'Exemple, a national organization that devoted itself to promoting children's health by disseminating hygienic instruction throughout the primary school network and renewing dilapidated school buildings and facilities. Under the auspices of this organization, de Failly set up a summertime "maison de campagne" in 1936, a kind of small-scale *colonie de vacances* in a rural boarding school in the Vosges that had recently been renovated by L'Hygiène par l'Exemple. The utter ineptitude of her staff (with the partial exception of one young girl whose experience in the scout movement provided a desperately needed repertoire of songs, games, and activities) convinced de Failly that goodwill was not enough; work with children in camps and *colonies de vacances* clearly required a formal preparation in the art of seizing the opportunities, and objects, available for pedagogical action. See de Failly, "Grandir," 22–28, and de Failly (then Gisèle Féry), "Maisons de campagne des écoliers," *L'hygiène par l'exemple* (Sept.–Oct. 1936): 170–84. André Lefèvre was the national commissioner of the Eclaireurs de France from 1922 to 1940, and cofounder, with Gisèle de Failly, of the CEMEA, in 1936–37. He was born in Angers and worked as an assistant accountant for the railway station at Angers, before migrating to Paris, where he found work in an office, as a *dessinateur.* In 1909, Lefèvre began his side-career as popular education militant when he joined the *silloniste* social action group organized around the *maison pour tous* "Chez Nous," located in the fifth arrondissement. After the 1911 papal condemnation of the Sillon, "Chez Nous" continued its work (which included organizing *colonies de vacances* and *caravanes scolaires* for children and adolescents) under Lefèvre's direction. See Jacques Scheer, "André Lefèvre," in Geneviève Poujol and Madeleine Romer, eds., *Dictionnaire biographique des militants, XIXe–XXe siècles: De l'éducation populaire à l'action culturelle* (Paris: Harmattan, 1996), 236–37.

101 De Failly notes that in order to preserve the principle of a training session that was open to all, she had had to struggle hard against the representatives of public education in the CEMEA's circle of patrons, who wished to see the entire venture placed squarely in the hands of qualified teachers. But the battle against the dominance of teachers was to be a losing one, since the militantly secular Ligue de l'Enseignement had recently manifested an interest in *colonies de vacances,* creating in 1934 its own national organization, the UFOVAL, which would soon become a powerful force

in organizing nonconfessional *colonies*. De Failly, "Grandir," 32–33. See
also G. de Failly, "1936, une époque riche de promesses," *Vers l'éducation
nouvelle* 112 (May 1957): 22–43, esp. 25.

102 De Failly, "Grandir," 36.

103 Cited in ibid., 37.

104 Juliette Pary, "Souvenirs du premier stage," *Vers l'éducation nouvelle* 112
(May 1957): 52 (excerpted from her original article on the *stage* at Beaurecueil, published in *Marianne*, 28 Apr. 1937).

105 Ibid., 53.

106 Ibid., 53.

107 Lefèvre had been using this technique since 1911, to train his scout chiefs
in pre-camp sessions where the would-be chiefs acquired the essential
techniques of the scout pedagogy while living the life of the camp.

108 De Failly, "Grandir," 29.

109 Ibid., 38. The CEMEA expanded quite rapidly, from two initial founding
stages in 1937, to four *stages* in 1938 and eleven in 1939. That year the first
stage for directors was introduced as well. The invasion of 1940 curbed
this expansion but did not snuff out the CEMEA altogether, which managed to organize six *stages* that year, despite the considerable obstacles
that the Occupation threw in their way. Gilles Gardaix, "Les CEMEA,
mouvement d'éducation. Esquisse d'une époque: 1945–1957" (Mémoire
de maîtrise, Université de Paris I, 1981), 10, 12.

110 De Failly, "Grandir," 40. De Failly and her colleagues at the CEMEA were
not alone in thinking they had waged pedagogical revolution; in 1955,
colonie de vacances pedagogue Philippe Rey-Herme would hail the *stage*
method as constituting "the most important progress realized in the *colonies de vacances* over fifty years." Philippe Rey-Herme, *La Colonie de vacances hier et aujourd'hui* (Paris: Editions Cap, 1955), 75.

111 Here she represents perfectly the viewpoint of the "milieux *laïques*"
(that is, the Ligue d'Enseignement, whose role in the founding tri-
umvirate of the CEMEA—Eclaireurs, Hygiène par l'Exemple, and Ligue
d'Enseignement—de Failly also represented), which, until the era of the
Popular Front, viewed the Eclaireurs as weird, paramilitary units marked
by Protestant spiritism and foreign (British) origins. Ory, *La Belle illusion*, 773.

112 Dr. R. M. Schalow, *Joues rouges et belle humeur*, 109 and 97–98. Schalow
had been an Eclaireur and served as *moniteur* in secular *colonies de vacances*
during the 1930s.

113 A. Lefèvre, introduction to R. M. Schalow, *Joues rouges et belle humeur*, 2.

114 Léon Tolstoi, *L'École de Iasnia-Poliana en Novembre et Decembre 1862*
(Paris: Stock, 1905). The Eclaireurs were of course quite pleased to find
themselves at the heart of the national popular education movement, a
fact which schoolteacher Albert Châtelet celebrated when he noted in his

speech before the Eclaireur Congrès Fédéral of August 1938 that "public officialdom" had at last begun to appreciate scouting "not just as a magnificent game, or even a method of *éducation nouvelle,* but in a broader sense they have begun to understand that these somewhat barbaric methods, these childish games, big hats and all the rest, have their function. For each time it is a question of organizing *colonies de vacances,* or children's leisure more generally, it is to the Eclaireur movement that public officials have turned, time and again." *Le chef* (official EDF organ), discours d'Albert Châtelet, Aug.–Sept. 1938.

115 Rey-Herme, *Les Colonies de vacances en France, 1906–1936,* 462.

116 Bordat, *Les C.E.M.E.A.,* 13–14. The term *health machine* is taken from an article on the *colonies de vacances* of the *banlieues rouges* titled "Les machines à fabriquer la santé: Voyages aux colonies de vacances enfantines de la banlieue rouge," *Regards 82* (8 Aug. 1935): 7–8.

117 Bordat, *Les C.E.M.E.A.,* 14.

118 Ibid., 14, emphasis original. Bordat's memories do not entirely accord with the records of the Ivry *colonie,* which in this period (early 1930s) refer constantly to the "comrades-surveillants" responsible for watching over this turbulent crew. See also Paul-Henry Chombart de Lauwe, *La Vie quotidienne des familles ouvrières, recherches sur les comportements sociaux de consommation* (Paris: CNRS, 1956), for a remarkable discussion of working-class food practices in Paris and its *banlieue* during the early 1950s.

119 Bordat, *Les C.E.M.E.A.,* 16 and 14, original emphasis.

120 Gisèle de Failly, "1937/1957," *Vers l'éducation nouvelle* 112 (1957): 39. The central state supported the expansion of the *centres de formation* by a subvention policy that, after 1945, increasingly redirected its funds away from individual *colonies* and municipalities and toward the various training centers. In 1945, the secular centers (CEMEA, JPA, UFOVAL) were the main beneficiaries of this policy; by 1986, the Catholic UFCV was receiving the largest single portion of state funds for the *colonies* and *centres de vacances.* For details, see Jean Houssaye, *Aujourd'hui les centres de vacances* (Vigneux: Editions Matrices, 1991), chap. 5.

121 André Schmitt and André Boulogne, *La Cure de santé et les jeux des enfants* (Paris: Editions du Scarabée, 1955).

122 Ibid., 11.

123 Ibid., 61.

124 Ibid., 55: "Adults play to amuse themselves or to gain a result. Children play to construct themselves." It would seem that Groosian functionalism had not been displaced by the postwar arrival of "psycho-pédagogie" in the *colonies de vacances.*

125 Ibid., 62.

126 Schmitt and Boulogne's *La Cure de santé* thus features but a single illustration: a frontispiece in the form of a close-up photo of one of these many

"Jeux Interdits dans le Square" signs. The expression "le peuple enfant" comes from philosopher and pedagogue Jean-Yves Château, whose doctoral thesis assessed the various theories that underwrote play-centered pedagogies against the results of his own fieldwork: eight years spent watching "le peuple enfant" as it played in villages around Angoulême and Pau (1937–45). His thesis, title "Le Jeu de l'enfant après trois ans: Sa nature, sa discipline," was published by the CEMEA's own Editions Scarabée in 1946 and was read by CEMEA militants, including Boulogne and Schmitt.

127 Schmitt and Boulogne, *La Cure de santé,* 61.

128 Ibid., 61.

129 Ibid.

130 Ibid., 62.

131 Ibid., 88. This revival of tradition did not necessarily imply miring the children inside of structures past; rather, the interest seemed to lie in hitching the educational virtues of traditional games to current society, including the postwar penchant for *mixité en colonie.* Hence, with *la galoche,* for example, the authors note that while it is originally a "boys' game," girls, too, enjoy playing and up to age twelve or thirteen, "join in on equal terms and with great pleasure." Ibid., 88. CEMEA activists also favored these old-fashioned games because they worked best in small groups, and after the Liberation small group activity in the *colonies de vacances* was the watchword among progressive pedagogues.

132 Ibid., 62.

133 Alain Boureau, "Propositions pour une histoire restreinte des mentalités," *Annales ESC* 6 (Nov.–Dec. 1989): 1491–1504.

134 "First and foremost, then, all play is a voluntary activity . . . By this quality of freedom alone, play marks itself off from the course of the natural process." Jan Huizinga, *Homo Ludens: A Study of the Play-Element in Culture* (Boston: Beacon Press, 1950), 7. The book was written in 1938 and first translated into English in 1949.

CHAPTER 6 Municipal Communism and the Politics of Childhood

1 It was the Bloc Ouvrier et Paysan—a united worker-peasant front that the Communists had forged with the Socialists in December 1923—that took a decisive majority that day.

2 Archives Municipales d'Ivry (hereafter A.M. d'Ivry), Raymond Lagarde, Interview 50, 7 Jan. 1982, 16 bis.

3 Save for the period of World War II, when President Edouard Daladier dismissed the Communist council and placed the city in the hands of a caretaker regime of appointed officials. For in August 1939, the Commu-

nist Party was outlawed in France and all Communist officials were driven from office. Throughout the war (1940–45), the *colonie* at Les Mathes would remain closed to the children of Ivry, not to reopen its doors until the summer of 1946.

4   "The real faith of the Communist militants after 1920 was syndicalist," wrote George Lichtheim in 1966. "Insofar as the working-class member of the French CP had a vision of the future, it was the old anarcho-syndicalist dream of a factory without bosses, a society without exploiters, and a nation without a state." George Lichtheim, *Marxism in Modern France* (New York: Columbia University Press, 1966), 70. See also Robert Wohl, *French Communism in the Making, 1914–1920* (Stanford: Stanford University Press, 1966).

5   Jean Lojkine and Nathalie Viet Depaule, *Classe ouvrière, société locale et municipalités en région parisienne. Eléments pour une analyse régionale et une approche monographique: Le cas d'Ivry-sur-Seine* (Paris: Centre d'études des mouvements sociaux, 1984), 173.

6   Louis Barron, *Les Environs de Paris* (Paris: Maison Quantin, 1886), 175. Even in 1866, the percentage of the population working in agriculture had already shrunk to 4.6 percent, while a full 58.6 percent were employed in industry. Lojkine and Viet Depaule, *Classe ouvrière,* 176.

7   Victor-Eugène Ardouin-Dumazet, *Voyage en France. Banlieue parisienne. 1. Région sud-est et est* (vol. 64 of *Voyage en France*) (Paris: Berger-Levrault, 1921), 33.

8   A.M. d'Ivry, Lucienne Ballerat, Interview 76–77–78, 28 Apr. 1982, 3; and René Guillard, Interview 101–102, 23 Nov. 1982, 2.

9   The population doubled again between 1896 and 1931, rising from 24,385 to 48,929. Lojkine and Viet Depaule, *Classe ouvrière,* 203, 273.

10 Jean Bastié, *La Croissance de la banlieue parisienne* (Paris: PUF, 1964), 200. Bastié further notes that in 1896, only 11 percent of these houses had their own *cabinets d'aisance.* The omnipresent mud of the Ivry winter was due to seasonal flooding of the Seine, which was not brought under control until the interwar period. On the eve of World War I, mortality rates from tuberculosis alone were 50 percent higher in the Paris *banlieue* than for the rest of France. Ibid., 219.

11 Jacques Valdour, *Ouvriers parisiens d'après-guerre* (Paris: A. Rousseau, 1921), 81–82. Jacques Valdour was the pen name of Dr. Louis Martin, a Catholic royalist and social investigator who is remembered for his remarkable series of books, "La Vie ouvrière, observations vécues."

12 Marques was editor-in-chief of *L'Aube sociale* (the Communist newspaper for the southern *banlieue*) and his café-hotel was a favorite meeting place for local militants.

13 "Thèses sur le programme municipale du B.O.P.," *Bulletin communiste,* 7 Nov. 1924, 1055–58. On working-class sociability in relation to politics,

see Maurice Agulhon, *La République au village* (Paris: Seuil, 1979). See also Maurice Cassier, "Classe ouvrière et municipalité en région parisienne. Montreuil ouvrier et républicain: Formation, évolution, et crise d'un 'bastion Communiste' " (thesis for the diplôme d'études approfondies, Ecole des Hautes Etudes en Sciences Sociales, 1981), esp. 115 ff., on the French Communist Party as heir to the Guesdist/Blanquist traditions of working-class self-organization, in the neighborhood as well as the workshop or factory.

14 Etienne Fouilloux, "Des chrétiens à Ivry-sur-Seine," in Annie Fourcaut, ed., *Banlieue rouge 1920–1960. Années Thorez, années Gabin: Archetype du populaire, banc d'essai de modernité* (Paris: Autrement, 1992), 163. Marrane remained extremely popular throughout his forty-one-year mayorship, garnering some 76 percent of the vote in successive municipal elections.

15 A.M. d'Ivry, *Bulletin municipal officiel d'Ivry* (hereafter *BMO d'Ivry*), special issues n. 18 (Apr. 1929) and 54 (Mar.–Apr. 1935). The *BMO d'Ivry* was published by the *mairie* and distributed free to all residents as a means of keeping the population in close touch with what the new administration was doing for them.

16 Jean Chaumeil, *Venise Gosnat: Un Militant exemplaire du mouvement ouvrier français* (Paris: Editions ouvrières, 1970), 175. The municipality's commitment to providing summer holidays for all young Ivryens must have seemed all the more remarkable to people for whom childhood ended at age thirteen, with the transition from school to factory: "I started work at age thirteen, and like all kids of that age, I was given a workcard. I began working at Vineau's sheet metal shop, on 54 rue Château des Rentiers. My apprenticeship was harsh and exhausting because I had to deliver automobile fenders by wheelbarrow all the way across to the other side of Paris. My work-day began at 5:30 A.M. and often ended at 10 P.M." A.M. d'Ivry, André Nidrecor, Interview 44, 8 Oct. 1981, 1.

17 Interviews conducted by the author at Les Mathes, June, 1998.

18 Scholars of municipal communism in interwar France agree on the important role that networks of sociability and notions of local and regional identity played in the implantation of Communism at the local level. Annie Fourcaut goes so far as to comment that "one could say that Communism in the interwar *banlieues* seemed far more like a form of popular culture than a political opinion." Annie Fourcaut, *Bobigny, banlieue rouge* (Paris: Editions ouvrières, 1986), 16. Michel Hastings and Gérard Noiriel make similar arguments about politics and local popular culture in the cities of Halluin and Longwy. See Michel Hastings, *Halluin-la-rouge, 1919–1939: Aspects d'un communisme identitaire* (Arras: Presses Universitaires de Lille, 1991); and Gérard Noiriel, *Longwy: Immigrés et prolétaires 1880–1980* (Paris: PUF, 1984).

19 The parishes of Ivry-Port and Petit-Ivry sent their children with the *colonie*

organized by Saint-Pierre-et-Saint-Paul. On the first Catholic *colonies* in Ivry, see Eugène Plantet and Arthur Delpy, *Les Colonies de vacances: Organisation et fonctionnement* (Paris: Hachette, 1910), 408.

20   Ivry's first *patronage* dates from about 1885.

21   This numeric equality was unusual, for Catholic parishes generally sent more boys than girls, according to Corinne Hubert, "Demain on part en colo . . ." (Mémoire de maîtrise, Paris VIII, 1986), 51. The gender imbalance probably reflects the Church's overweening concern with shoring up the faith among "de-Christianized" males.

22   A.M. d'Ivry, 6 PER, Abbé Garin, Curé d'Ivry-sur-Seine, *La Belle étoile,* Ivry, 1929, 1–2.

23   The Petits Ivryens à la Campagne continued to function after 1925 as a private program, sending several hundred children to the farms and villages of the Deux-Sèvres each summer until the outbreak of war in 1940. Local industrialists used the *colonie* as a form of social assistance with which they rewarded their most loyal workers.

24   These patrons were generally from wealthier parishes outside Ivry, in Paris or the bourgeois "banlieues vertes."

25   This is four years after taking office. One wonders why the town council waited so long, since relations with the local Catholic hierarchy had been openly hostile from the outset.

26   This was, after all, the golden age of *laïcité* in France (after the 1905 separation and before the Marie and Barangé laws of September 1951), when the republican state refused all support to Catholic educational institutions as a matter of principle.

27   Indeed, prewar Ivry was already famous for its rituals of ardent secularism, the civic baptisms and "red god-parents" that punctuated the rhythm of public rite organized around city hall. In 1906 radical Socialist mayor Jules Coutant went so far as to pass a local ordinance forbidding priests to wear their habits on the streets of the working-class city. This ordinance must later have fallen into desuetude, for the memoirs and oral histories of the interwar years are filled with tales of children chasing after priests in their habits, throwing stones and yelling "Hou, hou, la calotte," while in February 1934, Abbé Lorenzo tangled with a group of demonstrators on a street in Ivry. "They were escorted by a group of young women singing the Internationale. The sight of my habit unleashed a tempest of sarcasm and insult from these girls. A similar scene had unfolded just six days before, with a few minor variations." Archives Départementales du Val-de-Marne (hereafter A.D. 94), 9J Ivry 6C5, Abbé Lorenzo, *Le Lien des aînées,* Feb. 1934, 1.

28   A.M. d'Ivry, Abbé des Graviers, "Eclairez votre lanterne," *Le Courrier du patro,* June 1936. The *Courrier du patro* was founded in 1929 with the

explicit goal of countering Communist propaganda and activity among children.

29 Jean Millet, "En 1939, à quatorze ans, j'entre à la JOC," *Autrement* 8 (1977): 57.

30 *Le Courrier du patro,* 2nd fortnight of July, 1934.

31 Abbé Soutif, *Le Lien des aînées,* 15 July 1933. The JOC (Jeunesse Ouvrière Chrétienne and Jeunesse Ouvrière Chrétienne Féminine) were the Catholic organizations for apprentices and working youth (aged thirteen and up). They blended a profound sense of spiritual mission with militant class-based and syndicalist politics, which often earned them the suspicion of a hierarchy which viewed class conflict as the false and unnecessary creation of contemporary, materialist society. The girls' *patronage* put out two publications each month, the *Lien des aînées,* for those young teenagers who had already made their first communion (at age eleven to twelve), and the *Lien des jeunes,* for those still in catechism.

32 *Le Courrier du patro,* Mar. 1935, 4. As Madeleine Delbrêl later wrote: "To break with the Communist or para-Communist organizations in Ivry was to break with the practical life of the city, it was to become a 'man without a country' at the local level, it was to eliminate two thirds of the normal contact between Christians and non-Christians." Madeleine Delbrêl, *Ville marxiste, terre de mission* (Paris: Editions du Cerf, 1970), 53.

33 By the early 1930s, Ivry's three parishes boasted eight *patronages,* which taken together served over a thousand boys and girls. *Courrier du patro,* Feb. 1932, 696.

34 94 A.D., 9J Ivry 6C3, Supplément, *Courrier du patro,* June 1936, 13.

35 *Courrier du patro,* Feb. 1935, 3.

36 *Bulletin paroissial,* "Les *Colonies de vacances* dans les Alpes," June–July 1923, 203; supplément, *Courrier du patro,* 13. The youngest children were exempted from these chores.

37 "Journal des *colonies de vacances,*" *Bulletin paroissial,* Nov. 1922, 112.

38 "Les *Colonies de vacances* dans les Alpes," *Bulletin paroissial,* June–July 1923, 202.

39 A.M. d'Ivry, 6 PER, Abbé Garin, Curé d'Ivry-sur-Seine, *La Belle étoile,* Ivry, 1929, 5.

40 A.D. 94 9J Thiais 10 C 1, "La colonie Sainte-Thérèse à Saint-Servan de Bretagne," *L'Essor du Thiais,* Oct.–Nov. 1933, 11.

41 Supplément, *Courrier du patro,* 23.

42 Ibid., 7.

43 A.M. de Suresnes, "Souvenirs de Vacances," *Bulletin mensuel,* Notre-Dame-de-la-Salette, Suresnes, Sept. 1913, 3.

44 *Le Lien des aînées,* article by E. Travert, Guide *cheftaine,* June 1933.

45 *Bulletin paroissial,* "Réponses . . . sans Questions," Jan. 1933, 861. The puta-

tive question in this case was: "Scouting is good for boys, but is it good for girls? What does our curé think?"

46 Marie-Thérèse Chéroutre and Gérard Cholvy, eds., *Scoutisme féminin et promotion féminin, 1920–1990* (Paris: Les Guides de France, 1990). See also Marie-Thérèse Chéroutre, "Les Guides de France: Un projet chrétien d'éducation des filles," in Chéroutre and Cholvy, eds., *Le Scoutisme: Quel type d'hommes, quel type de femmes? Quel type de chrétiens?* (Paris: Editions du Cerf, 1994), 65–111.

47 Aline Coutrot, "La Naissance des Guides de France," in Françoise Mayeur and Jacques Gadille, *Education et images de la femme chrétienne en France* (Lyon: Editions l'Hermès, 1980), 183.

48 *Bulletin paroissial,* E. Travert, "Etre prête," Sept.–Oct. 1932, 803. Four years later, Abbé Lorenzo (who organized the activities and study circles at the girls' *patronage*) commented approvingly on this "virilizing" tendency among modern girls: "Bit by bit, we are witnessing the appearance of a modern Catholic girl. There is nothing languid or vaporous about her; she knows how to speak frankly, and to see things for what they are. She prefers action to dreams, and does not shrink in the face of sports, nor from the open road. She cultivates her intelligence and makes use of the study circles, and sometimes shows a greater taste for cultivating the spirit than boys of her own age. She has masculinized herself, but remains profoundly a woman. She dresses well—neither overly pious nor a scatterbrained fashionplate. She dreams of marriage and motherhood, and understands that she must be ready to greet these terrible joys. She retains the reserve of her sex and, without being prudish, she is so pure that she naturally commands respect. A genuine young girl with a steady gaze and a firm handshake is a noble human achievement." *Le Lien des aînées,* June 1936, 10.

49 Marrane and his deputies created the OVPE in order to protect children's vacations from the winds of political fortune. Hence, even if the right were to regain city hall, the Communist program could continue to send Ivry's children on holiday each summer. In addition, this separate organization made the OVPE eligible for state and departmental funds, under the Associations Law of 1901.

50 The staff included two men, three women, and a nurse, with a "master swimmer" hired to watch over the sea-bath.

51 *BMO d'Ivry* 2 (1 Oct. 1926): 46.

52 A.M. d'Ivry, *Association pour l'histoire d'Ivry,* Marius Prunières, Interview 3, 1980, 2.

53 The OVPE sent many children free of charge, and especially the children of the unemployed. (During the Depression, local unemployment rose as high as 16 percent, in 1938.)

54 A.M. d'Ivry, Br 451, Venise Gosnat, "Villanous," typescript account of the *colonie* at Les Mathes in 1948, written by the director, 1.

55 A.M. d'Ivry, *Le Travailleur* 68 (11 Aug. 1934): 3. This same reporter, Henri Biron, had earlier noted with some glee that the republican *colonie* (the Little Ivryens) had to beef up their contingents with children from the neighboring (and less proletarian) towns of Charenton and Courbevoie, in order to hide the feeble number of young Ivryens that these "enemies of the workers" had attracted. *Le Travailleur* 67 (4 Aug. 1934): 3.

56 The municipal *colonie* was financed through a combination of municipal and departmental funds, supplemented by whatever contribution the parents could muster, and, finally, the profits of the annual kermesse, held each June for the benefit of Les Mathes (about 25 percent of the *colonie* expenses were met by the kermesse profits alone).

57 A.M. d'Ivry, Vital Marques, Interview 103-104-105, 2-4.

58 Denis Bordat, *Les C.E.M.E.A., qu'est-ce que c'est?* (Paris: Maspéro, 1976), 14-15.

59 Vital Marques, Interview 103-104-105, 3.

60 Bordat, *Les C.E.M.E.A.,* 15.

61 Ibid., 15-16.

62 The *Cahier des surveillants* from the summer of 1952 recounts an incident in which one *moniteur* slapped another who had just insulted him, suggesting that *moniteurs* did not always take their disputes to the director's office. A.M. d'Ivry, 22Z, *Cahier des surveillants,* summer 1952, 65.

63 For details see the minutes of the June 1930 meeting of the OVPE, A.M. d'Ivry, 22 Z 11, Conseil d'administration, Procès-verbaux, 1926-76.

64 A.M. d'Ivry, *Association pour l'histoire d'Ivry,* Lucien Laborie, Interview 27, 8 July 1981, 15. Between 1949 and 1967, Laborie served first as *moniteur* (1949-52), then assistant director (1952-57), and, finally, director of Les Mathes (1957-67).

65 *BMO d'Ivry,* July 1931, 178; *BMO d'Ivry,* Oct. 1947, 7; *BMO d'Ivry,* Nov. 1949, 8.

66 A.M. d'Ivry, 22 Z 10, "Livres de bords de la *colonie,* 1949-53," Les Mathes, 1949, joint "livre de bords" kept by the *équipe des Bouchers* and the *équipe des Forgerons* (boys aged eleven to twelve), entries for 15 and 17 August 1949. The match of *ballon prisonnier* on 17 August set boys of eleven to twelve against older girls of fourteen to fifteen, "who naturally won the game," wrote the young male author of that day's entry in the collective journal, "but we defended ourselves very well." The *colonie* staff may have felt that giving the girls an age advantage was one way to make up for differences in strength, and so roughly equalize the teams.

67 Interview with Mme Clerville, A.M. d'Ivry, *Association pour l'histoire d'Ivry,* Clerville Interview, 13. The two sections (*masculine* and *féminine*)

were formed at the same time, ca. 1918–19. Sport held an important place in interwar municipal Communism in general (building the future generation), and the fact that Ivry's mayor, Georges Marrane, was an avid *footballeur* and militant in the Communist Fédération Sportive et Gymnastique du Travail (of which he became president in 1934) doubtless contributed to expanding the local cult of sport.

68   "Le Sport féminin considéré comme une forme d'assistance sociale," *BMO d'Ivry,* Feb.–Mar. 1929, 8. The article also points out how the regime of outdoor sport proposed — rhythmic dancing, javelin, high-jump, games, basketball, tennis, swimming — would develop women's "strength, grace, and flexibility," and so promote the health of France's future mothers.

69   *Bulletin municipal officiel de Villejuif,* Mar. 1934, 20. "A la *colonie* de Bernadoux." See also Gosnat, "Villanous," 23: "Authority . . . presupposes in all things the free consent of the child, and the absence of constraint and punishment. Hierarchical authority must therefore give way to moral authority."

70   *BMO d'Ivry* 50 (July 1934): 7.

71   Edwin Hoernle, *Manual for Leaders of Children's Groups* (Berlin, n.d. [ca. 1924]), 6 and 19.

72   Martin Gleisner, "Comment transformer les grands jeux en jeux collectifs," *L'Aide: Bulletin mensuel des Amis de l'Enfance Ouvrière,* Mar. 1937, 3.

73   Kurt Loewenstein, cited in Georges Monnet, "Cours de Loewenstein," *L'Aide: Bulletin mensuel des Amis de l'Enfance Ouvrière,* Dec. 1933, 16. For analogous conceptions of the Catholic *colonie* organized as one long game, "the game of the City of God," see Abbé Fillère, *La Cité paroissiale des jeunes,* Rapport présenté au Congrès de l'Union des Oeuvres Catholiques Ouvrières, Rennes, 1934.

74   The expression "le monde du flirt bourgeois" is taken from the article "Former des couples ou non," in *L'Aide: Bulletin mensuel des Amis de l'Enfance Ouvrière de France,* Apr. 1936, 10–12.

75   The partisans of a more direct and interventionist management of the children's groups thus strove to increase political conformity while maintaining a spirit of activism, which was always preferable to a mere passive transmission of orders. This tendency in Communist pedagogy emerged in the late 1920s, with the declaration by the Sixth Congress of the Communist International (in the summer of 1927) that Europe, having gone through a "First Period" of revolution (1917–23) and a "Second Period" of capitalist stabilization (1923–27) was now entering into a "Third Period" of capitalist crisis, with escalating international tension and a concomitant radicalization of revolutionary militancy among the masses. The International concluded that Communist parties across Europe had to break with the reformist circles of social democracy (now labeled "social fascism," the last bastion of capitalist defense) and prepare the intensified struggle that

would at last bring the system to its knees. The French Communist Party's loyal adoption of such hard-line tactics against the non-Communist left eliminated or alienated many of the libertarian and democratic revolutionary tendencies that had been attracted to the early Soviet regime, and so further homogenized the party's cultural politics.

76 *BMO d'Ivry,* July 1934, 7.

77 Kurt Loewenstein, cited in Georges Monnet, "Cours de Loewenstein," *L'Aide: Bulletin mensuel des Amis de l'Enfance Ouvrière,* 1 Dec. 1933 and Jan. 1934.

78 For a good example of "previous" pedagogy, see Emile Durkheim, *L'Education morale* (Paris: Alcan, 1926).

79 "Livres de bords de la colonie, 1949–53," Les Mathes, 1949, joint "livre de bords" kept by the *équipe des Bouchers* and the *équipe des Forgerons,* 19 Aug. 1949. The *étude du milieu* was drawn directly from the "pédagogie populaire" of Célestin Freinet.

80 "Livres de bords de la *colonie,* 1949–53," livre de bords de Clapet, 1951. The focus of the *équipes* at Les Mathes on semirural and archaic occupations is interesting. Perhaps they were intended to serve as examples of the "bad old days" of nineteenth-century capitalism.

81 Ibid. See A.M. d'Ivry, 22Z/6, dossier "Union des Vaillants et Vaillantes," 1952, "Le Chant," pt. 1, which celebrates the role of song in binding social movements while cautioning *moniteurs* against those mass-market songs "that are destined to steal from the child his impulse to struggle against those who exploit him." Ibid., 3. See also 22Z/6, dossier "Union des Vaillants et Vaillantes," 1952, "Réunion sur le chant," handwritten notes, n.d.

82 Gosnat, "Villanous," 23.

83 While the republic of Villanous clearly bore a strong resemblance to the Socialist *républiques enfantines* of the Faucons Rouges, the Communist pedagogues of Ivry never mentioned these recent Socialist predecessors, but rather traced the pedagogy of their *colonie* back to their common Bolshevik ancestor, soviet pedagogue Pistrak.

84 Gosnat's account of the first child republic at Les Mathes, "Villanous," stresses the choice of a political form, the town council, that would be familiar to the children, for each of them would have seen the mayor and his adjuncts distributing prizes at the close of school each summer. "Villanous," 11.

85 Gosnat, "Villanous," 19–20.

86 Ibid., 21.

87 Interview with the author, 18 June 1998, Ivry-sur-Seine. This is a most faithful translation of Pistrak's pedagogical prescription that "the school is not a bell-jar," found in Pistrak, *Les Problèmes fondamentaux de l'école du travail* (Paris: Desclée de Brouwer, 1973), 27.

88 Interview with the author, 18 June 1998, Ivry-sur-Seine. Created in 1948 in order to assure pedagogical continuity in the *colonie,* the *amicale* grouped all young adults who worked for the city's child-care centers (Les Mathes, and the municipal *patronage*) in an organization that combined militant activism "in defense of childhood" with intensive pedagogical discussion (based on lectures and on participants' practical experiences working with children) and a certain amount of socializing as well (the *amicale* met every Friday night, and the evening's activities often terminated in a small "pot").

89 A.M. d'Ivry, Denis Bordat, Interview 73, 18 Apr. 1982, 1.

90 Secrétariat de la Jeunesse, letter to Georges Marrane, 10 July 1951, quoted in the minutes of the Conseil Général de la Seine's meeting of 13–14 July 1951, reprinted in the *BMO d'Ivry,* 28 July 1951, 486.

91 Secrétariat de la Jeunesse, letter to Georges Marrane, 27 June 1951, quoted in the minutes of the Conseil Général de la Seine, meeting of 13–14 July 1951, 486. Departmental and state subventions to the *colonies* were normally assessed and paid out during the winter after the *colonie* in question had taken place.

92 Conseil Général de la Seine, meeting of 13–14 July 1951, 486. The seminarian he referred to was probably worker-priest Maurice Ducreux, who had served as *moniteur* at Les Mathes since 1949.

93 Marrane before the Conseil Général de la Seine, meeting of 13–14 July 1951, 486.

94 Secrétariat de la Jeunesse, letter to Georges Marrane, 27 June 1951, quoted in the minutes of the Conseil Général de la Seine, meeting of 13–14 July 1951, 486.

95 Marrane before the Conseil Général de la Seine, meeting of 13–14 July 1951, 486, 487.

96 Circulaire Morice, issued 29 June 1951 (though it was not sent out to the various mayors until 22 August 1951), which threatened to prevent "certain" (Communist) *colonies* from opening or to shut others down, "by force if necessary." Cited in A.M. d'Ivry, 22Z, dossier "Rapports V.P.E., 1952," Waldeck l'Huillier and H. Jambon, "Rapport sur les colonies de vacances à la suite des visites effectuées de 4 au 12 août 1952," typescript, 5. The PCF "Rapport sur les colonies" was directed explicitly at the Communist municipalities around Paris, urging them to put their respective houses in order so that they might avoid closure.

97 Conseil Général de la Seine, meeting of 13–14 July 1951, 487. It was common practice in red *colonies* to give the tents and dormitories names of militants "beloved by the working class." A.M. d'Ivry, 22Z/6, dossier "Divers," Réunion amicale des élus, 8 Mar. 1952, handwritten notes on the Rapport Pierrette Petitot, 2.

98 PCF *conseillère* Pierrette Petitot, speaking on behalf of the Commission

Mixte de la Famille et de la Population. Conseil Général de la Seine, meeting of 13–14 July 1951, 485. *Colonies de vacances* were, in Petitot's view, the sole public institution capable of providing real assistance in the struggle to improve children's health during the difficult years of inflation and ongoing food shortage that followed the war, and she pressed vehemently for an increase in the national and departmental subventions to the *colonies*. The national subvention had already fallen to the point where it was covering only 6.5 percent of the *colonies'* costs (though as recently as 1949 this subvention had been closer to 50 percent, according to Jean Houssaye, *Aujourd'hui les centres de vacances* [Vigneaux: Editions Matrices, 1991], 155–56). The municipalities were picking up the slack, covering as much as 50–60 percent of their *colonies'* budgets, but in a period of lagging wages, high prices, and persistent food shortage, the demand for the *colonies* was greater than ever, and municipal resources were sorely stretched. Nonetheless, Petitot's arguments failed, for the state had already begun channeling its funds toward the training centers (UFOVAL, JPA, CEMEA), rather than to individual *oeuvres de colonies. Départements,* municipalities, and parents thus continued to carry the cost of sending their children *en colonie.* This may explain the sudden surge (1950–51) in the numbers of children sent to the *colonies* of the *comités d'entreprises,* which often sent children for free. (l'Huillier and Jambon, "Rapport sur les colonies de vacances," 3).

99 To my knowledge, no such closures were in fact ever implemented. "Rapport sur les colonies de vacances." The authors visited the *colonies* of seventeen *banlieues* (Ivry among them), the twentieth arrondissement, and the Syndicat des Métaux's Château de Vouzeron.

100 Ibid., 5, emphasis original.

101 Ibid., 6, emphasis original.

102 "Les organisations d'enfants. II — La presse enfantine et les organisations prolétariennes d'enfants," *Cahiers de contre-enseignement prolétarien,* Sept. 1933, esp. 8.

103 l'Huillier and Jambon, "Rapport sur les colonies de vacances," 6. UJRF was the Union des Jeunes Républicains de France, UJFF was the Union des Jeunes Filles de France.

104 Ibid., 7.

105 A.M. d'Ivry, 22Z/6, dossier "Exposition de l'Enfance," "Rapport sur les travaux de la Commission," handwritten notes from the 25 October 1951 meeting, 6 and 4. See also A.M. d'Ivry, 22Z/6, dossier "Discussions à l'Amicale, 1952–60," "Rôle sociale de la colonie," handwritten notes, 4 pp. During the cold war, the "social role of the *colonie*" was a way to talk about the role of *moniteurs* in orienting children toward a life of political activism.

106 Ibid., "Rôle sociale de la colonie," 2.

107   A.M. d'Ivry, 22Z/6, dossier "Divers," "Réunion amicale des élus," 8 Mar.
      1952, handwritten notes on the Rapport Pierrette Petitot, 2.

108   In practice this meant a return to a round of sports competitions, dramatic
      games, and *grands jeux* in which the comic-book characters of the "Pen-
      sion Radicelle" from *Vaillants* found themselves up against a sinister team
      of Super-Boy, Tarzan, and other degenerate American imports. See A.M.
      d'Ivry, 22Z, *Cahier des surveillants,* 1952, 79 ff. for an account of the *grand
      jeu "Vaillant* versus the unhealthy comics." The game lasted for about a
      week, and featured numerous opportunities for various *moniteurs* (who of
      course played the bad guys) to repent by dressing up in silly outfits (e.g.,
      with their shirts and shorts on backwards) and clowning about for the
      amusement of the children.

109   "Rôle sociale de la colonie," 3–4.

110   "Réunion amicale des élus," 3.

111   A.M. d'Ivry, 2R3, dossier "Bilans, 1954–55–58"; "Rapport du Comrade
      Laluque sur la colonie des Mathes 1955," 1. See also A.M. d'Ivry, 2R3,
      dossier "V.P.E., Conseil d'Administration, 1959–60, Colonie des Mathes,
      Extraits Rapport R. Laluque," 25 Jan. 1959, 1. In 1981, Lucien Laborie
      remarked that the percentage of working-class *moniteurs* at Les Mathes
      had fallen from 75–80 percent in the mid-1930s to 70–72 percent by the
      early 1980s (which figures reflected the social composition of Ivry itself,
      he added). Lucien Laborie, Interview 27, 8 July 1981, 14.

112   A.M. d'Ivry, 22Z/6, dossier "V.P.E. Rapports, 1951–2," "Rapport du Pierre
      Feltz, Responsable du Camp 'Valmy,' Colonie des Mathes, 1952," 2, 9–10.

113   l'Huillier and Jambon, "Rapport sur les colonies de vacances," 7.

114   See the *Cahier des surveillants,* 1952, 81–82 for an account of the ceremony,
      which was made up of the same kinds of poems and songs invoking self-
      less militants and young martyred heroines that had constituted the peda-
      gogical structure of the *colonie* in its earlier incarnation as the republic of
      Villanous.

115   Lucien Laborie, interview, 1981, 17.

116   Ibid.

117   Lucien Laborie, interview with the author, June, 1998.

118   Jean Piaget, *La Formation du symbole chez l'enfant: Imitation, jeu et rêve,
      image et représentation* (Neuchâtel: Delchaux et Niestlé, 1970), pt. 2, chaps.
      4–7. See also Piaget, *Le Jugement moral chez l'enfant* (Paris: PUF, 1969).
      Donald Winnicott would later describe this space as a "neutral zone"
      which affords the child the opportunity for "formless experience, and for
      creative impulses, motor and sensory, which are the stuff of playing. And
      on the basis of playing is built the whole of man's experiential existence . . .
      We experience life in the area of transitional phenomena, in the exciting
      interweave of subjectivity and objective observation, and in an area that
      is intermediate between the inner reality of the individual and the shared

reality of the world that is external to individuals." From D. W. Winnicott, "Playing: The Search for the Self," reprinted in Winnicott, *Playing and Reality* (London: Tavistock, 1971), 64.

119 Lucien Laborie, Interview 27, 8 July 1981, 24–25.

120 Anna Davin, *Growing Up Poor: Home, School, and Street in London, 1870–1914* (London: Oram Rivers Press, 1996), 199–200.

121 A.M. d'Ivry, 22 Z, Amicale des Moniteurs, compte rendu de la réunion de 11 Dec. 1952.

122 Sylvie Chaperon, *Les Années Beauvoir, 1945–1970* (Paris: Fayard, 2000), 65.

123 Jean-Noël Luc, *L'Invention du jeune enfant au XIXe siècle: De la salle d'asile à l'école maternelle* (Paris: Belin, 1997).

Epilogue

1 From a municipal circular for Drancy-Bobigny "Vacances 76," cited in Henri Collet, "Action municipale et loisirs," *Cahiers de l'animation* 21 (3d trimester, 1978): 5. See also Jean Planchon, *Le Rhythme journalier de la vie des enfants à la colonie de vacances* (Grenoble, Doctorat d'Université, 1960), esp. 11. At the dawn of the twenty-first century, the rhetoric had hardly shifted: "Today, with the disappearance of boarding schools and military service, the *centre de vacances* remains the only site where the child can confront difference, living on a daily basis with other children in an environment that is, moreover, educational . . . Every child needs a social world, and some time independent of both school and family during which he can construct himself . . . by integration into a little society of comrades his own age. One never forgets the time he spent in the *colo*. This experience, which so many of us have lived, constructed in each of us that developing individual whom our parents greeted at the return with the words 'my, how you've grown!' " Daniel Séguret and Michel Claeyssen, national delegate and president (respectively) of the Fédération Générale des Associations des Pupilles de l'Enseignement Publique, interview by Carine Hahn, "Les Colos c'est unique," *Valeurs mutualistes* 212 (July 2001): 8. Séguret also discussed the ongoing decline in the *colonies,* which he attributes to the lack of state funding and to the recent "problem" of pedophilia, which had "degraded the *colonies'* image." Ibid., 7.

2 Philippe Rey-Herme, *La Colonie de vacances hier et aujourd'hui* (Paris: Editions Cap, 1955), 107–8.

3 After all, as Jean Houssaye put it, "to leave home is to grow up a bit." Jean Houssaye, *Aujourd'hui les centres de vacances* (Vigneux: Editions Matrices, 1991), 17. The author went on to note that parents found their children more self-reliant, outgoing, and easy-going ("less marked by emotional problems") after they'd spent a summer *en colonie*. Ibid., 18.

4   See Jacques Godard, *Nos enfants vont en colonie* (Paris: Editions Néret, 1959), 2: "It is better that children live in organized groups, led by trained *moniteurs,* rather than hanging about in the streets or running to the cinema."

5   Jean Houssaye, *Le Livre des colos: Histoire et évolution des centres de vacances pour enfants* (Paris: La Documentation Française, 1989), and Houssaye, *Un Avenir pour les colonies de vacances* (Paris: Les Editions ouvrières, 1977), 5. See also Robert Penin, "Les Colonies de vacances," *Ecole et socialisme* 7, no. 1 (July 1977): 18.

6   Report by M. A. Lavy, cited in L. Stehelin, *Essais de socialisme municipale* (Thèse de droit, Paris, 1901), 34. See also Marc Lazar, "La République à l'épreuve du social," in Marc Sadoun, ed., *La Démocratie en France, tome 2: Limites* (Paris: Gallimard, 2000), 309–406, which underscores the importance of the republican rooting of social aspirations in the public school: a secular, competitive, but also egalitarian institution intended to shape and educate a rational citizenry.

7   The *comités d'entreprises* were created after the Liberation in response to people's hopes for a broader transformation of social and economic life in postwar France. They are company-based welfare committees run by workers' delegates, and one of their most visible activities was sending workers' children *en colonie,* either with the local municipal program or with the company's own organization.

8   See Adrien Veber, *Le Socialisme municipal* (Paris: V. Giard and E. Brière, 1908), for a clear exposition of the steps by which municipal socialists pressed the logic of republican solidarity to its fullest extent, striving to create a shadow of the "social republic" on the local level.

9   Charity Organisation Society, *The Better Way of Assisting School Children* (1893), 27, cited in J. S. Hurt, *Elementary Schooling and the Working Classes, 1860–1918* (London: Routledge, 1979), 111. Hurt notes that school managers and teachers were quite prepared to distribute food, shoes, and clothing so that the children would pay attention in school. But the COS consistently opposed such action for fear that it would undermine parental, and especially paternal, responsibility.

10 Ibid., 111.

11 British advocates of school feeding were well aware of the French advance in this realm. See Mildred E. Bulkley, *The Feeding of Schoolchildren* (London: G. Bell and Sons, 1914), which recounts with envy the creation of the *caisses des écoles,* as well as the precocious arrival (1887) of systematic medical inspection in French primary schools. On the struggles around school meals, see Keith Laybourn, "The Issue of School Feeding in Bradford, 1904–1907," *Journal of Educational Administration and History* 14, no. 2 (July 1982): 30–39; and Bentley Gilbert, *The Evolution of National*

Insurance in Britain: The Origins of the Welfare State (London: Michael Joseph, 1966).

12 On the fin-de-siècle shift in the public valorization of children, see Viviana Zelizer, *Pricing the Priceless Child: The Changing Social Value of Children* (New York: Basic Books, 1985), which argues that in the United States the public value of children rose dramatically over the period 1870–1930. Precisely at the moment that their market value plummeted, thanks to obligatory schooling and labor laws that banned children from the workplace, children became "emotionally priceless," not only to their families but to a larger national community that was now investing in their education and training. Carolyn Steedman has described an analogous shift in fin-de-siècle England, with Independent Labour Party educator Margaret McMillan spearheading the efflorescence of such sentiments on the left. See *Childhood, Culture, and Class in Britain: Margaret McMillan, 1860–1931* (New Brunswick: Rutgers, 1990). For comparable developments in France, see Antoine Prost, *Histoire de la vie privée*, vol. 5 (Paris: Seuil, 1987), and Colin Heywood, *Childhood in Nineteenth-Century France: Work, Health, and Education among the "Classes Populaires"* (Cambridge: Cambridge University Press, 1988).

13 Rachel Fuchs and Sylvia Schafer both detect important changes in public assistance to orphaned and abandoned children in late-nineteenth-century France, especially with the state's assumption of a directly parental role vis-à-vis "morally abandoned" children. Rachel Fuchs, *Abandoned Children: Foundlings and Child Welfare in Nineteenth-Century France* (Albany: SUNY Press, 1984), and Sylvia Schafer, *Children in Moral Danger and the Problem of Government in Third Republic France* (Princeton: Princeton University Press, 1997).

14 Houssaye, *Aujourd'hui*, 15. The statistics he gives here are based on survey data collected by the SOFRES in 1982–83, cited in SOFCO, *Les Centres de vacances pour enfants: Enquête sur la clientèle actuelle et potentielle* (Paris: SOFRES, 1983).

15 Houssaye, *Aujourd'hui*, 16.

16 Penin, "Les Colonies de vacances," 18.

17 Ibid., 18.

18 Leaving aside the dispossessed 20 percent, who could not afford to leave at all. Ibid., 18.

19 Cited in Houssaye, *Aujourd'hui*, 56. The school half-holiday was moved from Thursday to Wednesday afternoons in the late 1950s.

20 By the 1960s, the term *animateurs* was starting to replace *moniteurs* in *colonies* and *centres de vacances* across France.

21 Hence the particular activities (sailing, horseback riding, camping) matter less than the personal development of the child, her capacity to take

on greater responsibility for herself, a development which is seen to owe primarily to the quality of the *animateur*. Taken from a 1985 report by the EDF-GDF *comité d'entreprise* on its *colonies,* cited in Houssaye, *Aujourd'hui,* 21.

22 The numbers of children and adolescents sent *en colonie* thus peaked at 1.4 million in the mid-1960s and remained fairly steady at 1.26 to 1.30 million until the very end of the decade, at which point they began to fall off gently. It was only in the mid-1980s that the numbers fell just below one million. See Houssaye, *Aujourd'hui,* especially 130–31 for details.

23 SOFCO, *Les Centres de vacances pour enfants,* cited in Houssaye, *Aujourd'hui,* 19. This same survey revealed that 46 percent of parents who continued to send their children *en colonie* believed that their children would prefer to spend their holidays otherwise, but sent them anyway, out of the conviction that it would benefit them educationally.

24 Mark Lilla, "Night Thoughts," *New York Review of Books,* 30 Nov. 2000, 20.

SELECT BIBLIOGRAPHY

PRIMARY SOURCES

Archives

Archives Municipales d'Ivry-sur-Seine

Series D: Deliberations of the Municipal Council, 1915–1960
Association pour l'histoire d'Ivry (Interviews with Ivryens covering the period
    1900–1970, conducted in 1980–82 under the direction of retired school-
    teacher and PCF militant Fernand Leriche)
Series BR: A collection of pamphlets, brochures, and unpublished manu-
    scripts, including the annual reports of the Petits Ivryens à la Campagne for
    1924, 1931, and 1936, and Venise Gosnat's unpublished report from the 1948
    colonie, "Villanous."
Series PER: A collection of periodicals and local publications, including the
    Bulletin paroissial d'Ivry-Centre.
Series 5 Fi: Photographs of Ivry and its *colonie de vacances*
Series 2R3: *La colonie scolaire,* 1940–45
Series 22 Z: "Vacances Populaires Enfantines" (18 boxes containing the
    records of the Oeuvre des Vacances Populaires Enfantines from 1925
    through 1976)
22 Z 1–2: Notes and reports from the Amicale des Moniteurs, 1949–61
22 Z 3: Construction at Les Mathes, 1936–38
22 Z 4: Reports and statistics from the Les Mathes *colonie,* 1959–66
22 Z 5: Budget and blueprints for construction at Les Mathes, 1928–43
22 Z 6–7: OVPE, notes, reports, and correspondence
22 Z 8–9: Les Mathes, 1949
22 Z 10: *Livres de bords* from the *colonie,* 1949–53; *Cahier des surveillants,* 1952
22 Z 11: Conseil d'administration de l'OVPE, *procès-verbaux,* 1926–76
22 Z 12–18: Material on the *colonies* at Theys, Le Bréau, and Héry-sur-Ugine
Bulletin municipal officiel d'Ivry
Le Travailleur de la banlieue sud

Archives Municipal de Suresnes

Series D: Deliberations of the Municipal Council, 1915–60; section L: Com-
    missions scolaires, folder 361, *colonies de vacances,* 1915–18

Series 26R: *Colonie municipale, 1919–31*
Series 27R: *Colonie municipale, 1932–39*
Series 28R: *Colonie municipale, 1940–45*
Series 29R: Budgets and statistics for the *colonie municipale, 1919–45*
Series 77R: *Colonie municipale de Bourdelas, 1945–54*
Series H 32: Wartime evacuation of children from Suresnes to refugee centers at Lanare, Vibraye, and St-Maixent (Sarthe), 1943–45
Series H 36: Wartime evacuation of children from Suresnes to refugee centers at Lanare, Vibraye, and St-Maixent (Sarthe), 1940–42
Le Suresnois

Archives Départementales du Val-de-Marne

Series 9J Ivry: Parish archives for Ivry-Centre, Ivry-Port, and Petit-Ivry

Bibliothèque Marguerite Durand

Dossier of press clippings on the *colonies de vacances, 1900–1940*

Le Musée Social

Collection of pamphlets, brochures, and reports on the national *colonie de vacances* movement, including the reports from the interwar meetings of the Congrès Nationaux des Colonies de Vacances

Bibliothèque Historique de la Ville de Paris

Collection of reports from the *colonies scolaires* of Paris, 1890–1914

Newspapers and Periodicals

L'Aide: Bulletin mensuel des Amis de l'Enfance Ouvrière de France
Air et soleil
Bulletin communiste
Bulletin de l'Association des Anciens Elèves de l'Ecole de Saint-Sulpice
Bulletin de la ruche
Bulletin de la Société Historique et Artistique de Suresnes
Bulletin de la Société de Saint-Vincent-de-Paul
Bulletin de l'Union Nationale des Colonies de Vacances et Oeuvres de Grand Air
Bulletin mensuel, Notre-Dame-de-la-Salette
Bulletin municipal officiel d'Ivry-sur-Seine

Bulletin municipal officiel de Villejuif
Bulletin paroissal d'Ivry-Centre
Cahiers de l'animation
Cahiers de bolchevisme
Cahiers de contre-enseignement
  prolétarien
Le Chef
Le Courrier du patro
Ecole et socialisme
L'Educateur prolétarien
Educateurs
L'Essor du Thiais
Le Front rouge
L'Hygiène par l'exemple
L'Idéal du foyer: Revue littéraire,
  artistique, economique et sociale de
  la famille
L'Information municipale
La Jeunesse par la joie
Le Lien, édition des aînées
Le Lien, édition des jeunes
Le Mouvement sanitaire
Les Nouvelles du Patronage Olier

Le Phare de Royan
Regards
Revue des patronages
Revue Médico-sociale et de la
  protection de l'enfance
Revue pédagogique
Saines vacances, Revue des patronages
  et des colonies de vacances
Le Suresnois
Le Temps
Le Travailleur de la banlieue sud
L'Univers
Urbanisme, special issue on Suresnes,
  January 1935
Valeurs mutualistes
Vers l'éducation nouvelle
La Vie au patronage, édition des filles
La Vie au patronage, édition des
  garçons
La Vie heureuse
Vous et vos enfants (supplement to the
  Bulletin paroissal d'Ivry-Centre)

Books and Articles

Administration Générale de l'Assistance Publique. Les Enfants assistés pupilles de la Département de la Seine. Montévrain: Ecole d'Alembert, n.d. (ca. 1930).

Armand-Delille, P. F., and Ch. Lestocquoy. "Le placement familial permanent dans la campagne." In Congrès national des colonies de vacances et oeuvres de plein air. St-Etienne, 1925.

Beauvisage, Dr. "Modes de placement." In Congrès national des colonies de vacances, ed. F. Gibon. Paris, 1910.

———. "Les Oeuvres d'assistance scolaire et les colonies de vacances de la région lyonnaise." In Congrès de l'Association Française pour le Développement des Sciences. Lyon, 1906.

Bion, Wilhelm. Les Colonies de vacances: Mémoire historique et statistique. Paris: Delgrave, 1887.

Blin, Ernest. "La Population dans le canton de Saint-Pierre-le-Moûtier." Paris et Nevers: Editions de la Revue du Centre, 1929.

Bouchet, Henri. Le Scoutisme: Bases psychologiques; Méthodes et rites. Paris: Alcan, 1933.

Bouchet, Henri. *Le Scoutisme et l'individualitè.* Paris: Alcan, 1933.

Boulonnois, Louis. "Histoire et systématique des fonctions de l'assistance scolaire." *Journées médico-sociales de l'enfance d'âge scolaire,* 4–6 April 1935, Paris.

———. *La Municipalité en service social: L'oeuvre de M. Henri Sellier à Suresnes.* Paris: Berger-Levrault, 1938.

Bourreau, Léa. "Le Travail parmi les enfants." *Cahiers de bolchevisme,* November 1926.

Brémond, Arnold. *Une Explication du monde ouvrier: Enquête d'un étudiant ouvrier dans la banlieue parisienne.* St-Etienne: Revue du christianisme social, 1927.

Brouet, V. "Les Colonies scolaires de la ville de Paris." *Revue pédagogique,* 15 January 1902.

Bruneau, Abbé Henry. "L'Oeuvre des Saines Vacances (Douvaine)." *Bulletin de l'Association des Anciens Elèves de l'Ecole de Saint-Sulpice,* 1902.

Caisse des Ecoles du Ve arr't. *La Colonie scolaire du Ve arrondissement, 1892.* Paris, 1893.

Caisse des écoles du VIII arr't. *Compte rendu de la 17e assemblée générale de la Caisse des Ecoles du VIIIe arrondissement: Colonie et voyages scolaires de 1889.* Paris, 1889.

Caisse des écoles, VIIIe arr't. *Compte rendu de la 39e assemblée générale.* Paris, 1911.

Caisse des écoles du XIe arr't. *La Colonie scolaire de Mandres-sur-Vair en 1889.* Paris, 1889.

Cambéssèdes, H., and J. Boyer. *Hygiène des institutions de plein air.* Paris: J.-B. Baillière et fils, 1945.

Centre de formation des moniteurs et de cadres des loisirs éducatifs. *La Colonie de vacances éducative.* Paris: Editions sociales françaises, 1942.

Chardavoine, Jean. "La Caisse des écoles." *L'Information municipale* 12 (December 1937): 8.

Le Comité Parisien des colonies de vacances. "Les Colonies de vacances à Paris." *Revue pédagogique,* 15 June 1887.

Comte, Louis. *L'Oeuvre des Enfants à la Montagne.* Saint-Etienne: Relèvement social, 1902.

Congrès international des colonies de vacances, Paris. Paris: Le Mouvement Sanitaire, 1937.

Congrès national des colonies de vacances, Pau. Paris: Le Mouvement Sanitaire, 1929.

Congrès national des colonies de vacances, Reims. Paris: Le Mouvement Sanitaire, 1927.

Congrès national des colonies de vacances, Saint-Etienne. Paris: Le Mouvement Sanitaire, 1925.

Congrès national des colonies de vacances, Strasbourg. Paris: Imprimerie Alsaci-
enne, 1923.

Conlombant, Louis. *Manuel du surveillant (à lire et à méditer avant le dé-
part et à relire pendant le séjour).* Paris: Oeuvre parisienne des Enfants à la
Montagne, 1931.

———. "Placement familial dans les colonies de vacances." *Revue médico-
sociale et de la protection de l'enfance* 6, no. 4 (1938).

Copin-Albincelli, Paul. "La Question des boy-scouts ou éclaireurs en France."
La Renaissance française, 1913.

Cottinet, Edmond. *La Colonie scolaire du IXe arrondissement.* Report to the
Caisse des Ecoles. Paris: Imprimerie Chaix, 1883.

———. *La Colonie scolaire du IXe arrondissement, rapport, 1884.* Paris: Imprimerie Chaix, 1885.

———. *La Colonie scolaire du IXe arrondissement, rapport, 1885.* Paris: Imprimerie Chaix, 1886.

———. *Les Colonies de vacances de la ville de Paris en 1887.* Paris: Delgrave, 1888.

———. *Les Colonies de vacances en France et à l'étranger.* Mémoires du Musée
Pédagogique, 2d series, part 47. Paris, 1889.

———. *Instruction sur la formation et le fonctionnement des colonies de vacances.* Paris: Imprimerie Chaix, 1887.

Cottinet, Edmond, and A. Cahen. *Les Colonies de vacances de la ville de Paris
en 1888 et 1889.* Paris: Hachette, 1890.

Courtois, Abbé Gaston. *Orientations actuelles de nos oeuvres de jeunesse,* doc. 43,
Union des Oeuvres Ouvrières Catholiques, supplement to *l'Union* of December 1931.

———. *Pour "réussir" auprès des enfants: Quelques conseils de pédagogie pratique.* Paris: J. Ruckert, 1938.

Delpy, Arthur. *Les Oeuvres de colonies de vacances.* Paris, 1903.

Delsuc, Pierre. *Plein jeu.* Fonteny-sous-Bois: Editions de l'Orme Rond, 1985.

Dequidt, Georges. "Colonies de vacances." *Air et soleil,* July, Aug., Sept. 1928.

Diémer, Marie. *Le Livre de la forêt bleue.* Montreuil-sous-Bois: Imprimerie de
la Seine, 1933.

———. "Pourquoi j'ai écrit le livre de la Forêt bleu." *La Cheftaine,* April 1936.

E. P., "Comment organiser une colonie de vacances." *Bulletin de l'Association
des Anciens Elèves de l'Ecole de Saint-Sulpice,* August 1905.

Evrard, Abbé. "Le Personnel des colonies de vacances." *Congrès national des
colonies de vacances catholiques.* Limoges, 1911.

Fabre, Commandant. "Allocution." *Congrès national des colonies de vacances
et d'oeuvres de plein air, Reims,* 22–24 April 1927. Paris: Le Mouvement
Sanitaire, 1927.

———. "La Discipline dans les colonies de vacances et oeuvres de plein air."

Congrès national des colonies de vacances et d'oeuvres de plein air, Pau, 5–7 April 1929. Paris: Le Mouvement Sanitaire, 1929.

Fillère, Abbé. *La Cité paroissiale des jeunes: Rapport présenté au Congrès de l'Union des Oeuvres Catholiques Ouvrières.* Rennes: Union des Oeuvres Catholiques Ouvrières, 1934.

Freinet, Célestin. "Des Lectures pour nos enfants?" *L'Educateur prolétarien,* December 1932.

———. "La Vraie place du jeu en éducation." *L'Educateur prolétarien,* 1 March 1940, 173–75.

Friedl, Berthold. "La Conscience de classe chez l'enfant." Part 1, *L'Educateur prolétarien,* 10 December 1935, 112–15 and Part 2, 25 December 1935, 137–38.

Garin, Abbé Joseph. *La Belle étoile.* Ivry, 1929.

Gaussin, Pierre. "Que peut-on attendre des patronages?" *La Vie au patronage,* 15 February 1912.

Gérard, Emile. "Rapport sur les colonies de vacances." *10e Conférence nationale des municipalités socialistes,* 11–13 September 1937.

Gibon, Eugène. "Les Enfants au soleil!" *Le Suresnois,* 28 July 1934.

———. "Nos Enfants aux colonies de vacances." *Le Suresnois,* 6 August 1932.

———. "Retour des colonies de vacances." *Le Suresnois,* 17 September 1932.

Gleisner, Martin. "Comment transformer les grands jeux en jeux collectifs (1)." *L'Aide: Bulletin des Amis de l'Enfance Ouvrière de France,* March 1937.

Godard, J. "Croissance et développement physique de l'enfant." *L'Aide: Bulletin mensuel des Amis de l'Enfance Ouvrière de France,* 1 February 1934.

Gosnat, Venise. "Villanous" (typescript, 1948, 50 pp.).

Guérin-Desjardins, Jacques. "Le Rôle éducatif des colonies de vacances." *Congrès internationale des colonies de vacances, Paris.* Paris: Le Mouvement Sanitaire, 1937.

Guillard, Etienne. "Les Conditions d'efficacité du placement familial." *Congrès international des colonies de vacances, Paris.* Paris: Le Mouvement Sanitaire, 1937.

Hazemann, R-H. "Assistantes familiales ou infirmières scolaires?" *L'Hygiène par l'exemple,* July–Aug. 1928, 183–87.

Héret, Réginald. *La Loi scoute: Commentaire d'après saint Thomas d'Aquin.* Paris: Spès, 1929.

Jarosson, G. "Oeuvres des Saines Vacances, notes complémentaires." *Bulletin de l'Association des Anciens Elèves de l'Ecole de Saint-Sulpice,* 1903.

Koeppé, Théo. "La Formation des cadres dans les colonies de vacances." *Congrès international des colonies de vacances, Paris.* Paris: Le Mouvement Sanitaire, 1937.

Krupskaya, Nadezhda. *De l'Éducation: Recueil d'articles (1920–1937).* Moscow, 1958.

Laisant, C-A. "Education libératrice." *Bulletin de la ruche* 1, no. 1 (10 March 1914).

Laroppe, Abbé. *Dans la vallée de Celles: Souvenir d'une colonie de vacances.* Paris: Bloud, 1911.

Lion, Dr. "Egalité et supériorité." *L'Aide: Bulletin mensuel des Amis de l'Enfance Ouvrière de France,* June 1937.

Loewenstein, Kurt. "Pédagogie socialiste (Cours des Aides, 7 nov 1933)." *L'Aide: Bulletin mensuel des Amis de l'Enfance Ouvrière de France,* 1 December 1933.

Lorette, Abbé. "Oeuvre des Saines Vacances." *Bulletin de l'Association des Anciens Elèves l'Ecole de Saint-Sulpice,* 1903.

Lorriaux, Suzanne. *Oeuvre de Trois Semaines, Rapport, 1892.* Paris: Imprimerie J. Lievens, 1893.

Lorriaux, Théodore and Suzanne. *Notice sur L'Oeuvre de Trois Semaines après 25 années d'existence.* Paris: Rasquin, 1906.

Maréchal, Hyacinthe. *Scouts de France et ordre chrétien.* Paris: Desclée de Brouwer, 1934.

Martin, Henri. "Les Colonies scolaires en France et à l'étranger." Review of W. Bion, *Die Ferienkolonien und Werwandte Bestrebungen auf dem Giebete der kinder-Gesundheitspflege.* Zurich, 1901. In *Revue pédagogique,* July 1903.

Monnet, Georges. " 'Notre tâche.' (Cours des Aides, 7 nov 1933)." *L'Aide: Bulletin mensuel des Amis de l'Enfance Ouvrière de France,* 1 December 1933.

Municipalité d'Ivry-sur-Seine. *Revoir les Mathes . . . Souvenirs et témoignages.* Ivry-sur-Seine: 1994.

Oeuvre de la Chaussée de Maine. *Rapport, 1905.* Paris, 1906.

Oeuvre de la Chaussée de Maine. *Rapport, Année 1918–1919.* Paris, 1919.

Oeuvre de Trois Semaines. *Rapport pour l'été 1897.* Saint-Maur: J. Lievens, 1898.

Oeuvre Louis Conlombant. *Rapport, 1951.* Paris, 1952.

Oeuvre Louis Conlombant. *Rapport, 1953–54.* Paris, 1954.

Perroy, Elia. "Le Jeu et les jeux." *Educateurs,* Jan.–Feb. 1949.

Petit, Edouard. *Premier rapport.* Published in the *Journal officiel,* 11 August 1896, 4601.

Les Petits Ivryens à la Campagne. Ivry, 1924.

Les Petits Ivryens à la Campagne. Ivry, 1931.

Les Petits Ivryens à la Campagne. Ivry, 1936.

Pistrak, Moses. *Les Problèmes fondamentaux de l'école du travail.* Paris: Desclée de Brouwer, 1973.

Poggioli, Antonin. "Les Colonies de vacances." Report to the Fédération Nationale des Municipalités Socialistes, 28 April 1931.

———. "Rapport de l'union des municipalités socialistes de la Seine." *56e Congrès administratif de la Fédération de la Seine du Parti socialiste,* 26–27 October 1935.

Ponsard, François. "Une Colonie scolaire." *Le Temps,* 15 August 1905.

Porcher, E. "Voyages de vacances." *Revue pédagogique,* June 1880.

———. "Voyages d'instruction des Ecoles Supérieures Municipales: L'Ecole Turgot au Havre en 1877." *Revue pédagogique,* March 1878.

Portiez, Louis François. *Des voyages: De leur utilité dans l'éducation.* Paris: Imprimerie Nationale, n.d.

———. *Sur l'instruction publique.* Paris: Imprimerie Nationale, n.d.

Rouget, L. "De l'éducation physique." *Bulletin de la ruche* 1, no. 1 (10 March 1914): 7–8.

Roumajon, M. J. "Le Rôle des colonies de vacances dans la formation intellectuelle de la jeunesse." *Congrès international des colonies de vacances, Paris.* Paris: Le Mouvement Sanitaire, 1937.

Roux, Mme Jean-Charles. "Les Colonies de vacances de la Chaussée de Maine." *Revue Médico-sociale et de la Protection de l'Enfance* 4 (1938).

Sautter, E. "Le Travail de l'éducation morale dans les colonies de vacances." *Congrès national des colonies de vacances et d'oeuvres de plein air, Reims, 22–24 April 1927.* Paris: Le Mouvement Sanitaire, 1927.

Schalow, Raymond. *Joues rouges et belle humeur.* Paris: Editions des Eclaireurs de France, 1946.

Schmitt, André, and André Boulogne. *La Cure de santé et les jeux des enfants.* Paris: Editions du Scarabée, 1955.

Ségur, A. de. "Un Patronage entre ciel et terre." *L'Univers,* 28 June 1896.

Sellier, Henri. "Le 'Citoyen' Vaillant." *Le Populaire,* 29 January 1940.

———. *Le Parti socialiste et l'action communale.* Paris: La Vie communale, 1925.

———. *Programme municipal pour les élections de 1935.* Paris: Union des Elus Municipaux Socialistes, 1935.

———. *Le Socialisme et l'action municipale.* Paris: La Vie communale, 1934.

Sevin, André. *Vers une éducation nouvelle: Réflexions sur le scoutisme.* Paris: G. Enault, 1930.

Société de Saint-Vincent-de-Paul. "Les Colonies des vacances de Saint-Etienne: Rapport du Comité." *Bulletin de la Société de Saint-Vincent-de-Paul* 697, January 1907.

———. "Lyon: Oeuvre des Enfants à la Montagne." *Bulletin de la Société de Saint-Vincent-de-Paul,* July 1904.

———. "Rapport à l'Assemblée Générale de Lyon, le 9 déc. 1904." *Bulletin de la Société de Saint-Vincent-de-Paul,* 676, April 1905.

———. *Rapport général sur les conférences et les oeuvres de la Société de Saint-Vincent-de-Paul.* Paris, 1904.

SOFCO. *Les Centres de vacances pour enfants: Enquête sur la clientèle actuelle et potentielle.* Paris: SOFRES, 1983.

Solages, Bruno de. "Philosophie du Scoutisme." In *Compte rendu des Journées nationales, 1934,* no. 120 (February 1935): 163–64.

Supplément, *Courrier du patro,* June 1936.

Turmann, Max. *Au Sortir de l'école: Les patronages.* Paris: Lecoffre, 1901.

———. *L'Education populaire, les oeuvres complémentaires de l'école en 1900.* Paris: Lecoffre, 1904.

Vallier, Abbé Charles. "Une Colonie de vacances dirigée par des séminaristes." *Bulletin pour le recrutement sacerdotal,* December 1904.

———. "Un Congrès de patronages tenu par des enfants." Part 2. *La Vie au patronage,* 15 February 1914.

Veber, Adrien. *Le Socialisme municipal.* Paris: V. Giard and E. Brière, 1908.

Veuillot, François. "Autour d'un patronage." *L'Univers,* 15 April 1897.

Vimard, Raoul. "Le Retour à la terre par les colonies de vacances." *Grand revue,* April 1911.

———. "Le Surveillant idéal." *Congrès national des colonies de vacances et d'oeuvres de plein air, Saint-Etienne,* 17–19 April. Paris: Le Mouvement Sanitaire, 1925.

Vuillemin, Louis. *Pour l'avenir de la race: Colonies scolaires et camps de vacances. Guide pratique pour leur organisation et leur fonctionnement.* Paris: Charles-Lavauzelles, 1927.

Wenger-Charpentier, Anne-Marie. *La Cheftaine des jeannettes (Dans la Forêt bleue).* Paris: Spès, 1933.

Willème, Emile. "L'Amélioration physique des enfants: Les colonies scolaires." *Rappel,* 6 July 1899.

SECONDARY SOURCES

Agulhon, Maurice. *La République au village.* Paris: Seuil, 1979.

Alain [pseud. of Emile Chartier]. *Propos sur l'éducation.* Paris: Reider, 1932.

Ardouin-Dumazet, Victor-Eugène. *Voyage en France: Banlieue parisienne. 1. Région sud-est et est.* Vol. 64 of *Voyage en France.* Paris: Berger-Levrault, 1921.

Audoin-Rouzeau, Stéphane, and Annette Becker. *La Grande guerre: 1914–1918.* Paris: Gallimard, 1998.

Barron, Louis. *Les Environs de Paris.* Paris: Maison Quantin, 1886.

Bastié, Jean. *La Croissance de la banlieue parisienne.* Paris: PUF, 1964.

Bazin, Germain. "La Rosière de Suresnes et le prix de vertu." *Bulletin de la société historique et artistique de Suresnes* 7 (1936).

Becker, Annette. *La Guerre et la foi: De la mort à la mémoire, 1914–1930.* Paris: A. Colin, 1994.

Becker, Jean-Jacques. *Les Français dans la grande guerre.* Paris: Laffont, 1980.

Betron, Christian. "Acteur de l'histoire locale à Suresnes." *La Banlieue en fête: De la marginalité urbaine à l'identité culturelle.* Paris, 1988.

Bimbi, Eric. "Le PCF et l'enseignement à l'école primaire de 1921 au milieu des années 1930." Mémoire de maîtrise, Université de Paris I, 1991.

Blackmer, Donald, and Sidney Tarrow, eds. *Communism in Italy and France.* Princeton: Princeton University Press, 1975.

Bodin, Louis, and Jean Touchard. *Front populaire 1936.* Paris: Armand Colin, 1985.

Boltanski, Luc. *Prime éducation et morale de classe.* Paris: Mouton, 1969.

Bonnefoi, Jean-Claude. *Les Colonies de vacances organisées par l'Etat et les collectivités publiques.* Rennes: Imprimerie Oberthur, 1959.

Bordat, Denis. *Les C.E.M.E.A., qu'est-ce que c'est?* Paris: Maspéro, 1976.

Boswell, Laird. *Rural Communism in France, 1920–1939.* Ithaca: Cornell University Press, 1998.

Boureau, Alain. "Propositions pour une histoire restreinte des mentalités." *Annales ESC* 6 (November–December 1989): 1491–1504.

Bredin, Jean-Denis. *L'Affaire.* Paris: Fayard, 1991.

Brunet, Jean-Paul. *Un Demi-siècle de gestion municipale à Saint-Denis-la-Rouge.* Paris: Editions Cujas, 1981.

———. *Saint-Denis, la ville rouge (1890–1939).* Paris: Hachette, 1980.

Buisson, Ferdinand. *Dictionnaire de pédagogie.* 2 vols. Paris: Hachette, 1887.

Bulkley, Mildred E. *The Feeding of Schoolchildren.* London: G. Bell and Sons, 1914.

Burlen, Katherine, ed. *La Banlieue oasis: Henri Sellier et les cités-jardins.* Vincennes: Presses Universitaires de Vincennes, 1989.

Cassier, Maurice. *Classe ouvrière et municipalité en région parisienne. Montreuil ouvrier et républicain: formation, évolution et crise d'un "bastion Communiste."* Thesis for the Diplôme d'études approfondies, Ecole des Hautes Études en Sciences Sociales, Paris, 1981.

Chambaz, Bernard. "L'Implantation du Parti communiste français à Ivry pendant l'entre-deux-guerres." Mémoire de maîtrise, Université de Paris I, 1971.

Chambelland, Collette, ed. *Le Musée social en son temps.* Paris: Presses de l'Ecole Normale Supérieure, 1998.

Chaperon, Sylvie. *Les Années Beauvoir, 1945–1970.* Paris: Fayard, 2000.

Château, Jean-Yves. *Le Jeu de l'enfant après 3 ans, sa nature, sa discipline: Introduction à la pédagogie.* Paris: Vrin, 1946.

Chaumeil, Jean. *Venise Gosnat: Un Militant exemplaire du mouvement ouvrier français.* Paris: Editions ouvrières, 1970.

Chéroutre, Marie-Thérèse, and Gérard Cholvy, eds. *Le scoutisme: Quel type d'hommes, quel type de femmes? Quel type de chrétiens?* Paris: Editions du Cerf, 1994.

———. *Scoutisme féminin et promotion féminin, 1920–1990.* Paris: Les Guides de France, 1990.

Cholvy, Gérard. *Histoire des organisations et mouvements chrétiens de jeunesse en France, XIXe-XXe siècles.* Paris: Editions du Cerf, 1999.

———. *Histoire des organisations et mouvements de jeunesse en France, XIXe-XXe siècles.* Paris: Editions du Cerf, 1999.

———. *Patronage: Ghetto ou vivier?* Paris: Nouvelle cité, 1987.

Cholvy, Gérard, and Yves-Marie Hilaire. *Histoire religieuse de la France contemporaine, vol. 2, 1880-1930.* Toulouse: Privat, 1987.

Chombart de Lauwe, Paul-Henry. *La Vie quotidienne des familles ouvrières: Recherches sur les comportements sociaux de consommation.* Paris: CNRS, 1956.

Ciuciu, Emile. *Préservation de l'enfance par le grand air.* Paris: Thèse en médecine, 1908.

Cochard, Martine. "La Politique éducative d'une municipalité pendant l'entre-deux-guerres: Suresnes, 1919-1939." Mémoire de maîtrise, Université de Paris V, 1983.

Cohen, Yves, and Rémi Baudouï, eds. *Les Chantiers de la paix sociale, 1900-1940.* Fontenay-Saint-Cloud: Editions de l'Ecole Normale Supérieure, 1996.

Collet, Henri. "Action municipale et loisirs." *Cahiers de l'animation,* no. 21, 3d trimester, 1978.

Corbin, Alain. *L'Avènement des loisirs.* Paris: Aubier, 1995.

Crubellier, Maurice. *L'Enfance et la jeunesse dans la société française, 1851-1950.* Paris: Armand Colin, 1979.

Dainville, François de. *L'Éducation des jésuites (XVIe-XVIIIe siècles).* Paris: Les Editions de Minuit, 1978.

Davin, Anna. *Growing Up Poor: Home, School, and Street in London, 1870-1914.* London: Oram Rivers Press, 1996.

de Failly, Gisèle. *Le Moniteur, la monitrice.* Paris: Editions du Scarabée, 1956.

de Felice, R. "L'Oeuvre des colonies de vacances." *L'Idéal du foyer: Revue littéraire, artistique, économique et sociale de la famille,* 1 May 1903.

Delahaye, Martine. *Les Enfants du Mont-Valérien.* Ardèche: Lienhart, 1997.

Delbrêl, Madeleine. *Ville marxiste, terre de mission.* Paris: Editions du Cerf, 1970.

Delpérier, Louis. *Les Colonies de vacances.* Paris: La Librairie Victor J. Gabalda et Cie., 1908.

Dessertine, Dominique. *La Société lyonnaise pour la sauvetage de l'enfance.* Toulouse: Erès, 1990.

Dessertine, Dominique, and Olivier Faure. *La Maladie entre libéralisme et solidarités: 1850-1940.* Paris: Mutualité française, 1994.

Dommanget, Maurice. *Edouard Vaillant: Un Grand socialiste, 1840-1915.* Mayenne: Floch, 1956.

Donzelot, Jacques. *La Police des familles.* Paris: Editions de Minuit, 1977.

Downs, Laura Lee. " 'L'Avenir de la jeune fille': Les filles dans les colonies de

vacances en France, 1884–1960." In Louise Bruit, Gabrielle Houbre, Chris-
tiane Klapisch-Zuber, and Pauline Schmitt-Pantel, *Le Corps des jeunes filles
(de l'Antiquité à nos jours)*. Perrin, 2001.

———. "Comment faire appel à 'l'instinct viril du garçon'? La pédagogie du
jeu et la formation de l'enfant au masculin: Les Scouts de France, 1920–
1940." *Cahiers Masculin/Féminin de Lyon 2,* no. 4, Presses Universitaires de
Lyon, autumn, 2001.

———. "Municipal Communism and the Politics of Childhood: Ivry-sur-
Seine, 1925–1960." *Past and Present* 166 (February 2000): 205–41.

Dreux, Hélène. *Les Colonies de vacances à placement collectif.* Thèse de médecine. Paris: A. Legrand, 1938.

Duclert, Vincent, Rémi Fabre, and Patrick Fridenson, eds. *Avenirs et avant-
gardes en France, XIXe–XXe siècles: Hommage à Madeleine Rébérioux.* Paris:
Editions de la Découverte, 1999.

Durkheim, Emile. *L'Éducation morale.* Paris: Félix Alcan, 1925.

Dutoit, Marie. *Madame de Pressensé: Sa vie.* Paris: Fischbacher, 1904.

Fabre, Rémi. "Les Mouvements de jeunesse dans la France de l'entre-deux-
guerres," *Le Mouvement social,* July–September 1994, 9–30.

Faron, Olivier. *Les Enfants du deuil: Orphelins et pupilles de la nation de la
première guerre mondiale (1914–1941).* Paris: Editions de la Découverte, 2001.

Feroldi, Vincent. *La Force des enfants: Des Coeurs Vaillants à l'A.C.E.* Paris:
Editions ouvrières, 1987.

Fishman, Sarah, Laura Lee Downs, Ioannis Sinanoglou, Leonard V. Smith,
and Robert Zaretsky, eds. *France at War: Vichy and the Historians.* London:
Berg, 2000.

Fourcaut, Annie. *Bobigny, banlieue rouge.* Paris: Editions ouvrières, 1986.

———, ed. *Banlieue rouge 1920–1960. Années Thorez, années Gabin: Archetype
du populaire, banc d'essai de modernité.* Paris: Autrement, 1992.

François, Pierre, and Pierre Kergomard. *Les Eclaireurs de France, 1911–1951.*
Paris: ESF, 1983.

Freinet, Madeleine, ed. *Célestin Freinet, Oeuvres pédagogiques.* Paris: Seuil,
1994.

Fridenson, Patrick, and Madeleine Rébérioux. "Albert Thomas, pivot du
réformisme français." *Le Mouvement social* 87 (1974).

Fuchs, Rachel. *Abandoned Children: Foundlings and Child Welfare in
Nineteenth-Century France.* Albany: SUNY Press, 1984.

Garaud, Marcel, and Romuald Szramkiewicz. *La Révolution française et la
famille.* Paris: PUF, 1978.

Gardaix, Gilles. "Les CEMEA, mouvement d'éducation. Esquisse d'une
époque: 1945–1957." Mémoire de maîtrise, Université de Paris I, 1981.

Garin, Joseph. *Histoire d'Ivry-sur-Seine des origines à nos jours.* Paris: Gabalda
et fils, 1930.

Gautier, Léon, trans. *Le Chanson de Roland.* Tours: Alfred Mame et Fils, 1897.

Gérôme, Noelle, Danielle Tartakowsky, and Claude Willard. *La Banlieue en fête: De la marginalité urbaine à l'identité culturelle.* Saint-Denis: Presses Universitaires de Vincennes, 1988.

Gilbert, Bentley. *The Evolution of National Insurance in Britain: The Origins of the Welfare State.* London: Michael Joseph, 1966.

Girault, Jacques. *Sur l'implantation du Parti communiste français dans l'entre-deux-guerres.* Paris: Editions sociales, 1977.

Girault, Jacques, ed. *Ouvriers en banlieue, XIXe–XXe siècle.* Paris: Editions ouvrières, 1998.

Godard, Jacques. *Nos enfants vont en colonie.* Paris: Editions Néret, 1959.

Godin, Daniel, and Yvan Daniel. *France, pays de mission?* Paris: Editions du Cerf, 1943.

Grafteaux, Serge. *Mémé Santerre.* Paris: Editions du Jour, 1975.

Groos, Karl. *Les Jeux des animaux.* Paris: Alcan, 1902.

———. *The Play of Man.* New York: D. Appleton, 1901.

Guérin, Christian. *L'Utopie: Scouts de France. Histoire d'une identité collective, catholique et sociale, 1920–1995.* Paris: Fayard, 1997.

Guignard-Perrein, Liliane. "Les Faucons rouges, 1932–1950." Thèse de 3e cycle, Université de Paris X, 1982.

Hahn, Carine. "Les Colos c'est unique." *Valeurs mutualistes* 212 (July 2001).

Halbwachs, Maurice. *La Classe ouvrière et les niveaux de vie: Recherches sur la hiérarchie des besoins dans les sociétés industrielles contemporaines.* Paris: Alcan, 1912.

———. *Classes sociales et morphologie.* Paris: Editions de Minuit, 1972.

———. *La Politique foncière des municipalités.* Paris: Librairie du Parti Socialiste, 1908.

Hall, Granville Stanley. "Recreation and Reversion." *Pedagogical Seminary,* 1915, 510–20.

Hastings, Michel. *Halluin-la-rouge, 1919–1939: Aspects d'un communisme identitaire.* Arras: Presses Universitaires de Lille, 1991.

Hayward, J. E. S. "The Official Social Philosophy of the French Third Republic: Léon Bourgeois and Solidarism." *International Review of Social History* 6 (1961): 19–48.

Heywood, Colin. *Childhood in Nineteenth-Century France: Work, Health, and Education among the "Classes Populaires."* Cambridge: Cambridge University Press, 1988.

Hoernle, Edwin. *Manual for Leaders of Children's Groups.* Berlin and New York, n.d., [ca. 1924].

Hoffman, Emmanuel. "L'Ecole primaire à Ivry-sur-Seine, 1944–1968." Mémoire de maîtrise, Université de Paris I, 1992.

Hoibian, Guillaume. "Le Patronage de St-Pierre-et-St-Paul d'Ivry-sur-Seine et l'oeuvre de la jeunesse de Charenton (1918–1939)." Mémoire de maîtrise, Université de Paris I, 1995.

Houssaye, Jean. *Aujourd'hui les centres de vacances.* Vigneux: Editions Matri-
    ces, 1991.

————. *Un Avenir pour les colonies de vacances.* Paris: Editions ouvrières, 1977.

————. *Le Livre des colos: Histoire et évolution des centres de vacances pour
    enfants.* Paris: La Documentation Française, 1989.

Hubert, Corinne. "Demain on part en colo . . . Les premières colonies de
    vacances de l'actuel Val-de-Marne sous la IIIe République." Mémoire de
    maîtrise, Université de Paris VIII, 1986.

Huizinga, Jan. *Homo Ludens: A Study of the Play-Element in Culture.* Boston:
    Beacon Press, 1950.

Hurt, J. S. *Elementary Schooling and the Working Classes, 1860–1918.* London:
    Routledge, 1979.

Irigaray, Luce. *Ethique de la différence sexuelle.* Paris: Editions de Minuit, 1984.

Knibiehler, Yvonne. *Nous les assistantes sociales: Naissance d'une profession.*
    Paris: Aubier Montaigne, 1980.

————. "Socialisme et service social: L'action d'Henri Sellier, Maire de
    Suresnes, Ministre du Front Populaire." *Sociologie du Sud-Est* 28–29
    (April–September 1982).

Lagrée, Michel. "Exilés dans leur patrie (1880–1920)." In François Lebrun,
    ed., *Histoire des catholiques en France du XVIe siècle à nos jours.* Toulouse:
    Privat, 1980.

Langignon, Martine. "Relations entre communistes et chrétiens à Ivry entre
    les deux guerres." Mémoire de maîtrise, Université de Paris XII, 1979.

Larkin, Maurice. *Church and State after the Dreyfus Affair.* London: Macmil-
    lan, 1974.

————. *France since the Popular Front.* Oxford: Oxford University Press, 1986.

————. *Religion, Politics, and Preferment in France since 1890.* Cambridge:
    Cambridge University Press, 1995.

Launay, M., Pierre Pierrard, and Rolande Trempé. *La J.O.C., regards
    d'historiens.* Paris: Editions ouvrières, 1984.

Lavarenne, Joseph. *Un Pionnier, une initiative: Le père Vallier et la Colonie de
    Verrières.* Lyon: Editions du Sud-Est, 1953.

Laybourn, Keith. "The Issue of School Feeding in Bradford, 1904–1907."
    Journal of Educational Administration and History 14, no. 2 (July 1982):
    30–39.

Lefebvre, Rémi. "Le Socialisme saisi par l'institution municipale." *Recherche
    socialiste* 6 (March 1999): 9–25.

Le Goff, Jacques, and René Rémond, eds. *Histoire de la France religieuse.*
    Vol. 4. Paris: Seuil, 1992.

Le Henaff, Geneviève. *La Vie quotidienne à la colonie de vacances.* Paris: Edi-
    tions du Scarabée, 1954.

Lequin, Yves. "L'Espace ouvrier: Le regard géographique." *Historiens et
    géographes* 350 (October 1995): 231–39.

Lhande, Pierre. *Le Christ dans la banlieue, enquête sur la vie réligieuse dans les milieux ouvriers de la banlieue de Paris.* Paris: Plon, 1927.

Lichtheim, George. *Marxism in Modern France.* New York: Columbia University Press, 1966.

Lilla, Mark. "Night Thoughts." *New York Review of Books,* 30 November 2000, 18–21.

Lojkine, Jean, and Nathalie Viet Depaule. *Classe ouvrière, société locale et municipalités en région parisienne. Eléments pour une analyse régionale et une approche monographique: le cas d'Ivry-sur-Seine.* Paris: Centre d'Études des Mouvements Sociaux, 1984.

Jean-Luc Noël. *L'Invention du jeune enfant au XIXème siècle: De la salle d'asile à l'école maternelle.* Paris: Belin, 1997.

Lurie, Alison. "Not for Muggles." *New York Review of Books,* 16 December 1999, 6–8.

Magri, Susanna, and Christian Topalov, eds. *Villes ouvrières, 1900–1950.* Paris: Harmattan, 1990.

Maitron, Jean. *Dictionnaire biographique du mouvement ouvrier français.* Paris: Editions ouvrières, 1964–92.

Makarenko, Anton. *Poème pédagogique.* 3 vols. Moscow: Editions en langues étrangères, 1953.

Mayeur, Françoise. *Histoire générale de l'enseignement et de l'éducation en France.* Vol. 3. Paris: G-V Labat, 1981.

Mayeur, Françoise, and Jacques Gadille. *Education et images de la femme chrétienne en France.* Lyon: Editions l'Hermès, 1980.

Mayeur, Jean-Marie. *La Question laïque, XIXe–XXe siècle.* Paris: Fayard, 1997.

Michaud, René. *J'avais vingt ans: Un jeune ouvrier au début du siècle.* Paris: Syros, 1983.

Millet, Jean. "En 1939, à quatorze ans, j'entre à la JOC." *Autrement* 8 (1977): 56–61.

Mishler, Paul C. *Raising Reds: The Young Pioneers, Radical Summer Camps, and Communist Political Culture in the United States.* New York: Columbia University Press, 1999.

Montessori, Maria. *The Montessori Method.* London: Heinemann, 1914.

Municipalité de Suresnes. *Il y a cinquante ans . . . Henri Sellier installait la première municipalité à direction socialiste à Suresnes, 1919–1969.* Saint-Ouen: Imprimerie Maubert, 1970.

Nord, Philip. *The Republican Moment.* Cambridge: Harvard University Press, 1995.

Noiriel, Gérard. *Longwy: Immigrés et prolétaires 1880–1980.* Paris: PUF, 1984.

Nye, Robert. *Crime, Madness, and Politics in Modern France: The Medical Concept of National Decline.* Princeton: Princeton University Press, 1984.

Ory, Pascal. *La Belle illusion: Culture et politique sous le signe du Front Populaire, 1935–1938.* Paris: Plon, 1994.

Pary, Juliette. *L'Amour des camarades.* Lille: Victor Michon, 1948.

———. *Mes 126 gosses.* Paris: Flammarion, 1938.

Penin, Robert. "Les Colonies de vacances." *Ecole et socialisme* 7, no. 1 (July 1977).

Piaget, Jean. *La Construction du réel chez l'enfant.* Paris: Delachaux et Niestlé, 1996.

———. *La Formation du symbole chez l'enfant: Imitation, jeu et rêve, image et représentation.* Neuchâtel: Delachaux et Niestlé, 1970.

———. *Le Jugement moral chez l'enfant.* Paris: PUF, 1992.

———. *Le Langage et la pensée de l'enfant: Études sur la logique de l'enfant.* Paris: Denoël, 1984.

Pieronne, Marie. "Les Premiers centres de vacances à Ivry-sur-Seine, 1925–1949." Mémoire de maîtrise, Université de Paris I, 1991.

Pierrard, Pierre. *L'Eglise et les ouvriers en France, 1840–1940.* Paris: Hachette, 1984.

———. *L'Eglise et les ouvriers en France, 1940–1990.* Paris: Hachette, 1991.

Planchon, Jean. *Besoins des enfants et rhythme des activités.* Paris: Editions du Scarabée, 1965.

———. "Le Rhythme journalier de la vie des enfants à la colonie de vacances." Doctorat d'Université, Grenoble, 1960.

Plantet, Eugène, and Arthur Delpy. *Les Colonies de vacances: Organisation et fonctionnement.* Paris: Hachette, 1910.

Prost, Antoine. *Histoire de l'enseignement en France, 1800–1967.* Paris: Armand Colin, 1968.

———. "Jeunesse et société dans l'entre-deux-guerres." *Vingtième siècle, revue d'histoire* 13 (January–March 1987): 35–43.

Prost, Antoine, and Gérard Vincent, eds. *Histoire de la vie privée.* Vol. 5. Paris: Seuil, 1987.

Poujol, Geneviève. *Le Métier d'animateur.* Toulouse: Privat, 1978.

Poujol, Geneviève, and Madeleine Romer, eds. *Dictionnaire biographique des militants, XIX–XXe siècles: De l'éducation populaire à l'action sociale.* Paris: Harmattan, 1996.

Pudal, Bernard. *Prendre parti: Pour une sociologie historique du PCF.* Paris: Presses de la Fondation Nationale des Sciences Politiques, 1989.

Rab, Sylvie. "Culture et banlieue: Les politiques culturelles dans les municipalités de la Seine, 1935–39." Thèse de doctorat, Université de Paris VII, 1994.

Rabinow, Paul. *French Modern: Norms and Forms of the Social Environment.* Cambridge, Mass.: MIT Press, 1989.

Ragache, Gilles. *Les Enfants de la guerre: Vivre, survivre, lire et jouer en France, 1939–1949.* Paris: Perrein, 1997.

Rauch, André. *Les Vacances en France de 1830 à nos jours.* Paris: Hachette, 1996.

Rey-Herme, Philippe-Alexandre. *La Colonie de vacances hier et aujourd'hui.* Paris: Editions Cap, 1955.

———. *Les Colonies de vacances: Origines et premiers développements.* Paris: privately published by the author, 1954.

———. *Les Colonies de vacances en France, 1906–1936: L'institution et ses problèmes.* Paris: Fleurus, 1961.

Riglet, Marc. "L'Ecole et la Révolution: Aspects du discours révolutionnaire sur l'école pendant l'entre-deux-guerres." *Revue française de la science politique* 3 (June 1978): 488–507.

Robrieux, Philippe. *Histoire intérieure du PC.* 4 vols. Paris: Fayard, 1980.

———. *Maurice Thorez: Vie secrète et vie publique.* Paris: Fayard, 1983.

Sadoun, Marc, ed. *La Démocratie en France. Vol. 2: Limites.* Paris: Gallimard, 2000.

Schafer, Sylvia. *Children in Moral Danger and the Problem of Government in Third Republic France.* Princeton: Princeton University Press, 1997.

Sellier, Henri. *Les Banlieues urbaines et la réorganisation administrative du Département de la Seine.* Paris: Imprimerie nationale, 1917.

———. *Le Crise du logement et l'intervention publique en matière d'habitation populaire dans l'agglomération parisienne.* Paris: OPHBM, 1921.

Seron, O. *Histoire de Suresnes.* Suresnes: published privately by the author, 1926.

Sordes, René. *Histoire de Suresnes.* Alençon: Imprimerie Corbière et Jugain, 1965.

Soriano, Marc. *Guide de la littérature enfantine.* Paris: Flammarion, 1959.

Steedman, Carolyn. *Childhood, Culture, and Class in Britain: Margaret McMillan, 1860–1931.* New Brunswick: Rutgers University Press, 1990.

———. *Strange Dislocations: Childhood and the Idea of Human Interiority, 1780–1930.* Cambridge: Harvard University Press, 1993.

Stehelin, L. *Essais de socialisme municipale.* Thèse de droit. Paris, 1901.

Swain, Gladys. *Dialogue avec l'insensé: A la recherche d'une autre histoire de la folie.* Paris: Gallimard, 1994.

Thorez, Paul. *Les Enfants modèles.* Paris: Lieu Commun, Collections Folio, 1984.

Thorez-Vermeersch, Jeanette. *La Vie en rouge: Mémoires.* Paris: Belfond, 1992.

Tolstoi, Léon. *L'École de Iasnia-Poliana en Novembre et Décembre 1862.* Paris: Stock, 1905.

Topalov, Christian. *Laboratoires du nouveau siècle: La nébuleuse réformatrice et ses reseaux en France, 1880–1914.* Paris: Editions de l'École des Hautes Études en Sciences Sociales, 1999.

Valdour, Jacques. *Ouvriers parisiens d'après-guerre.* Paris: A. Rousseau, 1921.

Vitry, Xavier. *Les Hommes aux mains vides (Dans la banlieue disgraciée).* Paris: Mignard, 1939.

Vulbeau, Alain. *Le Gouvernement des enfants.* Paris: Desclée de Brouwer, 1993.

Vygotsky, Lev. *Pensée et langage.* Paris: La Dispute, 1997.

Whitney, Susan Brewster. "The Politics of Youth: Communists and Catholics in Interwar France." Ph.D. diss., Rutgers University, 1994.

Winnicott, Donald W. *Playing and Reality.* London: Tavistock, 1971.

Wohl, Robert. *French Communism in the Making, 1914–1920.* Stanford: Stanford University Press, 1966.

Zelizer, Viviana. *Pricing the Priceless Child: The Changing Social Value of Children.* New York: Basic Books, 1985.

LAURA LEE DOWNS is Directeur d'Etudes,
Centre de Recherches Historiques, Ecole des Hautes
Etudes en Sciences Sociales, in Paris. She is the author
of *Manufacturing Inequality: Gender Division in the
French and British Metalworking Industries,
1914–1939* (1995).

Library of Congress Cataloging-in-Publication Data

Downs, Laura Lee.
Childhood in the promised land : working-class
movements and the colonies de vacances in France,
1880–1960 / by Laura Lee Downs.
p. cm.
Includes bibliographical references (p.) and index.
ISBN 0-8223-2928-x (cloth : alk. paper) —
ISBN 0-8223-2944-1 (pbk. : alk. paper)
1. Vacation schools — France — History.
2. Poor children — Education — France — History.
3. City children — Education — France — History.
4. Children — France — Social conditions.
5. Labor movement — France — History.   I. Title.
LC5771.F8 D69   2002
371.826'23'0944 — dc21   2002005513